40 QUESTIONS ABOUT
Bible Translation

Mark L. Strauss

Benjamin L. Merkle, Series Editor

KREGEL
ACADEMIC

40 Questions About Bible Translation

Published by Kregel Academic, an imprint of Kregel Publications, 2450 Oak Industrial Dr. NE, Grand Rapids, MI 49505-6020.

This book is a title in the 40 Questions Series edited by Benjamin L. Merkle.

For a complete list of titles in the 40 Questions series, go to 40questions.net.

The Greek font GraecaU and the Hebrew font New JerusalemU are from www.linguistsoftware.com/lgku.htm, +1-425-775-1130.

ISBN 978-0-8254-4750-1

Printed in the United States of America

23 24 25 26 27 / 5 4 3 2 1

"There is no better person to answer your questions about Bible translation than New Testament scholar Mark Strauss. Dr. Strauss draws from a deep well of knowledge and experience filled by many years of professional work as an English Bible translator. He writes in a clear, engaging style that brings clarity to even the most complicated questions. This book is an excellent addition to the 40 Questions series and deserves to be on the shelf of every serious student of biblical studies."

—Karen H. Jobes, PhD,
Gerald F. Hawthorne Professor Emerita of New Testament Greek and Exegesis,
Wheaton College

"Mark Strauss's book on Bible translation is an amazing source of information which covers translation philosophy, difficult issues in translating the biblical text, the various translations used, the history of English translations, and so much more. The book is also beautifully written and some of the examples used are quite humorous. Here is a resource, no matter what translation one prefers, that is invaluable and full of wisdom. I anticipate returning to this book often and hope it is read widely."

—Thomas R. Schreiner, PhD,
James Buchanan Harrison Professor of New Testament Interpretation,
Associate Dean, The Southern Baptist Theological Seminary

"Why are there so many Bible versions and what makes them different? These are just two of many questions that the gifted New Testament scholar and translator Mark Strauss answers for the interested reader. Strauss's well-written and compelling book is an amazing compendium of fascinating information about the process, issues, history, and more of the translation of the most important book in the world. If you want to understand your Bible better, I enthusiastically recommend *40 Questions About Bible Translation!*"

—Tremper Longman III, PhD,
Distinguished Scholar and Professor Emeritus of Biblical Studies,
Westmont College

"Mark Strauss has been studying, practicing, thinking, and teaching about Bible translation for many years. His thorough understanding of the key questions and his wisdom in addressing the challenges posed to translators can be seen on every page. He writes clearly and provides wonderfully helpful examples of all the issues he explains. This tremendously helpful book should be the first one to be read by anyone wondering what Bible translation involves and why we have different translations in the same language. It also provides a fine overview of the history of the translation of the Bible into English and the information needed to understand historical and current debates about Bible translation, whether in the English language or in other parts of the world."

—Roy E. Ciampa, PhD,
S. Louis and Ann W. Armstrong Chair of Religion,
Chair, Department of Biblical and Religious Studies,
Samford University

"For readers who feel overwhelmed by the present array of English Bible translations on offer, *40 Questions About Bible Translation* shines much needed light. Strauss answers every classic question raised about the why and the how of Bible translation. And he does so with that eminently readable style and clarity we have come to expect of his writing. Thorough. Crystal clear. Enjoyable. Everything you've asked about Bible translation gets an answer in *40 Questions About Bible Translation*."

—Jeannine Brown, PhD,
The David Price Professor of Biblical and Theological Foundations,
Director of Online Programs, Bethel Seminary of Bethel University

"Ever wondered all that goes into translating the Bible you use? And what is going on with all these different versions? If you have such questions, *40 Questions About Bible Translation* is for you. Using his years of experience in Bible translation work, Mark Strauss ably walks you through all it takes and should take to translate the Bible. Your understanding for the challenges of translation and appreciation for the service translators provide will cause you to read your Bible with more vigor, sensitivity, and understanding."

—Darrell L. Bock, PhD,
Executive Director for Cultural Engagement,
Howard G. Hendricks Center for Christian Leadership and Cultural Engagement,
Senior Research Professor of New Testament Studies, Dallas Theological Seminary

"Mark Strauss is my top-of-the-class, 'go-to' expert on Bible translation, and his *40 Questions* presents a remarkably clear, informative, and comprehensive treatment of one of the most underappreciated ministries in the history of the church—the ministry of putting the words of God in the hands and hearts of people. Although I have taught the topic of Bible translation for years, by reading this book I learned things I did not know and was challenged to think in fresh ways about both the challenges and glory of the translation process. This is a wonderfully accessible volume that will serve equally well in a church Bible study group or an academic classroom. I highly recommend it!"

—George H. Guthrie, PhD,
Professor of New Testament,
Regent College

To my colleagues on the Committee on
Bible Translation (CBT) for the
New International Version,
whose brilliance in all things
biblical, humility, wit, and wisdom
are a constant source of joy and inspiration.

Contents

Abbreviations

Bible Versions

ASV	American Standard Version (1901)
AV	Authorized Version (another name for the KJV)
CEB	Common English Bible (2011)
CEV	Contemporary English Version (1995)
CSB	Christian Standard Bible (2017)
ESV	English Standard Version (2001)
GNB/GNT	Good News Bible/Good News Translation (1976; 1992)
GW	God's Word (1995)
HCSB	Holman Christian Standard Bible (2004)
ICB	International Children's Bible (1986)
ISV	International Standard Version (1995)
JPS	Jewish Publication Society *Tanakh* (1985)
KJV	King James Version (1611)
LB	Living Bible (1971)
MSG	The Message (2002)
NAB	New American Bible (revised 1988, 1990)
NASB	New American Standard Bible (1970; 1995; 2020)
NEB	New English Bible (1970)
NET	New English Translation (2006; 2017)
NCV	New Century Version (1987)
NIV	New International Version (1978; 1984; 2011)
NIrV	New International Reader's Version (1996)
NIVI	New International Version, Inclusive Language Edition (1996)
NJB	New Jerusalem Bible (1985)
NKJV	New King James Version (1982)
NLT	New Living Translation (1996; 2004)
NRSV	New Revised Standard Version (1990; 2022)
PME	Phillips' New Testament in Modern English (1958)
REB	Revised English Bible (1989)
RSV	Revised Standard Version (1952)
RV	Revised Version (1885)
TEV	Today's English Version (same as GNB)

Other Abbreviations

b.	born
c.	*circa* (Latin), "around"
ch(s).	chapter(s)
d.	died
DSS	Dead Sea Scrolls
ed(s).	editor(s); edited by
e.g.	*exempli gratia* (Latin), "for example"
IBS	International Bible Society
i.e.	*id est* (Latin), "that is"
LXX	Septuagint (Greek OT)
MT	Masoretic Text (Hebrew)
NT	New Testament
OT	Old Testament
p., pp.	page, pages
UBS	United Bible Societies
RCC	Roman Catholic Church
SIL	Summer Institute of Linguistics (Wycliffe affiliate)
v., vv.	verse, verses
WH	B. F. Westcott and F. J. A. Hort

A Note on the Use of Italics and Underline in Biblical Quotations

Some Bible versions use italics to indicate words in their translation that do not have a corresponding Hebrew or Greek word (a practice we discuss in Question 15). So, for example: 2 Corinthians 9:7 in the NASB reads, "Each one *must do* just as he has decided in his heart." When quoting these verses, we retain the italics. To avoid confusion, therefore, in this book we will use underline instead of italics in biblical quotations to point out words or phrases under discussion. For example: "The Word became <u>flesh</u>" (John 1:14 NIV) is an example where the Greek word *sarx* means "human being."

Introduction

The Bible is the most influential book in human history. For two millennia, it has been the most read, most studied, most copied, most translated, most published, most purchased, most discussed, most debated, and most revered book of all time. The British and Foreign Bible Society estimates that since the invention of the printing press in the fifteenth century, somewhere between five to seven billion copies of the Bible have been printed.[1]

The Bible is many things. It is a library of great literature, comprised of a wide range of diverse genres: epic poetry, historical narrative, legal statutes, prophetic oracles, wisdom writings, psalms of praise and lament, proverbs and epigrams, philosophical discussion, letters, parables, allegories, apocalyptic imagery, and more. It is a story, the divine narrative of humanity's creation, rebellion, and restoration with their Creator God. It is a drama, the cosmic struggle of God versus Satan, right versus wrong, truth versus error. It is a guidebook, providing essential direction and guidance for human flourishing. For Christian believers, it is the Word of God, a divine self-revelation for the people of God.

Yet despite the great importance of this book, almost all readers access the Bible in translation rather than in its original languages. Even for those with some working knowledge of the Hebrew and Greek, their primary engagement with the text, whether for reading, study, teaching, or preaching, is with a translation in their native language.

When we consider these two facts—the great importance of this book and its access primarily through translation—the importance of Bible translation becomes obvious. This book is meant to provide answers to forty basic questions related to the nature, practice, and history of Bible translation.

While many of the topics and principles we cover relate to translation in general, our primary focus will be on *English Bible translation.* A sixth and final section will focus on issues specific to translations around the world. The forty questions have been divided into six categories: (1) the necessity, goals, and methods of Bible translation; (2) preparation for translation; (3) challenges for translators; (4) the history of (English) Bible translation; (5) contemporary English versions; and (6) international Bible translation.

1. "Best-Selling Book," Guinness World Records, accessed August 15, 2022, https://www.guinnessworldrecords.com/world-records/best-selling-book-of-non-fiction.

PART 1

The Necessity, Goals, and Methods of Bible Translation

QUESTION 1

Why Do We Need Bible Translation?

The "Real" Bible

A colleague of mine who has Swedish ancestry was describing his experience as a boy growing up in a Swedish Baptist church in Minnesota. One of his Sunday school teachers was an old Swede with a deep love for God's Word. As they read together in class, occasionally a difficult issue would come up in the text. The teacher would puzzle over the English for a while and then say, "Let's check the original." He would pull out his Swedish Bible, read the passage, and then say, "Oh, let me explain!" The Swedish Bible was the one he had grown up with, and so, for him, it was the *real Bible*. For people who grow up in a context where the Bible is regularly read and taught, the real Bible is the Bible they know and love. For most English speakers over the last four centuries, this has been the Authorized or King James Version. For many English-speaking millennials today, it might be the New International Version, the New American Standard Bible, the New King James Version, the English Standard Version, or the New Living Translation.

But, of course, none of these is the real Bible—or, we should say, the *original* Bible. They are all English translations. The original Bible was written in Hebrew, Aramaic, and Greek, many centuries ago. The vast majority of people in the world today read the Bible in translation, not in its original languages. So, the simple answer to the question, "Why do we need Bible translation?" is twofold: (1) the Bible is God's Word, his message for Christians today, yet (2) it was not written to us. It was written to people in diverse times and places and circumstances and in *different languages*. This being the case, the importance of Bible translation can hardly be overstated. Providing a translation that gets the meaning right is essential for hearing God speak today.

In translation studies, the language of the original text is called the *source language* or *donor language*. The text being translated from is the *source/donor text*. The language you are translating into is the *receptor* or *target language*, and the result is the *receptor/target text*. For the Bible, the source language of the Old Testament (OT) is primarily Hebrew, with a few passages in Aramaic, and the source text is the *Tanakh*, or Hebrew Scriptures, what Christians call the Old Testament. For the New Testament (NT), the source language is Koine Greek, and the source texts are the twenty-seven "books" that make up the NT canon. For Roman Catholic and Eastern Orthodox believers, there are also the deuterocanonical books, or the Apocrypha (see Question 7), which were written between the OT and the NT. These are mostly in Greek. The main receptor language we will deal with in this book is English. The last section will briefly discuss international Bible translation.

The Hebrew Bible (Old Testament)

Hebrew was the language of the Jewish people for as far back as we can trace their history. The Hebrew of the Old Testament, known as Biblical or Classical Hebrew, is from the Northwest Semitic family of languages, with close relationships to Aramaic, Phoenician, and Ugaritic. Our earliest examples of written Hebrew come from around the tenth century BC. Hebrew was originally written in what is known today as the Paleo-Hebrew script. This was gradually replaced between the fifth and third centuries BC with an alphabet derived from Aramaic. This new alphabet was the standard text of Jesus's day and is used today in modern Hebrew.

Hebrew is written and read from right to left, and so Hebrew books open on the right side and read from what in English is back to front. Here is Genesis 1:1 in Hebrew:

בראשית ברא אלהים את השמים ואת הארץ

[the earth] [and] [the heavens] [God] [created] [In the beginning]

The Hebrew alphabet contains twenty-two letters, all of which are consonants. The vowels were understood and pronounced when the text was read, based on the reader's prior knowledge of the spoken language. A vowel system, made up of dots, dashes, and other symbols placed around the consonants, was introduced during the Middle Ages by scholars known as the Masoretes. The text they standardized and edited is known as the Masoretic Text (MT). It is the standard Hebrew Bible today. Here's an example of Genesis 1:1 with its vowel points:

בְּרֵאשִׁית בָּרָא אֱלֹהִים אֵת הַשָּׁמַיִם וְאֵת הָאָרֶץ

Hebrew continued to be spoken by the Jews during the Persian, Greek, and Roman periods, although Aramaic gradually increased in usage among the common people (see discussion below). The Jewish culture of Palestine in

Jesus's day was trilingual, with Hebrew, Aramaic, and Greek all widely used.[1] Jesus likely taught mostly in Aramaic; he worshipped in synagogue services that used the Hebrew text; and he would have conversed with governmental officials, merchants, soldiers, and other foreigners mostly in Greek.

An interesting side note is that, following the two failed Jewish revolts against the Romans (AD 66–74; AD 132–135), Hebrew gradually declined in usage and disappeared as a spoken language somewhere between AD 200 and 400. It continued to be used, however, in liturgical and other religious contexts in Judaism. Modern Hebrew is actually the intentional revival of the ancient language, provoked especially by the Zionist movement to establish a Jewish homeland and the need for a common language among Jewish immigrants to Israel. Near the end of the nineteenth century, Eleazer Ben-Yehuda, an activist in the Jewish nationalist movement, began reviving Hebrew as a spoken language. This process utilized and modified biblical Hebrew, as well as Yiddish and other Jewish dialects, and introduced modern vocabulary to create what is today modern Hebrew—a remarkable revival of a "dead" language after almost two millennia!

The Aramaic of Scripture

While most of the Old Testament is in Hebrew, a few sections are in Aramaic, including Ezra 4:8–6:18 and 7:12–26, Daniel 2:4–7:28, and one verse in Jeremiah (10:11). Aramaic is a general term for a group of related dialects that are part of the larger family of Northwest Semitic languages, which includes Hebrew, Phoenician, and Ugaritic. Aramaic has been spoken in various forms for more than three thousand years. The term originally referred to the language of the Arameans, a people group from the region of Syria and Mesopotamia. During the period of the Assyrian Empire (911–605 BC), Aramaic gradually became the *lingua franca*, or common language, for trade and diplomacy. This continued throughout the Babylonian (605–539 BC) and Persian (539–334 BC) periods. Only after the conquests of the Greeks in the fourth century BC (see below) did Greek replace Aramaic as the common trade language of the Eastern Mediterranean.

The Aramaic material in the book of Ezra occurs mostly in governmental correspondence (4:8–6:18; 7:12–26), which would have been written in the common language of diplomacy. In compiling the text, the author(s) probably kept these sources in their original language. The Aramaic in Daniel (Dan. 2:4–7:28) is more puzzling. In Daniel chapter 2, King Nebuchadnezzar has a dream and asks his astrologers (known as "Chaldeans") to interpret the dream. Daniel 2:4 NASB reads, "Then the Chaldeans spoke to the King in Aramaic." Some translators consider the phrase "in Aramaic" to be part of the

1. Latin would also be spoken among Roman officials and soldiers based in Judea and Galilee; but few Jews would have understood Latin.

narrative, identifying the language that the astrologers spoke (NASB; NKJV; NRSV; ESV; NLT; CEB). Others consider it to be an editorial note added to identify the change in language at this point in the text (NIV; CSB; NET). The NIV drops the phrase and notes the change in language in the footnote. The CSB includes a parenthetic note: "The Chaldeans spoke to the king (Aramaic begins here)"; and the NET Bible has "The wise men replied to the king: [What follows is in Aramaic] . . . ". This latter interpretation seems most likely, since the text here switches to Aramaic, not just in the words of the astrologers but in the narrative that follows all the way through to the end of chapter 7 (2:4–7:28).[2] Chapter 8 then returns to Hebrew for the rest of the book.

The reason for this change in language is debated by scholars. Some think it is an intentional literary shift. These chapters relate to the Gentile nations and so are presented in the language they would understand. Others think the switch is not literary or theological but related to the transmission of the text and the sources used by the author or editor when compiling the book of Daniel.

By the time of Jesus, Aramaic had become the common language of Jews in Israel. Jesus probably spoke and taught mostly in Aramaic. Although the New Testament is written in Greek, occasional Aramaic words and phrases appear, transliterated with Greek letters. Examples include Jesus's words at the raising of Jairus's daughter, *Talitha koum* ("Little girl, arise!"; Mark 5:41), his command at the healing of a deaf man, *Ephphatha* ("Be opened!"; Mark 7:34), and his prayer in the garden of Gethsemane, *Abba* ("Father"; Mark 14:36). The apostle Paul picks up this last usage, occasionally referring to God as *Abba* (Rom. 8:15; Gal. 4:6). Paul also uses the Aramaic expression *Marana tha* ("Our Lord, Come!") in 1 Corinthians 16:22. This was likely a common prayer of the early Aramaic-speaking church in Jerusalem, praying for Christ's soon return.

The Greek New Testament

While the Old Testament is almost all in Hebrew, the New Testament is written entirely in Greek, and more specifically, Hellenistic or Koine Greek. The Greek language has the longest documented history of any Indo-European language, with roots going back to the Mycenaean civilization in the fifteenth century BC. The Greek alphabet was derived from the Phoenician alphabet, which also lies behind the alphabets of Latin, Cyrillic, Coptic, and other languages.

Greek proper can be divided into four main periods: Classical, Koine, Medieval (or Byzantine), and Modern. Classical Greek, which included various dialects (Attic, Ionic, Aeolic, and Doric), was the form of Greek used by

---

2. Stephen R. Miller further notes that the astrologers would likely have spoken in Akkadian, the common language of the city, rather than in Aramaic (*Daniel*, New American Commentary 18 [Nashville: Broadman & Holman, 1994], 81).

writers from Homer (eighth century BC) to Plato (fourth century BC). Koine, also known as Hellenistic Greek, developed in the decades following the conquests of Alexander the Great in the fourth century BC. Alexander became king of the Greek kingdom of Macedon at the early age of twenty, after his father Phillip II was assassinated. Alexander inherited from his father a brilliant military mind and quickly set out for conquest. Within ten years, he had conquered the mighty Persian Empire and most of the Eastern Mediterranean, including Anatolia (modern Turkey), Syria, Egypt, Mesopotamia, and a vast area reaching as far east as India.

Alexander had been tutored by the renowned Greek philosopher Aristotle, and he had a love for all things Greek, including language, culture, art, and philosophy. Wherever he went, he promoted Greek ways, establishing Greek-style cities, with gymnasiums, public baths, theaters, and stadiums. He aggressively promoted Greek culture, settling Greek colonists in various locations and encouraging his soldiers to intermarry with conquered peoples. As a result, Greek culture spread, and the Greek language became the *lingua franca* of the Eastern Mediterranean. It was a necessary tool of communication for anyone who needed to travel or who wanted to interact with merchants, soldiers, and government officials. *Koinē* in Greek means "common" and refers to the fact that this form of Greek became the common language of subject people groups. It was almost always second-language Greek, meaning that a local population would speak their native tongue and then use Greek for cross-cultural communication in travel, trade, and diplomacy.

The spread of Koine Greek and the translation of the Hebrew Scriptures into Greek (the Septuagint; see Question 23) had a profound impact on early Christianity. It allowed Christian missionaries to speak and write in this common language wherever they traveled and to defend the gospel using a Greek translation of the Hebrew Bible.

In general, the Koine is simpler and less precise than Classical Greek. It also has many different dialects and speech variations. The Greek of the New Testament varies in style and sophistication from author to author. The gospel of Mark and Johannine literature are written in a simpler, Semitic-style Greek. The letter to the Hebrews and Luke's two works, Luke and Acts, are written in a higher literary style. Each author has their own unique style, determined by their background and education.

Summary

Translation is necessary because the Bible was not written in today's languages. The Old Testament was written in Classical Hebrew, with a few passages in Aramaic. The New Testament was written in Koine Greek, with occasional words or phrases transliterated from Aramaic. Koine, or "common," Greek became the trade and diplomatic language following the conquests of Alexander the Great. Having a common language throughout the Eastern

Mediterranean broke down barriers of communication, creating a favorable context for the expansion of early Christianity.

REFLECTION QUESTIONS

1. What English translation, if any, did you grow up using? How did you view this version (positives and/or negatives)?

2. In what language(s) was the Old Testament originally written? What did you learn in this chapter about this language?

3. In what language was the New Testament originally written? What did you learn here about this language?

4. Who was Alexander the Great, and what did he accomplish?

5. How did the spread of Koine Greek impact the early Christian movement?

QUESTION 2

What Should Be the Goals of Bible Translation?

There is a broad consensus concerning the essential goals of Bible translation. Consider these quotes from the introductions of some of the most popular English Bible versions:

New American Standard Bible

The NASB strives to adhere as closely as possible to the original languages of the Holy Scriptures and to make the translation in a fluent and readable style according to current English usage.[1]

New King James Version

This principle of complete equivalence seeks to preserve *all* of the information in the text, while presenting it in good literary form. . . . Complete equivalence translates fully, in order to provide an English text that is both accurate and readable.[2]

Christian Standard Bible

The CSB places equal value on fidelity to the original and readability for a modern audience, resulting in a translation that achieves both goals.[3]

New International Version

We have prioritized accuracy, clarity and literary quality with the goal of creating a translation suitable for public and private reading, evangelism, teaching, preaching, memorizing and liturgical use.[4]

---

1. Foreword to the New American Standard Bible (La Habra, CA: Lockman Foundation, 2020).
2. Preface to the New King James Version (Nashville: Thomas Nelson, 1982); italics in original.
3. Introduction to the Christian Standard Bible (Nashville: Holman Bible, 2020).
4. Preface to the New International Version (Grand Rapids: Zondervan, 2011).

Common English Bible

Accuracy and clarity. The CEB translators balance rigorous accuracy in the rendition of ancient texts with an equally passionate commitment to clarity of expression in the target language.[5]

New Living Translation

The goal of any Bible translation is to convey the meaning and content of the ancient Hebrew, Aramaic, and Greek texts as accurately as possible to contemporary readers. . . . The resulting translation is easy to read and understand, while also accurately communicating the meaning and content of the original biblical texts.[6]

Good News Translation

The Good News Bible . . . seeks to state clearly and accurately the meaning of the original texts in words and forms that are widely accepted by people who use English as a means of communication.[7]

New Century Version

Two basic premises guided the translation process of the New Century Version. The first concern was that the translation be faithful to the manuscripts in the original languages. . . . The second concern was to make the language clear enough for anyone to read the Bible and understand it.[8]

Notice that all of these Bible versions agree on two fundamental goals of translation, *accuracy* and *readability*. One might think from this that there is a great deal of agreement and a single unified approach to translation. Yet these eight versions represent a broad spectrum of approaches, from very literal to very idiomatic. This is because, to a certain extent, they have different ideas of what is meant by accuracy and readability.

What Constitutes Accuracy?

The answer to the question, "What is the meaning of a text?" can be a complicated one in the modern field of literary criticism. Contemporary discussions of hermeneutics (the science and art of biblical interpretation) debate the relative roles of authors, texts, and readers in the creation and discernment of "meaning" in written texts.[9] For our (simplified) purposes, *accu-*

---

5. Preface to the Common English Bible (Nashville: Abingdon, 2013); italics in original.
6. "A Note to Readers," in the New Living Translation (Carol Stream, IL: Tyndale House, 2015).
7. Foreword to the Good News Translation (New York: American Bible Society, 1992).
8. Preface to the New Century Version (Nashville: Thomas Nelson, 2005).
9. See Jeannine K. Brown, *Scripture as Communication: Introducing Biblical Hermeneutics*, 2nd ed. (Grand Rapids: Zondervan, 2021), 1–131.

racy in translation may be defined as reproducing the meaning of the source text in the receptor language in a way that preserves, as much as possible, the author's intention.

Historical and Cultural Accuracy

An inaccurate translation is therefore one that misrepresents the historical or cultural meaning intended by the author. This can sometimes be seen in versions that seek immediate relevance over historical precision. In Romans 16:16, Paul encourages the believers in Rome to "Greet one another with a holy kiss" (most versions). J. B. Phillips contemporizes this as, "Give each other a hearty handshake all around" (PME; cf. 2 Cor. 13:12; 1 Thess. 5:26; 1 Peter 5:14). The Living Bible similarly has "Shake hands warmly with each other" (cf. 1 Cor. 16:20; 1 Thess. 5:26; 1 Peter 5:14). These versions are intentionally recontextualizing the text, seeking to communicate its message of mutual love and affection for contemporary cultures where kissing is not a sign of such hospitality. For more examples, see Questions 5 and 36.

Capturing as Much of the Meaning as Possible

Accuracy can also be compromised by simplifying or generalizing the text to the point that significant meaning is lost. Instead of "this is the Law and the Prophets" (ESV), J. B. Phillips translates Matthew 7:12 as "this is the essence of all true religion" (PME). The problem is Jesus is not here epitomizing all religion. He is distilling the many laws of the Hebrew Torah into their central theme. Similarly, instead of "But now apart from the law the righteousness of God has been made known" (Rom. 3:21 NIV), the Living Bible reads, "But now God has shown us a different way to heaven." But the manifestation of the righteousness of God for Paul is far more than a ticket to heaven.

Loss of Accuracy Through Obscurity

In the previous two examples, translations were deemed inaccurate because they translated the text too *freely*. But in many other cases, inaccuracy results from translating too *formally*. Esther 1:14 ESV describes advisors to the Persian king Xerxes as the seven princes of Persia and Media "who saw the king's face" (*ro'e pene hammelekh*). This Hebrew idiom, however, does not refer to literally seeing the king's face (which would apply to any number of servants), but rather to an authoritative position to give counsel. In English you would never say, "These were the White House officials who saw the President's face." The NASB translates more accurately as "who had access to the king's presence." The NAB has "who were in the king's personal service."

Similarly, in Luke 15:20, when the father of the prodigal son sees his son returning, the NKJV reads, "his father saw him and . . . ran and <u>fell on his neck</u>." The phrase "fell on his neck" is a literal rendering of the Greek phrase *epepesen epi ton tracēhlon autou*. But of course, in English we would never say it this way. It sounds like he is attacking his son (perhaps what we would expect from the father after the son squandered his inheritance!). In normal English, we would say, "he hugged him" (NET; CEB; CEV), "he embraced him" (NLT; ESV; NASB; REB), or "he threw his arms around him" (NIV; TEV).

What Constitutes Readability?

Like accuracy, readability is a goal affirmed by virtually all translators. Yet just as there are different perspectives on what constitutes accuracy, so there are different perspectives on what constitutes readability. As we will see, different kinds of translations (formal, mediating, functional; Question 3) set different standards of readability.

Readability as Comprehension

For some translators, readable means understandable or comprehensible. The meaning of the text may not be readily apparent, but can be determined when the overall context is observed and reflected upon. Compare Psalm 12:2 in the NRSV and NIV:

> NRSV They utter lies to each other; with flattering lips and a double heart they speak.
>
> NIV Everyone lies to their neighbor; they flatter with their lips but harbor deception in their hearts.

The Hebrew idiom to speak "with a heart and a heart" (*belev walev*) is translated by the NRSV as to speak "with . . . a double heart." While this may be understandable from the larger context, it is awkward and opaque English. I would never say of someone who distorts the truth or seeks to deceive that "they speak with a double heart." By seeking to retain the Hebrew idiom, the NRSV may (or may not) be *comprehensible*, but it is certainly not clear.

Readability as Clarity

Readability as *clarity* means that the text is not just understandable upon reflection but that its meaning is readily apparent to the reader. The ESV translates Isaiah 6:10 as "Make the heart of this people dull, and their ears heavy." The Hebrew verb translated "make . . . heavy" (*hakhbed*) in some contexts can mean to make something heavy or burdensome. It can also mean to "honor," "glorify," or "harden." When used of ears, it means to deafen or stop someone from hearing. The CSB reads, "deafen their ears." CEB has "make their ears deaf." These translations are both comprehensible *and clear*.

Readability as Natural Language

Taking readability a step further, a translation may be *clear*, but not *natural*. In the 1984 edition of the NIV, Psalm 23:1 reads, "The LORD is my shepherd, I shall not be in want." This translation may be clear (there is no confusion as to what it means), but it is not natural. No native speaker in English would say, "I am not in want today." They would say, "I have everything I need" or perhaps "I lack nothing." The likely reason for this translation is that Psalm 23 is one of the most beloved and well-known passages in the Bible, and many people know it by heart from the King James Version: "The LORD is my shepherd, I shall not want." Seeking to preserve as much of the familiar wording as possible, the original NIV translators rendered this as "I shall not be in want." The 2011 edition of the NIV changed this to a more natural reading, "The LORD is my shepherd, I lack nothing." The NLT is even more natural: "The LORD is my shepherd; I have all that I need."

The difference between a translation that is "clear" and one that is "natural" is subtle but important. I have a missionary friend who served for a number of years as a Bible translator in Guatemala. He described to me his experience of working on a particular verse and reading his first draft to one of his native-language consultants. He asked, "Does this make sense?" and the man replied, "Yes." Sensing some hesitation, my friend asked, "Is this how *you* would say it?" The consultant laughed and said, "No!" and responded how a native-language speaker would say the phrase. The draft translation "worked" grammatically and lexically. It was comprehensible and even clear. But it was not natural. This kind of natural fluency is something native speakers intuitively recognize, but it can take many years for new language learners to pick up.

So should a translation strive to be natural? Another way to ask this is whether a translation should sound like a translation from another language, or whether it should sound like an original composition in the receptor language. We will discuss this topic—sometimes called "domesticating" versus "foreignizing" translation—in Question 6 below.

Other Goals

While accuracy and readability are the most widely asserted goals of Bible translation, others, such as beauty and dignity, should also be noted.[10] "Beauty" usually refers to literary quality. A children's book or a simple

10. Ken Barker, for example, describes four goals of translation, using the acronym A-B-C-D: accuracy, beauty, clarity, and dignity. Kenneth Barker, *The Balance of the NIV: What Makes a Good Translation* (Grand Rapids: Baker, 1999), 41–55, 112–141; Kenneth Barker, "Bible Translation Philosophies with Special Reference to the New International Version," in *The Challenge of Bible Translation: Communicating God's Word to the World*, Festschrift Ronald F. Youngblood, eds. Glen G. Scorgie, Mark L. Strauss, Steven M. Voth (Grand Rapids: Zondervan, 2003), 51–63.

instruction manual might be easy to read and understandable, but would not be considered great literature. By contrast, a well-written essay may be difficult to understand, communicating complex ideas with sophisticated vocabulary and grammar, but be very fine in literary quality. The NT letter to the Hebrews is an example of high literary Greek (and a great challenge for my beginning Greek students!). Beauty can also refer to aesthetic appeal. One of the great challenges of translating poetry is that it often depends on formal features, such as assonance, alliteration, parallelism, rhyme, and rhythm, for its appeal. Translating poetry in a way that preserves both its cognitive content and its aesthetic appeal can be a great challenge (see Question 13).

Another goal often set forth by Bible translators is "dignity," translating the text in a manner appropriate for sacred Scripture. Translations that are colloquial, coarse, or trendy seldom gain wide support or staying power. Rob Lacey's *The Street Bible*, also known as *The Word on the Street*, was meant to translate the Bible in the hip language of the street. Instead of "In the beginning God created the heavens and the earth" (Gen. 1:1 NIV), the *Street Bible* reads, "First off, nothing. No light, no time, no substance, no matter. Second off, God starts it all up and WHAP! Stuff everywhere."[11] In Genesis 2:23, instead of Adam saying about Eve, "This is at last bone of my bones and flesh of my flesh" (ESV), the *Street Bible* has, "Woah! Now we're talking!" says Adam. "She's like me . . . only not. Same bones, same skin, same shape . . . only not. She's . . . uh . . . sexy."[12] Needless to say, this doesn't quite achieve the poetic dignity of the original text.

In the preface to the NRSV, the translators note the goal of producing a dignified translation and point to the significance of the KJV tradition in achieving this goal: "We have resisted the temptation to introduce terms and phrases that merely reflect current moods, and have tried to put the message of the Scriptures in simple, enduring words and expressions that are worthy to stand in the great tradition of the King James Bible and its predecessors."[13]

Summary

There are two main goals that virtually all Bible translators strive to achieve: accuracy and readability. "Accuracy" means interpreting the text according to the author's intended meaning, staying true to the original historical and cultural context, and using clear and accurate English to communicate that meaning. Translators (and readers), however, sometimes have different thresholds as to what constitutes "readability" in the target language, whether it means comprehension, clarity, or naturalness. Debate on this issue

---

11. Rob Lacey, *The Street Bible* (Grand Rapids: Zondervan, 2003), 20.
12. Lacey, *Street Bible*, 24.
13. Preface to the New Revised Standard Version (Nashville: Thomas Nelson, 1989).

centers especially on whether priority in the translation process is given to form or meaning. It is to this issue we turn in the next three questions.

REFLECTION QUESTIONS

1. What goals do virtually all English Bible versions claim for themselves?
2. What constitutes "accuracy" in translation?
3. The text talks about different degrees of "readability." What are these?
4. What, in your opinion, constitutes "readability"?
5. What other goals for translation are discussed here? Can you think of others that are important?

QUESTION 3

What Are the Main Philosophies or Methods of Translation?

The previous question discussed the primary goals of translation as accuracy and readability. In this question we discuss the various approaches that strive to achieve these goals.

Formal versus Functional Equivalence

Historically, there have been two main philosophical and methodological approaches to translation. *Formal equivalence*, also known as word-for-word, literal, or direct translation, seeks to reproduce the *form* of the source text as much as possible. *Functional equivalence*, also known as dynamic equivalence, sense-for-sense, free, idiomatic, or meaning-based, seeks to reproduce the *meaning* of the source text, regardless of form. Formal equivalence claims greater allegiance to the source text. Functional equivalence claims equal allegiance to both source text and receptor language but insists that communication fails if inadequate attention is given to reception by the target audience.

Lexical Concordance versus Word Meanings in Context

At the level of words, a formal equivalent translation seeks whenever possible to use the same English word to translate a particular Greek or Hebrew word. We can call this "lexical concordance." Consider the Greek word *nomos*, which is the word most commonly translated as "law." The word occurs seventy-four times in Paul's letter to the Romans. In the ESV, a more formal equivalent version, it is translated "law" in all seventy-four cases. Similarly, the NASB, another formal equivalent version, translates seventy-three of these as "law." By contrast, a functional equivalent version, like the New Living Translation (NLT), translates it in a variety of ways depending on the context. Consider Romans 7:21–23:

ESV So I find it to be a law [*nomos*] that when I do right evil lies close at hand. For I delight in the law [*nomos*] of God, in my inner being, but I see in my members another law [*nomos*] waging war against the law [*nomos*] of my mind and making me captive to the law [*nomos*] of sin that dwells in my members.

NLT I have discovered this principle of life [*nomos*]—that when I want to do what is right, I inevitably do what is wrong. I love God's law [*nomos*] with all my heart. But there is another power [*nomos*] within me that is at war with my mind. This power [*nomos*] makes me a slave to the sin that is still within me.

The ESV is more formally equivalent, consistently translating the Greek *nomos* as "law." The NLT seeks functional equivalence, translating *nomos* according to its closest English equivalent in context ("principle of life," "law," "power"). The ESV is closer to the source text; the NLT is clearer in the receptor language.

While the ESV and other formal equivalent versions seek to be consistent, no version achieves complete lexical concordance, since words often have different meanings in different contexts. The NASB, for example, while rendering *nomos* as "law" four times in these verses, uses "principle" in verse 21: "I find then the principle that evil is present in me" (Rom. 7:21). A footnote, however, alerts the reader that the word "principle" is "Lit. *law*." While this note is helpful in alerting readers that the Greek word used here is the same word that is translated "law" elsewhere, it is linguistically inaccurate. "Law" is not the "literal" meaning of *nomos*. According to the standard lexicons of New Testament Greek, *nomos* can mean many things: custom, rule, law, principle, norm, standard, regulation, command, legal system, sacred ordinance. It can also refer to the Pentateuch, the first five books of the Old Testament (as in "the Law and the Prophets"). As we will discuss later in detail (see Question 10), words don't have a single literal meaning; they have a range of possible senses—a semantic range. For this reason, it is almost never accurate to call something the "literal" meaning of a word.

Grammatical Form versus Semantic Function

While at the level of words, formal equivalence means seeking to translate in a one-to-one manner, at the level of syntax (the relationships between words), formal equivalence means reproducing the same grammatical constructions in the receptor text as in the source text. For example, in Romans 7:23a cited above, the ESV closely follows the Greek grammatical forms:

Greek:	*blepō*	*de*	*heteron*	*nomon*	*en tois melesin*	*mou*
English:	*I see*	*but*	*another*	*law*	*in the members*	*of me*
	verb	**conjunction**	**adjective**	**noun**	**prepositional phrase**	**pronoun**

ESV:	But	I see	in my members	another	law	
	conjunction	**verb**	**prep. phrase w/pos-sessive adj.**	**adjective**	**noun**	

Though the Greek and English have different word orders, the grammatical forms are the same, with only one exception: the Greek has a possessive pronoun in the genitive case (*mou*, "of me") while the ESV uses a possessive adjective "my." The potential difficulty is that, while reproducing the form of the Greek, the meaning in English can be obscured or misrepresented. For example, what does "I see in my members another law" mean? Is "the law" the Old Testament law? A rule or command? A principle or a power? Are "my members" body parts? As we shall see, one of the most significant problems with formal equivalence is the obscurity and inaccuracy that can result because of the differences between languages.

By focusing on the meaning (or *semantic function*) of each grammatical form, functional equivalent versions seek to answer these grammatical questions. For example, the NLT translates the phrase above as, "But there is another power within me." The Greek word *nomos* is here translated as "power" to make clear how the word is functioning in context. The perplexing phrase "in my members" (*en tois melesin mou*) is translated simply as "within me." The NIV is somewhere between the ESV and the NLT, translating the phrase, "but I see another law at work in me." The translation "law" is retained for *nomos* to capture Paul's wordplay, but the idiom "in my members" is translated more clearly as "in me," as in the NLT.

English Bible Versions on a Spectrum

All contemporary Bible versions lie on a spectrum between these two poles of form and function. The following chart shows the approximate place of the most popular contemporary English versions along this spectrum:

		Formal ◄	———	**Mediating**	———	——— ►	**Functional**			
ASV	RV	NKJV	KJV	NRSV	NAB	NIV	JB	NEB	GNT	CEV LB
Young's	RSV	ESV			NET	CEB	REB	NLT	NCV	PME
		NASB			(H)CSB	NJB			GW	MSG

In addition to formal and functional versions, we have introduced a third category—"mediating"—for the broad area in the middle of the spectrum. Versions like the NIV, NRSV, NET, (H)CSB, CEB, NAB, NJB, NEB, and REB represent a measure of balance between retaining the nuances of the Hebrew or Greek while preserving more idiomatic English. As the example from Romans 7:23a NIV above demonstrates, these versions are sometimes more literal and sometimes more idiomatic.

Using the categories of "readability" introduced in the previous question (Question 2), I suggest that formal equivalent versions tend to modify the form of the Hebrew or Greek until it is *comprehensible*. Mediating translations tend to modify the form until it is *clear*. And functional equivalent versions tend to modify it until it is *natural*.

A common slogan used for formal equivalent versions is, "As literal as possible; as free as necessary." The point is to render the text in a word-for-word manner until it becomes necessary to modify it. The challenge here is "as free as necessary" for what purpose? To achieve comprehension? clarity? natural language? A slogan for functional equivalence could be, "Translate the meaning; follow the form if it accomplishes this goal." Another way this has been expressed is, "As free as necessary, as faithful as possible."[1]

Historical Advocates for Meaning-Based Translation

On the surface of things, the most straightforward way to translate a text would seem to be to simply replace the words of one language with the words of another. Yet while this word-for-word approach has been practiced by many throughout the centuries, voices of dissent go back as far as we have records of translation discussion.

Cicero (106–43 BC)

The most famous statements from the Greco-Roman world for meaning-based translation come from Roman statesman and philosopher Marcus Tullius Cicero. For example, in introducing his own translation of several Greek orators into Latin, Cicero rejected "word-for-word" renderings and

1. Paul Cauer, *Die Kunst des Uebersetzens*, 4th ed. (Berlin: Weidmannsche Buchhandlung, 1909), 12.

instead claimed to reproduce the "same ideas" using Latin instead of Greek patterns of language:

> I did not translate them as an interpreter, but as an orator, keeping the same ideas and forms, or as one might say, the "figures" of thought, but in language which conforms to our usage. And in so doing, I did not hold it necessary to render word for word, but I preserved the general style and force of the language.[2]

Jerome (AD 342?–420)

In the late fourth century, the church father Jerome was commissioned by Pope Damasus to produce a new Latin version of the Bible. His translation, the Latin Vulgate, became the standard Bible of the Western church for a thousand years. In the course of his work, Jerome became a strong advocate for meaning-based translation, citing the authority of Cicero as a precedent. Jeremy Munday summarizes Jerome's translation philosophy:

> Jerome rejected the word-for-word approach because, by following so closely the form of the [source text], it produced an absurd translation, cloaking the sense of the original. The sense-for-sense approach, on the other hand, allowed the sense or content of the [source language] to be translated. In these poles can be seen the origin of both the "literal vs. free" and "form vs. content" debate that has continued until modern times.[3]

Martin Luther (1483–1586)

The Protestant Reformation in the sixteenth century saw the proliferation of vernacular translations of the Bible (see Question 24). The most famous of these was the German translation of Martin Luther (1483–1586). In the course of his work, Luther became a defender of an idiomatic translation approach. Describing his translation of the OT, he wrote:

> I must let the literal words go and try to learn how the German says that which the Hebrew expresses. . . . Whoever would speak German must not use Hebrew style. Rather he must see to it—once he understands the Hebrew author—that he concentrates on the sense of the text, asking himself,

2. Cicero, *De optimo genere oratorum*. Cited by Jeremy Munday, *Introducing Translation Studies: Theories and Applications*, 4th ed. (New York: Routledge, 2016), 31.
3. Munday, *Introducing Translation Studies*, 32.

> "Pray tell, what do the Germans say in such a situation?" . . . Let him drop the Hebrew words and express the meaning freely in the best German he knows.[4]

John Dryden (1631–1700)

Luther's intuitive sense of the importance of meaning over form was echoed and defined more specifically a century later by the English poet and translator John Dryden. In the preface to his translation of Ovid's *Epistles* in 1680, Dryden placed all translation in three categories: (1) *metaphrase*, a "word by word and line by line" approach; (2) *paraphrase*, which follows the "sense" of the text without strictly following its words, and (3) *imitation*, in which the translator uses the source text "as a pattern to write as he supposes that author would have done, had he lived in our age and in our country."[5] Dryer favored paraphrase as the right balance between metaphrase, which often distorted the meaning through servitude to the source text, and imitation, which betrayed "the memory and reputation of the dead."[6] These three categories are remarkably similar, respectively, to the categories of formal equivalence (= metaphrase), functional equivalence (= paraphrase), and what we will call "transculturation" or "recontextualization" (= imitation) (see Question 36).

Eugene Nida (1914–2011)

The most influential work on meaning-based translation in modern times came from the prolific pen of linguist and international Bible translator Eugene Nida (1914–2011), who is widely viewed as the "father of modern Bible translation." Influenced by Noam Chomsky's notion of deep structure in language, Nida and his colleagues sought to establish a "science" of translation. Nida's method was to break down a text into its basic meaning components or "kernel structures," which could then be restructured to transfer the semantic content of a source (or donor) text into the very different structures of a target (or receptor) language.[7] Nida originally called his method "dynamic equivalence" but subsequently renamed it "functional equivalence" because "dynamic" was being misused by some translators to focus on the response of the receptors to the exclusion of the meaning of the source text.[8]

---

4. *Luther's Works* (Philadelphia: Muhlenberg, 1960), 35:193.
5. Munday, *Introducing Translation Studies*, 43.
6. Munday, *Introducing Translation Studies*, 43.
7. Eugene A. Nida and Charles R. Taber, *The Theory and Practice of Translation* (Leiden: E. J. Brill, 1974).
8. For the reason for this terminological shift, see Jan de Waard and Eugene A. Nida, *From One Language to Another: Functional Equivalence in Bible Translating* (Nashville: Nelson, 1986), 7–8.

While these examples come from mostly European traditions, the debate between form and function is by no means limited to the West. Munday points to similar debates in imperial China, where the Eastern Han Dynasty and the Three Kingdom Period (c. 158–265) tended to produce word-for-word renderings, while the Jin Dynasty and the Northern and Southern Dynasties (c. 265–589) produced freer translations following target language usage.[9] Similarly, in the Arab world, Baghdad became a great center of translation during the ʾAbbāsid period (750–1250). While Greek scientific and philosophical words were originally translated in a word-for-word manner, this gave way to a more sense-for-sense approach, "creating fluent target texts which conveyed the meaning of the original without distorting the target language."[10]

Summary

Historically, the most significant debate related to Bible translation is that between formal and functional equivalence. Formal equivalence seeks to replicate the form of the original text as much as possible. Functional equivalence focuses on the meaning of the text, regardless of the form. Important early advocates of meaning-based translation include Cicero, St. Jerome, Martin Luther, and John Dryden. In the twentieth century, the work of Eugene Nida and his colleagues involved in international Bible translation has had a profound impact not only on translation of the Bible but on translation theory and practice in general.

An important caveat is in order here. While discussions about translation philosophy over the past two thousand years have focused especially on the question of form versus function, this has shifted significantly in recent years. Beginning in the second half of the twentieth century, linguists and translators sought to move beyond this historical debate to a more nuanced discussion that takes greater account of the complex nature of communication through language and cross-cultural communication. We will discuss some of these new directions in Question 6. Nevertheless, in the field of Bible translation, and especially in popular and nontechnical literature, the question of form versus function still dominates the discussion.

REFLECTION QUESTIONS

1. What is the goal of formal equivalence?
2. What is the goal of functional equivalence?

9. Munday, *Introducing Translation Studies*, 33.
10. Munday, *Introducing Translation Studies*, 36–37.

3. Which of these approaches makes the most sense to you? Why?

4. Where do the main Bibles you read lie on the spectrum between form and function? Have you read and used a Bible from a different place on the spectrum? What was your impression?

5. Who are some examples of historical advocates of a meaning-based rather than form-based approach to translation?

QUESTION 4

What Are the Strengths and Weaknesses of Formal Equivalence?

The previous question defined formal and functional equivalence. In this question and the next, we will note some strengths and weaknesses of each approach.

Strengths of Formal Equivalence

Identifying the Formal Structure of the Original Text

The first and most obvious strength of formal equivalence is allowing the reader to see the formal patterns of the original text. My beginning Greek students love formal equivalent versions like the NASB because they provide a crib or cheat sheet for their Greek translation assignments. For example, when you see the English word "flesh" in the NASB in the New Testament, you can be almost certain that it is translating the Greek word *sarx*. Similarly, when you see "flesh" in the Old Testament, it is almost always a rendering of the Hebrew word *basar*. This one-to-one correspondence provides a helpful window on the original text.

Tracing Recurrent Words and Verbal Allusions

Translating each word the same (lexical concordance) in turn allows the reader to trace repeated words and verbal allusions, even when words take on different shades of meaning in subsequent contexts. In an example given above (Question 3), reading the NLT alone would not enable the English reader to see that Paul is using the same Greek word (*nomos*) with various shades of meaning (principle, law, power). By consistently translating *nomos* as "law," the NASB reader can see that Paul is rhetorically playing with the Greek word to make a point about the Jewish law.

Another good example of this is the use of the Greek adverb *euthys* in the gospel of Mark. The word is characteristic of Markan style and the author uses it forty-two times. While *euthys* often means "immediately" or "just then," in some contexts it functions as a simple word of transition to the next scene.

***Euthys* in Mark 1**	
NKJV	**CEB**
1:10 And immediately, coming up from the water	1:10 While he was coming up out of the water
1:12 Immediately the Spirit drove Him into the wilderness.	1:12 At once the Spirit forced Jesus out into the wilderness.
1:18 They immediately left their nets and followed Him.	1:18 Right away, they left their nets and followed him.
1:20 And immediately He called them	1:20 At that very moment he called them.
1:21 Then they went into Capernaum, and immediately on the Sabbath He entered the synagogue	1:21 Jesus and his followers went into Capernaum. Immediately on the Sabbath Jesus entered the synagogue
1:23 Now there was a man in their synagogue with an unclean spirit. And he cried out	1:23 Suddenly, there in the synagogue, a person with an evil spirit screamed
1:28 And immediately His fame spread throughout all the region around Galilee.	1:28 Right away the news about him spread throughout the entire region of Galilee.
1:29 Now as soon as they had come out of the synagogue, they entered the house of Simon and Andrew, with James and John.	1:29 After leaving the synagogue, Jesus, James, and John went home with Simon and Andrew
1:30 Simon's wife's mother lay sick with a fever, and they told Him about her at once	1:30 Simon's mother-in-law was in bed, sick with a fever, and they told Jesus about her at once.
1:42 And immediately the leprosy left him, and he was cleansed.	1:42 Instantly, the skin disease left him, and he was clean.
1:43 And He sternly warned him and immediately sent him away	1:43 Sternly, Jesus sent him away

In eight of the eleven occurrences of *euthys* in Mark 1, the NKJV translates it as "immediately" (cf. NASB; ESV). The CEB, by contrast, translates the same word nine different ways. While the CEB may use more natural English, the NKJV captures something of Mark's rapid-fire style of writing.

Formal equivalence is also helpful for tracking verbal allusions. A good example is in 1 Corinthians 1–4, where Paul has been contrasting the world's claims of wisdom (*sophia*) with God's true wisdom.

> Where is the wise person [*sophos*]? Where is the teacher of the law? Where is the philosopher of this age? Has not God made foolish the wisdom [*sophia*] of the world? For since in the wisdom [*sophia*] of God the world through its wisdom [*sophia*] did not know him, God was pleased through the foolishness of what was preached to save those who believe. Jews demand signs and Greeks look for wisdom [*sophia*], but we preach Christ crucified: a stumbling block to Jews and foolishness to Gentiles, but to those whom God has called, both Jews and Greeks, Christ the power of God and the wisdom [*sophia*] of God. For the foolishness of God is wiser [*sophōteros*] than human wisdom, and the weakness of God is stronger than human strength. (1 Cor. 1:20–25 NIV)

The cross of Christ, which seems like foolishness from a human perspective, is in fact the great wisdom of God that saves us. In 1 Corinthians 3:10, Paul continues, "According to the grace of God which was given to me, as a wise master builder I have laid the foundation, and another builds on it" (NKJV). The Greek word translated "wise" here is *sophos*. Most versions, recognizing that builders or contractors are not usually described as "wise," translate this word as "skilled" (RSV; ESV; NRSV; CSB; NET) or "expert" (NIV 84; NLT; TEV; CEV). Yet while this is better in terms of contemporary English idiom, it misses an important verbal allusion. Paul is here alluding back to his previous discussion, where the true wisdom of God is the cross of Christ. It is the wisdom of the cross that he is building upon. Versions that translate *sophos* consistently as "wise" (NIV; NKJV; NASB; CEB) pick up this important allusion.

This example also illustrates how translators must make hard decisions and that translation involves compromise. Will you retain an important but awkward verbal allusion or translate more smoothly and miss the allusion? In either case, something will be lost and something gained. This also illustrates the helpfulness of using more than one version in your study. Formal equivalent versions tend to pick up more formal features—idioms, metaphors, verbal allusions, and wordplays—but may miss the most natural meaning in context. Functional equivalent versions tend to provide better English but may miss some of these nuances.

Identifying and Retaining Ambiguity

A third strength of formal equivalence is that it is less interpretive and so retains a greater degree of ambiguity. While ambiguity can be a bad thing, resulting in obscurity, it can also be viewed as a way to identify interpretational options for the reader. For example, the Greek genitive phrase that opens the book of Revelation, "The revelation of Jesus Christ" (*Apokalypsis Iēsou Christou*, 1:1), can be translated more precisely either as a subjective genitive, "The revelation from Jesus Christ" (NIV; NLT; cf. TEV) or as objective genitive, "The revelation about Jesus Christ."[1] Ambiguity is maintained by translating "of Jesus Christ" (NKJV; ESV; NASB; etc.).

Another example may be seen in 1 Corinthians 5:5, where Paul calls on the church to discipline a man involved in sexual sin. In the ESV, Paul says to "deliver this man to Satan for the destruction of the flesh [*sarx*], so that his spirit may be saved in the day of the Lord." The meaning of *sarx* here is greatly debated. While many versions consider it to refer in some sense to the man's body, others interpret it as referring to his fallen human nature. The NLT translates, "so that his sinful nature will be destroyed"; CEB has "to destroy his human weakness"; and GW reads, "to destroy his corrupt nature." While the 1984 NIV similarly had "so that the sinful nature may be destroyed," the 2011 NIV revision changes this to the more ambiguous "the destruction of the flesh."

Another example of retaining ambiguity can be seen in 1 Thessalonians 4:3–4, where the NASB translates, "For this is the will of God, your sanctification; *that is*, that you abstain from sexual immorality; that each of you know how to possess his own vessel in sanctification and honor." The interpretation of the last line is a difficult one. The Greek word translated "vessel" is *skeuos*, which can mean many things: "object," "thing" (Acts 10:11; Rom. 9:22; Rev. 18:12), "possession" (Mark 3:27), "pottery piece," "jar," "dish," "vessel" (Luke 8:16; Rom. 9:21; Rev. 2:27), "instrument," or "utensil" (Acts 9:15). It is sometimes used metaphorically of a person, including a person functioning as an instrument of God (2 Tim. 2:20–21) or as a man's wife (1 Peter 3:7). The verb translated "possess" can mean "get," "gain," "acquire," or "control," "gain mastery over." Most versions opt for a translation related to control or mastery over one's own body, interpreting the verse to refer to sexual self-control (NIV; CSB; NRSV; NJB; NET; ESV; NLT; etc.). A few favor "wife" and interpret the verse to mean faithfulness in marriage (TEV; NAB; GW). The NASB remains ambiguous by retaining the metaphor "vessel" without specifying the referent ("body" or "wife").

1. Daniel B. Wallace suggests this is "plenary genitive," meaning both objective and subjective (*Greek Grammar Beyond the Basics: An Exegetical Syntax of the New Testament* [Grand Rapids: Zondervan, 1996], 119–21).

There are potential assets and liabilities in retaining ambiguity. Positively, it doesn't force one interpretation on the reader, empowering them to make their own decision. Negatively, such ambiguity can confuse readers and promote a *wrong* interpretation. We should add that in this case, virtually all versions include footnotes providing alternatives. NASB has a footnote on "possess" that reads, "Or *acquire*" and a footnote on "vessel" that reads: "I.e., body; or wife."

Preserving Cultural Features Embedded in Metaphors and Idioms

A fourth potential strength of formal equivalence is the retention of Hebrew and Greek metaphors and idioms, which can preserve historical and cultural background material. Consider, Genesis 35:29, where the ESV reads, "Isaac . . . died and <u>was gathered to his people</u>" (cf. NIV; NASB; NKJV; NRSV). The Hebrew idiom means that "the deceased joins his ancestors in the realm of the dead" and probably reflects the practice of burying family members in a common tomb (cf. Gen. 25:17; 35:29; 49:33; Num. 20:24; Deut. 32:50).[2] Genesis 49:31 confirms that Isaac was buried in the family tomb at Machpelah. Meaning-based versions sometimes omit the idiom entirely (CEV; TEV) or use a more general expression like "He was buried with his ancestors" (CEB; cf. MSG) or "joining his ancestors in death" (NLT; cf. GW).

A New Testament example of preserving a cultural feature is seen in Luke 2:36–37, a passage that speaks of the pious and elderly prophetess Anna, who met Joseph and Mary when they brought the baby Jesus to the Jerusalem temple. Anna is described as "having lived with her husband seven years <u>from her virginity</u>, and as a widow until she was eighty-four. She did not depart from the temple, worshiping with fasting and prayer night and day" (RSV; cf. ESV). The Greek idiom "from her virginity" (*apo tēs parthenias autēs*) is an odd way in English to refer to a wedding day, and most English versions translate it instead as "after her marriage" (NIV; CSB; NRSV; NASB; cf. NLT; NET; CEB). Yet by retaining the Greek idiom, the RSV may preserve something of the religious and cultural background to Anna's deep piety, which is seen both in her purity as a virgin *before* her marriage and her celibacy and devotion to the Lord for many years *afterward*. Translators must decide whether to introduce awkward English to retain a cultural nuance.

Weaknesses of Formal Equivalence

While there are benefits of translating more formally, there are also weaknesses, including the potential for inaccuracy, obscurity, and unnatural language.

---

2. Kenneth A. Matthews, *Genesis 11:27–50:26*, New American Commentary (Nashville: Broadman & Holman, 2005), 356, 630.

Inaccuracy

Literal translation can misrepresent the original meaning. Romans 14:22 in the ESV reads, "The faith that you have, keep between yourself and God." By seeking lexical concordance in translating *pistis* as "faith," the ESV seems to be discouraging believers from sharing their faith. But the word *pistis* does not here refer to faith in Christ, but rather to one's personal *convictions* about issues in dispute in the Roman church, especially related to food and drink.[3] The REB reads more accurately, "If you have some firm conviction, keep it between yourself and God." The NIV similarly captures the meaning better: "So whatever you believe about these things keep between yourself and God."

In the NKJV Mark 1:2 and its parallels in Matthew 11:10 and Luke 7:27 read, "Behold, I send My messenger before your face" (cf. RSV; ESV). The English prepositional phrase "before your face" is a formal rendering of the Greek *pro prosōpou sou*. But this idiom has nothing to do with a literal face. It is a dead metaphor (see Question 13), which means "ahead of you" (NIV; NRSV; NAB; NLT; CSB; NET; REB; GNT; GW). While the 1971 NASB used "before your face," its 1995 update corrected this to "ahead of you." The NRSV similarly revised the RSV. Curiously, the ESV misses the idiom here (and parallels) but gets it right in Luke 9:52 and 10:1, where *pro prosōpou autou* is translated "ahead of him."

Awkward or Obscure Language

Literal translation often results in something that may not rise to the level of an inaccuracy, but sounds odd or awkward in English. Consider Genesis 18:11, where we learn that Abraham and Sarah are too old to have children:

> It had ceased to be with Sarah after the manner of women. (NRSV)
>
> Sarah was no longer menstruating. (CEB)
>
> Sarah had ceased to have her monthly periods. (NJB)
>
> Sarah was past the age of childbearing. (NIV)

The NRSV (cf. ESV) is the closest of these versions to the Hebrew, following it in an almost word-for-word manner. But the phrase "it had ceased to be with Sarah" is very awkward English, and the "manner of women" is a Hebrew euphemism (see Question 16) that would be obscure to most English readers. It refers to a woman's menstrual cycle. Together the two phrases indicate that Sarah had stopped menstruating and so could no longer produce children.

3. Douglas Moo, *The Epistle to the Romans*, New International Commentary on the New Testament, 2nd ed. (Grand Rapids: Eerdmans, 2018), 878.

The CEB states the meaning of the Hebrew idiom concretely in English: "Sarah was no longer menstruating." The NJB replaces the Hebrew euphemism ("manner of women") with an English one ("monthly period"). The NIV states the general point being made: "Sarah was past the age of childbearing." The NRSV, while close to the Hebrew form, is strange and obscure in English.

Unnatural Language

Sometimes a literal translation is clear enough to make sense but sounds unnatural in English. For example, Matthew 5:2 NASB reads, "And He opened His mouth and began to teach them, saying . . . ". The Greek phrase *anoixas to stoma autou* ("opening his mouth") is a common expression in Greek for starting a formal speech or teaching session. But we would never say it this way in English. While formal equivalent versions often translate the phrase literally (RSV; NASB; NRSV; NKJV), mediating and functional equivalent versions translate it more naturally as "he began to teach them" (NIV; TEV; NLT; NET; GW; NAB) or simply "he taught them" (CEB; CEV).

Another example of unnatural language is 1 Corinthians 9:16 ESV, which reads, "For if I preach the gospel, that gives me no ground for boasting. For necessity is laid upon me." This last sentence is very unnatural English. The Greek idiom indicates compulsion and would be more naturally translated as "since I am compelled to preach" (NIV) or "I am compelled by God to do it" (NLT).

Consistent Failure

The greatest weakness of formal equivalence is that while it may work adequately as a *method* of translation, it fails when set out as the *goal* of translation. The slogan "as literal as possible" means the translator proceeds methodologically by translating in a word-for-word manner, but the follow-up "as free as necessary" means that the translator changes the form *whenever* it is necessary to do so. And experience shows that this is in virtually every sentence in the Bible. Can formal equivalence be considered a "reliable" method if it fails so often, and translators must consistently default to functional equivalence? (See the next question.)

Summary

Formal equivalent versions can be helpful tools for students, providing a window on the formal features of the source language, tracing verbal allusions, identifying ambiguities in the text, and preserving cultural features associated with metaphors and idioms. Yet because of the many differences between languages, formal equivalence often results in inaccuracy, obscurity, and unnatural language. It fails as a consistent philosophy of translation.

REFLECTION QUESTIONS

1. Name some of the strengths of formal equivalence. Which of these do you think is most important and why?

2. Name some of the weaknesses of formal equivalence. Which of these do you think is most important and why?

3. How important is it for a translation to be clear to the receptor audience? How important is it to sound natural?

4. Did this chapter change your perspective on the relative merits of a literal translation? In what ways?

5. If you have ever studied a second language, consider some common phrases you have learned. How do these sound when translated word-for-word into English?

QUESTION 5

What Are the Strengths and Weaknesses of Functional Equivalence?

Functional equivalence seeks to reproduce the meaning of the source text in a way that is clear and natural in the receptor language, regardless of the form. Meaning in this case refers to the communicative intent of the speaker or author. Here are some of the strengths and potential weaknesses of functional equivalence.

Strengths of Functional Equivalence

Accurately Communicating the Meaning of the Text

Functional equivalence is most easily defended by looking at how language is translated around the world. The great majority of real-life translation across languages is functionally rather than formally equivalent. A visit to the United Nations could confirm this. When a speech is being simultaneously translated into dozens of languages, none of the translators are translating literally. All are translating idiomatically—changing the form of the words and grammar of the source language to communicate the meaning accurately in the receptor language. Another way to say this is that all are translating "sense-for-sense" rather than "word-for-word," comprehending the meaning of phrases and clauses, and utilizing equivalent words, phrases, and clauses to reproduce that sense. Any translator doing word-for-word translation in such a situation would be fired on the spot for incompetence and replaced with a true native speaker.

Anyone who has ever studied a foreign language soon recognizes that moving closer to the form of the source language can result in moving away from its meaning—if by meaning we mean the normal or standard way of speaking in the receptor language. Consider the common Spanish sentence *¿Cuántos años tienes?* A literal or word-for-word translation would be "How many years have you?" While this is good Spanish, it is very poor English. In English we would say, "How old are you?" Similarly, to ask someone's name in Spanish you would say, *¿Cómo se llama?,* literally "How yourself call?" Again, that is awkward and obscure in English. A good English translation is "What's your name?" To be literal (word-for-word) in form is to be inaccurate in meaning.

The same is of course true in biblical languages. Consider 2 Samuel 18:25, where King David is awaiting a report from a battle. A lone runner appears on the horizon. In the NKJV, a more formal equivalent version, David says, "If he is alone, <u>there is news in his mouth</u>" (cf. ESV; NASB; NRSV). The idiom "there is news in his mouth" may be good Hebrew, but it is very strange English. I would never say, "Here comes Johnny, and there is news in his mouth." The NET Bible more accurately renders it "<u>he brings good news</u>" (cf. NIV; CSB; CEB; NLT). King David assumes that since the man is alone, he is a messenger bringing a report of victory. A defeat would be signaled by many troops retreating. In this case, a formal equivalent translation is awkward and obscure. A functional equivalent one is clear and accurate. This example raises the question of idioms, which by definition have a different meaning than their literal parts. We will examine many more examples of Hebrew and Greek idioms in Question 12.

Clarity

The goal of functional equivalence is not just to be comprehensible but to be *clear*, so that the translation is readily understandable to the target audience. In Joshua 9, during the conquest of Canaan by Joshua and the Israelites, the Gibeonites trick the Israelites into making a pact with them by pretending to come from a far-off land. Joshua grudgingly accepts the legitimacy of the pact, but places the Gibeonites in a position of servitude (Josh. 9:22). When five Amorite kings subsequently attack the Gibeonites, the Gibeonites send a message to Joshua requesting help. The RSV translates the message as "<u>Do not relax your hand</u> from your servants; come up to us quickly, and save us, and help us" (Josh. 10:6; cf. ESV). By rendering the Hebrew phrase formally, the RSV and ESV have obscured its meaning. "Do not relax your hand" would likely be misunderstood to mean "don't stop squeezing us" or "don't stop putting pressure on us." This is almost the opposite of its meaning, which is "don't abandon" (HCSB; cf. NIV; NASB; NRSV, NET, NAB), "don't desert" (CEB), or "don't forsake" (NKJV). In this case, a functionally equivalent translation is clear, while a formally equivalent one is obscure.

Also notice that in this case even several formally equivalent versions (NASB; NKJV; NRSV) recognize that the Hebrew phrase is an idiom and so modify its form to reproduce its meaning. This illustrates an important point mentioned in Question 4: *Even formal equivalent versions consistently abandon form when necessary to reproduce the meaning.* In other words, while claiming their approach as formal equivalence (stay as close to the form as possible), they are operating with a *philosophy* of functional equivalence (change the form whenever necessary).[1]

Thousands of examples could be marshaled to show that formal equivalent versions frequently default to an idiomatic translation, contradicting the claim that literal equals accurate.[2] Consider 2 Corinthians 6:15, where Paul warns the Corinthians against associating with idolaters. As justification, he says, "What part/portion [*meris*] a believer with an unbeliever?" (word-for-word translation). Consider how various formal equivalent versions render this:

ESV	What portion does a believer share with an unbeliever?
NRSV	What does a believer share with an unbeliever?
RSV/NASB	What has a believer in common with an unbeliever?
NIV	What does a believer have in common with an unbeliever?

None of these is actually literal. The ESV is closest, retaining the word "portion" (*meris*) and adding a verb "does . . . share." Yet it is also the most obscure. It sounds like they are sharing a piece of pie. The NRSV drops "portion" and adds "does . . . share." The RSV and NASB drop "portion" and add "has . . . in common." All of these are modifying the form to communicate the meaning. In other words, they are practicing *functional equivalence.*

Natural Language

A third strength of functional equivalence is its goal of producing natural language. As discussed above (Question 2), this means not just clarity, but reproducing the text in a way that a native speaker would say it. Some critics challenge the appropriateness of this, claiming it "domesticates" the text and potentially deceives readers into confusing its values with their own. They argue for the need to "foreignize" the translation—retain its otherness—rather than to domesticate it, in order to protect indigenous cultures (see Question 6 for more on this). Most translators of the Bible, however, continue to seek to produce a translation that is natural. The reasoning is that since

1. International translator Dave Brunn repeatedly points this out in his book *One Bible, Many Versions: Are All Translation Created Equal?* (Downers Grove, IL: IVP Academic, 2013). He notes, "I began to realize that every 'literal' version frequently sets aside its own standards of literalness and word-for-word translation" (16).
2. Brunn, *One Bible*, 22–34 and passim.

the Classical Hebrew of the Old Testament and the Koine Greek of the New Testament would have sounded clear and natural to their original readers, the translator's text should sound clear and natural to its modern readers. Below are a few examples of the differences between a translation that is clear and one that is natural.

Luke 22:3 RSV reads, "Then Satan entered into Judas called Iscariot, who was of the number of the twelve." While it would almost certainly be clear to most readers that this means that Judas was one of Jesus's twelve disciples, no native English speaker would say it like this. It is not natural English. Instead, we would say that he was "one of the twelve" (most versions). Similarly, Isaiah 22:17 NRSV has "the Lord . . . will seize firm hold on you" (cf. RSV; ESV). A more natural translation would be "the Lord . . . will grasp you firmly" (NASB), "will take hold of you" (CSB), or "grip you firmly" (NAB).

In 2 Corinthians 6:12 Paul is making the point that he has not held back his affection toward the Corinthians, but they have held theirs back from him. The NKJV renders the verse as "You are not restricted by us, but you are restricted by your own affections" (cf. ESV). While this may be understandable, it is strange and unnatural English. The NIV is much more natural: "We are not withholding our affection from you, but you are withholding yours from us." The NLT similarly uses natural English: "There is no lack of love on our part, but you have withheld your love from us."

Weaknesses of Functional Equivalence

While functional equivalent versions in general represent more clear and natural renderings in English, they also have potential weaknesses.

More Interpretation Risks Misinterpretation

As noted above, one of the main strengths of functional equivalent versions is clarity. But clarity requires more interpretation, opening the possibility of *mis*interpretation. For example, in 1 Corinthians 15:32 Paul points out that the risk of death he experiences each day is worthwhile if there is a resurrection from the dead. He then refers to a specific event: "If I fought wild beasts in Ephesus with no more than human hopes, what have I gained? If the dead are not raised . . . " (NIV). Most scholars think this likely refers metaphorically to conflict with human opponents in Ephesus rather than fighting actual animals in the arena. The NLT makes this former meaning explicit by translating, "And what value was there in fighting wild beasts—those people of Ephesus—if there will be no resurrection from the dead?" While this interpretation may be right, it could also be wrong. A footnote alerts readers to this by noting the more literal reading: "Greek *fighting wild beasts in Ephesus*."

This example raises another question about the difference between translation and commentary. Since every Hebrew or Greek word or phrase must be interpreted before it can be translated, *all translation* involves interpretation.

So, to a greater or lesser degree, all translation is commentary. There is a fluid boundary rather than a hard and fast line between the two. We will discuss this distinction in more detail in Question 35.

Too much interpretation can also remove an author's intentional ambiguity. For example, John's gospel includes several wordplays that intentionally evoke two meanings of a word. For example, when Jesus says to Nicodemus, "You must be born again" (John 3:7), the Greek word translated "again" (*anōthen*) can also mean "from above." Since both a second spiritual birth (3:4–8) and Jesus's identity as "the one who comes from above" (John 3:31; cf. 3:13) are important themes in John's gospel, many scholars think John is making here a play on words and that both meanings are present. The NRSV translates "from above" and most versions provide footnotes to point out this alternate meaning (NIV; NLT; ESV; CSB; etc.).

Another example is when Jesus speaks in John's gospel about being "lifted up" (John 3:14; 8:28; 12:32–33). While this no doubt refers to Jesus's crucifixion, where he was lifted up on a cross, it also refers to Jesus's resurrection and ascension, where he was lifted up to heavenly glory. The NLT narrows the meaning in John 8:28 by adding the words "on the cross," which do not appear in the Greek: "When you have lifted up the Son of Man <u>on the cross</u> . . . ". While this makes the passage clearer to the reader, it also removes the potential for a double meaning. A footnote in the NLT, however, alerts readers to the absence of "on the cross" in the Greek.

Oversimplification Resulting in Loss of Meaning

Functional equivalent versions seek to make the text as accessible as possible in the receptor language. This, however, can result in oversimplifications or generalizations that lose important components of meaning. For example, in the Living Bible, Jesus's self-reference as the "Son of Man" often becomes "I, the Messiah" (Matt. 8:20; 9:5–6; etc.). While this simplification helps the uninformed reader to understand that Jesus's use of "Son of Man" is self-referential and messianic, a great deal of meaning is lost, including Jesus's intentional *avoidance* of the title "Messiah" in the Gospel tradition, and the rich Old Testament and Jewish background to the title "Son of Man."

A less egregious example of oversimplification appears in Mark 3:22 NLT, where the religious leaders respond to Jesus's exorcisms by saying, "He is possessed by Beelzebul! By the prince of demons he is driving out demons" (NIV). The NLT simplifies the text by translating, "He's possessed by Satan" (with a footnote noting that the Greek reads *Beelzeboul*). The reference here is clearly to Satan, since Jesus responds in the next verse, "How can Satan cast out Satan?" (Mark 3:23). "Beelzebul" was originally a title given to the Canaanite god Baal, meaning "Baal the Prince" or "Baal of the Exalted One," which over time came to be used as a name for Satan. The strength of the NLT here is clarity, since readers will immediately recognize that the leaders are referring to Satan. Its weakness is a lack of historical precision, since the text says "Beelzebul," a name that may carry historical or theological significance for Mark and his readers.

Historical or Cultural Inaccuracy

Focusing too much on the receptor culture can contemporize the translation in a way that misrepresents the historical or cultural context. For example, Psalm 119:105 in most English versions reads, "Your word is a lamp to my feet." Seeking to appeal to a modern audience, the Living Bible translates this, "Your words are a flashlight to light the path ahead of me." While "flashlight" may achieve contemporary relevance, it misrepresents the psalmist's cultural context. This problem is even more acute in a passage like 2 Timothy 4:6, where instead of "For I am already being poured out as a drink offering" (NIV), the Living Bible reads, "Very soon now I will be on my way to heaven." This simplification may help the reader understand Paul's general point, but loses the significance of Paul's life and ministry as an Old Testament priestly drink offering, being poured out as a sacrifice to God.

Summary

Functional equivalence, idiomatic, or meaning-based translations seek to represent the meaning of the source text as clearly and accurately as possible in the receptor language. The strength of this approach is that it focuses first and foremost on the primary goal of all translation, which is to reproduce the *meaning* of the text. Its main weakness is that overemphasis on simplicity or contemporary relevance can result in a loss of important historical, cultural, or theological meaning.

REFLECTION QUESTIONS

1. What are some important strengths of functional equivalence? Which of these do you think is most important?
2. What are some important weaknesses of functional equivalence? Which of these do you think is most important?
3. What is the danger of focusing too much on the receptor culture audience?
4. What is the potential danger of simplifying texts to reach all readers?
5. Did this chapter change your perspective on any Bible version? In what way?

QUESTION 6

Are There Approaches That Go Beyond Formal and Functional Equivalence?

Is the Translation Debate Over?

While formal equivalent versions are helpful tools for Bible study and remain popular among preachers and teachers, functional equivalence has come to dominate the world of international Bible translation. The reason for this was noted in a previous question: almost everyone who does actual translation in the real world—whether in the jungles of Irian Jaya or the halls of the United Nations—practices idiomatic or meaning-based translation. D. A. Carson, while expressing various cautions about functional equivalence, acknowledges its superiority as a translation philosophy:

> For the vast majority of people actually engaged in Bible translation, the importance of functional equivalence is a given and rightly so. Its victory is hailed by numerous pieces of evidence. There is widespread recognition of the inadequacy of merely formal equivalence in translation, buttressed by thousands and thousands of examples. . . . Functional equivalence displays its triumph in the publishing houses, in the continuing parade of helps, front rank research, manuals of problems, reflective textbooks, assorted popularizations, and sane assessments of recent translations.[1]

1. D. A. Carson, "The Limits of Functional Equivalence in Bible Translation—and Other Limits Too," in *The Challenge of Bible Translation: Communicating God's Word to the World*, eds. Glen G. Scorgie, Mark L. Strauss, Steven M. Voth (Grand Rapids: Zondervan, 2003), 91–92.

One might think from this kind of statement that the debate is over. Yet the goal set forth in the title of Eugene Nida's 1964 book, *Toward a Science of Translation*,[2] has proven elusive, and there is not yet a single unifying theory of translation. At the same time, the field of translation studies continues to develop in various directions. Here we will discuss some of the challenges to the dominance of functional equivalence.

Translation and Communication

Nida's dynamic and functional equivalent theories have sometimes been criticized as being based on an inadequate "code theory" of language.[3] Code theory operates under the assumption that communication through language is a matter of the encoding and decoding of messages. For every act of communication, there are three components, a sender, a receiver, and a message. The sender encodes the message in a particular form and transmits it to the receiver, who decodes the message in the receptor language.

TEXT *(Source Language)*—decode→MEANING—encode→TEXT *(Receptor Language)*

Formal equivalence consistently fails because it assumes that source and receptor languages *have the same code*, so that meaning is transferred automatically by reproducing forms. Functional equivalence correctly recognizes that the two codes are different, and so (1) the source language must first be decoded (interpreted/exegeted) to determine its meaning and then (2) re-encoded in the receptor language.

Critics have pointed out, however, that code theory has certain inadequacies, especially in relation to extra-lingual factors of communication. Consider, for example, the following scenario: My wife and I are having breakfast one morning, and she asks, "Are you home this evening?" I respond, "It's Monday." She says, "Oh, right," accepting my answer as a "no," and the conversation ends. But there is nothing inherent in my words that would indicate a negative answer. Linguistically, "It's Monday" does not mean "No, I won't be home this evening." The reason my answer was perceived correctly was because my wife and I share certain *assumptions*:

a. This semester I am teaching on Monday evenings.
b. Today is Monday, so I will be teaching tonight.
c. Therefore, I will not be home until late.

---

2. Eugene A. Nida, *Toward a Science of Translation with Special Reference to Principles and Procedures Involved in Bible Translating* (Boston: E. J. Brill, 1964).
3. On code theory of language, see Nida, *Towards a Science of Translation*, 120–44; cf. Eugene A. Nida and Charles R. Taber, *The Theory and Practice of Translation* (Leiden: Brill, 1982), 22–24.

To understand how a message is transmitted we must expand our definition of communication beyond linguistic entities. We must include not only *semantics*—the meaning of the words, phrases, and clauses—but also *pragmatics* and the shared *assumptions* of sender and receiver. Pragmatics refers to all the accompanying circumstances of communication, including tone of voice, inflection, gesture, and proxemics (personal space).[4] Assumptions refer to the shared knowledge that sender and receiver bring to bear on a particular utterance, including knowledge of the language system, family and societal knowledge, worldview, and so on. These assumptions are drawn from the total *cognitive environment*, which means everything sender and receiver know about the world. If *translation* is the reproduction of written communication across languages, then bringing the author's and readers' assumptions in line is essential to the task.[5]

Relevance Theory

Various theories have been proposed to take account of this phenomenon of communication and translation. One that has raised special interest with reference to Bible translation is relevance theory. Relevance theory was developed by Deirdre Wilson and Dan Sperber, who drew from Paul Grice's theory of pragmatics and implicatures. Relevance theory affirms that communication begins with the thoughts or intentions of the speaker or author. The sender's *intention* is communicated to the receiver, who *infers* the meaning. While recognizing the necessity of linguistic code (words and syntax), relevance theory argues that communication is more than just the encoding and decoding of messages. Sperber and Wilson write,

> According to the code model, a communicator encodes her intended message into a signal, which is decoded by the audience using an identical copy of the code. According to the inferential model, a communicator provides evidence of her intention to convey a certain meaning, which is inferred by the audience on the basis of shared knowledge of the context.[6]

Context means not just the co-text (the surrounding words), but also the set of *assumptions* shared by sender and receiver. Sperber and Wilson present

---

4. In written language, pragmatics are more limited than in oral communication, since no speaker is present. Yet some features, such as bowing down or tone of voice, may be explicitly narrated.
5. It should be noted that Nida is by no means unaware of these nuances and discusses the importance of cultural context at length. The point is that his foundational code theory has been subject to this criticism.
6. Deirdre Wilson and Dan Sperber, "Relevance Theory," in *Handbook of Pragmatics*, eds. G. Ward and L. Horn (Oxford: Blackwell, 2004), 607.

two key principles of relevance, a *cognitive* principle related to the hearer and a *communicative* principle related to the speaker. The cognitive principle is that *human cognition tends to be geared to the maximization of relevance.*[7] This means that we attend to the information that seems most relevant. The communicative principle is that *every act of ostensive communication communicates a presumption of its own optimal relevance.* The speaker expects the hearer to consider their statement relevant enough to be worth the effort expended in processing it. The hearer, in turn, expects their attempts at interpretation to yield *positive cognitive effects* at *minimal processing cost.* When these expectations are met, communication succeeds.

While relevance theory was developed as a general theory of communication, it has been applied to Bible translation by Ernst-August Gutt and others.[8] Gutt's basic premise is that if communication is best described as an *inferential* process, then Bible translators should not seek "equivalence" in the receptor language, but should instead seek to replicate this inferential process. This is done by providing the reader with sufficient communicative clues to infer the author's meaning.

Gutt distinguishes between two kinds of translation, *direct* and *indirect.* Direct translation retains as many of the source language clues as possible, thus allowing the receptor language reader to infer the meaning from the source language context. Since readers may be unaware of that context, direct translation must be supported by supplemental materials like book introductions, footnotes, glossaries, study guides, and so on. In indirect translation, by contrast, the translator chooses which parts of the source text are deemed most relevant for the receptor audience and adds or omits content to direct them to that material.

Some critics have suggested that Gutt has simply renamed the two sides of the age-old debate and is seeking to smuggle literal translation in by the back door. Instead of formal and functional equivalence, we have direct and indirect translation.[9] But Gutt and other supporters of relevance theory explicitly reject that they are advocating for literal translation. Gutt writes, "Direct

7. Wilson and Sperber, "Relevance Theory," 610.
8. Ernst-August Gutt, *Translation and Relevance: Cognition and Context* (Oxford: Basil Blackwell, 1991); Ernst-August Gutt, *Relevance Theory: A Guide to Successful Communication in Translation; Lectures Delivered at the Triennial Translation Workshop of UBS Zimbabwe, 1991* (Dallas: UBS; New York: SIL, 1992). Cf. Harriet Hill, *The Bible at Cultural Crossroads: From Translation to Communication* (Kinderhook, NY: St. Jerome, 2006). For the application of relevance theory to the training of international Bible translators, see Harriet Hill, Ernst-August Gutt, Margaret Hill, Christoph Unger, and Rick Floyd, *Bible Translation Basics: Communicating Scripture in a Relevant Way* (Dallas: SIL, 2011).
9. In an early review, Ernst Wendland criticized relevance theory as "an elaborate, theoretically-based effort to justify a return to formal equivalence" ("A Review of 'Relevance Theory' in Relation to Bible Translation in South-Central Africa, Part 2," *Journal of Northwest Semitic Languages* 23, no. 1 [1997]: 86).

translation cannot be understood in terms of resemblance in actual linguistic properties for the simple reason that languages differ in those properties."[10] Rather, the goal is to replicate the ostensive-inferential process of human communication more closely.

Skopostheorie and Functionalism

Skopostheorie and functionalism (not to be confused with functional equivalence) are two closely related theories that may be treated together. Like relevance theory, they challenge some of the basic premises of functional equivalence. *Skopostheorie* was developed by Hans J. Vermeer and Katharina Reiss,[11] and functionalism by Christiane Nord.[12] *Skopos* is Greek for "purpose" or "aim," and both *Skopostheorie* and functionalism claim that "the prime principle determining any translation process is the purpose (*Skopos*) of the overall translation action."[13] Vermeer writes:

> Each text is produced for a given purpose and should serve this purpose. The *Skopos* rule thus reads as follows: translate/interpret/speak/write in a way that enables your text/translation to function in the situation in which it is used and with the people who want to use it and precisely in the way they want it to function.[14]

The most important question to ask of a translation, then, is, Does this translation accomplish its purpose and fulfill its communicative intent? This may be contrasted with an equivalency approach to translation. To say a receptor language translation is "equivalent" to a source text begs the question of what kind of equivalence. Does it mean structural or formal equivalence? Does it produce the same cognitive effect? Does it produce the same emotional response? Does it make the text relevant and applicable for a contemporary reader? *Skopostheorie* and functionalism seek not equivalence but the fulfillment of the *purpose* (= *skopos*) or *function* set out by the translator or their client.

For example, a children's translation would be successful if it achieved its stated goal, which may be to communicate the message of a source text using

---

10. Gutt, *Translation and Relevance*, 170. Cf. Gutt, *Relevance Theory*: "Meaning-based translation is in fact the only kind of translation possible" (65).
11. Katharina Reiss and Hans J. Vermeer, *Grundlegung einer allgemeinen Translationstheorie* (Tübingen: M. Niemeyer, 1984).
12. Christiane Nord, *Translation as Purposeful Activity: Functionalist Approaches Explained*, Translation Theories Explored (Manchester: St. Jerome, 1997).
13. Nord, *Translation as Purposeful Activity*, 27.
14. Hans Vermeer, *Skopos und Translationsauftrag—Aufsätze*, 2nd ed. (Heidelberg: Universität, 1990); translation from Nord, *Translation as Purposeful Activity*, 29.

language and concepts that children understand. A formal equivalent translation may have as its goal the replication of source language idioms. Nord speaks of the critical importance of the "translation brief" developed by the patron and client, outlining in detail the purpose of the translation with reference to the target audience and the method to be utilized to accomplish this goal.

Positively, *Skopostheorie* and functionalism provide the theoretical foundation for different kinds of translations for different audiences and situations. Negatively, they have been criticized for elevating the translator's purpose over the author's original intent. Nord responds to this criticism by introducing the concept of "loyalty," which she claims fits the method better than terms like "fidelity" or "equivalence." Loyalty means responsibility to both source language text and receptor language partners. Loyalty is not the same as fidelity, which concerns the relationship between texts. Loyalty concerns the relationship between people. Loyalty to the source language author means that "target-text purpose should be compatible with the original author's intention."[15]

Foreignizing, Domesticating, and Post-Colonial Approaches to Translation

As we have seen, functional equivalence has as its goal the production of a translation that is as clear and natural to the contemporary reader as it was to its original readers. Some scholars, however, challenge this goal as potentially destructive to the receptor language culture. Lawrence Venuti, a strong critic of Eugene Nida and international Bible translation, claims that a translator's goal should not be to "domesticate" a text, but rather to "foreignize" it, making it clear that it comes from a different time and place. Venuti approaches the issue from a post-colonial perspective that sees language and translation as a common means of hegemonic domination by colonial powers.[16] Since the 1970s there has been increasing interest by anthropologists, social scientists, and linguists in post-colonial translation theory in recognizing the role language and translation play in colonial dominance.[17] Communication is essential to maintaining empire and controlling communication is an important means of maintaining power. A dominant culture's decision on which trade languages to use, which translators/interpreters to train and how, which works to translate and how to translate them are critical to hegemonic domination. Venuti writes, "By producing the illusion of transparency, a fluent [= domesticating] translation masquerades as a true semantic equivalent when it in

15. Nord, *Translation*, 27.
16. Lawrence Venuti, *The Translator's Invisibility: A History of Translation*, 2nd ed. (London: Routledge, 2008), 15–18.
17. For a good survey of authors and issues, see Douglas Robinson, *Translation and Empire: Postcolonial Theories Explained*, Translation Theories Explained, ed. Anthony Pym (Manchester, UK: St. Jerome, 1997).

fact inscribes the foreign text with a partial interpretation, partial to English-language values."[18] Venuti argues that as a restraint on the "ethnocentric violence" of translation, foreignizing

> is highly desirable today, a strategic intervention in the current state of world affairs, pitched against the hegemonic English-language nations and the unequal cultural exchanges in which they engage their global others. Foreignizing translation in English can be a form of resistance against ethnocentrism and racism, cultural narcissism and imperialism, in the interests of democratic geopolitical relations.[19]

In response, there are no doubt potential dangers in domesticating translation. As we have seen, simplifying language to make it immediately relevant to the receptor audience can distort its meaning and miss important cultural features in the source language (see Questions 2, 5, 36). We must also acknowledge the important role that language and translation play in the shaping of cultures, and the potential for hegemonic domination. I remember during Russia's 2022 invasion of Ukraine, one of the first things Russian troops did was change the road signs and street names to Russian as a way of claiming captured territory that was (in their view) historically Russian land. Language control is certainly part of imperial domination.

Yet Venuti's criticisms are also open to critique. As Stan Porter points out, "It strikes some as odd in light of Nida's own cross-cultural experience and anthropological background that his program of translation is seen . . . to impose a cultural hegemony."[20] Nida's anthropological and cultural sensitivities would seem to make him *less* likely to impose ethnocentric and hegemonic values onto the receptor culture. Venuti, however, does not like the fact that to him a fluent translation "seems less an exchange of information than an appropriation of a foreign text to serve a purpose in the receiving culture."[21] He also does not like that Nida's theories go hand in hand with an "evangelistic zeal" and "a Christian understanding of the Bible."[22] Of course Christian missionaries and linguists who do Bible translation have a very different perspective, believing that the introduction of Christianity is not an imperialistic imposition that destroys cultures, but rather an ethical and spiritual asset

18. Venuti, *Translator's Invisibility*, 16.
19. Venuti, *Translator's Invisibility*, 16.
20. Stanley E. Porter, "Assessing Translation Theory: Beyond Literal and Dynamic Equivalence," in *Translating the New Testament*, eds. S. E. Porter and M. J. Boda (Grand Rapids: Eerdmans, 2009), 139–40.
21. Venuti, *Translator's Invisibility*, 17.
22. Venuti, *Translator's Invisibility*, 17–18.

that enriches them, no less valuable than supplying lifesaving medicine, clean water, or crop-growing technology.

Summary

While functional equivalence remains the dominant approach among international Bible translators today, various challenges to its preeminence have been made. Advocates of relevance theory claim that translation is not just the replacement of one language code with another, but rather an ostensive-inferential process whereby receptors *infer* the speaker's or author's meaning based on a complex set of linguistics, pragmatics, and shared assumptions. *Skopostheorie* and functionalism depart from traditional translation goals by claiming that a translation is successful not by achieving formal or functional *equivalence* but by accomplishing the purpose or goal (*Skopos*) set out by its initiators. Finally, postcolonial approaches to translation claim that cross-cultural translation, especially those done by dominant colonial powers, should be intentionally foreignized rather than domesticated to minimize the imposition of foreign values and beliefs on subject peoples.

REFLECTION QUESTIONS

1. Communication involves more than words and sentences. What else does it involve? Provide some examples.

2. According to relevance theory, communication through language is an *inferential* process rather than simply a decoding of signs. Can you illustrate what this means and how it relates to Bible translation?

3. According to *Skopostheorie*, what makes a translation successful? Can you see any potential problems with this related to translating the Bible?

4. What does Venuti mean by a "domesticating" translation? Why does he think we should "foreignize" translations?

5. In what ways might "foreignizing" run counter to the goals of Bible translators? In what ways might it be helpful for translators?

PART 2

Preparing to Translate

QUESTION 7

Which Books Should Be Included in a Bible Version?

We have been discussing different philosophies or approaches to Bible translation, but in fact the *first task* of the Bible translator is to determine *what* to translate, that is, which books to include and what Hebrew and Greek manuscripts to translate them from. In this chapter and the next, we will discuss questions of the *canon* and the *text* of Scripture.

The word "canon" means a rule or standard and refers to those books acknowledged by the people of God to be the inspired and authoritative Word of God. Here we will not discuss in detail *how* these books came to be recognized and acknowledged as holy Scripture (a complex question beyond our scope),[1] but rather which books are included in the Bibles of Judaism and the major branches of Christianity.

The Jewish Bible (*Tanakh*)

Jewish Bibles only include the Hebrew Scriptures (the Christian "Old Testament"), since Jews do not recognize the authority of the New Testament. Most Jewish Bibles are organized according to the traditional Hebrew order of the books, which includes twenty-four books arranged in three sections, *Torah* (Law), *Nevi'im* (Prophets), and *Kethuvim* (Writings). The Hebrew Bible is known as the *Tanakh*, an acronym taken from the first letter of each section (TNK). The Christian Old Testament contains the same books as the Hebrew Bible, but they are arranged differently (see discussion below).

1. See F. F. Bruce, *The Canon of Scripture* (Downers Grove, IL: InterVarsity, 1988); Michael W. Holmes, "From Books to Library: The Formation of the Biblical Canons," in *Scripture and Its Interpretation*, ed. Michael J. Gorman (Grand Rapids: Baker, 2017), 115–32; L. Scott Kellum and Charles L. Quarles, *40 Questions About the Text and Canon of the New Testament* (Grand Rapids: Kregel, 2023).

The two most popular Jewish Bibles in English have both come from the Jewish Publication Society (JPS). Its first edition, *The Holy Scriptures according to the Masoretic Text*, was published in 1917 and produced by a committee led by Max Margolis, Professor of Biblical Philology at Dropsie College. This edition was styled after the King James Version. By the middle of the century, a more contemporary version was deemed necessary, and the JPS authorized a new edition, with Harry M. Orlinsky, Professor of Bible at Hebrew Union College, serving as editor-in-chief. The Torah was published in 1962, and the full Hebrew Bible in 1985. This version, commonly referred to as "JPS," is a respected version that utilizes a high level of Jewish scholarship.

The Christian Bible and the Question of the Apocrypha

All three major branches of Christianity—Protestant, Roman Catholic, and Eastern Orthodox—accept the same twenty-seven books of the New Testament and the whole of the Hebrew Scriptures as authoritative Scripture.[2] The only significant question of canon for contemporary Bible translators is whether to include the books of the Apocrypha.

Answering the question "What is the Apocrypha?" is actually quite complicated. The first problem is the name. "Apocrypha" means "hidden" and is often used by Protestants to identify these books as outside the accepted canon of Scripture. Roman Catholic and Eastern Orthodox believers refer to them instead as "deuterocanonical books," meaning part of a "second canon."

The term "Apocrypha" is also ambiguous with reference to its contents. The books of the Apocrypha are all Jewish works written between the Old Testament and the New. As such, they are part of a much larger body of Second Temple Jewish literature, including the Pseudepigrapha, the Dead Sea Scrolls, and the works of Jewish authors like Josephus and Philo. All these writings provide important background material for the NT and the world in which Jesus lived. The Pseudepigrapha refers to dozens of Jewish writings produced by various groups during the latter part of the Second Temple period (approx. 200 BC–AD 100).[3] The name means "falsely written," since many of these works are pseudonymously named after an Old Testament character. Like the Apocrypha, the term "Pseudepigrapha" contains wisdom literature, apocalyptic literature, expansions on Old Testament narratives, prayers, psalms, and a variety of other genres. The only significant difference between the Apocrypha and the Pseudepigrapha is that the former are those Second Temple works that were accepted as

---

2. While the Eastern Orthodox Church does not read the NT book of Revelation as part of its liturgy, the church still considers it part of the Bible.
3. See J. H. Charlesworth, ed., *The Old Testament Pseudepigrapha*, 2 vols., 2nd ed. (New Haven, CT: Yale University Press, 2009); cf. J. H. Charlesworth, *The Pseudepigrapha and Modern Research*, rev. ed. (Missoula, MT: Scholars, 1981).

part of the authoritative canon by various Christian traditions. By contrast, with very few exceptions, the books of the Pseudepigrapha are not accepted as Scripture by any branch of Christianity today, although many of these books have been read, respected, and even revered by Jews and Christians through the ages.

Contents of the Apocrypha in Different Traditions

Further complicating the definition and scope of the Apocrypha is that various Christian traditions include some books that others do not. The following are the apocryphal books of the Roman Catholic and Eastern Orthodox traditions.

Roman Catholic Deuterocanonical Books	Eastern Orthodox Deuterocanonical Books
Tobit	Tobit
Judith	Judith
Additions to Esther (6 additions in 10:4–16:24)	Additions to Esther (6 additions in 10:4–16:24)
1 Maccabees	1 Maccabees
2 Maccabees	2 Maccabees
Wisdom of Solomon	Wisdom of Solomon
Sirach (Ecclesiasticus)	Sirach (Ecclesiasticus)
Baruch (chs. 1–5)	Baruch (chs. 1–5)
Letter of Jeremiah (Baruch, ch. 6)	Letter of Jeremiah (Baruch, ch. 6)
Additions to Daniel • The Prayer of Azariah and the Song of the Three Jews (Dan. 3:24–90) • Susanna (Daniel 13) • Bel and the Dragon (Daniel 14)	Additions to Daniel • The Prayer of Azariah and the Song of the Three Jews (Dan. 3:24–90) • Susanna (Daniel 13) • Bel and the Dragon (Daniel 14)
	1 Esdras
	2 Esdras
	3 Maccabees
	Psalm 151
An appendix in the Latin Vulgate includes 3 Esdras, 4 Esdras, and the Prayer of Manasseh.	An appendix in the Greek Orthodox canon includes 4 Maccabees and the Prayer of Manasseh.

In the Roman Catholic and Orthodox Bibles, the books of the Apocrypha are embedded within the Old Testament. For example, Tobit and Judith follow Nehemiah in the historical books of the OT, and Wisdom of Solomon and Sirach follow the Song of Songs in the OT books of wisdom and poetry.

Summary of Contents of the Main Deuterocanonical Books

Tobit (c. 200 BC) is a historical novel named after its main character, a pious Israelite who faces various challenges after being carried into exile to Nineveh following the Assyrian conquest of Israel in the eighth century BC.

Judith (c. 150 BC) is another Jewish novel; it is about Judith, a beautiful heroine who saves the besieged city of Bethulia from the Assyrians by slaying the enemy commander Holofernes.

The Wisdom of Solomon (c. 30 BC) was written pseudonymously in Solomon's name, probably by a Jew of Alexandria in the first century BC. It is a wisdom book similar to Proverbs, but with significant influence from Greek philosophical thought.

The Wisdom of Jesus Son of Sirach (c. 180 BC), also known as Sirach, or Ecclesiasticus, is a Jewish book of wisdom presenting the wise sayings of Yeshua Ben Sira. It was originally written in Hebrew in about 180 BC and was translated into Greek by the author's grandson around 130 BC.

First Maccabees (c. 100 BC) tells the story of the victory of the Maccabees, a Jewish priestly family, over the Seleucid ruler Antiochus IV Epiphanes, who sought to assimilate Judaism into Greek culture and religion.

Second Maccabees (c. 100–70 BC) provides additional details about the events leading up to and following the revolt under Judas Maccabeus.

Baruch (c. 150–50 BC) is a pseudepigraphic work that purports to be a letter from Baruch, the secretary of Jeremiah, from exile in Babylon to the priests and people of Jerusalem.

Letter of Jeremiah (= Baruch 6; c. 300–100 BC) is a pseudonymous letter purporting to be from Jeremiah to the Jewish exiles in Babylon. The letter draws its inspiration from Jeremiah 29:1–23.

Additions to Esther (c. 140–130 BC) include six passages that appear in the Greek edition of Esther, not found in the Hebrew text. Most significantly, these passages speak of God's providence in saving and delivering his people. By contrast, the Hebrew text never speaks directly of God or his actions.

Additions to Daniel (c. 100 BC) include three passages from the Greek version of Daniel that are not found in the Hebrew/Aramaic version. *The Prayer of Azariah and the Song of the Three Jews* occurs between Daniel 3:23 and 3:24. It recounts the story of Daniel's three friends who are miraculously delivered from the fiery furnace, including a prayer by Azariah, one of the three, and a song of praise by all three (Dan. 3:24–90 LXX). *Susanna*, chapter 13 of the Greek version of Daniel, tells the story of a woman who is falsely accused of immorality by two Jewish elders until Daniel defends her in court and unmasks her accusers as liars. *Bel and the Dragon* tells of Daniel's exploits in revealing the false priests of the Babylonian god Bel, slaying a dragon, and surviving the lions' den.

First Esdras (c. 150–100 BC; *Esdras* A in the LXX; 3 Ezra in the Vulgate) is a compilation of various stories related to Judah's religious history, including reforms under Josiah and the rebuilding of Jerusalem and the temple under the leadership of Ezra and Zerubbabel. (Esdras is the Greek form of the Hebrew name Ezra.) Certain portions follow almost exactly material from 2 Chronicles, Ezra, and Nehemiah.

Debating the Apocrypha

The status of the Apocrypha as authoritative Scripture is an ancient debate. Against its inclusion is the evidence for an established threefold division of the Hebrew canon that did not include the Apocrypha. The prologue to Sirach, written in the second century BC, refers to "the Law and the Prophets and the other books of our ancestors." Jesus, too, speaks in Luke 24:44 of "the Law, the Prophets and the Psalms." This seems to assume the same threefold division, with the Psalms heading up the Writings and appearing as shorthand for them. This identification of the Jewish canon also seems to be assumed by the author of 4 Ezra (c. AD 100), who speaks of twenty-four books (4 Ezra 14:45). Although today we speak of the thirty-nine books of the Old Testament, twenty-four is the traditional count, treating the twelve minor prophets as a single book, Ezra and Nehemiah as one, and Samuel, Kings, and Chronicles as single books, before they were split in two in the Septuagint. Josephus similarly refers to the "twenty-two" books of sacred Scripture (*Against Apion* 1:38), a small difference that probably resulted from treating Ruth with Judges and Lamentation with Jeremiah. The point is that all these descriptions imply an established Hebrew canon by the first century, which did not include the books of the Apocrypha.

This identification of the OT with the traditional Jewish canon is reflected among some early Christian leaders. Athanasius, in the thirty-ninth of his *Festal Letters*, identifies the extent of the Old Testament as essentially those books found in the Hebrew canon. Most influentially, Jerome, the translator of the Vulgate, affirmed the traditional Hebrew canon. Having studied Hebrew in Palestine under a Jewish rabbi, Jerome was well aware of the Jewish perspective. He argued that while the additional books might be viewed as "ecclesiastical" and could be read for edification, only the books of the Jewish canon should be viewed as "canonical" and used for the confirmation of doctrinal truth.[4]

---

4. David deSilva, *Introducing the Apocrypha: Message, Context, and Significance*, 2nd ed. (Grand Rapids: Baker, 2018), 1–31; Bruce, *Canon of Scripture*, 77–80, 87–93.

On the other side of the debate, books of the Apocrypha were popular in the early church, and our earliest copies of the Septuagint contain various books of the Apocrypha. The three great majuscule manuscripts from the fourth and fifth centuries AD—Codex Sinaiticus (א), Codex Vaticanus (B), and Codex Alexandrinus (A)—all include books that are now part of the Apocrypha (and some from the Pseudepigrapha). Codex Sinaiticus includes Tobit, Judith, 1 and 4 Maccabees, Wisdom, and Sirach. Codex Vaticanus includes 1 Esdras, Wisdom, Sirach, Judith, Tobit, Baruch, and the Letter of Jeremiah. Codex Alexandrinus includes Baruch, Letter of Jeremiah, Tobit, Judith, 1 Esdras, 1–4 Maccabees, Wisdom, Sirach, Psalm 151, the Odes of Solomon, and in an appendix, the Psalms of Solomon.

This does not necessarily mean that earlier Jews viewed these texts as authoritative Scripture. The Septuagint was translated in the third century BC, long before most books of the Apocrypha were written. The most we can say is that Christians who copied these manuscripts in the fourth and fifth centuries AD viewed certain Jewish works that are now part of the Apocrypha and Pseudepigrapha as having great value and worth reading beside other sacred Jewish works. We can also surmise that, for Christians at least, the extent of the Old Testament canon was not as clearly delineated as it would eventually become.

In contrast to Jerome, the great fourth-century theologian Augustine of Hippo strongly encouraged the use of the Septuagint and with it an expanded canon that included the books of the Apocrypha. His reasons were more pragmatic, to encourage unity with the Eastern churches, which strongly supported the Greek text. Augustine's perspective was followed by many church leaders, and his canon was recognized by the Third Council of Carthage in 397 and affirmed again by the Sixth Council of Carthage in 419.[5]

Other Christian leaders, however, continued to follow Jerome's perspective, including Gregory the Great (540–604), John of Damascus (675–749), and Hugh of St. Victor (1096–1141). The Protestant Reformers were generally skeptical and sometimes hostile toward the Apocrypha. In his German translation, Martin Luther included the books of the Apocrypha, but moved them to a section between the Testaments. In his preface to the Apocrypha, he affirms Jerome's perspective: "These are books that, though not esteemed like the holy Scriptures, are still both useful and good to read."[6] John Calvin more explicitly rejected the Apocrypha, and the Westminster Confession of 1646 reflected his perspective: "The books commonly called the Apocrypha, not being of divine inspiration, are no part of the canon of the Scripture; and therefore are of no authority in the

5. deSilva, *Introducing the Apocrypha*, 26; Bruce, *Canon of Scripture*, 97.
6. deSilva, *Introducing the Apocrypha*, 27.

Church of God, nor to be in any otherwise approved, or made use of, than other human writings."[7] This adamant dismissal of the Apocrypha was no doubt due in part to the Counter-Reformation and its affirmation of these books. The Council of Trent in 1546 had ruled that all books of the (Roman Catholic) Apocrypha were canonical.

Despite this polarization, nearly all the early English versions of the Old Testament included the Apocrypha, including Wycliffe, Coverdale, Matthew's Bible, the Great Bible, the Bishops' Bible, the Geneva Bible, and the King James Version (see Questions 24 and 25). The Coverdale Bible of 1535 was the first English version to separate the Apocrypha from the rest of the Old Testament and print it as an appendix after the Old Testament. Other Protestant versions followed suit, including the King James Version. The Geneva Bible included a warning that these books were not themselves canonical and should not be used to prove any point of doctrine. Yet "as books proceeding from godly men, [they] were received to be read for the advancement and furtherance of knowledge of the history and for the instruction of godly manners."[8] What can be agreed on by all is that the books of the Apocrypha provide great insight into the historical, literary, cultural, and religious life of the Jewish people between the Old and New Testaments (see also Questions 24, 25, and 29).

Summary

The Apocrypha, or deuterocanonical books, comprises various Jewish works written after the Old Testament period that are accepted as part of the canon of Scripture by Roman Catholicism and Eastern Orthodoxy (in slightly different forms) but rejected as authoritative Scripture by most Protestants. While the Hebrew canonical tradition excluded this material, the Greek tradition was more open to them. Whether translators today include them as part of their Bible translations is largely determined by the constituents to which that translation is directed (whether Catholic, Orthodox, or Protestant readers).

REFLECTION QUESTIONS

1. What books does the Jewish Bible contain?

2. What is the Apocrypha? Which Christian traditions include the Apocrypha as part of the Bible?

---

7. Cited by deSilva, *Introducing the Apocrypha*, 27.
8. F. F. Bruce, *History of the Bible in English*, 3rd ed. (New York: Oxford University Press, 1978), 89–90.

3. How is the Apocrypha useful for understanding Jesus and his world?

4. Does the primary Bible you use include the Apocrypha? Does the preface explain why or why not?

5. What do you think are the best arguments for including or excluding the Apocrypha from the Bible?

QUESTION 8

Which Manuscripts Should a Bible Version Follow?

In addition to the question of which books to translate (the question of canon), translators must also decide which Hebrew and Greek manuscripts to follow. The decision is necessary because prior to the invention of the printing press in the fifteenth century, all literary documents were hand-copied. A handwritten copy is known as a *manuscript*. The laborious task of transcribing texts inevitably results in errors, and no manuscript of the Bible (or any other work of ancient literature) is identical to another. These errors may be insignificant issues of spelling or minor grammar, or they may be more significant ones related to the meaning of the text. They may be accidental errors caused by a slip of the eye or mishearing a word. Or they may be intentional changes meant to smooth out a difficult passage or to correct what the scribe thought was an error made by a previous copyist.

Many Bible translations include footnotes that read something like, "Some manuscripts read . . . ". These notes alert readers when the text behind the translation is in dispute because of manuscript variants. So how do translators choose which Hebrew, Aramaic, and Greek words to translate? The method used to retrieve the original text of Scripture is known as *textual criticism*. Textual criticism is necessary because we do not have the original copy—known as the *autograph*—of any book of the Bible. This is not surprising, since the vast majority of ancient documents have decayed and turned to dust over time.[1]

There are two kinds of evidence that textual critics analyze, external and internal. External textual evidence relates to the value given to the manuscripts themselves, based on their age and relationships to other manuscripts.

1. See L. Scott Kellum and Charles L. Quarles, *40 Questions About the Text and Canon of the New Testament* (Grand Rapids: Kregel, 2023).

Internal evidence evaluates the variant readings found in these manuscripts based on the tendencies of authors and copyists. In the discussion that follows, we will survey the textual evidence for the Old Testament and the New Testament and will then summarize the method of textual criticism.

Old Testament Manuscript Evidence

The Masoretic Text

The standard Hebrew text of the Old Testament is called the *Masoretic text* because it is based on the *Masora*, the textual tradition of the Jewish scholars known as the Masoretes, who copied and preserved the text from the fifth to the tenth centuries. The Masoretes are well known for their obsessive accuracy in preserving the text, keeping records such as the number of words in each book.[2] The Masoretic text is abbreviated as MT or designated with the sigla 𝔐. The standard edition is the *Biblia Hebraica Stuttgartensia* (BHS), which is based on the Codex Leningradensis (B 19ª or L), a Hebrew manuscript copied around AD 1010 in Cairo, Egypt, and now housed in the Russian Public Library in Leningrad. It is the oldest dated manuscript of the complete Hebrew Bible.

The Samaritan Pentateuch

When the Samaritans separated themselves from the Jews in the postexilic period, they took the Pentateuch, the first five books of the Old Testament, with them. Unlike most Jews, they only viewed these five books as authoritative Scripture. The value of the Samaritan Pentateuch is disputed among scholars. Some view it as a revision of the Masoretic text. Others consider it to represent an important independent witness to the pre-Masoretic tradition. The earliest extant copy of the Samaritan Pentateuch is MS Add.1846, a copy produced in the early twelfth century. It is written on vellum in the Samaritan alphabet, which developed from the Paleo-Hebrew script. The manuscript is located in Cambridge University Library.

The Dead Sea Scrolls

The Dead Sea Scrolls (DSS), the greatest archeological find of the twentieth century, were discovered in eleven caves near the shores of the Dead Sea between 1947 and 1956. The scrolls are believed by most scholars to be the library of a Jewish group known as the Essenes, who lived in the ancient monastic settlement of Qumran from around 250 BC to AD 68. The Qumran community likely buried their library to keep it from falling into the hands of the Romans during the Jewish revolt of AD 66–74. Presumably, the

2. See Paul Wegner, *The Journey from Texts to Translations: The Origin and Development of the Bible* (Grand Rapids: Baker, 1999), 173–74.

community was wiped out by the Roman legions during the war, and no one was left to retrieve the library. The caves were subsequently forgotten until their discovery by Bedouin shepherds two thousand years later! The caves contained tens of thousands of manuscript fragments, the vast majority from caves 1, 4, and 11.

The DSS are important because of the insight they give us into the historical, religious, and cultural life of a particular first-century Jewish community and because they contain a wealth of information on the text of the Old Testament. The scrolls can be categorized into three groups: (1) *books of the Hebrew Bible* (the Old Testament); (2) *extrabiblical Jewish literature*, included today in the Apocrypha and the Pseudepigrapha; and (3) *sectarian literature*, writings produced by the community itself, reflecting their beliefs and community life.

Fragments from almost every book in the Old Testament were discovered at Qumran, mostly in Hebrew, but some in Aramaic and Greek. The greatest find was a magnificent scroll containing almost the entire text of Isaiah. The biblical scrolls were dated from approximately 250 BC to AD 50. Prior to this discovery, the oldest Hebrew Old Testament manuscripts available were from the Middle Ages. So the DSS pushed our textual evidence for the Old Testament back more than one thousand years. While it is clear that the Hebrew text was less uniform in the first century than during the Masoretic period, the scrolls confirm the care with which the Hebrew Bible has been passed down for two millennia.

The Septuagint (Greek Old Testament; LXX)

On the origin and nature of the Septuagint, the Greek translation of the Hebrew Bible, see Question 23. The Septuagint is a valuable witness to the Old Testament because it represents a translation that was originally made in the third century BC, long before the Masoretic period. The challenge is that the Septuagint itself has its own complicated history of translation and transmission. Scholars debate the nature of the Hebrew source text(s) behind the Septuagint and its relationship to the Masoretic tradition.

Other Witnesses

While the four groups above represent the primary textual witnesses for the Hebrew Bible, other texts have been found in the Judean desert, including at Masada, the last holdout of the Jewish revolutionaries in the Jewish war (AD 66–74), and in caves at Wadi Murabba'at, and Wadi Habra. A large storehouse of Hebrew manuscripts was also discovered in the late nineteenth century at the genizah (a synagogue storage room) at the ancient Ben-Ezra synagogue in Cairo.

Other versions (translations into other languages) are also consulted for Old Testament textual evidence, including the targums (Aramaic paraphrases of Hebrew Scripture), the Aramaic Peshitta, the Old Latin translation, the Latin Vulgate, and various other versions, including translations into Coptic, Ethiopic, Armenian, and Arabic (see Question 23).

New Testament Manuscript Evidence

There are four main kinds of New Testament textual evidence: Greek manuscripts, Greek lectionaries, versions, and Patristic quotations. Greek manuscripts are copies of all or part of the New Testament. Lectionaries are collections of Scripture used for liturgical reading in the church. Versions are translations of the Greek New Testament into various other languages. Patristic quotations are Scripture passages cited by early church writers.

Greek Manuscripts

There are four kinds of Greek manuscripts: papyri, majuscules, minuscules, and lectionaries. The number of extant manuscripts is constantly changing as new manuscripts are discovered, identified, or recategorized. Each manuscript is given a number from the Gregory-Aland numbering system.[3] The following indicates the number of extant Greek manuscripts of each type:[4]

Papyri	141
Majuscule (Uncial) MSS	324
Minuscule MSS	3017
Lectionary MSS	2486
Total	**5968**

Papyri (𝔓). Our oldest Greek New Testament manuscripts are known as the papyri because they were written on papyrus, a paperlike writing material made from the papyrus plant, a reed grown in marshy conditions in Egypt. To make papyrus, strips of the plant are glued together in cross sections and then flattened together in a press to form a smooth writing surface. Because of the arid conditions in the Nile Delta in Egypt, papyrus manuscripts buried

3. This is known as the *K-Liste*, standing for *Kurzgefasste Liste der griechischen Handschriften des Neuen Testaments* (Short list of Greek manuscripts of the New Testament). It is maintained by the *Institut für Neutestamentliche Textforschung* (Institute for New Testament Textual Research) at the University of Münster, Germany (http://ntvmr.uni-muenster.de/liste). See also the Center for the Study of New Testament Manuscripts at www.csntm.org.
4. Lists of these manuscripts may be found most conveniently on the Wikipedia page "Lists of New Testament Manuscripts" and the links provided there to papyri, majuscules, minuscules, and lectionaries. Numbers cited here were accessed from these lists on March 21, 2023.

there have survived for thousands of years. The New Testament papyri are designated by an Old English "p" (𝔓) with a superscript number identifying the manuscript. For example, $𝔓^{52}$, a small fragment from John's gospel, is our earliest NT manuscript, perhaps dating to the first quarter of the second century. The papyri date from the second to the seventh centuries AD.

Majuscules (A B C D Θ Ψ). The great majority of Greek New Testament manuscripts come from the fourth century onward and were written on *parchment* or *vellum*, a more durable writing material made from animal skins. Parchment NT manuscripts are divided into two groups based on their handwriting style. The older *majuscules* (previously called "uncials"), date from approximately the fourth to the tenth centuries AD and use a square and upright Greek script that looks somewhat like modern Greek capital letters. This was the formal writing style of that time for literary works. There was also another cursive "running" hand, which could be written rapidly, and was used for everyday documents, such as notes, letters, receipts, and so on. Our oldest NT manuscripts, including the papyri, are written in the majuscule book hand. More than three hundred Greek parchment manuscripts are NT majuscules. They are classified with a number beginning with a "0" (e.g., 01, 02, 03). Approximately forty-five of the more important majuscules are also identified with capital Latin letters, Greek letters, or, in one case (Codex Sinaiticus), with the Hebrew letter *aleph*. Here are some examples:

01	A	Codex Alexandrinus
02	א	Codex Sinaiticus
03	B	Codex Vaticanus
04	C	Codex Ephraemi
05	D	Codex Bezae
043	Θ	Codex Koridethi
045	Ψ	Codex Arthous Laurae

Minuscules (33 61 81 157, etc.). About the beginning of the ninth century, a new style of cursive or running hand called "minuscule" gradually replaced the majuscules in formal literary works. While the majuscules are sometimes called "capital" letters and the minuscules "lower-case," these are misnomers, since they are different handwriting styles, not upper- and lowercase letters. The great majority of our NT manuscripts are written with miniscule letters. The miniscule manuscripts are categorized using Arabic numerals, from 1 to 3017.

Lectionaries (ℓ68; ℓ253; ℓ672, etc.). In addition to these Greek biblical manuscripts, there are almost 2,500 Greek lectionary manuscripts. Lectionaries are church reading books containing selected texts to be read on particular days of the church calendar. They date from the ninth to the fourteenth centuries.

Versions (lat, vg, syr, cop, arm, geo, sla, eth)

Versions are translations of the New Testament into various ancient languages to aid Christian missionaries. These include manuscripts in Latin, Syriac, Coptic, Armenian, Georgian, Slavic, Ethiopic, Arabic, and other languages. Although not written in Greek, these versions can help to establish the original Greek text. For example, in Mark 1:41 some Greek manuscripts read that Jesus "was indignant" (*orgistheis*) while others say he "was compassionate" (*splagchnistheis*). Noting how the version translates as either indignation or compassion in its own language confirms the Greek word behind it.

Patristic Quotations

Quotations from the early church fathers can also be a great benefit in textual criticism. Early church leaders quote from Scripture so often it has been suggested that we could construct practically the whole Greek New Testament from their writings. Quotations from church fathers are particularly helpful in determining the date and geographical location of certain readings, since we know when and where many of them lived.

The Method of Textual Criticism

The Evaluation of External Evidence

Because the Masoretic Text (MT) is so standardized, with few variations between manuscripts, English versions generally follow it closely in the Old Testament. At the same time, when two or more significant witnesses—such as the LXX and DSS—agree against the MT, textual critics are more inclined to go against it. For example, in 2 Samuel 24:17 David says to the Lord, "I have sinned; I, the shepherd, have done wrong" (NIV). A footnote in the NIV indicates that while "the shepherd" is absent from the Masoretic text, it appears in *both* the Dead Sea Scrolls and the Septuagint. The translators concluded that this agreement meant the word was likely part of the pre-Masoretic Hebrew text.

We should also note that the Masoretes themselves developed a system to point out verses in the Hebrew Bible that they believed had been corrupted in transmission. As a sign of reverence for the received text, they would keep the consonantal text as it stood, but would identify it as *ketiv* ("what is written"), and then note the preferred text as *qere* ("what is to be read").

The evaluation of external evidence is somewhat different in the New Testament, since there is more variation among manuscripts. New Testament textual critics have historically grouped manuscripts into three main "families," based on their similarities and likely genealogical relationships. These are the Alexandrian, Western, and Byzantine families. A fourth, the Caesarean, is sometimes considered a distinct family, although its homogeneity has been disputed.

Our earliest manuscripts, including most papyri and the oldest majuscules (esp. B, א), are from the Alexandrian family, so most textual critics consider this to be the earliest and most reliable family. The great majority of later manuscripts are from the Byzantine family, which most textual critics consider to be a later and less reliable standardization of the text.

A small minority of scholars hold to a "majority text" view, where manuscript readings are counted rather than weighed. Whichever reading appears in the most manuscripts is considered the original. This inevitably results in Byzantine family readings, since the vast majority of manuscripts are Byzantine. Most text critics, however, reject this method as invalid. They favor older manuscripts that conform to the rules of textual transmission (see below and Question 27).

The Evaluation of Internal Evidence

While external evidence evaluates the value of manuscripts based on their age and genealogical relationships (families), internal evidence evaluates the readings themselves based on the tendencies of authors (intrinsic evidence) and copyists (transcriptional evidence).

(1) *Intrinsic* internal evidence refers to the tendencies of authors. An example would be the textual question in Mark 1:1, which reads, "The beginning of the gospel of Jesus Christ, the Son of God" (1:1). While some manuscripts do not have the phrase "Son of God," the importance of the title "Son of God" elsewhere in Mark's gospel would be an intrinsic (authorial) argument for its inclusion here.

(2) *Transcriptional* internal evidence refers to the tendencies of copyists/scribes. The goal is to work backwards and undo the mistakes copyists made. For a description of these rules and examples of their use, see Question 27. Following these rules tends to result in readings found in the Alexandrian family. Since both the external evidence (the earliest manuscripts) and the internal evidence (scribal and authorial tendencies) tend to favor the Alexandrian family, almost all textual critics consider this to be the most reliable family. This is not to say that Alexandrian readings are *always* best, but in general these readings are favored.

More will be said on this issue in Question 27, when we discuss the Greek text behind the King James Version. Most translators use as their base Greek texts the latest editions of the United Bible Societies *Greek New Testament*

(5th ed.) and the *Nestle-Aland, Novum Testamentum Graece* (28th ed.), both of which have an apparatus identifying important textual variants.

Summary

The method used to determine the original text of Scripture is known as textual criticism. For the Old Testament, translators generally follow the Hebrew Masoretic Text, occasionally departing from it when two or more reliable witnesses (such as the DSS and the LXX) agree against it. For the New Testament, most textual critics utilize an eclectic method that considers both external evidence (age and family relationship of manuscripts) and internal evidence (tendencies of authors and scribes). Both kinds of evidence tend to favor the Alexandrian family of manuscripts, which most textual critics consider to be the earliest and most reliable family.

REFLECTION QUESTIONS

1. What is the purpose and goal of textual criticism?

2. What textual evidence do Old Testament text critics use?

3. What textual evidence do New Testament text critics use?

4. What is external textual evidence? Internal evidence?

5. Why is the Alexandrian family favored by most NT textual critics?

QUESTION 9

What Other Decisions Must Translators Make?

Various decisions must be made in preparation for translation, including which translation philosophy or approach to use (see Questions 3–5), which books should be included (Question 7), and which Hebrew and Greek texts to translate (Question 8). Here we discuss five additional factors that distinguish versions from one another. Translators must decide (1) whether to revise an existing version or produce a new translation; (2) whether to work as a committee or an individual; (3) what their theological or ecclesiastical perspective is; (4) who the intended audience is and the desired reading level; and (5) the degree of priority given to source and receptor cultures.

Revision or New Translation?

One key factor that distinguishes Bible versions from one another is whether they are a new version translated from the original languages or a revision of a previous version. Most Bible versions are periodically revised to keep up with changes in the language and to improve their style and accuracy. Dates provided on a version's copyright page identify these revisions. For example, the New International Version has as its copyright dates: "Copyright © 1973, 1978, 1984, 2011." The first date (1973) was the release of the New Testament; 1978 was the publication of the full Bible; 1984 was the first significant revision; and 2011 was the latest revision. While these revisions tend to be relatively minor, major revisions to a text sometimes result in a name change. Most famously for English, there have been a series of revisions of the King James Version, including the Revised Version (1885), the American Standard Version (1901), the Revised Standard Version (1952), the New American Standard Bible (1971), the New King James Version (1982), the New Revised Standard Version (1990), and the English Standard Version (2001). The KJV was itself a revision of the Bishops' Bible, with input from other versions (see Question 25). We will survey all these versions and more when we examine the history of English Bible translation (part 4).

While revisions start with a previous version, new translations are rendered directly from the Hebrew and Greek. Some new Bible versions produced in the late twentieth and early twenty-first centuries include the New English Bible (1970), the Living Bible (1971), Today's English Version (1976), the New International Version (1978), the Holman Christian Standard Bible (2004), and the New English Translation (2006). Of course these versions are not wholly original, since translators are well aware of established English versions and are impacted by them. There is no completely original translation of the Bible!

New versions are often subsequently revised in minor ways under the same name, or given a new name after a major revision. Examples of the latter include the NEB revised as the Revised English Bible (1989); the LB revised as the New Living Translation (1996); Today's English Version revised as the Good News Bible (1976), and the Holman Christian Standard Bible (2004) revised as the Christian Standard Bible (2017).

Committee Work or Individual Translation?

While most translations tend to be produced under the oversight of a committee, some are done by individuals. For example, the Living Bible was primarily the work of Kenneth Taylor, *The Message* was translated by Eugene Peterson, and the NT of Today's English Version was translated by Robert Bratcher, while the Old Testament was done by a committee of seven scholars. For other single-translator versions see Question 30.

The most respected and widely used English versions today are almost all committee works, including the NEB, NASB, NIV, NKJV, REB, NAB, NJB, NRSV, NLT, ESV, NET, (H)CSB, and CEB. The benefits of a committee translation are many, but especially important are its checks and balances. An error missed by one scholar may be caught by another. Having a measure of diversity among committee members also helps to protect against idiosyncratic or tendentious readings. Committees also enable members to have expertise in a variety of genres and fields of study and thus a broader range of scholarship. Committees also normally have a mix of Old and New Testament scholars and sometimes include English stylists. Having committee members with a good ear for English is important, since a translation can be precise in terms of its scholarship, yet awkward for public reading. Committees work in a variety of ways, almost always in stages. An individual or small team may do the initial translation of a book or section of Scripture, which then goes to another committee for review and evaluation. There is usually a senior oversight committee that approves the final translation.

Potential benefits of a single-translator version are uniformity of style and readability. Both Kenneth Taylor (the Living Bible) and Eugene Peterson (*The*

Message) were gifted writers. Their translations are a delight to read, which is one reason for their enormous popularity. The danger of a single translator, of course, is the inevitable gaps in that person's knowledge and experience. To help redress this, both Taylor and Peterson at times consulted with outside biblical experts.

Theological or Ecclesiastical Perspective?

A third factor that distinguishes Bible versions from one another is the theological or ecclesiastical perspective of the translators. While we would like to think that all translators are objective and free of bias, everyone comes to the task of translation with certain beliefs, values, and a variety of life experiences. No one translates from a blank slate, and the translator's theological perspective and view of Scripture will inevitably impact the translation to one degree or another.[1] Some English versions could be called "evangelical," since their translators affirm certain assumptions about the authority and inspiration of Scripture (e.g., NASB; NIV; NLT; NET; ESV; CSB). Such presuppositions are often noted in the preface or introduction to the translation. Other English versions were produced in broader, more ecumenical circles (e.g., REB; RSV; NRSV; CEB).

Despite these differences, there remains a remarkable amount of agreement on the basic meaning of the biblical text. There are very few English versions—whether produced by Roman Catholic or Protestant scholars, evangelical or more liberal—that I would not recommend as useful and reliable tools for students of the Bible. A few exceptions to this are versions that are clearly agenda-driven, seeking to assert a particular theological perspective. One example of this is the New World Translation, produced by the Jehovah's Witnesses, which skews its translation to their unorthodox theological perspectives.

Audience, Reading Level, and Register

A fourth important issue that distinguishes Bible versions is the intended audience. Some versions make grandiose claims that their version is perfect for all readers—children and adults, remedial readers and intellectuals, novices and scholars, new believers and seasoned Christians. Yet different kinds of versions can be more helpful for different audiences. A version that uses technical theological terms like justification, sanctification, and propitiation may be appropriate for someone who has grown up in the church but difficult for a new Christian or someone unfamiliar with Christian theology.

---

1. See my article, "Ideology and Bible Translation, Part 1: Evangelicals and the Ethics of Translation" (Beekman Lectures, Bible Translation Conference, October 16–20, 2015, Dallas, Texas), available at MarkLStrauss.com.

Some versions are geared especially for children or for those with limited reading skills. The International Children's Bible (ICB), an edition of the New Century Version, first published in 1986, was adapted from a version originally developed for the deaf (see Question 32). The goal was to establish a text that was both accurate and simple to read and understand. Sentences are kept short, and a limited vocabulary is utilized. Another example is the New International Reader's Version (NIrV), a simplified revision of the New International Version. It is geared not only for children but for anyone with remedial reading skills, including those learning English as a second language and those with reading disorders (see Question 34).

Translations are often rated according to their grade level. The KJV is sometimes said to be a twelfth-grade reading level, the NIV a seventh- or eighth-grade level, and the NCV a third-grade level.[2] These categories, however, are somewhat arbitrary. Does grade level refer to complexity or obscurity? One translation may be difficult to understand because it is overly literal, with nonstandard English and confusing grammar. Another may be hard to understand because it is written for a more educated audience, utilizing more technical vocabulary and complex but accurate grammar.

The linguistic term "register" refers to style or level of writing. Register in this sense has been defined as "a variety of a language or a level of usage, as determined by degree of formality and choice of vocabulary, pronunciation, and syntax, according to the communicative purpose, social context, and social status of the user."[3] A "high" register would be something written with greater complexity in terms of vocabulary and grammar, or directed to those with technical expertise in a particular field.

An extreme example of a unique register is a translation of the New Testament published in 1768 by classical scholar Edward Harwood. Harwood's version, which has been referred to as a "literary curio,"[4] has the fulsome title *Liberal Translation of the New Testament: Being an Attempt to Translate the Sacred Writings with the Same Freedom, Spirit, and Elegance, with Which Other English Translations from the Greek Classics Have Lately Been Executed.* Harwood sought to improve "the bald and barbarous language of the old vulgar version" (meaning the KJV) with a style that "might induce persons of liberal education and polite state to peruse the sacred volume."[5] Bruce

---

2. See, for example, "Translation Reading Levels," Christian Book, accessed January 31, 2023, www.christianbook.com/page/bibles/about-bibles/bible-translation-reading-levels.
3. Encyclopedia.com, s.v. "register," updated May 21, 2018, https://www.encyclopedia.com/science-and-technology/computers-and-electrical-engineering/computers-and-computing/register#:~:text=3.,social%20status%20of%20the%20user.
4. F. F. Bruce, *History of the Bible in English*, 3rd ed. (New York: Oxford University Press, 1978), 130.
5. Cited by Bruce M. Metzger, *The Bible in Translation: Ancient and English Versions* (Grand Rapids: Baker, 2001), 82.

Metzger provides an example of Harwood's opulent style from the Magnificat of Mary (Luke 1:46–48):

> My soul with reverence adores my Creator! and all my faculties with transport join in celebrating the goodness of God my savior, who hath in so signal a manner condescended to regard my obscure and humble station—Transcendent goodness! Every future age will now conjoin in celebrating my distinguished happiness!

Imagine such exalted prose coming from a Palestinian peasant girl! Metzger concludes that Harwood "aimed at elegance, perspicuity, and propriety, and achieved pomposity."[6]

Source-Culture or Receptor-Culture Priority?

While all Bible versions lie on a spectrum between form and function, they also lie on a spectrum between replicating the original context and recontextualizing it to a contemporary one. Translators must decide how much to bridge the gap between the source culture and the receptor culture and how much to let readers navigate these cultural differences on their own. We have noted several examples of this in previous questions (2, 5). When the Living Bible uses "flashlight" for "lamp" in Psalm 119:105, and when the Phillips' translation replaces a kiss of greeting with a handshake (Rom. 16:16 PME), they are intentionally identifying with the receptor culture. Extreme examples of this are the radical recontextualizations of the biblical story found in versions like *The Cotton Patch Version* produced by Clarence Jordan, P. K. McCary's *Black Bible Chronicles*, and *The Street Bible* by Rob Lacey (see Question 36).

While these are extreme examples, all versions must wrestle with the question of how much to modify the cultural context to make the text understandable to the receptor audience. For example, do you translate weights using Hebrew or Greek terms like *shekel*, *mina*, and *talent*, or do you use contemporary American or metric equivalents like ounces, pounds, grams, and kilograms? Similarly, should lengths be given in biblical measurements like *spans*, *cubits*, and *stadia*, or in their contemporary equivalents like inches, feet, yards, miles, meters, and kilometers? For more on the translation of measurements see Question 17.

Summary

In addition to choices concerning methodology, canon, and text, translators must also decide several other issues: whether to revise an older version or produce a new one; whether to work as an individual or a committee; to

6. Metzger, *Bible in Translation*, 82.

what extent their theological position will affect their translation; the audience and reading level to which they are aiming; and to what degree they will accommodate to the receptor culture.

REFLECTION QUESTIONS

1. Consider the primary Bible translation you use. Where does it stand on each of the five factors discussed in this question?
2. What are the benefits of a committee translation?
3. What are the benefits of a single-translator Bible version?
4. What are the benefits of a translation that closely follows the culture of the biblical world? What might be its weaknesses?
5. What are the benefits of a translation that accommodates to the receptor culture? What are its weaknesses?

PART 3

Challenges for Translators

SECTION A

Lexical Issues

Words, of course, are the basic building blocks of language. To do good translation requires an understanding of how words work. The challenge for translators is that the various meanings of words in one language seldom overlap exactly with the meanings of words in another.

QUESTION 10

What Are the Challenges of Translating Words?

The study of word meanings is known as "lexical semantics." A "lexeme" is the basic dictionary entry of a word, which includes its various forms. For example, the verb "run" is a lexeme, which includes such forms as "ran," "runs," and "running." The word "semantics" relates to meaning, so lexical semantics is the study of word meanings. Here are some basic principles of lexical semantics.[1]

Basic Principles of Lexical Semantics

(1) *Most words in any language have a semantic range—a range of possible senses—not one "literal" or core meaning.* The reason for this is that every language has a limited number of words (or "lexical stock") with which to express an almost infinite number of ideas.[2] Consider just a few of the many senses of the English word "board":

A flat piece of wood (n.):	"Saw that board in half."
A control panel (n.):	"Check the circuit board."

1. For lexical semantics in biblical studies see, James Barr, *The Semantics of Biblical Language* (Philadelphia: Trinity, 1961); Moisés Silva, *Biblical Words and Their Meaning*, rev. ed. (Grand Rapids: Zondervan, 1995); Peter Cotterell and Max Turner, *Linguistics and Biblical Interpretation* (Downers Grove, IL: InterVarsity, 1989), 106–87.
2. To be sure, some languages have a large number of words and others a smaller lexical stock. According to one website, the language with the fewest words is Taki Taki (also called Sranan Tongo), an English-based Creole spoken in the South American country of Suriname. Taki Taki only uses 340 words ("Language Statistics and Facts," Vistawide, accessed January 31, 2023, www.vistawide.com/languages/language_statistics.htm). By contrast, the Oxford English Dictionary lists more than 200,000 English words!

A leadership team (n.):	"The board voted on new officers."
Any number of flat surfaces (n.):	"skateboard," "surfboard," "backboard," "blackboard"
Daily meals (n.):	"Does that include room and board?"
To get on a vehicle (v.):	"It's time to board the plane."

Since most words have multiple senses, it is almost never correct to speak of the "literal" meaning of a word. Words have a semantic range, not a single literal meaning.

(2) *The meanings of words in one language do not necessarily line up with the meaning of words in another language.* So, for example, in Spanish if you want to refer to a flat piece of wood, you might say *la tabla* or *el tablón*. But if you mean a leadership board, you would say *el consejo* or *la junta*. If you mean a skateboard, you might say *monopatín* or *patineta*; a blackboard would be *la pizarra* or *el pizzarón*; and if you meant daily meals, you might say *pensión* or *habitación y comida*. To embark on a ship, you could say *subir a bordo*. There is no one Spanish word that encompasses all the senses of the English word "board."

The same is true for almost all words in any language, including Hebrew and Greek. The Greek verb *pherō* most commonly means "bring" or "carry." But consider the diverse ways this verb is translated. We use the NASB here to show that even formal equivalent Bible versions acknowledge this multiplicity of word senses:

Mark 2:3	some people came, <u>bringing</u> [*pherō*] to Him a man who was paralyzed
Mark 4:8	Other seeds . . . <u>produced</u> [*pherō*] thirty, sixty, and a hundred times as much.
John 2:8	Draw some [wine] out now and <u>take</u> [*pherō*] it to the headwaiter.
John 15:2	Every branch in Me that does not <u>bear</u> [*pherō*] fruit
John 20:27	He said to Thomas, "<u>Place</u> [*pherō*] your finger here."
Acts 2:2	Suddenly a noise like a violent <u>rushing</u> [*pherō*] wind came from heaven.
Acts 12:10	They came to the iron gate that <u>leads</u> [*pherō*] into the city.

Acts 27:15	The ship was . . . driven [*pherō*] by the wind.
Rom. 9:22	What if God . . . endured [*pherō*] with great patience . . . ?
Heb. 1:3	He . . . upholds [*pherō*] all things by the word of His power.
Heb. 6:1	Let us press on [*pherō*] to maturity.
Heb. 12:20	For they could not cope [*pherō*] with the command
2 Peter 1:21	Men moved [*pherō*] by the Holy Spirit spoke from God.

So what is the "literal" meaning of the Greek word *pherō*? Bring? Carry? Produce? Take? Bear? Place? Rush? Lead? Drive? Endure? Uphold? Press on? Cope? Move? The answer is none of these, since words don't have a "literal" meaning. They have a semantic range. If that is the case, how do you determine the meaning of a particular word? The answer, of course, is *context.*

(3) *Context indicates which sense the author intended.* Authors or speakers choose particular words because they communicate the meaning they wish to express in a particular context. Look at the examples above with the Greek *pherō*. The translator chose an English word *in each context* to approximate the meaning of the Greek word in that context.

Notice also that other words might work equally well. John 2:8 could have been translated "bring it to the headwaiter" instead of "take it to the headwaiter." John 15:2 could have been translated "produce fruit" instead of "bear fruit." John 20:27 could have read "put your finger here" instead of "place." Translation is choosing a word that approximates the meaning intended by the author in a particular context.

(4) *Lexical choices in translation are approximations of the meaning of a word.* Since there is no exact one-to-one correspondence between languages, there is no single "correct" translation. Language by its very nature has a measure of ambiguity and imprecision. One word might pick up certain nuances of the original meaning, while another might pick up other nuances. Just as there is no such thing as a truly literal translation, so there is no such thing as a *perfect* translation. As the saying goes, "Something is lost in the translation." The goal, however, is to approximate the meaning of the original as closely as possible. And a translation can be *accurate* and *reliable* without being perfect.

(5) *Words may overlap in their semantic ranges but seldom correlate exactly.* Since no two languages are identical, words seldom mean exactly the same thing. In the example given above, the English word "board" may overlap in a number of its senses with the Spanish *la tabla,* but not always.

In those cases, to translate "literally" or in a one-to-one manner would be inaccurate.

Another way to say this is that words can be synonymous in some contexts but not in others. This is true both across languages and within a language. Consider the English words "house" and "home." These words can in many cases be synonymous. I could say, "He builds homes" and mean exactly the same thing as "He builds houses." But if I said, "She turned that house into a home," I would be using the words with two different senses. Similarly, in the sentences "He had an accident" and "He had a crash," "crash" and "accident" are synonyms, both meaning "an automobile collision." But if I said, "That crash was no accident," the word "accident" now means "something unintentional." If I wanted to be clever, I could even make a play on words by saying, "That accident was no accident." Here I am using the same lexeme with two different senses.

(6) *The meaning of words changes over time, so translations must be periodically updated.* While the meaning of the Hebrew and Greek texts of Scripture do not change, contemporary languages do, and this requires translation updates. For English readers, these changes are most easily seen in the King James Version, where words like "descry" (Judg. 1:23), "collops" (Job 15:27), "neesings" (Job 41:18), "churl" (Isa. 32:7), and "chambering" (Rom. 13:13) are unknown to most contemporary readers. Other words and phrases would be recognized but communicate the wrong meaning to contemporary readers: "strange women" (1 Kings 11:1), meaning foreign women; "the voice of the turtle" (Song 2:12), meaning the cooing of doves; "quick" (2 Tim. 4:1), meaning alive, and so on (see Question 26 for more of these).

Contemporary versions must also be updated, because English continues to change. There are some humorous examples of this. In the 1984 NIV, 2 Chronicles 14:14 reads, "They plundered all these villages, since there was much <u>booty</u> there." For obvious reasons, the 2011 edition changed this to "They looted all these villages, since there was much <u>plunder</u> there." Similarly, in Judges 16:7–8, when Delilah is trying to get Samson to reveal the source of his strength, the 1984 NIV reads,

> Samson answered her [Delilah], "If anyone ties me with seven fresh <u>thongs</u> that have not been dried, I'll become as weak as any other man." Then the rulers of the Philistines brought her seven fresh <u>thongs</u> that had not been dried, and she tied him with them.

The English word "thong" once referred to various kinds of straps or strips of material for fastening things, but the primary referent today is to women's underwear or a skimpy swimsuit. In the NIV 2011 this was changed to the more accurate "bowstrings."

The Challenge of Wordplays and Verbal Allusions

These principles confirm that it is important to translate words according to their meaning in context, rather than according to some "literal" or etymological sense. Yet there are times when the form of a word becomes an important part of textual meaning. This is especially so in the case of wordplays and verbal allusions. An example of wordplay appears in the account of the creation of the woman in Genesis 2:23, where the Hebrew words for "man" (*'ish*) and "woman" (*'ishah*) are etymologically related. When God brings Eve to Adam, he says,

> This is now bone of my bones
> and flesh of my flesh;
> she shall be called "woman" [*'ishah*]
> for she was taken out of man [*'ish*].

Coincidentally, the wordplay works in English, because as in Hebrew the words "woman" and "man" are etymologically related. It does not work in every language, however, since the words for "man" and "woman" are not always formally similar. The Greek Old Testament, for example, does not reproduce the Hebrew wordplay since "man" in Greek is *anēr* and "woman" is *gynē*. The LXX reads, "She will be called 'woman' [*gynē*] for she was taken from her 'man/husband' [*anēr*]."

Another example of Hebrew wordplay appears in Genesis 40, where Joseph is in prison and meets two former servants of Pharaoh, the king's chief cupbearer and chief baker. Each has a dream, which Joseph interprets. In interpreting the cupbearer's dream, Joseph uses a Hebrew idiom, which reads quite literally, "Pharaoh <u>will lift your head</u> and restore you to your office." The idiom "lift your head" means "to reinstate to your position." Idiomatic translations often change this to natural English. The NET reads, "In three more days Pharaoh <u>will reinstate you</u> and restore you to your office." GW reads, "In the next three days Pharaoh <u>will release you</u> and restore you to your position." Both are good, idiomatic translations. But in the narrative that follows, Joseph interprets the chief baker's dream and says, "Pharaoh <u>will lift your head</u>—off you—and will hang your body on a stake." The same idiom that meant to restore is now used for decapitation! Many versions translate the idiom quite literally to preserve the Hebrew wordplay. The NIV reads in verse 13, "Within three days Pharaoh <u>will lift up</u> your head and restore you to your position," and then in verse 16, "Within three days Pharaoh <u>will lift off</u> your head and impale your body on a pole." The NET, while giving an idiomatic translation, provides a footnote explaining the Hebrew wordplay.

For a NT example of a Greek verbal wordplay, see the example of *sophos* in 1 Corinthians 3:10 in Question 4.

Translating Words

From this discussion we can summarize the basic steps necessary to translate words:

1. *Determine the word's semantic range in the source language.* What various meanings does the word have in context? For those who have studied the original languages, this can be done using a Hebrew or Greek lexicon.[3] For others, an exhaustive concordance, word study book, or commentary can be used.
2. *Identify which sense the author intended by examining the context.* Context means especially the immediate sentence and paragraph, but also the way the word is used in the larger context of the book and the author's other writings, as well as similar writings and genres.
3. *Choose the closest meaning equivalent in the receptor language.* Decide what word or phrase best communicates the meaning most clearly for your target audience.
4. *Consider other factors that might influence word choice, such as wordplays, verbal allusions, or connotations.* Consider how the word or its cognates are used elsewhere. Also, for a New Testament word, consider how similar words are translated in the Old Testament.
5. *Make a final decision.* What is the best translation? If the decision is debated by scholars or a wordplay is present that cannot be easily communicated in translation, a footnote may be in order.

Summary

Words don't have "literal" meanings. They have a semantic range, a range of possible senses. The context in which the word occurs must be used to determine which sense the author intended. Translators must therefore be in a constant state of interpretation (all translation involves interpretation!), examining words in their contexts to determine which words or phrases to use to translate them. Translators should also be alert to verbal allusions and wordplays in the source text and must determine whether it is possible and/or desirable to reproduce that allusion or wordplay in the receptor language.

---

3. Some standard Hebrew lexicons include Ludwig Koehler and Walter Baumgartner, *Hebrew and Aramaic Lexicon of the Old Testament* [HALOT], 5 vols. (Leiden: Brill, 1994–2000), and F. Brown, S. R. Driver, and C. A. Briggs, *The New Brown-Driver-Briggs-Gesenius Hebrew and English Lexicon* [BDB] (Peabody, MA: Hendrickson, 1979). The most important dictionary for NT Greek is W. Baur, F. W. Danker, W. F. Arndt, and F. W. Gingrich, eds., *A Greek-English Lexicon of the Greek New Testament and Other Early Christian Literature*, 3rd ed. (Chicago: University of Chicago Press, 2001), abbreviated as BDAG.

REFLECTION QUESTIONS

1. What is the semantic range of a word?
2. What enables us to determine which sense of a word an author intended in a particular context?
3. Have you heard Bible teachers or preachers speak of the "literal" meaning of Hebrew or Greek words? Why is this problematic?
4. Why is it difficult to reproduce verbal allusions and wordplays in translation?
5. What are the basic steps necessary to translate words?

QUESTION 11

What Are the Challenges of Translating Collocations?

What Are Collocations?

The term "collocation" refers to linguistic elements, especially words, that are used together with other words to express a particular meaning. John Beekman and John Callow point out the many collocations in the Vagla language of Ghana that use the common Vagla word for "eat" (*diy*).[1]

Literal Vagla Translation	Meaning in English
He ate his self	He enjoyed himself
He ate his case	He judged his case
He ate shame	He was ashamed
He ate chieftainship	He became the chief
He ate two goals	He scored two goals
He ate a friend	He chose him as a friend
He ate him an argument	He argued with him
It is eating	It is sharp
You should eat	It's your turn

You can see that in Vagla "eat" (*diy*) has a large semantic range. It can mean many different things, depending on the word(s) it is paired with—its collocate. Few of these collocations work in English. The same thing occurs in all languages. Consider, for example, some of the words that are commonly paired with the English word "have":

1. John Beekman and John Callow, *Translating the Word of God* (Grand Rapids: Zondervan, 1974), 29.

Collocation	**Meaning**
have a car	own a car; *or* have rented a car; *or* have access to a car
have time	able to invest a certain amount of time
have an excuse	consider justified in something you did
have an opinion	hold a particular view
have a wife	be married to a woman
have at it	fight about something
have enough	be fed up
have a fit	throw a tantrum
have my eye on someone	be interested in a relationship
have a cold	be sick with a virus
have the right	be justified in doing something

These examples not only show that the word "have" has a very large semantic range; they also show that its meaning is derived from its collocations. "Have" means something very different when paired with "a fit" than it does when paired with "a car." Notice, too, that I can take almost any meaning in the right column and find many other collocations that go with it. I can "throw a tantrum," "throw a ball," "throw up," "throw my arms around you," or "throw the game" (meaning intentionally lose).

The great challenge for translators is that collocations seldom stay the same across languages. For example, in English you "take" a walk. But in Spanish you "give" a walk (*dar un paseo*). In English you "take a trip," but in Spanish you "make a trip" (*hacer un viaje*). In English, a drug "takes effect" or "works," but in Spanish it "supplies effect" (*surtir efecto*).[2] Or consider the example above with the English word "have." In my beginning Greek courses, I teach my students that the Greek word for "have" is *echō*. But you can't use *echō* with most of the English expressions with "have" above. And, conversely, there are many expressions with *echō* in Greek that don't translate well as "have" in English. Consider these Greek collocations:

Reference	**"Literal" Rendering of Greek** ***echō***	**Meaning in English**
Mark 3:22	He <u>has</u> Beelzeboul	He <u>is possessed by</u> Beelzeboul
Matthew 21:26	The people <u>held</u> John as a prophet	The people <u>considered</u> John a prophet
Mark 5:23	My daughter <u>has lastly</u>	My daughter <u>is dying</u>

2. These examples come from Gordon D. Fee and Mark L. Strauss, *How to Choose a Translation for All Its Worth* (Grand Rapids: Zondervan, 2007), 52.

Reference	"Literal" Rendering of Greek *echō*	Meaning in English
John 9:21	He has age	He is old enough
Luke 7:2	A servant was having badly	A servant was sick
Acts 17:11	These things had thusly	These things were true

You can imagine how difficult it is for someone learning a new language to figure all this out. You can't just learn the meaning of words. You must learn how those words interact in various collocations. I once asked a missionary friend working with a tribal language in Irian Jaya whether the idioms were difficult in his language. He responded that the idioms weren't bad, but the collocations were a nightmare! The problem is that common words like "eat" or "have" or "throw" or "make" or "keep" or "run" have a great many different meanings depending on their collocations. And these meanings often do not overlap in other languages.

Translators must therefore be in a constant mode of interpretation. Consider the first line of Matthew's gospel in Greek and how it is translated/interpreted in these English versions:

Matthew 1:1

Greek	*Biblos geneseōs Iēsou Christou*
KJV	The book of the generation of Jesus Christ (cf. ASV)
RSV	The book of the genealogy of Jesus Christ (cf. NKJV; ESV; NAB)
TEV	This is the list of the ancestors of Jesus Christ
NASB	The record of the genealogy of Jesus the Messiah
NIV	This is the genealogy of Jesus the Messiah
CEB	A record of the ancestors of Jesus Christ
HCSB	The historical record of Jesus Christ
CSB	An account of the genealogy of Jesus Christ
GW	This is the list of ancestors of Jesus Christ
MSG	The family tree of Jesus Christ
NET	This is the record of the genealogy of Jesus Christ
NJB	Roll of the genealogy of Jesus Christ
NLT	This is a record of the ancestors of Jesus the Messiah
NRSV	An account of the genealogy of Jesus the Messiah

The Greek collocation *Biblos geneseōs* is translated fourteen different ways in these eighteen versions! The Greek word *Biblos* is translated five different ways: "book," "list," "record," "account," and "roll." *Geneseōs* is translated three different ways: "generation," "genealogy," and "ancestors." In three versions, the two words are translated *together* as "family tree" (MSG) "historical record" (HCSB) or simply "genealogy" (NIV). This illustrates that translators must first ask, "What does this collocation as a whole *mean* in Greek (the source language)?" Then they must ask, "What is the clearest and most accurate way to reproduce that meaning in English (the receptor language)?"

Collocational Clashes

When translators pair up words that do not work well in the receptor language, this is called a collocational clash.[3] Collocational clashes are most common in formal equivalent versions, where translators often seek one-to-one correspondence between words in the source and receptor languages. Beekman and Callow write,

> The nonequivalence of collocational ranges between languages may seem obvious enough. Nevertheless, translators often use words outside their normal collocational range because they have, usually quite unconsciously, assumed that the particular collocation they are translating—the original collocation—is transferable to the [Receptor Language]. The translator therefore needs to be alert to collocations in the original which are potential trouble spots and to avoid transferring them into the [Receptor Language].[4]

Consider these examples of collocational clashes in various Bible versions. In each we pair up a more formal equivalent version with a mediating or functional equivalent version.

Exodus 21:7

ESV	When a man sells his daughter as a slave, she shall not <u>go out</u> as the male slaves do.
CEB	When a man sells his daughter as a slave, she shouldn't <u>be set free</u> in the same way as male slaves are set free.

The Hebrew verb translated "go out" in this collocation means "to be set free from slavery." No one speaking English would say, "The slaves *went out* after Lincoln issued his emancipation proclamation."

Judges 16:17

NASB	"<u>A razor has never come on my head</u>, for I have been a Nazirite to God from my mother's womb."

3. Beekman and Callow, *Translating the Word of God*, 160–174.
4. Beekman and Callow, *Translating the Word of God*, 164.

NLT "My hair has never been cut," he confessed, "for I was dedicated to God as a Nazirite from birth."

In English we would never speak of a haircut as "a razor coming on" someone's head ("Did you get a razor on your head today?"). We might say (awkwardly), "No razor has ever been used on my head" (NIV) or "No razor has ever touched my head" (CEB), but normal English is, "My hair has never been cut" (CSB; NLT; TEV; cf. GW).

Isaiah 1:15

NRSV even though you make many prayers, I will not listen; your hands are full of blood.
NET when you offer your many prayers, I do not listen, because your hands are covered with blood.

In English someone's guilt might metaphorically be described as "hands covered with blood" (NET; CSB; NASB; NLT; TEV; GW) or "stained with blood" (CEB; JPS). But we would not normally say they are "full of blood" (RSV; ESV; NRSV; NIV; NCV)—unless the image here is cupped hands holding a quantity of blood. But this seems unlikely.

Isaiah 56:1

NKJV Thus says the LORD: "Keep justice, and do righteousness
NET This is what the LORD says, "Promote justice! Do what is right!

To "keep" justice is not a normal English collocation. We might "promote justice" (NET) or "maintain justice" (NIV; REB) or "preserve justice" (CSB). Or one might "act justly" (CEB) or "do what is just" (TEV). Similarly, "Do what is right" (NIV; NET; NLT) is a more natural collocation than "do righteousness."

Amos 1:11

NKJV Edom . . . pursued his brother with the sword. . . . His anger tore perpetually
NET Edom . . . chased his brother with a sword. . . . In his anger he tore them apart without stopping to rest

The Hebrew is puzzling here, and commentators debate its meaning. But we would never speak in English about someone's anger "tearing." Some versions translate this as his anger "raged" (NIV; REB). The NET Bible suggests that in anger they tore their enemies apart.

Nahum 1:15

ESV	Behold, upon the mountains, the feet of him who brings good news, <u>who publishes peace</u>!
NASB	Behold, on the mountains, the feet of him who brings good news, <u>Who announces peace</u>!

Peace is not normally something you publish (especially centuries before the printing press!). Peace is "announced" or "proclaimed."

Mark 4:29

NASB	Now when <u>the crop permits</u>, he immediately <u>puts in the sickle</u>, because the harvest has come.
TEV	When <u>the grain is ripe</u>, the man <u>starts cutting it with his sickle</u>, because harvest time has come.

In English we would never say that a "crop permits" when it is ready for harvest. We would say it is "ripe" or "full grown" or "ready to be harvested." Furthermore, in English we would not say at harvest time a farmer "puts in a sickle." The farmer might "cut the grain with a sickle" or "harvest with a sickle."

Mark 10:22

ESV	Disheartened by the saying, he went away sorrowful, for he had <u>great possessions</u>.
NRSV	When he heard this, he was shocked and went away grieving, for he had <u>many possessions</u>.

To say he had "great possessions" in English would normally refer to the quality of the possessions. They are "great." But the collocation is referring to quantity. He had "many possessions" (NRSV; NLT; CSB), "much property" (NASB), or "great wealth" (NIV).

John 8:51

CSB	Truly I tell you, if anyone <u>keeps my word</u>, he will never <u>see death</u>.
NLT	I tell you the truth, anyone who <u>obeys my teaching</u> will never <u>die</u>!

The collocation "keeps my word" may be clear enough to someone steeped in "Bible language" (= KJV idiom), but it is not natural English for obedience in response to instruction. I would never say, "The police officer told me to pull over and I kept his word." To "keep my word" in English means to be faithful to my own promise, not for someone else to obey my teaching. The second collocation, "see death," is also unnatural English. It is unlikely I would ever say, "My grandfather saw death when he was 85 years old." I would simply say, "He died."

John 17:11

ESV	Holy Father, <u>keep</u> them in your name.
NLT	Holy Father, <u>protect</u> them by the power of your name.

The collocation "keep them in your name" makes little sense in English. The Greek word translated "keep" (*tēreō*) here means to "guard" or "protect," and one's "name" indicates their power and authority.

Hebrews 11:33

ESV	<u>stopped</u> the mouths of lions
NIV	<u>shut</u> the mouths of lions

In English we would not normally say that a lion's mouth is "stopped" but rather that it was "shut" or "closed."

Summary

Collocations are words that get their meaning when paired with other word(s), their collocate. The challenge for translators is that collocations seldom stay the same between languages. What you can "make" or "keep" or "have" in one language often does not work for another language. Translators must therefore be in a constant state of interpretation, determining the meaning of the collocation in the source language and then finding an equivalent word or phrase in the receptor language.

REFLECTION QUESTIONS

1. What is a collocation?

2. What makes it difficult to translate collocations?

3. Consider a common English verb, and list as many of its collocations as you can. You might want to check a dictionary to find more.

4. If you speak a second language, make a list of common phrases and then write out their English translations. Note any collocations you come across.

5. Or, open a computer translator (for example, type into the Google search engine: "English to German"). Put in some phrases that you might say on a visit to that country. Does the form change to reproduce the meaning?

SECTION B

Figurative Language

One of the great beauties of language is that words can be used in many ways beyond their most common, concrete, or “literal” meanings. Figurative language, while a great enhancement for communication through language, presents unique challenges for translators.

QUESTION 12

What Are the Challenges of Translating Idioms?

What Is an Idiom?

Merriam-Webster's online dictionary defines an idiom as "an expression in the usage of a language that is peculiar to itself either in having a meaning that cannot be derived from the conjoined meanings of its elements (such as *up in the air* for 'undecided') or in its grammatically atypical use of words (such as *give way*)."[1] By definition, an idiom cannot be understood "literally" since it functions as a whole rather than at the level of its individual parts. Consider Matthew 22:16, where a group of leaders approach Jesus in an attempt to trap him. They begin by flattering him. The NIV reads:

> "Teacher," they said, "we know that you are a man of integrity and that you teach the way of God in accordance with the truth. You aren't swayed by others, <u>because you pay no attention to who they are</u>."

The last phrase, translated word-for-word, is something like, "For you do not look into the face/appearance of men/people" (*ou gar blepeis eis prosōpon anthrōpōn*). This is an idiom. Consider the following versions:

KJV	for thou regardest not the person of men
NKJV	for You do not regard the person of men
ESV	for you are not swayed by appearances (footnote: Greek *for you do not look at people's faces*)

1. *Merriam-Webster*, s.v. "idiom," accessed March 4, 2023, www.merriam-webster.com/dictionary/idiom.

NASB for You *are not partial to anyone (footnote: Lit. *do not look at the face of people*)
NRSV for you do not regard people with partiality
CEB because you don't show favoritism

None of these versions is strictly speaking word-for-word. The KJV and the NKJV are perhaps closest in form to the Greek, but they are also the most obscure. The NASB and the ESV translate idiomatically, then provide footnotes that claim to provide either a "literal" meaning (NASB) or the "Greek" behind the English (ESV). In fact, neither of these descriptions is accurate. The ESV footnote claims to be providing the "Greek" but in fact gives only English words! Of course, what the translators mean is that this is a *word-for-word translation of the Greek*. But then they should say "word-for-word" rather than "Greek." The NASB footnote reads, "Lit. *do not look at the face of people*," but this, too, is problematic, since the NASB is simply giving one of many possible meanings for each Greek word, none of which is its "literal" meaning. As we have seen in Question 10, words don't have a single "literal" meaning; they have a semantic range. Here is the Greek sentence with some of the various possible senses below each word.

ou	*gar*	*blepeis*	*eis*	*prosōpon*	*anthrōpōn*
not	for	you see	into, to	face	of/from people
no	since	you observe	toward	appearance	of/from men
	because	you regard	for, on behalf	in front of	of/from humanity
	indeed	you beware	resulting in	in the presence of	
	but	you watch out	for purpose of	on the surface of	
		you pay attention			

Which one of these is the "literal" meaning? The answer is there can be no truly "literal" (single/core) translation since every word has multiple possible senses. Even if we had only one sense for each word, it would still be impossible to understand the idiom by translating its individual words. This is because idioms work as a whole, rather than through their individual parts.

To translate an idiom, then, the idiom must first be interpreted in the source language to determine its meaning (all translation requires interpretation). This meaning must then be transferred into the receptor language by either (1) restating the meaning concretely, or (2) using an idiom in the receptor language. A concrete statement would be something like the NRSV ("for you do not regard people with partiality") or the CEB ("because you don't show favoritism"). An equivalent idiom in English might be "You are not a respecter of persons," an English idiom that means "a person whose attitude and behaviour is uninfluenced by consideration of another's rank, power, wealth, etc."[2]

Consider these idioms, with a more formal equivalent version in the center column and a more functional or idiomatic one on the right. Underlining indicates the words representing the Hebrew or Greek idiom. As you read through the idiomatic translations, try to determine whether the translation on the right is using an English idiom or a concrete statement.

Reference	Formal Translation of Idiom	Idiomatic Translation into English
Exod. 13:2	whatever opens the womb among the children of Israel (NKJV)	the first offspring of every womb among the Israelites (NET)
Deut. 15:7	you shall not . . . shut your hand against your poor brother (RSV)	do not be . . . tightfisted toward your poor brother (CSB)
Josh. 2:11	as soon as we heard it, our hearts melted, and there was no spirit left in any man because of you (ESV)	When we heard this, we lost heart, and everyone's courage failed because of you (CSB)
Josh. 10:6	Do not relax your hand from your servants (RSV)	Do not abandon your servants (NIV)
Judg. 9:33	do to them as your hand finds to do (ESV)	seize the opportunity to attack them (NIV)
Judg. 11:3	worthless fellows collected around Jephthah and went out with him (ESV)	some worthless men joined Jephthah and went on raids with him (CSB)
2 Sam. 18:25	If he is alone, there are tidings in his mouth (NRSV)	If he is alone, he must have good news (NIV)
1 Kings 2:10	Then David slept with his fathers and was buried in the city of David (NRSV)	Then David died and was buried with his ancestors in the City of David (NLT)

2. Dictionary.com, s.v. "respecter," accessed January 31, 2023, https://www.dictionary.com/browse/respecter#:~:text=%2F%20(r%C9%AA%CB%88sp%C9%9Bkt%C9%99)%20%2F,rank%2C%20power%2C%20wealth%2C%20etc.

Reference	Formal Translation of Idiom	Idiomatic Translation into English
Esth. 1:14	the seven princes of Persia and Media who saw the king's face (RSV)	the seven officials of Persia and Media, who had access to the king (NRSV)
Ps. 12:2	they speak with flattering lips and a double heart (NASB)	they flatter with their lips but harbor deception in their hearts (NIV)
Ps. 75:5	Do not lift up your horn on high; Do not speak with a stiff neck (NKJV)	Do not flaunt your strength so proudly, do not talk with that arrogant stance (NJB)
Isa. 52:8	for eye to eye they see the return of the LORD to Zion (RSV)	for they see with their very own eyes the LORD's return to Zion (NET)
Isa. 58:13	If you turn away your foot from the Sabbath (NKJV)	If you stop trampling the Sabbath (CEB)
Ezek. 5:11	My eye will not spare, nor will I have any pity (NKJV)	I will not look on you with pity or spare you (NIV)
Jonah 1:2	cry out against it [Nineveh]; for their wickedness has come up before me (NRSV)	cry out against it, for their evil has come to my attention (CEB)
Matt. 23:32	Fill up, then, the measure of your fathers (ESV)	Go ahead and finish what your ancestors started (NLT)
Acts 8:23	For I see that you are in the gall of bitterness and in the bond of iniquity (ESV)	For I see that you are bitterly envious and in bondage to sin (NET)
Acts 9:28	So he went in and out among them in Jerusalem (NRSV)	Saul moved freely among the disciples in Jerusalem (CEB)

The Problem of "Half-Idioms"

There is a tendency among biblical scholars—those who live in the world of Hebrew and Greek—to think they are getting it right if they can preserve a part of the idiom whenever possible. The result can be "half-idioms" (half-English and half-Hebrew/Greek), transferring a few words of the original, but missing its meaning in English.

We have seen examples of this before. The Hebrew idiom "with a heart and a heart" (*belev walev*) means to think or speak *with deceptive motives* (Ps. 12:2; see Question 2). When formal equivalent versions translate this as speaking "with a double heart" (NASB; NKJV; NRSV; ESV), they are trying to preserve a part of the idiom (two hearts). But idioms work *as a whole* rather than through their individual parts. More often than not, preserving bits of the idiom results in a translation that is awkward or obscure in English.

Consider Luke 2:36 ESV, which reads that "Anna . . . was advanced in years." The Greek idiom is word-for-word something like "advanced in many days" (*probebēkuia en hēmerais pollais*). The ESV seeks to preserve the words "advanced" and "days" by translating with the half-idiom "advanced in years." But this is not normal English. I would never say someone is "advanced in years." I would say they are "very old" (NIV; NLT; NET; CEB) or perhaps "along in years" (CSB). The attempt to preserve some of the words of the original idiom results in awkward English.

The "Son of X" Idiom

While the English phrase "son" normally denotes a male child, the Hebrew word for "son(s)" (*ben*; plural *banim*) and its Greek counterpart (*huios*; plural *huioi*) have much wider semantic ranges, including children and more distant relationships. So "son of ____" can mean a child, grandchild, or descendant of someone. Of special note is the plural expression "sons/children of Israel" (*bene-yisraʾel*), which occurs more than six hundred times in the Hebrew Bible. Its Greek counterpart (*huioi Israēl*) occurs fourteen times in the NT. While these expressions can refer to the twelve physical "sons" of Jacob (who was renamed Israel in Genesis 32:28), more often they refer to all the descendants of Jacob, that is, to the nation Israel (compare Exod. 1:1 and 1:9). The KJV consistently translates the latter as "children of Israel." Formal equivalent versions are divided in how they translate it: "sons of Israel" (NASB), "children of Israel" (KJV; NKJV), or "people of Israel" (RSV; NRSV; ESV). Most mediating and functional equivalent versions use "Israelites" (NIV; NET; CEB; CSB; NAB; CEV; TEV) or "people of Israel" (see CEV; TEV; NLT). (For more on the inclusive nature of these terms, see Question 19).

"Son(s) of God" also has a wide range of meanings and can refer to angelic beings (Job 1:6; Ps. 29:1; perhaps in Gen. 6:2); the nation Israel (Exod. 4:22; Hosea 11:1); the king from David's line (2 Sam. 7:14); Adam, the first man (Luke 3:38); the Messiah (Luke 1:35); Jesus's followers (Luke 6:35); or Christian believers (Rom. 8:19).

"Son of man" (Hebrew *ben-ʾadam*) is an idiom referring to humanity. Though it can refer to males, most commonly it is used generically for human beings. Possible translations include "son of man," "child of Adam," "person," "human being," "humanity," "mankind," and "humankind." God addresses the prophet Ezekiel as "son of man" approximately ninety times in the book of Ezekiel. The address seems to point to Ezekiel as a lowly mortal in contrast to the sovereign God. In the Gospels, Jesus's most common term of self-reference is also "son of man." The Greek phrase (*huios tou anthrōpos*) is a literal translation of the Hebrew *ben-ʾadam*, or the Aramaic *bar ʾenash*. Jesus appears to have adopted this title especially from Daniel 7:13–14, where "one like a son of man" (= in human form) comes before the Ancient of Days (God himself) and is given authority, glory, and sovereign power.

In addition to these special uses, the expression "son of x" is used in a wide range of idioms in Hebrew and Greek. Here is a sampling:

Reference	Formal Rendering	Probable Meaning
Num. 17:10	sons of rebellion	rebellious people
Deut. 25:2	son of beating	one who deserves a beating
1 Sam. 14:52	son of valor	a brave warrior
1 Sam. 20:31	son of death	one worthy of death
1 Sam. 25:17	son of wickedness	a wicked person
1 Kings 20:35	sons of the prophets	members of a group of prophets
2 Kings 6:32	son of murder	a murderer
2 Kings 14:14	sons of pledges	hostages
2 Chron. 25:13	sons of the troop	soldiers
Ezra 2:42	sons of gatekeepers	gatekeepers
Ezra 2:61	sons of priests	priests
Ezra 4:1; 6:19	sons of the exile	those who have returned from exile
Neh. 3:8	sons of perfumers	members of the perfumers' trade
Neh. 12:28	sons of singers	singers
Job 30:8	sons of foolishness	foolish people
Job 30:8	sons of no-name	disreputable people
Ps. 89:22	sons of wickedness	wicked people
Prov. 31:5	sons of affliction	those who are oppressed
Prov. 31:8	sons of passing away	those destitute or dying
Isa. 19:11	a son of the wise	a wise person
Zech. 4:14	sons of oil	anointed leaders
Matt. 8:12	sons of the kingdom	subjects of the kingdom
Matt. 12:27	sons of the Pharisees	disciples of the Pharisees
Mark 2:19	sons of the wedding hall	wedding guests or groomsmen
Luke 10:6	sons of peace	those who promote peace

Reference	Formal Rendering	Probable Meaning
Luke 20:34	sons of this age	people of the present age/world
John 17:12; 2 Thess. 2:3	son of destruction	person doomed to destruction
Acts 3:25	sons of the prophets	heirs of the prophets
Eph. 2:2	sons of disobedience	disobedient people
Eph. 2:3	children of wrath	people subject to God's wrath
Eph. 5:8	children of light	people who live in God's light

These many and diverse references confirm the idiomatic (nonliteral) sense of "son" (*huios/ben*) in Hebrew and Greek expressions. Translators need to consider carefully from the context how best to render the idiom in the receptor language.

When Idioms Cross Languages

As we have seen, languages change over time. One of the key catalysts for change in English has been the profound influence of the King James Version (see Question 26). As a result, many Hebrew and Greek idioms and expressions have become familiar to English readers and may now be viewed as common or standard English. Consider the following examples:[3]

> "put words in his mouth" (Exod. 4:15; cf. 2 Sam. 14:3)
> "a scapegoat" (Lev. 16:9–10)
> "fall flat on his face" (Num. 22:31)
> "escaped with the skin of my teeth" (Job 19:20)
> "the land of the living" (Job 28:13)
> "pour out your heart" (Ps. 62:8)
> "lick the dust" (Ps. 72:9)
> "at their wits' end" (Ps. 107:27)
> "pride goes before . . . a fall" (Prov. 16:18)
> "nothing new under the sun" (Eccl. 1:9)
> "a fly in the ointment" (Eccl. 10:1)
> "a drop in a bucket" (Isa. 40:15)
> "see eye to eye" (Isa. 52:8)

3. Some of these were taken from Alister McGrath, *In the Beginning: The Story of the King James Bible and How It Changed a Nation, a Language, and a Culture* (New York: Anchor, 2001), 263–64; others were found at "Biblical Idioms and Sayings with Origins Explained," Improving Your English, September 21, 2021, https://improving-your-english.com/vocabulary/idioms/bible-idioms.

"no rest for the wicked" (Isa. 57:20–21)
"like a lamb . . . to the slaughter" (Jer. 11:19)
"can the . . . leopard change its spots?" (Jer. 13:23)
"the salt of the earth" (Matt. 5:13)
"an eye for an eye" (Matt. 5:38)
"go the extra mile" (Matt. 5:41)
"the blind leading the blind" (Matt. 15:14)
"give up the ghost" (Mark 15:37)
"gird up your loins" (1 Peter 1:13)
"the powers that be" (Rom. 13:1)
"a thorn in the flesh" (2 Cor. 12:7)

One of the challenges translators have is determining whether idioms like these have become sufficiently familiar to English speakers that they can be used as they are, or whether they need to be reworded in more natural English. For more on this issue, see the section on "dead metaphors" in Question 13.

Summary

Idioms are a particular challenge for translators since the definition of an idiom is a group of words whose meaning differs from the meaning of its parts. Idioms don't "mean" what they "say." To reproduce an idiom, translators must first determine its meaning in the source language and then find a parallel word, phrase, clause, or idiom in the receptor language that means the same thing.

REFLECTION QUESTIONS

1. What is an idiom?

2. Why is it inappropriate to translate idioms "literally"?

3. Why, based on the nature of word meanings (see Question 10), is there no such thing as a truly "literal" translation?

4. We sometimes say, "All language is idiomatic." What do you think this means?

5. Read an article from a web page, journal, or magazine carefully and look for idioms. How would you identify them?

QUESTION 13

What Are the Challenges of Translating Poetry and Metaphorical Language?

Translating Poetry

More than a third of the Hebrew Scriptures come to us in poetic form. Poetry occurs not only in the books of Poetry and Wisdom (Job, Psalms, Proverbs, Ecclesiastes, Song of Songs), but also in the Prophets (Isaiah–Malachi), where many prophetic oracles are set in poetic verse. Poetry also appears in scattered poems and songs throughout the Bible's narrative literature (e.g., Genesis 49; Exodus 15; Deuteronomy 32; Judges 5; 1 Samuel 2; 2 Samuel 22, 23; etc.).

What Is Poetry?

Merriam-Webster defines poetry as "writing that formulates a concentrated imaginative awareness of experience in language chosen and arranged to create a specific emotional response through meaning, sound, and rhythm."[1] The communicative power and emotional response produced through "meaning, sound, and rhythm" can be illustrated in the opening stanza of Edgar Allen Poe's famous poem "The Raven":

> Once upon a midnight dreary, while I pondered, weak and weary,
> Over many a quaint and curious volume of forgotten lore,
> While I nodded, nearly napping, suddenly there came a tapping,
> As of some one gently rapping, rapping at my chamber door.

1. *Merriam-Webster*, s.v. "poetry," accessed January 31, 2023, https://www.merriam-webster.com/dictionary/poetry.

> "'Tis some visitor," I muttered, "tapping at my chamber door—
> Only this, and nothing more."

The basic events described in the poem may be presented in prose as: "One night while falling asleep reading an old and obscure book, I heard someone knocking on the door and assumed it was a visitor." While this may correctly represent the "meaning" of the poem, it hardly serves as an adequate translation, since it does nothing to achieve the emotional affect produced by the words, rhythm, and sound of the original. Much of the poem's literary force is conveyed through *rhyme* and *alliteration*. "Dreary" rhymes with "weary"; "napping" with "tapping" and "rapping"; "lore" with "door" and "more." There is also much alliteration: weak and weary, quaint and curious, nearly napping. Concerning meaning, the introductory, "Once upon a . . . " evokes the beginning of a fairytale and so sets a mood of fantasy. There is also a pessimistic tone set by words like dreary, weak, and weary, and by the speaker's need for self-assurance: "only this, and nothing more."

Challenges in Translating Poetry

Poetry can be among the most difficult of genres to translate. This is primarily because (1) poetry functions at the emotive level as well as at the analytic level, and (2) poetry depends a great deal on its *form* to produce these emotive effects. This creates a challenge for translators, because of the formal differences between the source and receptor languages. What rhymes in one language does not usually rhyme in another. What is alliterated in one language may be nearly impossible to alliterate in another. Generally, Bible translators do not try to replicate these kinds of formal features but rather translate the basic meaning of words and phrases while seeking to retain some sense of the rhythm and meter of poetry.

I am aware of only one Bible translation that has tried to reproduce the poetic quality of Scripture by using rhyming verse. This is the New Testament of the International Standard Version (ISV). The "Christ Hymn" of Philippians 2:6–11 ISV is reproduced below.[2] For the purpose of comparison, I have placed the NRSV beside it. The NRSV, like some other versions (cf. NIV; CSB; CEB; NET), puts the hymn in metered verse, but does not try to rhyme the words.

2. On the nature, structure, and history of this "hymn," see R. P. Martin, *Carmen Christi: Philippians ii:5–11 in Recent Interpretation and in the Setting of Early Christian Worship*, 2nd ed. (Grand Rapids: Eerdmans, 1983). On its character as poetry, see Moisés Silva, *Philippians*, Baker Exegetical Commentary on the New Testament, 2nd ed. (Grand Rapids: Baker Academic, 2005), 92–116; Gordon D. Fee, "Philippians 2:5–11: Hymn or Exalted Pauline Prose?," *Bulletin for Biblical Research* 2 (1992): 29–46.

ISV	NRSV
5 Have the same attitude among yourselves that was also in Christ Jesus: 6 In God's own form existed he, and shared with God equality, deemed nothing needed grasping. 7 Instead, poured out in emptiness, a servant's form did he possess, a mortal man becoming. In human form he chose to be, 8 and lived in all humility, death on a cross obeying.	5 Let the same mind be in you that was in Christ Jesus, 6 who, though he was in the form of God, did not regard equality with God as something to be exploited, 7 but emptied himself, taking the form of a slave, being born in human likeness. And being found in human form, 8 he humbled himself and became obedient to the point of death— even death on a cross.
9 Now lifted up by God to heaven, a name above all others given, this matchless name possessing. 10 And so, when Jesus' name is called, the knees of everyone should fall, wherever they're residing.	9 Therefore God also highly exalted him and gave him the name that is above every name, 10 so that at the name of Jesus every knee should bend, in heaven and on earth and under the earth,
11 Then every tongue in one accord, will say that Jesus the Messiah is Lord, while God the Father praising.[3]	11 and every tongue should confess that Jesus Christ is Lord, to the glory of God the Father.

It should first be noted that the Greek text does not rhyme. The ISV translators are not trying to replicate the Greek style of poetry (non-rhyming), but rather to introduce an English style of poetry (rhyming) as a way to "translate" not only the words but also the genre.[4] The reader will have to judge the success or failure of this attempt. Especially in poetry, beauty is in the eye of the beholder.

---

3. From the International Standard Version on Biblegateway.org.
4. The ISV preface says, "The ISV treats subtle nuances of the original texts with special care. For example, several passages of the Bible appear to have been rendered in poetic form when first penned by their authors. The ISV has meticulously crafted these original passages as true poems—thus communicating a sense of their original literary form as well as translating the original intent of the author" (*The Holy Bible: International Standard Version* (Yorba Linda, CA: Davidson Press, 2011). Poetic passages noted in the ISV preface are Luke 7:32, 35; 1 Cor. 13:4–7; Phil. 2:6–11; 1 Tim. 1:15; 3:1, 16; 4:8; 2 Tim. 2:11; Titus 1:12; 3:4–7. It is, of course, dubious to suggest that "true poems" (even in English!) should rhyme.

Parallelism in Hebrew Poetry

Fortunately for Bible translators, Hebrew (and Greek) poetry almost never rhymes. Instead, the primary poetic structure of Hebrew poetry is parallelism, where two or more lines express parallel thoughts. There are three main kinds of Hebrew parallelism: (1) synonymous parallelism, where two lines say something similar; (2) antithetical parallelism, where two lines represent a contrast; and (3) synthetic parallelism, where the thought of the second line develops the thought of the first. Since these kinds of parallelism concern conceptual content rather than verbal form, they can be reproduced quite well in translation. Consider these examples of the three main kinds of parallelism from Isaiah 40 (CSB):

Synonymous Parallelism	Look, the nations are like a drop in a bucket; they are considered as a speck of dust on the scales (v. 15)
Antithetical Parallelism	God is enthroned above the circle of the earth; its inhabitants are like grasshoppers (v. 22)
Synthetic Parallelism	He brings out the stars by number; he calls all of them by name (v. 26)

Bible translators often seek to reproduce Hebrew poetry by placing the text in poetic stanzas and then trying to retain the poetic cadence, rhythm, and meter of the original. Compare the first four verses of Psalm 24 in the NIV, which like many modern versions uses poetic verse, with the KJV, which does not.

Psalm 24 NIV		Psalm 24 KJV
1The earth is the LORD's, and everything in it, the world, and all who live in it; 2for he founded it on the seas and established it on the waters. 3Who may ascend the mountain of the LORD? Who may stand in his holy place? 4The one who has clean hands and a pure heart, who does not trust in an idol or swear by a false god.	A B A B A B A B B	1 The earth is the LORD's, and the fulness thereof; the world, and they that dwell therein. 2 For he hath founded it upon the seas, and established it upon the floods. 3 Who shall ascend into the hill of the LORD? or who shall stand in his holy place? 4 He that hath clean hands, and a pure heart; who hath not lifted up his soul unto vanity, nor sworn deceitfully.

We have added scansion marks to show the rhythmic pattern of the psalm in the NIV (ABAB ABABB). The NIV uses these scansions to mark the rhythm and poetic parallelism (B repeats the thought of A). The NIV also divides the psalm into stanzas based on the changes in subject matter.

Various additional challenges face translators of biblical poetry. One is identifying what is and is not poetry. For example, the book of Haggai is widely acknowledged as containing exalted prose, but scholars debate whether some passages should be considered true poetry and formatted as such.[5]

Another unique challenge for Bible translators is acrostic or alphabetical psalms (e.g., Psalms 25, 34, 37, 119, 145). These Hebrew psalms have lines or stanzas starting with consecutive letters of the Hebrew alphabet. So, for example, Psalm 119 is made up of twenty-two stanzas, with each stanza representing one of the twenty-two letters of the Hebrew alphabet. Every line of the first stanza begins with a word starting with the Hebrew *aleph* (א); every line of the second stanza begins with a word starting with *beth* (ב), and so on, continuing through the Hebrew alphabet. Trying to replicate the form of this psalm in English is a major challenge, not only because of the difficulties in composing meaningful sentences with all the English letters (Q and X?!), but also because one would need to expand the psalm to twenty-six stanzas for the English alphabet.[6]

Translating Metaphors and Similes

Poetry often uses metaphorical language. Metaphors and similes are comparisons or analogies. For example, Jesus was using simile when he said, "The kingdom of heaven is like a mustard seed" (Matt. 13:31) or "The kingdom of heaven is like yeast" (Matt. 13:33). While a simile makes the comparison explicit by using "like" or "as," a metaphor directly equates the two. Jesus was using metaphor when he said, "You <u>are</u> the salt of the earth," "You <u>are</u> the light of the world" (Matt. 5:13–14), "I <u>am</u> the bread of life" (John 6:35–48), and "I <u>am</u> the vine" (John 15:1, 5). This, of course, does not mean that his followers were literally salt and light. Like similes, metaphors compare one thing to another to identify certain shared attributes. Just as bread provides physical nourishment and life, so Jesus brings spiritual nourishment and life.

Translating metaphors and similes can be a challenge, especially in cultural contexts where the thing being compared is unknown or where the metaphoric image carries a different sense. Isaiah's statement "Though your sins are like scarlet, they shall be as white as snow" (Isa. 1:18) would be inexplicable in a tropical context where readers have never seen or heard of snow. It would also be problematic in a context where whiteness (of snow and wool) is

---

5. Eugene Merrill notes that "according to some scholars the book consists largely of poetic material. . . . Though Hebrew prose and poetry are not always easy to distinguish from each other" ("Haggai," in *The Expositor's Bible Commentary: Daniel–Malachi*, rev. ed., ed. T. Longman III and D. E. Garland [Grand Rapids: Zondervan, 2008], 8:703).
6. For an innovative solution, see the Knox translation in Question 29.

not associated with spiritual purity. There are various approaches a translator can take: (1) retain the metaphor, but introduce explanatory phrases to make the comparison clear: "Though your sins are like scarlet, the color of blood-stained hands, they shall be washed clean like pure-white snow"; (2) replace the metaphor with one that works in the receptor culture: "Though your sins are like scarlet, they shall be made white as a gardenia flower"; or (3) replace the metaphor/simile with a concrete statement: "Though you are guilty of sin, you will be forgiven and made pure." In cases like this, footnotes may be appropriate to alert readers to the original metaphor and its meaning.

Some biblical metaphors are not so easily replaced. Jesus's statement "I am the good shepherd" who "lays down his life for the sheep" (John 10:11) may be difficult to translate in a cultural context where sheep and shepherds are unknown. Yet images related to sheep and shepherds are so pervasive and important in Scripture (see Psalm 23; Isa. 53:6; Luke 15:4; John 10, etc.) that it would do more harm than good to try to replace them with analogous images. It would be better to educate readers on the nature of sheep and shepherds than to lose such an important metaphor. For more on this example and other challenges cross-cultural translators face see Question 39.

Most English Bible versions—whether formal, functional, or mediating—retain most metaphors in Scripture. There are occasional exceptions, as when translators of versions designed for children or remedial readers decide a metaphor might be misunderstood. For example, the GNT renders "The Lord is my rock" as "The Lord is my protector" (2 Sam. 22:2).

Live versus Dead Metaphors

While we would suggest that most metaphors in Scripture should be retained, there is one important qualification. This is in the case of "dead" metaphors. A live metaphor is one where the metaphorical image is retained, and the comparison is envisioned by the reader. When Jesus said, "I am the vine; you are the branches" (John 15:5), his hearers would have envisioned an actual vine with its branches. But when I say in exasperation, "That's the last straw!" no English speaker would envision an actual piece of straw. In this case the idiom has become so well-known and familiar that the word picture is lost. The metaphor is "dead." Here are a few other examples of dead metaphors in English:

> That's just sour grapes!
> He's a couch potato.
> That's a far cry from what I said.
> We're in a pickle.
> It's raining cats and dogs.

> That's the cat's pajamas.
> That'll cost you an arm and a leg.

To translate a dead metaphor as live is to mistranslate it. For example, I would never translate "That's the last straw" as "That's the only remaining piece of hay." Nor would I translate "He's a couch potato" as "He's a spud lying on the sofa," or "We're in a pickle" as "We're in a cucumber preserved in brine." The metaphorical images of straws, potatoes, and pickles have been forgotten in these idioms, so to translate them literally is to mistranslate them. They are "dead" metaphors.

The challenge for biblical translators is distinguishing between live and dead metaphors.[7] One of the most difficult examples is the Greek verb commonly translated "walk" or "live" (*peripateō*). While this verb can mean literally to "walk" (Matt. 4:18), it is often used in the metaphorical sense of "behave" or "live." Does Colossians 4:5 mean (literally) to "walk in wisdom toward outsiders" (ESV) or does it mean to "conduct yourselves with wisdom toward outsiders" (NASB)? Does Romans 6:4 mean "we also should walk in newness of life" (NKJV) or "we too may live a new life" (NIV)? Does Paul in Ephesians 4:1 urge believers to "walk worthy of the calling you have received" (CSB) or "to lead a life worthy of the calling to which you have been called" (NRSV)? In each of these cases, the translator must decide whether the speaker first envisioned the literal act of walking and then by analogy applied this to a person's behavior, or whether their mind went immediately to lifestyle or behavior.

Summary

Poetry can be among the most challenging of genres to translate because it functions more at the level of aesthetics and emotion than prose, and because much of its affect is accomplished through formal features like rhythm and sound, which are difficult to reproduce across languages. Some of this is mitigated since Hebrew poetry does not usually rhyme, but rather is marked by parallelism of content. Metaphors and similes can also be a challenge to translate, especially in cross-cultural contexts where the thing compared is unknown to the receptor audience. Translators must especially be alert for dead metaphors, in which the metaphoric "picture" has been lost. To translate a dead metaphor as live would be to mistranslate it.

---

7. See John Beekman and John Callow, *Translating the Word of God* (Grand Rapids: Zondervan, 1974), 131–36.

REFLECTION QUESTIONS

1. What are some challenges in translating poetry?
2. What is the primary feature of Hebrew poetry?
3. What is an acrostic psalm and why is it difficult to translate?
4. What is a metaphor? A simile?
5. What is a "dead" metaphor? Can you give some examples in English?

QUESTION 14

What Are the Challenges of Translating Other Figures of Speech?

Rhetorical Questions

Rhetorical questions are a kind of nonliteral speech since they are not real questions. A real question is a request for information. "What time is it?" is a true question, since I expect an answer. "What would you like for lunch?" is also a real question, since I am soliciting a response. On the other hand, if I said to someone who did something reckless, "What were you thinking?" I would not be asking for information. I would be criticizing. My question is rhetorical—meant to make a point or achieve a response. It means, "You obviously were not thinking about the consequences of your actions." Here are a few rhetorical questions in English, together with their meaning and their purpose or function:

Rhetorical Question	Meaning	Function
Are you out of your mind?	What you are saying/ doing is crazy.	Rebuke or criticism
Isn't that sunset gorgeous?	That sunset is gorgeous.	Statement
Would you mind closing the door?	Please close the door.	Request
Do you think I'm a fool?	Your words/actions are demeaning.	Indignation
Won't you stay for coffee?	Please stay for coffee.	Invitation

The Bible uses many rhetorical questions with a wide range of functions. In Genesis 30:15 Jacob's wife Leah says to her sister Rachel, "Wasn't it enough that you took away my husband? Will you take my son's mandrakes too?"

These are not real questions but expressions of indignation and rebuke. Here are a few other biblical examples:

Reference	Rhetorical Question	Meaning	Function
Gen. 38:17	"Will you give me . . . a pledge?"	Please give me a pledge.	Request
1 Sam. 16:1	"How long will you mourn for Saul?"	Stop mourning for Saul.	Rebuke
Mark 3:23	"How can Satan drive out Satan?	Satan would not drive out Satan.	Assertion
Mark 5:35	"Why bother the teacher anymore?"	Stop bothering the teacher.	Command
Luke 12:51	Do you think I came to bring peace on earth?	I did not come to bring peace on earth.	Statement
Gal. 3:3	Are you so foolish?	You are being foolish!	Exclamation

Rhetorical questions can be a challenge for international Bible translators, since some languages rarely use them or use them very differently from the biblical authors. John Beekman and John Callow give several examples where rhetorical questions have been misunderstood by receptor audiences. Readers from the Cora tribe in Mexico took Jesus's statement "What shall we say the kingdom of God is like?" as a request by Jesus for more information about the kingdom, instead of as an introduction to his teaching about the kingdom. To the Guarani of Brazil, Jesus's rhetorical question and rebuke "Don't you understand?" (Mark 4:13) was thought to mean "I don't understand these parables; can you help me?"[1]

Since rhetorical questions in English function much the same as they do in Hebrew and Greek, most English versions retain the question format. This is especially true of formal equivalent and mediating versions. Functional equivalent versions occasionally replace them with statements to avoid confusion. For example, at Jesus's trial in John 18:35, Pilate demands from Jesus whether he is the king of the Jews. When Jesus asks whether this question is coming from Pilate or others (the religious leaders), Pilate answers with the rhetorical question, "Am I a Jew?" (NIV and most versions). The CEV provides a functional equivalent rendering: "I am not a Jew!" Several mediating versions (CEB; NET; NAB) retain the rhetorical question but add clarification: "I am not a Jew, am I?" For the rhetorical question "Can the blind lead

1. John Beekman and John Callow, *Translating the Word of God* (Grand Rapids: Zondervan, 1974), 245, 247.

the blind?" the GNT has "One blind man cannot lead another one." In John 7:19, instead of "Didn't Moses give you the law?" (CEB), the NLT has "Moses gave you the law."

Irony and Sarcasm

Irony means expressing meaning by using language that normally signifies the opposite. Irony can be either *situational* or *verbal*. Situational irony is when the events in a story are themselves ironic. In John 4:12 the Samaritan woman asks Jesus rhetorically, "Are you greater than our father Jacob?" What she means is "You are not greater than Jacob," but the reader knows that Jesus is greater! Her question is unintentionally ironic in the context of the story. At the cross the religious leaders mock Jesus by saying, "He saved others . . . but he can't save himself! Let this Messiah, this king of Israel, come down now from the cross, that we may see and believe" (Mark 15:31–32). The informed reader knows that, ironically, it is by *staying* on the cross that Jesus is going to save others.

Verbal irony is when a speaker or author intentionally uses irony. Jesus is speaking ironically when he commends the religious leaders for how well they have learned to set aside God's commands for their own traditions. The New Jerusalem Bible captures this well: "How ingeniously you get round the commandment of God in order to preserve your own tradition!" (Mark 7:9). In 1 Corinthians 1:18–25 Paul points out that the apparently foolish message of the cross is (ironically) the power of God to save us. The message he preaches, "Christ crucified" (1 Cor. 1:23), is itself ironic, since no one would expect the anointed king to suffer such a humiliating defeat and death.

Sarcasm is almost always ironic, but it is also intended to mock, ridicule, or deride someone for their words or actions. David's wife Michal, the daughter of Saul, speaks sarcastically when she criticizes David for dancing with unbridled joy when he was bringing the ark into Jerusalem: "How the king of Israel has distinguished himself today, going around half-naked in full view of the slave girls of his servants" (2 Sam. 6:20). Paul also uses ironic sarcasm when he responds to the pride and arrogance of the church at Corinth. How wonderful it is, he says, that they are already reigning as kings, while Paul and the other apostles continue to suffer pain, hardship, and persecution (1 Cor. 4:8).

As with other nonliteral language, irony and sarcasm can at times be tricky to translate. If readers miss the ironic or sarcastic intention, they might accept the statement as true. But in fact, Jesus was *not* commending the religious leaders for setting aside God's commands, and the Corinthian dissenters were not already reigning with Christ. In most cases the context makes this clear, and English versions can expect readers to figure it out. Occasionally, however, functional equivalent versions will add clarifying phrases to bring out the irony or sarcasm. For example, in 2 Samuel 6:20, while the Hebrew simply says that Michal "said" these words to David, the NLT notes that she "said in disgust." Similarly, following Jesus's trial, while the Greek of Mark 15:18 says simply that the soldiers "began to salute him, 'Hail, king of the Jews!'" the NLT says, "they saluted him and taunted 'Hail, king of the Jews!'"

Litotes

This relatively uncommon figure of speech may be defined as *an emphatic statement made by saying that the opposite is* not *true*. For example, Luke's assertion that Paul and Barnabas "remained no little time with the disciples" in Antioch (Acts 14:28 ESV) means "they spent a long time with the disciples" (NASB; cf. NRSV; NKJV). When Paul preaches so long at Troas that a young man named Eutychus falls asleep and falls to his death from a three-story window, Paul rushes down, embraces the man, and raises him up. In response, "they took the youth away alive, and were not a little comforted" (Acts 20:12 ESV); "not a little" here means they were "greatly comforted" (Acts 20:12 NASB). Similarly, while defending himself before a crowd in Jerusalem, Paul says he is a Jew "from Tarsus in Cilicia, a citizen of no obscure city" (Acts 21:39 ESV), meaning "an important city" (Acts 21:39 NRSV).

Notice several things. First, Luke is fond of this literary device and most NT examples of litotes appear in the book of Acts. Second, while formal equivalent versions like the NASB, NKJV, and NRSV tend to retain Hebrew and Greek figures of speech, in the case of litotes, these versions frequently turn the negative statement into a positive one. This is because these expressions are easily misunderstood in English. A citizen of "no obscure city" sounds like Paul is a man without a city, rather than that his home city is a large and important one. "Not a little comforted" could easily be taken to mean "not comforted *even* a little" rather than greatly comforted. This is a case where these versions often choose clarity over formal equivalence. Only the RSV and ESV consistently retain the litotes.[2]

Metonymy and Synecdoche

Metonymy and synecdoche are parts of speech where one thing stands for another. Synecdoche is the more specific term and refers to a part standing for the whole, or the whole for a part. In English if I say, "He owns a nice set of wheels," wheels (a part) stands for a car (the whole). Similarly, "nice threads!" means nice clothes. "We need boots on the ground" means we need soldiers, with boots (part) standing for the whole (soldiers). An example of the whole for a part would be "San Diego beat L.A.," where the whole city stands for its sports team.

---

2. The NASB, while often eliminating the litotes, always provides a footnote indicating the "literal" reading.

Metonymy is a broader term, where one thing represents another in some more general way. In the proverb "The pen is mightier than the sword," the pen stands for words expressing powerful ideas, while the "sword" stands for physical or military might. The proverb means that ultimately ideas win over authoritarian force. In the sentence "The White House issued a press release," the White House stands for the executive branch of government. It is not always easy (or important) to distinguish synecdoche and metonymy. "White House" could be viewed as the whole for the part (since the president lives there) or simply as representing the executive branch. The important thing to identify is *what* the term stands for rather than precisely how it relates to it.

There are many examples of metonymy and synecdoche in the Bible. Consider a few here:

Reference	Metonymy or Synecdoche	Meaning
Gen. 42:22	Now we must give an accounting for his blood.	death
2 Sam. 7:13	He . . . will build a house for my Name.	me
2 Sam. 7:13	I will establish the throne of his kingdom forever.	royal reign
Job 2:10	Job did not sin with his lips.	the things he said
Ps. 8:6	You put everything under their feet.	authority
Hos. 11:12	Ephraim has surrounded me with lies.	Israel (Northern Kingdom)
Matt. 6:11	Give us this day our daily bread.	food for sustenance
Matt. 23:37	Jerusalem, you who kill the prophets	the people of Jerusalem
Luke 16:29	They have Moses and the Prophets	the Torah

As with most figures of speech, metonymy and synecdoche are handled somewhat differently by different kinds of translations. Formal equivalent versions tend to retain the figure of speech and let readers figure out its meaning. Mediating versions will often retain the image but might add clarifying phrases. Functional equivalent versions often go further and replace the metonymy with the thing to which it points. Consider these examples of the different approaches. In each case, I have presented at least one example from a formal, mediating, and functional equivalent version.

Genesis 42:22

ESV	So now there comes a reckoning for his blood.
NET	So now we must pay for shedding his blood!
GNT	And now we are being paid back for his death.

While the formal equivalent ESV refers simply to reckoning for "his blood," the mediating NET explains this as payback for "shedding his blood" and the functional GNT asserts more specifically that this is payback for "his death."

2 Samuel 7:13

NASB	I will establish the throne of his kingdom forever (also NIV)
NET	I will make his dynasty permanent
CEV	no one will be able to take his kingdom away from him

The metonymy "throne" (for ruling authority) is retained by formal equivalent (NASB) and some mediating versions (see NIV). Other mediating versions like the NET make clear that "throne" refers to dynastic reign. The functional equivalent CEV uses a less technical description.

Job 2:10

NKJV	In all this Job did not sin with his lips.
CSB	Throughout all this Job did not sin in what he said.
GNT	Even in all this suffering Job said nothing against God.

The formal equivalent versions retain the metonymy "lips," while mediating versions explain this as sinning with "what he said" (CSB; cf. NIV; NET). Functional equivalent versions take this either as saying nothing wrong (NLT) or more specifically of speaking against God (GNT; CEV). The following three examples follow a common pattern, where formal equivalent and mediating versions retain the metonymy (flesh and blood, finger, sword), while functional equivalent versions provide its concrete meaning. Identify the metonymy and its meaning in each of the following.

Matthew 16:17

NRSV	flesh and blood has not revealed this to you
NIV	this was not revealed to you by flesh and blood
CEB	no human has shown this to you

Luke 11:20

NASB	if I cast out the demons by the finger of God
NIV	if I drive out demons by the finger of God
NLT	if I am casting out demons by the power of God

Romans 13:4

NKJV	for he does not bear the sword in vain
NET	because government does not bear the sword for nothing
CEB	because it doesn't have weapons to enforce the law for nothing

Summary

Figures of speech make language more interesting, colorful, and engaging. Rhetorical questions, unlike real questions, are not requests for information, but function to make statements, assertions, commands, invitations, and so on. Irony and sarcasm make a point through words or actions that are contrary to what is expected. Litotes makes an assertion by noting that its opposite is *not* true. Synecdoche and metonymy use one thing to refer to another. Because of their nonliteral means of communication, all these present some challenges to translators. In general, formal equivalent versions tend to retain the figure of speech, while more functional versions clarify its concrete meaning. Mediating versions commonly retain the figurative language, except in cases like litotes, where there is a greater likelihood of confusion by readers.

REFLECTION QUESTIONS

1. What are rhetorical questions? How do they function?
2. Define irony, and give some examples from Scripture.
3. What is litotes? Did you find it not a little bit challenging to understand?
4. What is synecdoche? What is metonymy?
5. How do formal equivalent and functional equivalent versions tend to translate these figures of speech?

SECTION C

Cultural Differences

All translation, to one degree or another, involves cross-cultural communication. Some translation challenges, however, are particularly related to the differences between cultures.

QUESTION 15

What Are the Challenges of Translating Implicit Material?

We can define "implication" as meaning that is not apparent in the words themselves, but is assumed by the author and would be immediately recognized by the original readers. For example, when Matthew 3:13 (NIV) says that "Jesus came from Galilee to the Jordan to be baptized by John," the author implies but does not explicitly state that this is the Jordan *River*. To make this clear, various Bible versions add the word "River" (cf. NET; CEB; NLT; CEV; GW). Similarly, when we learn that Paul and his associates were "forbidden by the Holy Spirit to speak the word in Asia" (Acts 16:6 NASB), the author expects readers to know that this is the *Roman province* of Asia (western Turkey today), not the continent of Asia. The NIV makes this explicit by translating "the province of Asia."

Making Implicit Material Explicit

So when is it appropriate to include additional content that is implied by the author but not explicitly stated? The simplest answer would be whenever the original readers would have recognized and understood the implied material, but the intended audience is likely to miss it. Take the example of Acts 16:6. For contemporary English readers, the word "Asia" almost always means the continent, not the Roman province (which no longer exists). It is likely to be misunderstood unless clarified in the translation or in footnotes.

Taking account of implications is especially important in cross-cultural contexts, since implicit meaning is often culture specific. Words in a particular language and culture often have not only *denotative* meaning but also *connotative* meaning. For example, the word "dog" in American English usually has positive connotations, a loving family pet ("man's best friend"). In ancient Jewish contexts, however, dogs were generally viewed as filthy scavengers. To call someone a dog was a grave insult (Matt. 7:6; Luke 16:21; Phil. 3:2; Rev. 22:15).

The story line of Jesus's parable of the "good Samaritan" (Luke 10:25–37) is well known: a man traveling by foot from Jerusalem to Jericho is attacked by robbers. The man is beaten and left for dead. Two men, a priest and a Levite, come along, but pass by on the other side of the road. A third man, identified as "a Samaritan," then comes along and helps the man. While the story may seem straightforward, there is much implicit content here. A contemporary reader who sees the traditional title, "the good Samaritan," might be prone to think that Samaritans are people who do good deeds. But essential to understanding the story is the historical animosity between Jews and Samaritans. To make this clear, the New Living Translation adds various details: the traveler is identified as "a Jewish man"; the Levite is called "a Temple assistant," to confirm his Jewish religious credentials; and the Samaritan is called "a despised Samaritan." Although these terms are not explicit in the Greek, they are part of the implicit meaning that the original readers would have immediately recognized. And all are essential to understand Jesus's point. The Samaritan demonstrates by his remarkable act of love and sacrifice that God's command to "Love your neighbor as yourself" (Luke 10:27; Deut. 6:5) includes loving *even your enemies.*

Translators must make hard decisions concerning which implications and connotations to express and which to leave implicit. This is because all translation involves interpretation, and there is no strict line between translation and commentary (see Question 35). Consider Acts 12:1–4 in the ESV:

> About that time Herod the king laid violent hands on some who belonged to the church. He killed James the brother of John with the sword, and when he saw that it pleased the Jews, he proceeded to arrest Peter also. This was during the days of Unleavened Bread. And when he had seized him, he put him in prison, delivering him over to four squads of soldiers to guard him, intending after the Passover to bring him out to the people.

The passage is full of implicit meaning. "Herod the king" is not Herod the Great, who ruled at the time of Jesus's birth (Luke 1:5). Nor is this Herod Antipas (Luke 3:1), who reigned in Galilee during Jesus's public ministry. This is Herod Agrippa I, the grandson of Herod the Great and nephew of Herod Antipas. The idiom "to lay violent hands on" means to arrest using force. "He killed James . . . with the sword" doesn't mean he killed him himself but that he ordered the execution of James. To kill "with the sword" likely means to publicly execute by beheading. The expression "it pleased the Jews" may be referring to the Jewish leadership or the Jewish population in general. The "days of Unleavened Bread" refers to the weeklong festival leading up to the Passover, which celebrated the Exodus from Egypt. A "squad" of soldiers was made of four soldiers, so this is a rotation of four squads of four soldiers each. To "bring him out to the people" means to put Peter on public trial. The decision to wait until after Passover to execute Peter likely resulted from Jewish opposition to a public execution during the festival. Formal equivalent versions like the ESV tend to leave implications like these unexpressed, allowing the reader to work them out through the study of external sources, teaching or preaching in the church, or exposure to the larger context of Scripture.

Functional equivalent and mediating versions tend to include implicit meaning to a greater or lesser extent, either in the text or using footnotes. For example, the NLT translates "Herod the King" as "King Herod Agrippa," identifies "the Jews" as "the Jewish people," describes the four squads as "four squads of four soldiers each," and translates "to bring him out to the people" as "to bring Peter out for public trial." The NET Bible says Herod "had James executed" instead of the ESV's "he killed James" (cf. NIV; CEB) and, like the NLT, says that Herod planned to bring him out for public trial" (cf. NIV; CEB). For much of the rest of the implicit material, the NET relies on footnotes.[1]

Translators of all versions must decide how much implicit material to include and how much to let readers discover through other means. Here are a few more examples showing ways in which translators include implicit meaning.

Reference	Formal Rendering	Implicit Meaning Added
Gen. 44:13	they tore their clothes (NIV)	they tore their clothing in despair (NLT)
Josh. 2:11	our hearts melted (ESV)	our hearts melted in fear (NIV)
Luke 18:10	tax collector (NIV)	despised tax collector (NLT)
Luke 18:13	beat his breast (NKJV)	beat his chest in sorrow (NLT)
1 Cor. 5:2	mourning (NIV)	mourning in sorrow and shame (NLT)

1. A footnote on "King Herod" reads, "*King Herod* was Herod Agrippa I, the grandson of Herod I (Herod the Great). His mediocre career is summarized in Josephus, *Ant.* 18–19. This event took place in A.D. 42 or 43." A footnote on "executed with a sword" reads, "The expression *executed with a sword* probably refers to a beheading. James was the first known apostolic martyr (Eusebius, *Eccl. Hist.* 2.9.1–3). On James, not the Lord's brother, see Luke 5:10; 6:14. This death ended a short period of peace noted in Acts 9:31 after the persecution mentioned in 8:1–3." A footnote on "the Jews" reads, "This could be a reference to the Jewish people (so CEV) or to the Jewish leaders (so NLT). The statement in v. 4 that Herod intended to bring Peter 'out to the people' (i.e., for a public trial) may suggest the former is somewhat more likely."

The Use of Italics for Words Not Found in the Original Hebrew or Greek

As noted above, formal equivalent translators are more reluctant to include implicit meaning, since their focus is on replicating the *words* of the text, and implied meaning is not directly represented by Hebrew or Greek words. Some of these versions seek to resolve this by putting words that do not have a direct counterpart in Hebrew or Greek in italics.

This practice can be traced back to Sebastian Münster of Basel (1489–1552), who in 1534–35 produced a German translation of the Hebrew Bible, accompanied by his own Latin translation and notes.[2] In this Latin version, Münster introduced small roman type to distinguish inserted words from the black-letter (or Gothic) type used for the main body of the text. A similar practice was followed by Olivetan (1506–38), the cousin of John Calvin, for a French translation of the Bible that appeared in June 1535, and by Miles Coverdale in The Great Bible of 1539 (see Question 24). Coverdale's practice, however, was to use brackets and smaller type to show where readings found in the Latin Vulgate had been introduced into his English Bible, which otherwise followed the Hebrew and Greek texts.

The first English version to use italics for words without equivalents in the Greek was William Whittingham's New Testament of 1557. Whittingham subsequently adopted this practice in the Geneva Bible of 1560, for which he served as the main editor (see Question 24). Similar practices became common in English versions of the sixteenth century. The Bishops' Bible of 1568 and the original King James Version of 1611 used black-letter script for the main text and roman type for words not found in the original languages. A smaller sized "octavo" edition of the KJV published in 1612 followed the practice of the Geneva Bible in printing the main text in roman type and using italics for additions. This would become the standard practice in various editions that followed, including the Revised Version (RV) of 1885 and the American Standard Version (ASV) of 1901. The Revised Standard Version (RSV, 1952) abandoned this practice, as also did the NRSV and the ESV (for reasons we will discuss below). Among widely used versions today, only the KJV, NKJV, and NASB still follow this practice.

There are various problems with using italics in this way. For one thing, it confuses readers who generally think that italics indicate emphasis. Unless they read the preface that explains the practice, they will likely misunderstand it. A more fundamental problem, however, is that using italics in this way is linguistically flawed and misrepresents the goal of translation, which is to reproduce the *meaning* of the text in a different language. Since the words in

---

2. Much of the material that follows comes from the excellent article of Walter F. Specht, "The Use of Italics in English Versions of the New Testament," *Andrews University Seminary Studies (AUSS)* 6, no. 1 (1968): 88–109, https://digitalcommons.andrews.edu/auss/vol6/iss1/6.

italics are intended to represent the meaning more accurately in English, they really function no differently from the other words and so the italics are unnecessary. Consider the following five examples taken from the NASB:

> For God, whom I serve in my spirit in the *preaching of the* gospel of His Son, is my witness. (Rom. 1:9)

The words "preaching of the" are placed in italics by the NASB editors because the Greek, when read word for word, has "in the spirit of-me in the gospel" (*en tō pneumati mou en tō euangeliō*). There are no unique Greek words for "preaching of the." But the Greek word *euangelion* can mean not only "the gospel" (the message itself) but also "the preaching of the gospel." See, for example, Romans 15:19, where Paul uses *euangelion* to mean to "preach the gospel" with no separate word for "preach" in Greek (cf. 2 Cor. 2:12). The NASB there translates, "I have fully preached the gospel of Christ" with no italics! So the words in italics in Romans 1:9 are not in fact something added but are fundamental to the meaning of the Greek words.

> I do not want you to be unaware, brothers *and sisters*, that often I have planned to come to you. (Rom. 1:13)

This example involves a change made in the 2020 edition of the NASB. While previous editions translated the Greek word *adelphoi* as "brothers" or as "brethren," the NASB 2020 changed this to "brothers *and sisters*" in contexts like this. This is because it is now universally recognized that in passages like this, *adelphoi* refers to both men and women, meaning "siblings" or "brothers and sisters" (see Question 19). That is part of its semantic range. The NASB, however, continues to put "*and sisters*" in italics to signal to readers that these words are not in the Greek. But this is wrong. They *are* in the Greek, because in these contexts *adelphoi* means "siblings" = "brothers and sisters." The NASB translators seem to think that *adelphoi* "literally" means "brothers" and that "and sisters" is some sort of add-on. But that is a literal or root-meaning fallacy (see Question 10). *Alelphoi* does not have a single literal meaning. It has a semantic range; "siblings" is just as much part that range as "brothers." Neither of these is more literal than the other.

> For in it *the* righteousness of God is revealed from faith to faith. (Rom. 1:17)

The NASB translators here place "the" in italics because there is no article in Greek before the word translated "righteousness" (*dikaiosynē*). But this represents a misunderstanding of Greek grammar. Greek has no indefinite article ("a/an") and the Greek article (*ho*, *hē*, *to*) functions very differently from the

English definite article "the."[3] Many Greek words without the article are definite and words with the article can be indefinite.

> To those who by perseverance in doing good seek glory, honor, and immortality, *He will give* eternal life; but to those who are self-serving and do not obey the truth, but obey unrighteousness, *He will give* wrath and indignation. *There will be* tribulation and distress for every soul of mankind who does evil, for the Jew first and also for the Greek. (Rom. 2:7–9)

The italics here suggest that the phrases "He will give" (twice) and "There will be" are absent from the Greek. But in fact, these are ellipses, where the meaning carries over from the previous context. In verse 6, Psalm 62:12 (cf. Prov. 24:12) is quoted, saying that God "will repay/give back" (*apodōsei*) to each person according to their deeds. This verb then carries forward for each of the subsequent clauses: "he will give . . . eternal life," "he will give . . . wrath and indignation," "he will give . . . tribulation and distress." The repetition of the verb is unnecessary in the Greek but helpful to clarify the meaning in English.

> And immediately the girl rose and *began* to walk. (Mark 5:42)

Jesus here raises Jairus's daughter from the dead. "Began" is placed in italics in the NASB to indicate that there is no separate Greek word here that means "to begin." But again, this represents a misunderstanding of Greek grammar. The Greek verb for "walk" (*peripateō*) is in the imperfect tense (*periepatei*), which can function in a variety of ways. In this context, it is functioning as an ingressive or inceptive imperfect, emphasizing the beginning of the action.[4] It *means* "began to walk." To say that the word "began" is not in the Greek is to misrepresent how the Greek imperfect tense functions. "Began to walk" is precisely what *periepatei* means in context.

Thus, the philosophy behind using italics to mark additions to the Hebrew and Greek text is linguistically flawed, since it assumes that there is a one-to-one correspondence between languages and that if you stray from that correspondence, you are adding something extra. In fact, there is no one-to-one correspondence, since Hebrew, Greek, and English use *different* words, grammar, and idioms to communicate the *same* meaning. In fact, to

---

3. The multiple functions of the Greek article are far too complex to discuss here. Suffice it to say that Daniel B. Wallace, in his intermediate-level *Greek Grammar Beyond the Basics: An Exegetical Syntax of the New Testament* (Grand Rapids: Zondervan, 1996) devotes two chapters and 84 pages to its function (pp. 206–90).
4. See Wallace, *Greek Grammar Beyond the Basics*, 544–45.

be consistent, *all* the English words should be in italics since none of them appear in the Hebrew or Greek texts! The goal of translation is not to make sure that individual English words line up with individual Hebrew and Greek words (that is an interlinear, not a translation). The goal is to accurately reproduce the meaning of the text, whether that takes one word or a dozen.

Summary

Implicit meaning is meaning that is not explicitly stated in the text but would have been assumed by the original author and readers. Cultural connotations are a type of implicit meaning. All versions must decide how much implicit meaning to include to make their translation understandable to their receptor audience. In general, formal equivalent versions tend to include less implicit content than their functional equivalent counterparts.

Some versions use italics to indicate words that are implicit but not present in the Hebrew or Greek text. This practice, however, is linguistically flawed, since it assumes a one-to-one correspondence between languages. Any words that are necessary to communicate the *meaning* of the text are an essential part of the translation and therefore are no different than any other words in the translation. The goal must be to replicate the *meaning* of the text, no matter how many words it takes.

REFLECTION QUESTIONS

1. What is implicit meaning?
2. When is it appropriate to include implicit meaning in a translation?
3. Can you think of a situation where it would be inappropriate to include implicit meaning in a translation?
4. Is it appropriate in the translation of the parable of the good Samaritan to refer to "the despised Samaritan," even though no Greek word for "despised" is present in the text? Why or why not?
5. Why does the author suggest that italics should *not* be used to indicate words in the translation that are not present in the Hebrew or Greek?

QUESTION 16

What Are the Challenges of Translating Euphemisms and Other Cultural Features?

Euphemisms

Euphemisms are a special kind of idiom or figure of speech used with things that are considered distasteful, shameful, overly explicit, or taboo. They are especially common around matters of sex, death, and the toilet. Euphemisms are often unique to cultures. In American English, for example, we refer to sexual relations as "sleeping with" or "making love to" someone; we speak of genitals as "private parts"; someone who has died has "passed away," "is no longer with us," "has gone to their reward," or (in slang) "kicked the bucket." "Going to the bathroom/restroom" or "relieving yourself" is a polite way to say urinating or defecating.

Different cultures and languages use different euphemisms, which can sometimes create humorous misunderstandings. For example, in the United Kingdom, they more commonly refer to the "WC" (water closet) or the "toilet" rather than the "bathroom" or "restroom." When my wife and I were living in Scotland, we once drove all night to a vacation destination with some British friends. When we stopped at a petrol (= gas) station, I mentioned how grungy I felt. One of our friends turned to me and said, "If you like, you can go splash your face in the toilet." I naturally declined. (She meant, of course, that I could splash my face in the *sink* in the *restroom*!)

There are many euphemisms in the Hebrew and Greek Bibles. In Hebrew, sexual relations with someone can be described as "knowing" them (Gen. 4:1), "laying" with them (Gen. 19:33; 30:16; 34:2; Deut. 22:25), "going/coming" in to them (Gen. 16:2; 19:31; 29:23), "approaching/drawing near" them (Gen. 20:4; Lev. 18:14; Deut. 22:14; Isa. 8:3), or "uncovering her/his nakedness" (Lev. 18, 20). In 1 Corinthians 7:1, to "touch" a woman means to have sex with her.

A woman's monthly period is referred to as "the way/custom of women" (Gen. 18:11; 31:35). To "cover your feet" (Judg. 3:24; 1 Sam. 24:3; 1 Kings 18:27) means to relieve yourself, either urinating or defecating. "Sleep" is a common euphemism for death in both the Old and New Testaments (Job 7:21; Ps. 13:3; 90:5; Dan. 12:2; John 11:11; 1 Cor. 11:30; 15:51; 1 Thess. 4:14; 5:10). Other euphemisms for death and burial are to "go to your fathers in peace" (Gen. 15:15) and to be "gathered to your fathers/ancestors" (Judg. 2:10).

There are three main ways to translate euphemisms: (1) Translate them literally, that is, retain the Hebrew or Greek euphemism. Formal equivalent versions tend to do this. For example, the NKJV translates Genesis 4:1 as "Now Adam knew his wife Eve" (cf. NRSV; ESV; JPS). (2) Translate the euphemism directly, dropping the euphemism and describing explicitly what is happening. In Genesis 4:1 the TEV reads, "Then Adam had intercourse with his wife." The NLT has, "Now Adam had sexual relations with his wife." (3) Third, replace the Hebrew or Greek euphemism with a common euphemism in the receptor language. The NIV in Genesis 4:1 reads, "Adam made love to his wife Eve." *The Message* reads, "Adam slept with Eve his wife."

Either the second or third options are usually best, since readers may be unfamiliar with the Hebrew or Greek euphemism and so misconstrue its meaning. In Genesis 19:31 ESV, after the destruction of Sodom, Lot's daughter says to her younger sister, "Our father is old, and there is not a man on earth to come in to us" (cf. NKJV; NRSV). The euphemism "come in to" will likely be obscure or unknown to contemporary readers. The CSB is much clearer when it uses an English euphemism: "there is no man in the land to sleep with us" (cf. NIV; CEB). The NIV skips the euphemism and states the goal of producing offspring: "there is no man around here to give us children."

A similar misunderstanding is likely in Judges 19:22, a passage meant to demonstrate the decadence of Israel during the period of the judges. When a Levite and his concubine find lodging with an old man in the town of Gibeah, "the men of the city, worthless fellows, surrounded the house, beating on the door. And they said to the old man, the master of the house, 'Bring out the man who came into your house, that we may know him'" (ESV; cf. RSV; ASV). "Know" here does not mean to get acquainted, as most contemporary readers would understand it, but rather to "have sex with" (NLT; NIV; CSB; GW; GNT).

Another passage that would easily be misunderstood is Genesis 31:35, where Rachel conceals the household idols she has stolen from her brother Laban by hiding them on her camel's saddle. She sits on them and pretends to be unable to get up because of her monthly period. She says to Laban, "May my lord not be angry that I cannot stand in your presence, because the way of women is upon me" (Gen. 31:35 NASB; cf. ESV; NKJV). The NIV and other versions read more clearly "I'm having my period" (cf. CSB; CEB; NET; NLT), replacing the Hebrew euphemism with an English one.

Translating Unknown Cultural Practices

Like euphemisms, other cultural practices found in the Bible may be different or unknown in the receptor culture, presenting challenges for translators. Different versions seek to bridge this cultural gap in different ways.

Gird Your Loins (1 Kings 18:46)

The phrase "gird your loins" is one of those classic idioms from the King James Version, well known to traditional Bible readers but obscure in contemporary English. To "gird" means to prepare for action and can refer to putting on armor or fastening a sword to one's side. "Girding one's loins" comes from the practice of tying up loose fitting garments around one's waste or into the belt to allow greater freedom for running. The idiom occurs seventeen times in the KJV. Among contemporary versions, only the NKJV retains the idiom (twice: 1 Kings. 18:46; 1 Pet. 1:13). The phrase is used literally in 1 Kings 18:46, where following his defeat of the priests of Baal on Mount Carmel, "the hand of the LORD was on Elijah and he girded his loins and ran before Ahab to the entrance of Jezreel" (KJV). Other translations read:

NKJV	he [Elijah] <u>girded up his loins</u> and ran ahead of Ahab
ESV	he <u>gathered up his garment</u> and ran before Ahab
CSB	he <u>tucked his mantle under his belt</u> and ran ahead of Ahab
NIV	<u>tucking his cloak into his belt</u>, he ran ahead of Ahab

The idiom is used in a metaphorical sense in 1 Peter 1:13, where the KJV has "Wherefore <u>gird up the loins</u> of your mind, be sober." This is obviously a "dead metaphor" (see Question 13), since one can hardly conceive of tying your mind up under your belt! It means to be alert or ready for action:

NKJV	Therefore <u>gird up the loins</u> of your mind
ESV	Therefore, <u>preparing</u> your minds <u>for action</u>
NIV	Therefore, with minds <u>that are alert</u>
NLT	<u>So prepare</u> your minds <u>for action</u>

Anoint Your Head (Matthew 6:17)

In Matthew 6:16–18, Jesus criticizes those hypocrites who, when they are fasting, make themselves look terrible to show everyone how much they are suffering for the Lord. They have already received their reward, he says, which is the praise they receive from people. Instead, he says, you should make yourself look good, so that no one except God knows you are fasting. Then your reward will come from God. The point is that the purpose of fasting is to deepen your personal walk with God, not to impress others. To make yourself look good, Jesus says, you should wash your face and "anoint" or "pour a liquid" (*aleiphō*) on your head. While this could refer to perfume, more likely it refers to oil. Olive oil was used for many things in the ancient Near East: as fuel for lamps, for cooking, as a condiment, for medicinal purposes, for cosmetics, and as a sign of hospitality for an honored guest (Ps. 23:5: Luke 7:46). Since Jesus refers to doing this to oneself, it presumably refers to using oil as a cosmetic. Notice how various versions translate this:

ESV	But when you fast, anoint your head and wash your face (cf. NASB; NKJV; NET; NAB; REB)
NIV	But when you fast, put oil on your head and wash your face (cf. NRSV; CSB)
NLT	But when you fast, comb your hair and wash your face (cf. CEB; CEV; NCV; GW; LB; PME)

Most formal versions and a number of mediating ones use the traditional "anoint" here. While this fits with the use for hospitality, it seems strange to anoint oneself. Some mediating versions use "put oil on your head," apparently trying to retain the cultural practice, but make it clear that this is self-care. Most functional equivalent versions seek a contemporary parallel, where care for the hair means combing or brushing it.

Engaged or Betrothed? (Luke 1:27)

In Luke 1:27 (cf. Matt.1:18) many English versions describe Mary as "engaged" (*mnēsteuō*) to a man named Joseph (NRSV; NET; H/CSB; CEB; NLT; CEV). The problem with this translation is that it is anachronistic, since first-century marriages were contractual arrangements between families, not engagements in the modern sense. Most formal equivalent versions use the term "betrothed" (KJV; NKJV; NASB; REB; NJB; NAB; ESV), which may be closer to the historical meaning but sounds archaic to modern ears. Other versions use "pledged to be married" (NIV) or "promised in marriage" (TEV; GW) to try to capture the contractual sense.

Reclining at Table (Mark 2:13–17)

Cultural factors are also at play in Mark 2:13–17, where Jesus calls Levi the tax collector to be his disciple. In the next scene, we learn that Jesus "reclined in his house" (v. 15; formal Greek translation). To understand this phrase, we need to know not only the meaning of the words but also their cultural connotations. To "recline" commonly meant to recline on low cushions around a table during a formal dinner party. In the Greco-Roman world, meals were rituals of social status, where to share a meal meant to accept someone as a peer. For a rabbi like Jesus to accept an invitation from a despised tax collector was viewed as scandalous since it apparently meant accepting his immoral lifestyle (see v. 16). Consider how various versions translate this:

> as <u>he reclined at table</u> in his house (ESV)
>
> it happened that <u>He was reclining at the table</u> in his house (NASB)
>
> as <u>he sat at dinner</u> in Levi's house (NRSV)
>
> While <u>Jesus was having dinner</u> at Levi's house (NIV)
>
> Later, Levi <u>invited Jesus and his disciples to his home as dinner guests</u> (NLT)

None of these versions capture all the meaning. The ESV and NASB note the prone position and the table, but don't say whose house this is or anything about the meal. The NIV and the NRSV make it clear that this is dinner and that it is at Levi's house, but don't mention the posture of the guests. The NLT, which is furthest from the Greek in form, gives the clearest description of the cultural situation (a dinner party), but does not mention the reclined position of the guests. In this case translators must decide which cultural connotations are important to include.

Wearing Large Phylacteries (Matthew 23:5)

In Matthew 23:5 Jesus illustrates the hypocrisy of the Pharisees with examples of how they show off their religious devotion. The NRSV reads, "They do all their deeds to be seen by others; for they make their <u>phylacteries</u> broad and their <u>fringes</u> long." Phylacteries were small boxes with Scripture passages inside, which pious Jews wore on their foreheads and arms during prayer times. This practice was meant to fulfill the commands of Deuteronomy 6:8 and 11:18 to keep God's commands always in mind. Fringes or tassels on robes were another sign of Jewish devotion commanded by God in Numbers 15:38–39 and Deuteronomy 22:12. Consider how various versions translate the verse:

> They enlarge their <u>phylacteries</u> and lengthen their <u>tassels</u>. (CSB)

> They make their phylacteries wide and the tassels of their garments long. (NIV).
>
> They make extra-wide prayer bands for their arms and long tassels for their clothes. (CEB)
>
> On their arms they wear extra wide prayer boxes with Scripture verses inside, and they wear robes with extra long tassels. (NLT)
>
> Their lives are perpetual fashion shows, embroidered prayer shawls one day and flowery prayers the next. (MSG)
>
> They strut in their robes and display their degrees. (*Cotton Patch Version*)

Notice how these versions move progressively from the first-century context to the contemporary world. Most versions retain the technical term "phylacteries" (NRSV; NIV; CSB; etc.). Others, aware that many modern readers will not know the term, provide an explanation (CEB; NLT). A few others, like *The Message* and the *Cotton Patch Version* replace the original cultural image with a contemporary parallel. These last two make the passage more directly culturally relevant for modern readers, but at the expense of historical and cultural accuracy (see Question 36).

Whitewashed Tombs (Matthew 23:27)

A similar example can be seen in Matthew 23:27, where Jesus criticizes the Pharisees: "Woe to you, teachers of the law and Pharisees, you hypocrites! You are like whitewashed tombs, which look beautiful on the outside but on the inside are full of the bones of the dead and everything unclean" (NIV). *The Message* reads, "You're like manicured grave plots, grass clipped and the flowers bright, but six feet down it's all rotting bones and worm-eaten flesh." A modern cemetery, rather than a first century rock-hewn tomb, is now in view.

Summary

A euphemism is an idiom used to avoid language that is considered coarse, vulgar, or taboo. English euphemisms include expressions like "make love," "sleep with," "go to the bathroom," and "pass away." Like other idioms, euphemisms present a challenge for translators since they often differ between cultures and languages. Euphemisms can be translated literally ("Adam knew his wife"), directly ("Adam had sexual relations with his wife"), or using an English euphemism ("Adam made love to his wife"). The latter two are generally the most effective. Along the same lines, cultural practices that are unknown in the receptor culture can present challenges for translators. The tension here is between preserving the cultural context while communicating clearly in the receptor language.

REFLECTION QUESTIONS

1. What is a euphemism? What are some English euphemisms?
2. What makes euphemisms difficult to translate?
3. What three ways can euphemisms be translated? Which do you prefer?
4. What other kinds of cultural challenges do translators face?
5. How do formal equivalent, mediating, and functional equivalent versions tend to handle cultural issues like those discussed in this question?

QUESTION 17

What Are the Challenges of Translating Weights, Measures, Money, and Time?

Some of the most challenging cultural items for translators are measurements and quantities, since these units differ from culture to culture and across time. We will discuss three broad categories: (1) weights and measures, (2) money, and (3) time.

Weights and Measures

Modern readers will recognize the challenges of weights and measures in the contemporary attempts to adopt the metric system. While the United States steadfastly holds to inches, feet, yards, and miles, most of the world speaks of distances in terms of millimeters, centimeters, meters, and kilometers. For weight the United States retains ounces, pounds, and tons, while most of the world speaks of grams, kilograms, and so on. Liquid volume in pints, quarts, and gallons converts in the metric system to liters and kiloliters.

This conversion challenge is magnified in the Bible both because there are a variety of units across the biblical cultures and because we are not always sure of the value these units had. Most Bibles provide conversion charts of some kind for weights and measures. For example, the NIV 2011 provides the following table:

Table of Weights and Measures[1]

	Biblical Unit	Approx. American Equivalent		Approx. Metric Equivalent	
Weights	talent (60 minas)	75	pounds	34	kilograms
	mina (50 shekels)	1 1/4	pounds	560	grams
	shekel (2 bekas)	2/5	ounce	11.5	grams
	pim (2/3 shekel)	1/4	ounce	7.8	grams
	beka (10 gerahs)	1/5	ounce	5.7	grams
	gerah	1/50	ounce	0.6	gram
	daric	1/3	ounce	8.4	grams
Length	cubit	18	inches	45	centimeters
	span	9	inches	23	centimeters
	handbreadth	3	inches	7.5	centimeters
	stadion (pl. stadia)	600	feet	183	meters
Capacity					
Dry Measure	cor or homer (10 ephahs)	6	bushels	220	liters
	lethek (5 ephahs)	3	bushels	110	liters
	ephah (10 omers)	3/5	bushel	22	liters
	seah (1/3 ephah)	7	quarts	7.5	liters
	omer (1/10 ephah)	2	quarts	2	liters
	cab (1/18 ephah)	1	quart	1	liter
Liquid Measure	bath (1 ephah)	6	gallons	22	liters
	hin (1/6 bath)	1	gallon	3.8	liters
	log (1/72 bath)	1/3	quart	0.3	liter

1. Appendix to the New International Version (Grand Rapids: Zondervan, 2011). The table is followed by the following clarifications:

"The figures of the table are calculated on the basis of a shekel equaling 11.5 grams, a cubit equaling 18 inches and an ephah equaling 22 liters. The quart referred to is either a dry quart (slightly larger than a liter) or a liquid quart (slightly smaller than a liter), whichever is applicable. The ton referred to in the footnotes is the American ton of 2,000 pounds. These weights are calculated relative to the particular commodity involved. Accordingly, the same measure of capacity in the text may be converted into different weights in the footnotes."

"This table is based upon the best available information, but it is not intended to be mathematically precise; like the measurement equivalents in the footnotes, it merely gives approximate amounts and distances. Weights and measures differed somewhat at various times and places in the ancient world. There is uncertainty particularly about the ephah and the bath; further discoveries may shed more light on these units of capacity."

There are two main ways Bible versions translate weights and measures: they either (1) retain the ancient unit, usually with a footnote providing a modern equivalent; or (2) provide a modern equivalent, usually with a footnote identifying the ancient unit. Compare the NIV and NLT on Isaiah 5:10, which describes the desolation to agriculture that God's judgment of Israel will bring:

> NIV A ten-acre vineyard will produce only a bath[1] of wine;
> a homer[2] of seed will yield only an ephah[3] of grain.
> Footnotes: [1] That is, about 6 gallons or about 22 liters
> [2] That is, probably about 360 pounds or about 160 kilograms
> [3] That is, probably about 36 pounds or about 16 kilograms
>
> NLT Ten acres of vineyard will not produce even six gallons[1] of wine.
> Ten baskets of seed will yield only one basket[2] of grain.
> Footnotes: [1] Hebrew *a bath* [21 liters]
> [2] Hebrew *A homer* [5 bushels or 220 liters] *of seed will yield only an ephah* [20 quarts or 22 liters]

The NIV transliterates the Hebrew units, with footnotes providing modern equivalents. The NLT does the reverse, providing modern equivalents in the text and the Hebrew units in the footnotes.[2]

For units of distance, consider Luke 24:13:

> NASB And behold, on that very day two of them were going to a village named Emmaus, which was <u>sixty stadia</u> from Jerusalem.
>
> ESV That very day two of them were going to a village named Emmaus, about <u>seven miles</u> from Jerusalem.

The Greek unit of measurement *stadion* (pl. *stadia*) was equivalent to about six hundred feet. The NASB retains the Greek "sixty stadia" (*stadious hexēkonta*), with a footnote reading, "Possibly about 7 miles or 11.3 km; a Roman stadion perhaps averaged 607 ft. or 185 m." Most versions, like the ESV here, convert this to its modern equivalent: "seven miles." The ESV provides a footnote reading, "Greek *sixty stadia*; a *stadion* was about 607 feet or 185 meters."

Translating using modern equivalents generally works fine, except when the numbers have symbolic or theological significance. Consider Revelation 21:16, which is describing the dimensions of the New Jerusalem:

2. The Hebrew word for "acre" (*tsemed*) is also interesting. It means a "pair" or "yoke" of oxen and evidently referred to the amount of ground a team of oxen could plow in a day.

> NIV The city was laid out like a square, as long as it was wide. He measured the city with the rod and found it to be 12,000 stadia[1] in length, and as wide and high as it is long.
> Footnote: [1]That is, about 1,400 miles or about 2,200 kilometers
>
> NLT When he measured it, he found it was a square, as wide as it was long. In fact, its length and width and height were each 1,400 miles.[1]
> Footnote: [1]Greek *12,000 stadia* [2,220 kilometers]

While the NLT's 1,400 miles may be an accurate calculation of the length in contemporary miles, numbers in the book of Revelation often carry symbolic significance. This is especially true for the numbers seven and twelve. So, in this case the number 12,000 should probably be retained in the text, with a modern equivalent placed in the footnote.

For some biblical measurements, the ancient unit is retained but is given a traditional name rather than a transliteration from the Hebrew. This is especially common with names of measurements that have a long history in English, like "cubit" and "span." In 1 Samuel 17:4, Goliath is described:

> NIV A champion named Goliath, who was from Gath, came out of the Philistine camp. His height was six cubits and a span.[1]
> Footnote: [1]That is, about 9 feet 9 inches or about 3 meters

A cubit was the length from a man's elbow to the end of his hand, about 18 inches. A span was the distance between the tip of a man's thumb and his little finger, about nine inches. So Goliath is described as six cubits (6 x 18" = 9 feet) and a span (= 9 inches) tall. But the English word "cubit" is not a Hebrew transliteration (the Hebrew word is *'amma*. It is from the Latin *cubitum*, meaning "elbow" or "forearm." Similarly, "span" is not derived from the Hebrew (the Hebrew is *zeret*), but rather comes from a Germanic root. Words like "cubit" and "span" were early translations of these Hebrew words that came to be identified with the ancient measurements.

Money

Before discussing the translation of terms for money, a little background is necessary. Coins first came into use as monetary units around the seventh century BC in western Asia Minor.[3] This means that Old Testament references to "money"—such as shekels, minas, and talents—never refer to coins, but

---

3. John W. Betlyon, "Coinage," in *Anchor Yale Bible Dictionary* (New York: Doubleday, 1992), 1:1079.

always to weight, a volume of precious metals.[4] In Genesis 23:16, for example, Abraham pays Ephron the Hittite 400 shekels of silver for a burial place for Sarah. While standards varied from times and places, a shekel weighed about 2/5 ounce (12 grams). A mina equaled 50 shekels, so weighed about 20 ounces or 1¼ pounds (560 grams). A talent was worth 60 minas, so weighed about 75 pounds (34 kilograms).

When these terms came to be used for currency, a talent (= 75 lbs. of gold, silver, or bronze) represented a vast sum. This is crucial for understanding the parable of the unmerciful servant in Matthew 18:21–35. According to the parable, a servant owed his master "ten thousand talents." Modern readers might see this and think of something like $10,000, a manageable debt. But in the NT period, a Tyrian talent was worth 6,000 denarii, or the equivalent of 6,000 days of work for a laborer.[5] This servant owes his master 60,000,000 days of work, an absurdly vast debt! The point of the parable is that if God is willing to forgive the impossibly large debt we owe to him, how much more should we forgive the tiny debts owed to us by others? Formal equivalent versions tend to translate the phrase as "ten thousand talents" and depend on footnotes to instruct readers of the value (NASB; ESV; NKJV; NRSV; CSB; NET). Functional equivalent and mediating versions struggle with how to make the meaning clear, translating in various ways: "a huge amount" (NAB), "millions of dollars" (NLT; GW), "fifty million silver coins" (CEV), "ten thousand bags of gold" (NIV; CEB).

While most monetary units are not this difficult to translate, money does provide unique challenges for translators. As with other kinds of measurements, translators have two main options: they can either transliterate the name of the ancient currency in the text and provide a footnote describing its value, or they can introduce a modern equivalent, sometimes putting the ancient name in the footnote. For example, in the parable of the workers in the vineyard (Matt. 20:1–16), the NIV says that the landowner "agreed to pay them a denarius for the day and sent them into his vineyard" (v. 2). A footnote explains, "A denarius was the usual daily wage of a day laborer." The NLT does the reverse, stating in the text, "He agreed to pay the normal daily wage" with a footnote reading, "Greek *a denarius*, the payment for a full day's labor."

Two other factors complicate translations related to money. The first is that different countries use different currencies, making conversion values difficult. While "dollars" might work for the United States, Canada, and Australia, the United Kingdom uses "pounds," India uses "rupees," and so on. So translators need to find ways to represent the value of money without

---

4. While "shekel" and "mina" are transliterations of Hebrew words, "talent" (*talanton*) was a Greek word that was used in the LXX as a translation for the Hebrew *kikkar*.
5. S.v. τάλαντον, in *A Greek-English Lexicon of the Greek New Testament and Other Early Christian Literature*, 3rd ed., eds. W. Baur, F. W. Danker, W. F. Arndt, and F. W. Gingrich (Chicago: University of Chicago Press, 2001), 988.

limiting it to modern currency. The most common way of doing this is to refer to the average wage for a day laborer.

Another complicating factor is that the value of money changes over time, so that translations can quickly become out of date. For example, in Matthew 10:29 (cf. Luke 12:6), many contemporary English versions translate Jesus's words as, "Are not two sparrows sold for a penny?" (NIV; cf. ESV; CSB; NET; NRSV). In terms of contemporary value, this is way off. The Greek word translated "penny" here is *assarion*, which was a coin worth one-sixteenth of a denarius, the latter being the wage for a laborer for a day. So an *assarion* would be the normal pay for about a half hours' worth of work, the equivalent today (in US currency) of a few dollars. Sparrows were certainly cheap, but they weren't "sold for a penny" (essentially given away for free!). A similar reference occurs in the story of the so-called widow's mite in Mark 12:41–44 (cf. Luke 21:1–4), where Jesus commends the poor widow's gift of "two small copper coins" (Greek: "two lepta"). The lepton was the smallest coin in circulation in Palestine, worth only 1/64 of a denarius. But in today's currency, this would still be worth much more that "a penny" (NRSV; CEB; ESV) or even "less than a penny" (NET)! The CSB captures the sense better with, "two tiny coins worth very little."

A similar problem appears is the parable of the pounds in Luke 19:11–27, traditionally called this because early English versions used the British currency of a pound for the Greek term *mina:* "A certain nobleman . . . called his ten servants, and delivered them ten pounds" (Luke 19:12–13 KJV). The problem here is that a *mina* was worth 100 denarii, or about three and a half months' wages for each servant who receives one—far more than a British pound is worth today. Surprisingly, the RSV, NRSV, and NJB retain the word "pound," perhaps because of the traditional title of the parable. Other contemporary versions transliterate the Greek *mina* and provide modern equivalents in the footnotes (NIV; NASB; ESV; NET; NKJV). Some others use more general descriptions: NAB and TEV: "a gold coin"; GW: "a coin"; MSG: "a sum of money"; CEB: "money worth four months' wages." The NLT retains "pound" but modifies this to "a pound of silver," greatly increasing its value!

Time

Compared to money, measurements of time are relatively straightforward for English Bible translators. This is because people in the Greco-Roman world divided the day into twenty-four-hour units much the same way we do today, a system apparently going back to the ancient Egyptians and Babylonians. The "first hour," however, was not 1 am, as on our clocks. It was the beginning of the daylight hours, 6 am.

There are actually very few references to specific hours of the day in the Bible. One of the few is Mark's division of the crucifixion account into three three-hour periods: (1) In Mark 15:25, the narrator announces, "Now it was the third hour when they crucified Him" (NASB). Since the day began at approximately 6 am, the third hour was about 9 am. Most formal equivalent versions retain the Greek reading, "the third hour" (RSV; NASB; NKJV; ESV), while most functional and mediating versions either have "nine in the morning" (NIV; CSB; CEB) or "9 o'clock in the morning" (TEV; CEV; NLT; NET). (2) Mark next reports (15:33) that darkness covered the land from "the sixth hour . . . until the ninth hour" (RSV; NASB; NKJV; ESV), that is, "noon . . . until three in the afternoon" (NIV; CSB; NET; CEB; NRSV). (3) Finally, at "the ninth hour" (RSV; NASB; NKJV; ESV), or "three in the afternoon" (NIV; NRSV; NET; cf. CSB), Jesus cried out, "My God, my God, why have you forsaken me?" and died shortly afterward (15:34–37).

Another Greco-Roman way of reckoning time appears in Mark 6:48 (cf. Matt. 14:25), where the narrator reports that the disciples were in a boat on the Sea of Galilee straining against the wind when, "about the fourth watch of the night" (ESV), Jesus came to them, walking on the water. This time reference comes from the Roman division of the night into four "watches" of three hours each: *vigilia prima*, *vigilia secunda*, *vigilia tertia*, and *vigilia quarta*.[6] These are sometimes called "evening," 6–9 pm; "midnight," 9 pm–12 am; "cockcrow," 12–3 am; and "morning," 3–6 am. Most formal equivalent versions retain the more technical "fourth watch" language (ESV), while mediating and functional equivalent versions use more contemporary language like "about three o'clock in the morning" (NLT), "very early in the morning" (CSB; cf. NRSV), "shortly before dawn" (NIV), or "as the night was ending" (NET).

Summary

Weights, measures, money, and time can be a challenge for translators, since units of measurement and measurement values vary between times, places, and cultures. To reproduce the meaning, translators generally either transliterate the original unit with a footnote providing a contemporary equivalence, or they provide the contemporary equivalence in the text with a footnote identifying the original unit. Translating money can be a particular challenge. Not only do money units vary in name and value across time and culture, but the value of units (like a penny) change over time, potentially misrepresenting the meaning of the text.

REFLECTION QUESTIONS

1. How does your favorite Bible version handle the translation of weights, measures, and money?

---

6. For links to Roman authors, see "Hours and Other Divisions of Day and Night in Ancient Rome," Telling Time in Ancient Rome, accessed January 31, 2023, https://sites.google.com/site/dilucinum/home.

2. What are the most significant challenges translators face with reference to measurements?
3. What two ways are measurements typically translated?
4. What are the most significant challenges translators face with reference to money? Time?
5. What did you learn in this chapter about the value of a talent? In what way might using the word “talent” in a translation confuse readers?

SECTION D

Gender Issues

While gender issues in translation could be treated under the broader category of cultural issues, we have introduced a separate category here because of the importance of this issue related to English Bible translation and the controversies that have surrounded it in recent years.

QUESTION 18

What Are the Issues Related to Gender Language in Bible Translation?

Perhaps the greatest controversy in the world of English Bible translation in recent years has been the debate over "gender-inclusive" language. Simply defined, this means using inclusive rather than masculine terms in generic references. A generic reference means a passage where the author is referring to members of both sexes. For example, Romans 3:28 in the RSV reads, "For we hold that a man is justified by faith apart from works of law." The ESV, a revision of the RSV, renders the verse, "For we hold that one is justified by faith apart from works of the law." The Greek word translated "man" in the RSV is *anthrōpos*, which in this context clearly means "person," not male. While in the past "man" was understood as generic, including both men and women, English has changed, and today many readers hear it as male-oriented, referring only to men. The ESV therefore changed the translation to "one" to reflect this inclusive sense. Virtually all versions have moved in this direction to a greater or lesser extent in recent years. The question, then, becomes to what extent this is legitimate.

Historical Background to the Debate

The use of gender-inclusive terms for masculine generics in translation is not a new phenomenon, and every English translation since Wycliffe (see Question 24) has used some inclusive terms for masculine generics. The King James Version commonly used the gender-neutral "children" instead of "sons" for masculine plural terms in Hebrew (*banim)* and Greek (*huioi*). Yet the dramatic increase in the use of inclusive language in Bible translation is the result of two main factors: (1) changes in English usage, prompted especially by the women's rights movement in the 1960s and '70s, and (2) increased acceptance of meaning-based (functional equivalent) versions.

Alongside the push for greater equality for women in society came a similar push for language to reflect this equality. Using "men" when referring to both women and men was considered to be sexist and inaccurate. As a result, there has been a significant shift in English usage—even among those who oppose a feminist perspective. If I were preaching today and said, "All men should follow Jesus," I think the majority of the congregation would hear this as a reference to males. This would be especially true for the young people present, who have grown up in a context where masculine generics are seldom used. I would do better to say, "All people should follow Jesus." While there is nothing inherently wrong or evil about masculine generic terms (many languages use them), neither is there anything wrong or evil with using inclusive language. In fact, in a generic context "people" is more precise and so more accurate. Indeed, many refer to this kind of usage as "gender-*accurate*" rather than "gender-inclusive" or "gender-neutral." The goal is not to abolish gender distinctions but to define them more precisely.

Of course what makes this topic so controversial is that it has been closely linked to the debate over the role of men and women in the church and the home. On one side are egalitarians, who claim that women and men share equal status as God's image-bearers and so should be given equal roles in the church. Leadership should be based on a person's gifts and calling rather than on gender. On the other side are complementarians, who claim that while men and women are equal *ontologically* (that is, in essence), *functionally* they have different and complementary roles in the church and the home. Men should lead while women should nurture and support.

A number of complementarians have opposed the use of gender-inclusive language because they consider it to be part of a wider feminist agenda in the church. Yet this issue does not split on party lines, and a number of prominent complementarian scholars have come out in support of gender-inclusive language in Bible translation.[1] These scholars claim that using gender-inclusive language is simply sound translation policy and should not be confused with the promotion of an egalitarian or feminist agenda.[2]

A second reason for the increase in inclusive language is the rise of functional equivalence as a translation approach.[3] Recent translations that focus more on the *meaning* of the text than its *form* have tended to introduce inclusive terms more frequently than their more literal counterparts. For example,

1. See, for example, D. A. Carson, *The Inclusive Language Debate: A Plea for Realism* (Grand Rapids: Baker, 1997); Craig Blomberg, "Today's New International Version," CBE International, February 1, 2004, www.cbeinternational.org/resource/article/todays-new-international-version; Darrell Bock, "You Make the Call: Are Gender-Sensitive Translations Safe or Out?," *Bible Translator* 56, no. 3 (July 1, 2005): 169–87.
2. For a fuller discussion, see Mark L. Strauss, *Distorting Scripture? The Challenge of Bible Translation and Gender Accuracy* (Downers Grove, IL: InterVarsity, 1997).
3. See Grant Osborne, "Do Inclusive-Language Bibles Distort Scripture? 'No,'" *Christianity Today* 41, no. 12 (October 27, 1997), 33 and passim, https://www.christianitytoday.com/ct/1997/october27/7tc33a.html.

in the NASB 1977, Romans 2:6 read that God "will render to every man according to his deeds." The more idiomatic NIV 1984 had "God will give to each person according to what he has done." Without any agenda or mandate to introduce inclusive language, the NIV translators recognized that in this context *anthrōpos* meant "person," not "man." While in most cases the NIV 1984 retained the masculine generic "man," in many contexts a more inclusive term was used.

While these kinds of gender-inclusive renderings arose incidentally in the course of translation, by the mid-1980s steps were being taken by translators to introduce such language more consistently. Almost every major Bible version produced or revised over the last forty years has adopted a significant amount of gender-inclusive language. Of the early gender-inclusive versions, the New Revised Standard Version (NRSV) was the most widely anticipated and heralded. As a major revision of the widely used Revised Standard Version (RSV), its appearance was already much anticipated. When publicity went out that the revision would introduce the systematic use of gender-inclusive language, its 1989 release generated even more attention. Reviews of the new version were generally favorable, with one commentator calling the NRSV "the finest American translation yet."[4] Among evangelicals reaction was mixed. On the positive side, D. A. Carson, research professor of New Testament at Trinity Evangelical Divinity School, noted, "On the whole, their efforts [at inclusive language] are judicious, thorough and effective. . . . Most of the changes introduced by these commitments are happy ones."[5] More negative assessment came from Robert Thomas, professor of New Testament at the Master's Seminary, who expressed concern both for the revision's liberal bias and its use of inclusive language.[6] Wayne Grudem, research professor of theology and biblical studies at Phoenix Seminary, wrote an even more critical article, claiming that by making the goal of eliminating masculine-oriented language more important than the goal of accuracy in translation, the NRSV has made thousands of intentional changes in the sense of the text, and in so doing it has become a translation that cannot be trusted.[7] Grudem's criticisms turned out to be a preview of things to come. Prior to this, the sweeping trend toward gender-inclusive language in

---

4. Walter Wink, "The New RSV: The Best Translation, Halfway There," *Christian Century*, Sept. 19–26, 1990, 829.
5. D. A. Carson, "A Review of the New Revised Standard Version," in *Reformed Theological Review* 50, no. 1 (1991): 8; cf. John Stek, "A Review of the New Revised Theological Standard Version," *Reformed Theological Review* 50, no. 1 (1991): 8–10.
6. Robert L. Thomas, review of the NRSV in *Master's Seminary Journal* 2 (Spring 1991): 111–15.
7. Wayne Grudem, "What's Wrong with 'Gender Neutral' Bible Translations?" (paper, Evangelical Theological Society Annual Meeting, Jackson, Mississippi, November 1996), 17.

Bible translation had gone mostly unnoticed by the evangelical public. Events in March 1997 were about to change that.

The NIV and the "Stealth Bible" Controversy

On March 29, 1997, the cover of *World* magazine ran the headlines, "The Stealth Bible: The Popular *New International Version* Bible Is Quietly Going 'Gender-Neutral.'" The article, written by assistant editor Susan Olasky, noted that a "gender-neutral" version of the NIV had been recently published in Great Britain and a similar version would soon be introduced in North America. Olasky's description of the NIV Inclusive Language Edition (or NIVI) as a "stealth" Bible created a sensation (there was a picture of a stealth fighter on the cover). The repeated use of the explosive term "unisex" to describe the version, together with its link to creeping feminism in the church, provided all the ingredients for controversy. The actual title of the article was "The Feminist Seduction of the Evangelical Church." Indeed, most of the article was devoted not to the NIV but to a critique of what it termed the dangerous trend toward feminism in the church.

Complaints began to pour in at the International Bible Society (IBS), the NIV copyright holder, and Zondervan, the primary publisher. One man even drilled holes through several NIVs—meant to look like bullet holes—and sent these Bibles to the IBS.[8] Zondervan and the IBS moved rapidly for damage control, releasing press statements explaining that gender language was being introduced only when warranted by the meaning of the original text and in line with contemporary English usage. Yet public outrage grew. When the nation's largest denomination, the Southern Baptist Convention, threatened to drop the NIV from its Sunday school curriculum, the IBS reversed course, issuing a statement abandoning all plans for gender-related changes in future editions of the NIV.

A few days later, on May 27, 1997, James Dobson convened a conference of interested parties at Focus on the Family headquarters in Colorado Springs. The participants drafted a series of guidelines, which came to be known as "the Colorado Springs Guidelines." These guidelines were subsequently revised and published in a two-page advertisement in *Christianity Today*. At this point I became involved in the controversy. The guidelines seemed to me ideologically motivated and full of linguistic and hermeneutical errors. So I wrote a paper critiquing the guidelines and presented it at the 1997 Annual Meeting of the Evangelical Theological Society.[9] I subsequently wrote a book and various articles on the topic.[10]

---

8. Doug LeBlanc, "Hands Off My NIV!," *Christianity Today* 41, no. 6 (June 16, 1997), 53.
9. Subsequently published as "Linguistic and Hermeneutical Fallacies in the Guidelines Established at the 'Conference on Gender-Related Language in Scripture,'" *Journal of the Evangelical Theological Society* 41, no. 2 (1998): 239–62.
10. See, for example, Strauss, *Distorting Scripture?* and Mark L. Strauss, "Current Issues in the Gender-Language Debate," in *The Challenge of Bible Translation: Communicating God's*

The TNIV and Its Opponents

Since the International Bible Society had agreed to freeze the NIV in its 1984 version, the IBS decided to produce a new version to carry forward changes deemed necessary to maintain accuracy and contemporary English. This version was entitled Today's New International Version (TNIV). The NT was released in 2001 and the whole Bible in 2005.[11] While many critics viewed the TNIV simply as a "gender-neutral" version of the NIV, in fact it represented the scholarly discussions and votes of the NIV's Committee on Bible Translation (CBT) over the previous twenty years (1984–2005). Its purpose was to continue the NIV's legacy of accuracy and clarity.

Yet the TNIV was ferociously attacked by its opponents. This level of anger and opposition might seem overblown, since there were already a dozen or so English versions that had introduced the same kind of gender-inclusive language. But this was different. The TNIV was in the lineage of the NIV, which had become the premier Bible for evangelicals (see Question 34). The gender language of the NRSV could be shrugged off because it, like its predecessor the RSV, was viewed by many evangelicals as a "liberal" version. Similarly, the gender-inclusive language in versions like the GNT, NLT, and NCV could be forgiven, since these were viewed by many as mere "paraphrases," unsuitable for serious study. But the NIV was the *real Bible*—the primary text of Scripture for millions of evangelicals. When the NIV translators were accused of caving in to a feminist agenda, the response was overwhelming. The title of one article in *Christianity Today* sums up the evangelical response: "Hands Off My NIV!"[12]

The NIV 2011

Sales of the TNIV never really got off the ground. Despite a strong marketing push, the translation never achieved more than 1 percent of the English Bible market. This was likely due to two main factors: the strong opposition against it in some circles, and its relative obscurity in others. People either hated it or had never heard of it. Many Christian bookstores refused to stock it. In the face of little support for the TNIV and declining NIV sales, in 2009 the IBS and Zondervan changed course. They brought in a consultant who reviewed the entire history of the debate and advised that the TNIV should be discontinued, and the NIV moderately revised to take into account gender-language changes in English. Not wanting to be accused of producing another "stealth" version, Zondervan and the IBS widely publicized this new direction. In addition, Zondervan commissioned the Collins Dictionary group to

---

Word to the World, eds. Glen G. Scorgie, Mark L. Strauss, and Steven M. Voth (Grand Rapids: Zondervan, 2003), 115–41.

11. I was invited to join the CBT about this time and did so in 2005, after the release of the TNIV.
12. LeBlanc, "Hands Off My NIV!"

conduct a major study of contemporary English to gain empirical data concerning the present state of gender language. The CBT used the findings of this study to help guide their decisions.

After several years reexamining and discussing every gender reference in the Bible, the CBT produced the next generation of the NIV. It was published in 2011, coincidentally during the four hundredth anniversary year of the publication of the King James Version. The 2011 NIV retained many of the gender changes introduced in the TNIV but rolled back others that were viewed as controversial. For some of the more challenging gender-related issues, see Question 19.

Recent Developments: The CSB and the NASB Go Gender-Inclusive

The two and a half decades since the "Stealth Bible" controversy of 1997 have seen significant changes. In 2017, the Holman Christian Standard Bible (HCSB) was significantly revised and renamed the Christian Standard Bible (CSB) under the editorship of Tom Schreiner. The original HCSB had arisen in a context of general antipathy toward gender-inclusive language. The introduction stated, "The goal of the translators has not been to promote a cultural ideology but to faithfully translate the Bible" and warned against those who by removing traditional masculine terms like "man" and "men" had "begun a program to engineer the removal of a perceived male bias in the English language."

The CSB 2017 revision has a markedly different tone. This is evident in the first line of the introduction. While the HCSB introduction had read "The Bible is God's revelation to *man*," the CSB now reads "The Bible is God's revelation to *humanity*" (italics mine). The introduction goes on to say, "Recognizing modern usage of English, the CSB regularly translates the plural of the Greek word *anthrōpos* ('man') as 'people' instead of 'men.'" An electronic search of both editions confirms the extent of these changes. While the HCSB used the terms "man" or "men" 3,097 times, the CSB uses them only 2,551 times, a reduction of 546. Consider the following examples:

Matthew 12:12

HCSB	A <u>man</u> is worth far more than a sheep.
CSB	A <u>person</u> is worth far more than a sheep.

Romans 3:28

HCSB	For we conclude that a <u>man</u> is justified by faith.
CSB	For we conclude that a <u>person</u> is justified by faith.

Romans 4:8

HCSB	How joyful is the <u>man</u>
CSB	Blessed is the <u>person</u>

Perhaps the most striking gender-language change in the CSB is its rendition of the Greek plural *adelphoi*. While the HCSB consistently translated *adelphoi* as "brothers," the CSB changes this to "brothers and sisters" 145 times.[13]

These revisions should perhaps not be too surprising, since the CSB is a mediating version, whose goal is to communicate the meaning of the text in contemporary English. More surprising, however, was the announcement in 2020 that the (much more literal) NASB had revised its text to include gender-accurate language. Whereas the NASB (1977) had used "man" or "men" 3,896 times throughout the Bible and the 1995 revision just slightly fewer at 3847 times, the 2020 has these masculine terms only 2,625, a reduction of 1,226! Similarly, whereas the NASB consistently translated *adelphoi* as "brethren," the NASB 2020 now frequently renders it as "brothers *and sisters*" (131 times; with "and sisters" in italics; see Question 15).

Ironically, many of those who twenty years ago were vehemently attacking the revisers of the NIV for their use of gender-inclusive language are now adopting this same language in their own versions. This would seem to provide a measure of vindication for those who insisted all along that the goal was to achieve gender *accuracy*, not gender-neutrality.

Summary

Gender-inclusive Bible translation seeks to avoid masculine terms when the authors of Scripture were referring to both men and women. The first English version to consistently adopt gender-inclusive language was the NRSV, a 1989 revision of the RSV. Almost all versions produced or revised in the last forty years have adopted a generous amount of this kind of language. This trend erupted into public controversy in 1997, with articles attacking the publication of a gender-inclusive edition of the NIV in the United Kingdom. After abandoning plans to update the 1984 NIV with inclusive language, and then launching but soon abandoning the gender-inclusive Today's New International Version (TNIV), the International Bible Society commissioned the NIV committee to reexamine all gender changes in the NIV and produce a new edition. The result was the 2011 NIV. The trend toward the adoption of gender-inclusive language has continued with the 2017 revision of the HCSB as the CSB and the 2020 revision of the NASB.

13. For more details, see Mark L. Strauss, "A Review of the Christian Standard Bible," *Themelios* 44, no. 2 (2019): 258–77.

REFLECTION QUESTIONS

1. What is "gender-inclusive" Bible translation?

2. What two factors does the author say provoked the increase in gender-inclusive language in Bible translation?

3. What was the first major English translation to consistently adopt gender-inclusive language?

4. What was the "Stealth Bible" controversy? What was its cause? What was its result?

5. What has been the general trend since this controversy?

QUESTION 19

What Are the Main Translation Issues in the Gender-Language Debate?

Many languages use grammatically masculine terms in a generic sense to refer to people in general. This is true of Hebrew and Greek, and it is also true of English. In the sentence "Early man was a hunter and gatherer," the word "man" means "humans." Similarly, "Man shall not live on bread alone" means "people" shall not live on bread alone. Masculine generics are used in Hebrew and Greek not only for human beings generally, but also for a variety of relationships, including siblings, children, and parents. To understand how masculine generics work, it is important to distinguish between grammatical and biological gender.

Grammatical versus Biological Gender

In many languages, including Hebrew and Greek, all nouns are categorized according to gender. Hebrew has two genders: masculine and feminine. Greek has three genders: masculine, feminine, and neuter. This is *grammatical* gender and has nothing to do with biological sex. Consider the gender of various Hebrew and Greek words used for body parts and inner human life:

English	Hebrew	Gender	Greek	Gender
HEAD	*ro'sh*	masculine	*kephalē*	feminine
FACE	*paneh*	masc./fem.	*prosōpon*	neuter
EYE	*'ayin*	masc./fem.	*ophlamos*	masculine
EAR	*'ozen*	feminine	*ous*	neuter

English	Hebrew	Gender	Greek	Gender
MOUTH	*peh*	masculine	*stoma*	neuter
HAND	*yad*	masc./fem.	*cheir*	feminine
ARM	*zeroa'*	feminine	*brachiōn*	masculine
FOOT	*regel*	feminine	*pous*	masculine
BODY	*basar*	masculine	*sōma*	neuter
FLESH	*basar*	masculine	*sarx*	feminine
SOUL	*nefesh*	feminine	*psychē*	feminine
SPIRIT	*ruach*	feminine	*pneuma*	neuter
HEART	*lev*	masculine	*kardia*	feminine
MIND	*levav*	masculine	*dianoia*	feminine
LIFE	*chay*	masculine	*zōē*	feminine

Notice that (1) the gender of Hebrew and Greek words do not necessarily agree with each other, and (2) neither have anything to do with being male or female. Grammatical gender is an arbitrary category that has nothing to do with biological sex. While many modern languages like French, Spanish, and German retain grammatical gender, English has mostly lost its gender distinctions (Old English had three genders—masculine, feminine, and neuter). In languages with grammatical gender, words that modify these nouns—like adjectives, articles, and participles—agree in gender with the noun they modify. Similarly, pronouns agree with their antecedents in gender. This does not mean that the thing referred to suddenly becomes a "he" or a "she." It is simply grammatical agreement with the thing to which it refers.

With reference to persons, grammatical gender tends to agree with biological gender. The Greek word *gynē* means "woman" or "wife" and is feminine. Similarly, the Greek word *anēr* means "man" or "husband" and is masculine. But there are exceptions. While the Greek word for "person" (*anthrōpos*) is masculine, the Spanish word is feminine (*la persona*), as also is the German word (*die Person*). The Greek word *tekna*, which means "children," is neuter. The German word for a young woman (*Mädchen*) is also neuter. In Greek the word for Spirit (*pneuma*) is neuter; in Hebrew it is feminine (*ruach*). This does not mean that the Holy Spirit is an impersonal force in Greek or a female in Hebrew. Nor is the Spirit a male! The common use of "he" is traditional, identifying the Spirit as a person, not a male. Since the Greek word for "deacon" (*diakonos*) is masculine, one might conclude that all deacons were male. But in Romans 16:1 a woman named Phoebe is identified as a *diakonos*. My favorite example of a clash in grammatical and biological gender comes from German, where the term *die Männlichkeit*, meaning "manliness" or "masculinity," is feminine! For Germans, this is not odd or unusual, since they immediately recognize this is grammatical, not biological, gender.

"Man" or "Person"? Gender in Translation

As noted above, the default gender for generic terms in Hebrew and Greek is masculine. This has also been true historically in English, where terms like "man," "mankind," "(fore)fathers," "brethren," and so on have traditionally been used generically to refer to men and women. Feminists and egalitarians often claim this is a bias built into language because of patriarchy and male dominance. They encourage the use of more "inclusive" language to promote a more egalitarian society. Some complementarians, by contrast, claim that masculine generics are a God-ordained feature of language meant to reflect male priority and authority, and so they seek to retain masculine generics in translation.[1] This perspective is hard to defend globally, since languages around the world have a broad range of gender systems.[2] Some do not specify gender at all. Are these languages theologically inferior or deficient?

I would suggest a mediating approach to gender language, which focuses on the two main goals of translation: accuracy and readability (see Question 2). To achieve readability, translators should generally follow a *descriptive* rather than *prescriptive* approach. The goal should be to identify *how* people actually speak rather than to mandate how they *ought* to speak. If masculine generics like "man" are being replaced by more inclusive terms in contemporary English, then translators should follow suit. Concerning accuracy, gender-inclusive language should be used if it more accurately reflects the meaning of the text. When the author is referring to males, the word "men" should be used. When both men and women are included, "persons" or "people" are more precise and so more accurate.

'adam and anthrōpos

The most common Hebrew word for "human being" or "person" is *'adam*. This word has a range of possible meanings, including human being,

1. See Vern S. Poythress and Wayne A. Grudem, *The Gender-Neutral Bible Controversy: Muting the Masculinity of God's Word* (Nashville: Broadman & Holman, 2000), 192–93.
2. See D. A. Carson, *The Inclusive Language Debate: A Plea for Realism* (Grand Rapids: Baker, 1997), 77–98.

humankind, male human being, and the proper name "Adam." Consider the difference between the NASB 1995 and 2020 in the following examples. Notice that no change is made in the first two, since both use *ʾadam* to refer exclusively to the male. In the next two examples, however, the word is generic, so an inclusive term is introduced.

Genesis 3:21

NASB 1995 — The LORD God made garments of skin for Adam and his wife

NASB 2020 — And the LORD God made garments of skin for Adam and his wife

Genesis 2:15

NASB 1995 — Then the LORD God took the man and put him into the garden of Eden

NASB 2020 — Then the LORD God took the man and put him in the Garden of Eden

Genesis 1:26

NASB 1995 — Then God said, "Let Us make man in Our image . . . "

NASB 2020 — Then God said, "Let Us make mankind in Our image . . . "

Psalm 32:2

NASB 1995 — How blessed is the man to whom the LORD does not impute iniquity

NASB 2020 — How blessed is a person whose guilt the LORD does not take into account

Like Hebrew *ʾadam*, the Greek term *anthrōpos* is grammatically masculine but most commonly refers to a person rather than a male. Consider these examples from the NIV 1984 and 2001. In the first example, there is no change, since John was in fact a man.

John 1:6

NIV 1984 — There came a man who was sent from God; his name was John.

NIV 2011	There was a man sent from God whose name was John.

Mark 7:15

NIV 1984	Nothing outside a man can make him "unclean" by going into him.
NIV 2011	Nothing outside a person can defile them by going into them.

John 1:4

NIV 1984	In him was life, and that life was the light of men.
NIV 2011	In him was life, and that life was the light of all mankind.

Of course, none of these translations is "wrong," since "man" and "men" can still function generically in English. Yet the translations "person" or "mankind" are more precise and so more accurate.

'ish and anēr

While *'adam* and *anthrōpos* are usually inclusive, meaning "person" or "human being," there are other terms in Hebrew and Greek that have stronger male connotations. The Hebrew *'ish* is the most common word for "man" and is most often used of males. In Adam's famous statement at the creation of Eve he says,

> This is now bone of my bones
> and flesh of my flesh;
> she shall be called "woman [*'ishah*],"
> for she was taken out of man [*'ish*] (Gen. 2:23).

This is a play on words since the word for man is *'ish* and the word for woman is its cognate *'ishah*. As we have noted before (see Question 10), it is a happy coincidence of translation that the English terms "man" and "woman" are also phonetically similar.

While *'ish* frequently means "man" (male) or "husband," in many other contexts it is used generically to mean "person," "someone," or "anyone." Consider these examples.

Psalm 1:1

NASB 1995	How blessed is the man [*'ish*] who does not walk in the counsel of the wicked

NASB 2020	Blessed is the <u>person</u> [*'ish*] who does not walk in the counsel of the wicked

Proverbs 16:25

HCSB	There is a way that seems right to a <u>man</u> [*'ish*], but its end is the way to death.
CSB	There is a way which seems right to a <u>person</u> [*'ish*], But its end is the way of death.

Like the Hebrew *'ish* in the Old Testament, in the New Testament the Greek *anēr* carries stronger male connotations than *anthrōpos*, and its default translation is "man" or "men." Yet on some occasions it too has an inclusive sense. The letter of James in particular uses *anēr* in a generic sense:

James 1:12

NIV 1984	Blessed is the <u>man</u> [*anēr*] who perseveres under trial
NIV 2020	Blessed is the <u>one</u> [*anēr*] who perseveres under trial

James 1:20

NIV 1984	for <u>man's</u> [*anēr*] anger does not bring about the righteous life that God desires
NIV 2020	because <u>human</u> [*anēr*] anger does not produce the righteousness that God desires

In James 1:12 the author clearly has in mind *people* who persevere, and James 1:20 is speaking of human anger, not male anger.

"Brothers" or "Brothers and Sisters"?

The Greek term *adelphoi* can mean "brothers" in the sense of male siblings. But it is most commonly used in the New Testament in an inclusive sense of "siblings" or "brothers and sisters." Examples from Greek literature confirm that *adelphoi* is more inclusive than the English "brothers." A passage from the Oxyrhynchus Papyri (713, 20–23; AD 97) reads, "My father died leaving me and my siblings [*adelphoi*] Diodorus and Thais as his heirs." While Diodorus is a man's name, Thais is a woman's name. In English I would never say, "my brothers Bob and Jill"; but in Greek I can say "my *adelphoi* Diodorus and Thais." The Greek term is thus fully inclusive in this context, meaning "brother and sister" or "siblings." Consider these NT examples:

Matthew 4:18

NASB 1995	Now as Jesus was walking by the Sea of Galilee, He saw two brothers [*adelphoi*], Simon who was called Peter, and Andrew his brother
NASB 2020	As Jesus was walking beside the Sea of Galilee, he saw two brothers [*adelphoi*], Simon called Peter and his brother Andrew

Romans 12:1

NASB 1995	Therefore I urge you, brethren [*adelphoi*], by the mercies of God, to present your bodies a living and holy sacrifice
NASB 2020	Therefore, brothers *and sisters* [*adelphoi*], in view of the mercies of God, I urge you to present your bodies as a living sacrifice

The NASB 1995 translated *adelphoi* as "brothers" when referring to male siblings, but switched to "brethren" when referring to fellow Christians (perhaps assuming that the archaic "brethren" sounded more inclusive to Christian readers). The 2020 revision finally acknowledged that the word *adelphoi* in these contexts is referring to "brothers and sisters" and so should be translated this way. Notice, however, that the NASB still errs by placing "and sisters" in italics. As discussed in Question 15, the purpose of italics in the NASB is to identify words that don't have a parallel in the Greek. But this is simply wrong: "and sisters" *does* have a parallel in the Greek, because *adelphoi* means "siblings" (= brothers and sisters) in this context.

"Fathers," "Parents," "Forefathers," or "Ancestors"?

Terms for lineage in Hebrew and Greek tend to be less precise than their English counterparts. The Hebrew term for father (*'av;* plural: *'avot*) can also mean grandfather, forefather, or ancestor. Similarly, the Greek *patēr* (plural: *pateres*) is commonly used in the same way. It is different in English. Occasionally we might speak of someone as a "father" figure. George Washington is called the father of the United States and the "founding fathers" established the American form of government. Yet apart from these traditional uses, we use "father" almost exclusively for our immediate male parent. For more distant relatives we speak of grandfathers, great-grandfathers, forefathers, or ancestors.

More traditional and formal equivalent Bible versions have tended to retain "father(s)" in translation even when speaking of more distant relatives. This results from the tendency to seek one-to-one correspondence between

Hebrew and Greek words and English ones. Consider Deuteronomy 10:22 in various versions:

NKJV	our fathers went down to Egypt with seventy persons
ESV	Your fathers went down to Egypt seventy persons
NASB	Your fathers went down to Egypt seventy persons *in all*
HCSB	Your fathers went down to Egypt, 70 people in all
CSB	Your ancestors went down to Egypt, seventy people in all
NIV 1984	Your forefathers who went down into Egypt were seventy in all
NIV 2011	Your ancestors who went down into Egypt were seventy in all
NET	When your ancestors went down to Egypt, they numbered only seventy
NLT	When your ancestors went down into Egypt, there were only seventy of them

The formal equivalent versions (NKJV; ESV; NASB), in seeking one-to-one correspondence between Hebrew and English, translate the term as "fathers," even though it refers to generations past and to both male and female ancestors. There is a tension seen in the HCSB, which normally tends toward more contemporary language but here has "fathers" to preserve the masculine gender. Its 2017 revision, the CSB, switched to "ancestors." Some mediating versions, like the NIV 1984 (cf. REB), use "forefathers," seeking to retain the sense of past generations but remaining less attuned to the gender-exclusive sound of the term for many readers. The rest of the versions use "ancestors," recognizing both that these were past generations and they included men and women.

The same issue occurs in Greek, where *pateres* has this same semantic range (fathers, parents [see Heb. 11:23], grandfathers, forefathers, ancestors). In John 6:31 some Galilean Jews request a sign from Jesus, recalling God's gift of manna from heaven.

NKJV	Our fathers ate the manna in the desert
ESV	Our fathers ate the manna in the wilderness
NASB	Our fathers ate the manna in the wilderness

HCSB	Our fathers ate the manna in the wilderness
CSB	Our ancestors ate the manna in the wilderness
NIV 1984	Our forefathers ate the manna in the desert
NIV 2011	Our ancestors ate the manna in the wilderness
NET	Our ancestors ate the manna in the wilderness
NLT	After all, our ancestors ate manna while they journeyed through the wilderness

The formal equivalent versions (NKJV; ESV; NASB) seek one-to-one correspondence with the Greek by translating *pateres* as "fathers." Yet this is less precise and so less accurate than "ancestors," missing both the sense of past generations, as well as the inclusion of women among those who ate manna in the wilderness.

"Sons" or "Children"?

As with terms of ancestry, terms for descendants in Hebrew and Greek are less precise and have a much larger semantic range than their English counterparts. For example, the Hebrew word *ben* (plural: *banim*) can mean "son(s)" (= male offspring), but it can also mean "child(ren)" (= offspring of either gender); "grandson(s)" or "grandchild(ren)"; and "descendant(s)" (= several generations removed). The inclusive nature of *banim* is clear in a passage like Genesis 3:16, where Eve is told, "In pain you shall bring forth children [*banim*]" (ESV). Since pain is produced by babies of either sex, the masculine plural *banim* must here mean "children," not just "sons." The Greek counterpart *huios* ("son"; "child"; plural *huioi*) can be used in the same variety of ways. While the singular *huios* usually has male connotations ("son"), its plural is more often generic ("children"). The Greek *teknon* ("child"; plural *tekna*) and its diminutive *teknion* ("little child") are also more generic. Long before the gender-language debate, the King James Version often translated both *banim* and *huioi* as "children." The phrase "children of Israel" occurs more than six hundred times in the KJV. (For more on the "son of x" idiom, see Question 12.)

Summary

It is important to distinguish between grammatical and biological gender. In many languages, like Hebrew, Greek, Spanish, and German, all nouns are tagged for gender. This has nothing to do with biological gender, or sex. So the masculine gender of Greek *anthrōpoi* ("people") does not mean "males" any more than the feminine gender of Spanish *las personas* ("people") means "females." Gender-inclusive translation means using inclusive (non-gender-specific) terms when members of both sexes are intended by the author. Some examples include (1) using terms like "people" instead of "men" when both males and females are intended; (2) using "brothers and sisters" instead of "brothers" when siblings of both sexes are being referred to; (3) using "child(ren)" instead of "son(s)" when both boys and girls are present; and (4) using "ancestors" instead of "fathers," when both males and females are in view.

REFLECTION QUESTIONS

1. What is the difference between grammatical and biological gender? What does this have to do with the gender-language debate?

2. What different meanings can the Hebrew word *ʾadam* and the Greek word *anthrōpos* have?

3. In what way does gender-inclusive language make translation more precise than male-oriented language?

4. Two problems are noted when "fathers" is used when ancestors are intended. What are these?

5. Why might someone choose the translation "forefathers" over "ancestors," or vice versa?

QUESTION 20

What Are Some Controversial Issues Related to Gender Translation?

The two previous questions have shown that introducing gender-inclusive language can make translations more precise and more accurate by clarifying gender distinctions. When both men and women are intended, "person" is more precise than "man," since the latter could be misconstrued as limited to a male. Similarly, when past generations are in view, "ancestors" is more accurate than "fathers." While most translators would agree with this, other issues related to gender-inclusive language are more controversial.

Unnecessary Use of Inclusive Language

Some versions tend to introduce inclusive language in a broad and comprehensive manner, sometimes even when the original authors were likely referring to men. In Luke 5:18, the NIV reads, "Some *men* came carrying a paralyzed man on a mat." Luke here uses the term *andres* (plural of *anēr*), which, as we have seen, usually (but not always) means "men" rather than "people." The CEV translates, "Some <u>people</u> came carrying a crippled man on a mat." While the loss of meaning is slight, there seems no reason to avoid the word "men" in a case like this. A similar example appears in Luke 14:16, where the NIV begins a parable, "<u>A certain man</u> was preparing a great banquet and invited many guests." The NRSV reads, "<u>Someone</u> gave a great dinner and invited many." Again, while a small issue, it is unnecessary to replace "man" with "someone," since Luke is surely referring to the patriarch or male head of the household. In the qualifications for church leaders in 1 Timothy 3:1–7 and Titus 1:5–9, the CEV removes all masculine references. While it is legitimate to debate whether both men and women can hold these leadership offices today, *in these passages* Paul is likely referring to men. The patriarchal context of the first-century Greco-Roman world was a reality, and seeking to remove or mute that patriarchy results in a loss of meaning for the reader.

In many other contexts, it is difficult to discern whether both men and women are intended. In Exodus 32:28, did three thousand "men" (NASB) or three thousand "people" (NIV) die in the plague following the golden calf incident? The Hebrew word here is *'ish*, which could go either way. In Acts 4:4, had the church grown to five thousand "men" (NIV; CSB; NLT) or five thousand "people" (NRSV; CEV; GNT)? Since *andres* is used here, Luke may be referring to male heads of households. This is likely the case in the feeding of the five thousand. The Gospels refer to five thousand "men" (*andres*), using a word that most often refers to males. Matthew confirms this meaning in his gospel when he adds, "besides women and children" (Matt. 14:21).

Resumptive Masculine Pronouns

Another issue in the gender-language debate that has caused significant controversy is the matter of resumptive masculine pronouns. It is relatively easy to avoid the generic use of "man" by replacing it with "person" or by using indefinite pronouns like "anyone" or "whoever." For example, instead of saying, "A man must work hard," you can say, "A person must work hard." But what if the sentence continues, "if he wants to succeed." While "person" is gender-inclusive, "he" is masculine. The problem is that English does not have a singular gender-neutral pronoun. "It" will not do, since it does not refer to persons. There are various ways to handle this situation:

(1) *Keep the masculine singular pronoun: "A person must work hard if he wants to succeed."* Some Bible versions that have adopted a moderate use of gender language have continued to retain masculine resumptive pronouns. This is common, for example, in the Revised English Bible (REB 1989). In Psalm 1 the resumptive masculine pronouns are retained after the initial inclusive phrase: "Happy is <u>the one</u> who does not take the counsel of the wicked . . . <u>he</u> is like a tree . . . <u>he</u> prospers in all <u>he</u> does" (Ps. 1:1–3 REB). The Christian Standard Bible (CSB 2017), while adopting more gender-inclusive language than its predecessor (HCSB), retains masculine resumptive pronouns. The introduction reads: "While the Holman CSB avoids using 'man' or 'he' unnecessarily, the translation does not restructure sentences to avoid them when they are in the text. For example, the translators have not changed 'him' to 'you' or to 'them.'"[1]

(2) *Use "he or she": "A person must work hard if he or she wants to succeed."* While this might work in contemporary writing, few Bible translators have chosen this option since it quickly becomes redundant, awkward, and artificial-sounding.

(3) *Make the construction plural: "People must work hard if they want to succeed."* This works because the plural pronoun "they" is gender-neutral. The NRSV commonly uses this construction. For example, Job 15:14 in the RSV

1. Introduction to *Christian Standard Bible* (Nashville: Holman Bible Publishers, 2017).

reads, "What is man, that he can be clean?" The NRSV revises this to, "What are mortals, that they can be clean?" Similarly, where the RSV in Proverbs 13:24 reads, "He who spares the rod hates his son," the NRSV has "Those who spare the rod hate their children."

(4) *Change to a first- or second-person construction: "We must work hard if we want to succeed" or "You must work hard if you want to succeed."* This works in English because the first- and second-person pronouns (I, we, you) are gender-neutral and can be used to make general and proverbial statements. While the RSV translates Proverbs 20:24 as "A man's steps are ordered by the LORD," the NRSV revises this to "All our steps are ordered by the LORD." Similarly, RSV in Galatians 6:7 has "Whatever a man sows, that will he also reap." This becomes, in the NRSV, "You reap whatever you sow."

(5) *Use a "singular they": "A person must work hard if they want to succeed."* Perhaps the most common way to avoid a masculine resumptive pronoun in contemporary English is with the singular "they." In the sentence that begins, "Everyone likes pizza," most people would continue with "don't they?" rather than "doesn't he?" Although some English stylebooks have traditionally opposed this use for formal writing, it has been used in English since the fourteenth century and has now become the pronoun of choice in contemporary English. This usage has become so pervasive that in 2015 the American Dialect Society named "singular they" their word of the year![2] The seventh edition of the *Publication Manual of the American Psychological Association* (APA), published in 2020, endorses singular they for scholarly writing. *Merriam-Webster* now affirms this usage as well:

> We will note that *they* has been in consistent use as a singular pronoun since the late 1300s; that the development of singular *they* mirrors the development of the singular *you* from the plural *you*, yet we don't complain that singular *you* is ungrammatical; and that regardless of what detractors say, nearly everyone uses the singular *they* in casual conversation and often in formal writing.[3]

The first Bible translation to consistently introduce the "singular they" was the NIV 2011. Romans 8:9 NIV reads, "And if <u>anyone</u> does not have the Spirit of Christ, <u>they</u> do not belong to Christ." The singular indefinite pronoun "anyone" is followed by the singular "they." Though plural in form, "they" is

2. Jeff Guo, "Sorry, Grammar Nerds: The Singular 'They' Has Been Declared Word of the Year," *Washington Post*, January 8, 2016, https://www.washingtonpost.com/news/wonk/wp/2016/01/08/donald-trump-may-win-this-years-word-of-the-year.
3. *Merriam-Webster*, "Singular 'They,'" Words We're Watching, accessed January 31, 2023, https://www.merriam-webster.com/words-at-play/singular-nonbinary-they.

singular in function. Similarly, John 11:10 NIV reads, "It is when a person walks at night that they stumble."

Some have claimed this usage is grammatically inaccurate, since a singular antecedent ("person") is followed by plural pronoun ("they"). But this fails to recognize the difference between form and function. Though "they" is plural in form, it is *functioning* as a singular pronoun. In reality, using "he" is equally inaccurate, since a *gender-neutral* antecedent ("person") would be followed by a *masculine* pronoun ("he"). So both "they" and "he" have a grammatical anomaly. The translator must pick their poison (or is it "pick his poison"?) by deciding whether to agree in number or in gender. As always, translation involves give and take, and something (very minor in this case) will be lost in the translation.

God Language

Another concern sometimes expressed about the use of inclusive language is its application to God. There is a fear among some that progressive translators will refer to God as "she" or apply feminine terms like "mother" and "goddess" to God. Several clarifications are in order. First, these kinds of changes with reference to God would run counter to the goal of gender accuracy, which is to reflect the meaning of the text as accurately as possible. None of the dozen or so English versions we have identified in Question 18 as "gender-inclusive" or "gender-accurate" change any language related to God. There are indeed a few feminist versions, such as *The New Testament and Psalms: An Inclusive Version* (1995) and *The Inclusive Bible* (2007), that do change language related to God.[4] But these versions have a very different agenda than the mainstream versions discussed in Questions 18–20.

A second important clarification is that while God is not a woman, neither is God a man. Numbers 23:19 reads, "God is not man, that he should lie, or a son of man, that he should change his mind" (ESV). Of course in this passage "man" and "son of man" both mean "a human being." God is not a human being, yet both masculine and feminine imagery is used to describe him. God gave birth to the people of Israel (Deut. 32:18) and comforts them like a mother comforts her children (Isa. 66:13). Just as a mother cannot forget the baby at her breast, so God cannot forget his people (Isa. 49:15). On the other hand, most of the imagery related to God is masculine. God is king and Lord of all. Jesus especially emphasizes father language, referring to God as his father and inviting his disciples to pray to him as "our Father in heaven" (Matt. 6:9). This masculine imagery is perhaps why masculine pronouns are used to refer to God. But it is important to emphasize that God is not a "he" or a "she."

---

4. See Mark L. Strauss, *Distorting Scripture? The Challenge of Bible Translation and Gender Accuracy* (Downers Grove, IL: InterVarsity, 1997), chap. 3, "The Feminist Versions," 60–73.

The Humanity of Jesus Christ

While God is neither male or female, the Second Person of the Trinity is identified as "the Son," and he became incarnate as a male human being. Sometimes gender-inclusive versions have been accused of downplaying the maleness of Jesus by describing him as a "human being" rather than a man. Consider the following examples.

John 10:33

RSV	"We aren't stoning you for a good work," the Jews answered, "but for blasphemy, because you—being a man—make yourself God."
NRSV	The Jews answered, "It is not for a good work that we are going to stone you, but for blasphemy, because you, though only a human being, are making yourself God."

1 Timothy 2:5

RSV	For there is one God, and there is one mediator between God and men, the man Christ Jesus
NRSV	For there is one God; there is also one mediator between God and humankind, Christ Jesus, himself human

In both of these examples, the NRSV changes the RSV's "man" to "human (being)." Yet the NRSV is probably the better translation in both cases, since the emphasis here is not on Jesus's maleness but on his humanity. In John 10:33 the contrast is between the divine and the human. In 1 Timothy 2:5, the point is that Jesus has the power to save human beings not because he is male but because he himself is fully human as well as divine.

Messianic Passages

Another criticism sometimes leveled against gender-inclusive versions is that they obscure the connection between OT messianic prophecies and their NT fulfillment.[5] Compare Psalm 34:19–20 in the RSV and NRSV:

RSV	Many are the afflictions of the righteous; but the LORD delivers him out of them all. He keeps all his bones; not one of them is broken.
NRSV	Many are the afflictions of the righteous, but the LORD rescues them from them all. He keeps all their bones; not one of them will be broken.

5. For a fuller discussion, see Strauss, *Distorting Scripture?*, 190–93.

Some interpreters have criticized the NRSV and other versions (see NLT; GNT; CEV; CEB; NJB) for pluralizing Psalm 34:20, claiming it distorts the individual application of this verse to Jesus in John 19:36. In this passage the soldiers break the legs of the two criminals crucified with Jesus to hasten their death, but when they come to Jesus, they find he has already died. The narrator notes that: "These things occurred so that the scripture might be fulfilled, 'None of his bones shall be broken'" (NRSV).

Does pluralizing the reference in Psalm 34:20 obscure this messianic prophecy? Two responses are in order. First, it is not at all certain that John 19:36 is referring to Psalm 34:20. Many commentators see instead an allusion to the Passover lamb, whose bones were not to be broken (Exod. 12:46; Num. 9:12). Even if we assume the reference is to Psalm 34:20, however, the plurals are not inaccurate. This is because this OT passage is being fulfilled *typologically* rather than uniquely by Jesus. In its original context, Psalm 34 is a psalm of righteous sufferers. This is clear in Psalm 34:18, which reads: "The LORD is near to the brokenhearted, and saves the crushed in spirit" (NRSV). The Hebrew text uses plurals here, confirming that the singulars in verses 19–20 are generic, referring to righteous sufferers generally. This is clearly how the Septuagint translators interpreted the psalm, since they used plurals throughout. Jesus fulfills this prophecy typologically rather than uniquely. He is the ultimate righteous sufferer.[6]

The same point can be made about Psalm 8:4, which the NRSV similarly pluralizes:

RSV what is man that thou art mindful of him, and the son of man that thou dost care for him?

NRSV what are human beings that you are mindful of them, mortals that you care for them?

Some have claimed that changing "man" to "human beings" and "son of man" to "mortals" distorts the individual application to Jesus in Hebrews 2:6–9. But this is missing the point of Psalm 8, which is to affirm the exalted status and ultimate destiny of human beings. "Son of man" is not a messianic title for Jesus here. It is a reference to humanity in general. The point made in Hebrews 2:6–9, then, is that through his life, death, and resurrection, Jesus fulfills the ultimate destiny of human beings.[7]

Summary

In this section we have discussed some of the more controversial issues related to gender-inclusive translation. Some versions have been criticized

6. See Strauss, *Distorting Scripture?*, 191–93.
7. See Strauss, *Distorting Scripture?*, 190–91.

for using gender-inclusive language across the board, even in some passages that likely originally referred only to men. Another debated issue is how to translate resumptive pronouns after a generic antecedent, since English does not have a gender-nonspecific singular pronoun. Of the various options discussed, the most common solution in contemporary English is the singular "they," which the NIV 2011 frequently introduces. Some critics have expressed concerns that language related to God will be feminized, but this would be a very different goal than that of gender accuracy. Similarly, language related to Jesus remains masculine in these versions, except in those places where his humanity is being referred to. Finally, there have been concerns expressed that messianic prophecies are muted when plural language is introduced. In response, advocates of gender-inclusive language point out that these passages are typologically, rather than uniquely, fulfilled by Christ.

REFLECTION QUESTIONS

1. When might it be inappropriate to introduce gender-inclusive language?

2. Why is it a challenge to translate resumptive pronouns in an inclusive manner? What solutions have been proposed?

3. How is language related to God treated in the gender-inclusive versions discussed here?

4. When does the author say it is appropriate to use gender-inclusive language with reference to Jesus?

5. Why does the author say plural pronouns are appropriate in certain messianic prophecies?

SECTION E

Issues of Style, Structure, and Format

Beyond the words themselves, translators must be concerned with a host of issues concerning the manner in which divisions of text are marked and words are presented.

QUESTION 21

How Do Translators Determine Chapters, Verses, Paragraphs, and Sections?

Today we cite biblical passages by their chapters and verses. It seems so natural to speak of "Jeremiah 29:11" or "John 3:16." We also refer positively to "verse-by-verse" exposition, meaning systematically teaching through a text; and to "know chapter and verse" means to have in-depth biblical knowledge. So it may surprise some to learn that the original books of the Bible did not contain chapters or verses.

Yet this should not be surprising, since the biblical writings were intended as normal human communication. We would not expect someone writing an email or letter to us to divide it into chapters and verses; nor would we expect someone writing a novel to number every line as a separate verse. While chapters and verses are essential for helping us to find things in the Bible, they can distract us from reading the text as it was intended to be read. Here we will look at chapters, verses, and other structural features that are added to the biblical text to mark divisions and to aid in the reading experience.

Ancient Chapter Divisions

The system of chapters used in Bibles today was not developed until the thirteenth century. Yet divisions of various kinds do appear in early texts. The Hebrew Masoretic Text (see Question 1) had various chapter-like divisions. Shorter units similar to paragraphs are called *parashoth*. These are clearly ancient, since manuscripts from the Dead Sea Scrolls have them (c. 250 BC–AD 50), although they are not always the same as the Masoretic divisions. Other somewhat longer chapter-like units are called *sedarim*.

These were used to mark off the three-year lectionary cycle for synagogue reading.[1]

Many ancient Greek manuscripts also have chapter-like divisions.[2] Codex Vaticanus (B), one of our earliest Greek manuscripts of the whole Bible (fourth century AD), has alphanumeric symbols (letters used for numbers—see chart below) in its margins dividing the text into various sections or chapters (Greek: *kephalaia*).[3] There are 170 sections in Matthew, 62 in Mark, 152 in Luke, and 50 in John. Codex Alexandrinus (A), a fifth-century manuscript, uses a different system, with marginal numbers dividing Matthew into 68 sections, Mark into 48, Luke into 83, and John into 18. These examples confirm that early copyists divided the text into numbered sections and that there were competing systems.

This is also evident in the book of Acts, where Codex Vaticanus includes two different numbering systems, one dividing the text into 36 chapters and the other into 69 chapters. The style of writing of the former system resembles the handwriting found in the Gospels and was likely added shortly after the manuscript was produced, while the latter was added by a later copyist. Codex Sinaiticus, the other great fourth-century majuscule manuscript, uses the 69-chapter scheme for the first half of Acts (chs. 1–15), but the numbering stops midway through the book. Perhaps the scribe got bored! Many manuscripts of Acts have a third system, dividing the book into 40 chapters.

In Codex Vaticanus, the New Testament Epistles also have two numbering systems, an older and a newer one. Interestingly, in the older schema the letters of Paul are numbered consecutively, treating the Pauline letters as a single corpus. So, for example, the last section of Romans is number "21" (Greek: KA´), and the first section of First Corinthians is number "22" (KB´).

Alphanumeric System

Chapters in early Greek manuscripts are commonly numbered using an alphanumeric system that was developed around the fourth century BC (sometimes called the Ionic system to distinguish it from the earlier Attic system). The chart below shows the value given to each letter. To illustrate, chapter 139 of Matthew in Codex Vaticanus is identified in the margin as section ΡΛΘ (100 + 30 + 9). A bar across the top of the letters indicates the use of an alphanumeric. This system required 27 letters, so the 24-letter Greek alphabet was expanded by using three archaic letters: digamma/wau Ϝ for 6, koppa Ϟ for 90, and sampi Ϡ for 900.

1. Ernst Würthwein, *The Text of the Old Testament* (Grand Rapids: Eerdmans, 1979), 20–21.
2. Bruce M. Metzger and Bart D. Ehrman, *The Text of the New Testament: Its Transmission, Corruption, and Restoration*, 4th ed. (New York: Oxford University Press, 2005), 34–36.
3. Photos of Codex Vaticanus have been digitized and can be examined at the Vatican library website: https://digi.vatlib.it/view/MSS_Vat.gr.1209?ling=en.

Greek Letter	Name	Numeric Value	Greek Letter	Name	Numeric Value	Greek Letter	Name	Numeric Value
Α	alpha	1	Ι	iota	10	Ρ	rho	100
Β	beta	2	Κ	kappa	20	Σ	sigma	200
Γ	gamma	3	Λ	lambda	30	Τ	tau	300
Δ	delta	4	Μ	mu	40	Υ	upsilon	400
Ε	epsilon	5	Ν	nu	50	Φ	phi	500
Ϝ	digamma/ wau	6	Ξ	xi	60	Χ	chi	600
Ζ	zeta	7	Ο	omicron	70	Ψ	psi	700
Η	eta	8	Π	pi	80	Ω	omega	800
Θ	theta	9	Ϟ	koppa	90	Ϡ	sampi	900

Modern Chapter Divisions

The chapters found in our Bible were first introduced into the Latin Vulgate by Stephen Langton (1150–1228), archbishop of Canterbury. These were transferred, with some modification, to the Hebrew text by Salomon ben Ishmael (1330).[4] Langton's divisions have sometimes been criticized for missing important conceptual divisions, and some have joked that he made the divisions while riding on horseback. This story actually has some historical basis, since Stephanus's son claimed that his father had made the verse divisions *inter equitandum* ("while riding") on a journey from Paris to Lyons. Yet Bruce Metzger suggests this does not mean "while on horseback" (bumping along) but rather that Langton did the work during his journey to Lyons, likely while resting at inns along the way.[5]

Verse Divisions

Verse divisions were added very early to the Hebrew text, although there was significant variation among different scribal centers. Standard verse divisions were established by the Masoretic scribal tradition of the family of Ben Asher around AD 900 and these are found in manuscripts like Codex Cairensis (895) and the Aleppo Codex (930). In this system verse divisions were indicated with a large colon (:) called a *sôph pāsûq*, meaning "end of the verse." The Hebrew Bible contains 23,100 of these verses.[6]

---

4. Paul Wegner, *The Journey from Texts to Translations: The Origin and Development of the Bible* (Grand Rapids: Baker, 1999), 174.
5. Bruce M. Metzger, *Manuscripts of the Greek Bible: An Introduction to Greek Palaeography* (Oxford: Oxford University Press, 1981), 41 note 106; Wegner, *Journey from Texts to Translations*, 174–75.
6. Wegner, *Journey from Texts to Translations*, 175.

Our modern Old Testament text generally follows these verse divisions, though with some variation. For example, in Hebrew the superscripts of the Psalms are treated as verse 1, while modern translations start numbering with the Psalm itself. So, for example, Psalm 4 has eight verses in the English text but nine verses in the Hebrew text, with verse 1 reading:

לַמְנַצֵּחַ בִּנְגִינוֹת מִזְמוֹר לְדָוִד

For the director of music. With stringed instruments. A psalm of David.

The New Testament verse divisions we have today were first introduced in 1551, in the fourth edition of the Greek New Testament published by Robert Estienne (1503–1559). Estienne's edition contained his Greek text with two Latin versions, the Vulgate on one side and Erasmus's Latin translation on the other. The first English New Testament to introduce verses was the edition produced by William Whittingham in 1557. The first full English Bible with verses was the Geneva Bible of 1560, also produced by Whittingham (see Question 24).[7] Subsequent versions adopted this system of numbering, and it has become the standard.

Sentences and Paragraphs

In normal prose writing today, we use sentences and paragraphs rather than verses to mark off divisions in the text. While a verse is a rather arbitrary division intended to help the reader find a place in the text, a sentence is meant to indicate a complete thought.[8] And a paragraph is one or more sentences that together comprise a single idea or theme. Older Bible versions, including the KJV and some of its revisions (cf. NASB; NKJV), set each verse apart as a separate paragraph. The problem with this is that it wrongly focuses on the verse, rather than the paragraph, as the natural unit of thought. These versions sometimes add a paragraph symbol (¶) to mark off paragraph divisions within the text.

Most contemporary versions use normal indented paragraph divisions and minimize the significance of verse divisions by putting verse numbers in smaller font and superscript within the text (see chart below). This has the advantage of emphasizing paragraphs as the primary sense units in the progress of the text.

---

7. Wegner, *Journey from Texts to Translations*, 211.
8. Defnitions of a "sentence" vary, but tend to focus on a group of words that express a complete thought. Dictionary.com defines it as "a grammatical unit of one or more words that expresses an independent statement, question, request, command, exclamation, etc., and that typically has a subject as well as a predicate" (https://www.dictionary.com/browse/sentence; accessed 3/1/2023).

Mark 1:14–20	
KJV	**NIV**
14 Now after that John was put in prison, Jesus came into Galilee, preaching the gospel of the kingdom of God, 15 And saying, The time is fulfilled, and the kingdom of God is at hand: repent ye, and believe the gospel. 16 Now as he walked by the sea of Galilee, he saw Simon and Andrew his brother casting a net into the sea: for they were fishers. 17 And Jesus said unto them, Come ye after me, and I will make you to become fishers of men. 18 And straightway they forsook their nets, and followed him. 19 And when he had gone a little further thence, he saw James the son of Zebedee, and John his brother, who also were in the ship mending their nets. 20 And straightway he called them: and they left their father Zebedee in the ship with the hired servants, and went after him.	14 After John was put in prison, Jesus went into Galilee, proclaiming the good news of God. 15 "The time has come," he said. "The kingdom of God has come near. Repent and believe the good news!" 16 As Jesus walked beside the Sea of Galilee, he saw Simon and his brother Andrew casting a net into the lake, for they were fishermen. 17 "Come, follow me," Jesus said, "and I will send you out to fish for people." 18 At once they left their nets and followed him. 19 When he had gone a little farther, he saw James son of Zebedee and his brother John in a boat, preparing their nets. 20 Without delay he called them, and they left their father Zebedee in the boat with the hired men and followed him.

A few Bibles have removed chapters and verses entirely, or have relegated them to the margins, to provide a more natural reading experience. Some of these include the Message (chapters but no verses); the Books of the Bible, an edition of the NIV published by Biblica (2011); and the ESV Reader's Bible (2016), published by Crossway.

Section Headings

Modern Bibles often add section headings to describe the topic or theme of that section and summarize its content. For example, the NIV has five headings for the first five chapters of Genesis, including "The Beginning," "Adam and Eve," "The Fall," "Cain and Abel," and "From Adam to Noah." These headings sometimes coincide with chapter divisions, but not always, since contemporary scholars and translators may not agree with the chapter divisions. For example, the heading "Adam and Eve" begins at chapter 2 verse 4. The NIV translators considered this a more natural break than chapter 2 verse 1.

Punctuation and Spacing

Our earliest Greek manuscripts have only occasional marks of punctuation. In fact, although there is some variation, ancient scribes writing Greek normally left no spaces between words, a style known as *scriptio continua*.[9] This is not as problematic as it might at first seem. If I wrote, "forgodsolovedtheworld," most readers would quickly recognize the first phrase of John 3:16, "For God so loved the world." Of course, confusion is also possible, as in the often-used example "godisnowhere," which could be read by a theist as "God is now here" and by an atheist as "God is nowhere." (Note that "a theist" and "atheist" are also merely a difference in spacing!) Metzger points to several examples of possible confusion in the Greek New Testament. For example, Mark 10:40 could be read in two different ways, depending on how it is spaced: "but it is for those for whom it has been prepared" (*all' hois ētoimastai*) or "it has been prepared for others" (*allois ētoimastai*).[10] During the sixth and seventh centuries, scribes began to use more punctuation, but still to a limited extent. According to Metzger, question marks were rarely used before the ninth century.[11]

Punctuation is used today in printed copies of the Greek New Testament, introduced by the editors to make the best sense of the text. Occasionally, differences in punctuation can change the sense of the text. A good example is John 1:3–4:

> *panta di' autou egeneto, kai chōris autou egeneto oude hen ho gegonen. en autō zoē ēn, kai hē zoē ēn to phōs tōn anthrōpōn.*
>
> All things came into being through him; and without him not one thing came into being that has come into being. In him was life, and the life was the light of all people.
>
> *panta di' autou egeneto, kai chōris autou egeneto oude hen. ho gegonen en auto zōē ēn, kai hē zōē ēn to phōs tōn anthrōpōn·*
>
> All things came into being through him; and without him not one thing came into being. What has come into being in him was life, and the life was the light of all people.

The difference here is the placement of the period, whether it should come before or after the relative clause "what/that has come into being" (*ho gegonen*).

---

9. Metzger and Ehrman, *Text of the New Testament*, 22.
10. Metzger and Ehrman, *Text of the New Testament*, 22. The first reading takes the Greek *ALLOIS* as two words, an adversative conjunction (*all'*, "but") and a relative pronoun in the dative case (*hois*, "for whom"). The second reading takes it as a single word, a substantival adjective in the dative case (*allois*, "for others").
11. Metzger and Ehrman, *Text of the New Testament*, 41.

While most English versions follow the former (see NIV; NASB; NKJV; NET; ESV), a significant minority follow the latter (NRSV; NLT; NAB; CEB).

Greek punctuation has some similarities and some differences to English punctuation. The Greek comma and period are the same, but a Greek semicolon is a raised dot, and a question mark is an English semicolon:

,	=	Greek comma
.	=	Greek period
·	=	Greek semicolon
;	=	Greek question mark

This issue of pronunciation, spacing, and other aids to reading is a very different issue for the Hebrew Masoretic text, which has a wide range of notes on orthography (spelling), pronunciation, and cantillation (chanting patterns for ritual readings). Hebrew also generally has spaces between words, something that is true for both the Masoretic Text and the much older Hebrew manuscripts of the Dead Sea Scrolls. For the Hebrew consonantal system, see Question 1.

Parentheses

English Bible translators sometimes use parentheses for the same reasons that other writers do, to set material off from the flow of the text. For example, in Mark 13:14, in the middle of Jesus's end-times discourse on the Mount of Olive, the CSB reads,

> "When you see the abomination of desolation standing where it should not be" (let the reader understand), "then those in Judea must flee to the mountains."

The parentheses are introduced by the CSB translators to indicate that these words are not part of Jesus's speech, but are a narrative aside introduced by the author, perhaps to point his readers to the fact that these events are unfolding in Jerusalem at that time. Many other versions do the same thing (see CEB; NLT; NRSV; ESV).

Another example of parentheses introduced by translators appears in Revelation 20:4–5. The NIV reads:

> 4 I saw thrones on which were seated those who had been given authority to judge. And I saw the souls of those who had been beheaded because of their testimony about Jesus and because

> of the word of God. They had not worshiped the beast or its image and had not received its mark on their foreheads or their hands. They came to life and reigned with Christ a thousand years. [5] (The rest of the dead did not come to life until the thousand years were ended.) This is the first resurrection.

The parentheses are introduced by the translators to set off the beginning of verse 5 as a narrative aside that interrupts the flow of thought. They are necessary because the next sentence, "This is the first resurrection," refers back to verse 4 and the resurrection that takes place *before the thousand years.* Without the parentheses, the statement would seem to be saying that "the rest of the dead" are raised in the first resurrection, when in fact they are raised in the second (see v. 13).[12]

Summary

The original texts of Scripture did not have chapter and verse divisions. These were added later to help readers find things. While various ancient manuscripts use different systems of divisions, the chapters used in our modern versions were first introduced into the Latin Vulgate by Stephen Langton, archbishop of Canterbury, in the thirteenth century. Verse divisions for the OT go back to the Masoretic text. New Testament verse divisions were first introduced by Robert Estienne into the fourth edition of his Greek NT in 1551. Sentence and paragraph divisions are introduced by modern editors to mark off natural units of thought. Section headings and punctuation are also the work of translators and editors.

REFLECTION QUESTIONS

1. Did ancient manuscripts ever have chapter divisions? What are some examples?

2. When and by whom were the chapter and verse divisions used in Bibles today first introduced?

3. How are verses different from sentences?

4. What do paragraphs mark off, and why are they important?

5. What are parentheses used for in modern Bible translations?

---

12. The NLT solves the problem in a simpler way, by moving the sentence "This is the first resurrection" before the parentheses.

QUESTION 22

What Challenges Arise in Translating Language Related to God?

In Exodus 3, the burning bush episode, Moses has an encounter with God where the Lord identifies himself as the God of Moses's ancestors, Abraham, Isaac, and Jacob, and tells him to return to Egypt and demand from Pharaoh to set God's people free. Moses responds that when he returns to the people of Israel, they will surely ask about the name of this God who sent him. God replies,

> I AM WHO I AM. This is what you are to say to the Israelites: "I AM has sent me to you." . . . Say to the Israelites, "The LORD, the God of your fathers—the God of Abraham, the God of Isaac and the God of Jacob—has sent me to you."
>
> This is my name forever,
> the name you shall call me
> from generation to generation. (Exod. 3:14–15 NIV)

The word translated LORD (with small caps) is the Hebrew word YHWH (יהוה), commonly pronounced "Yahweh." It is also known as the *Tetragrammaton*, which means "four letters," because it is made up of four Hebrew consonants. The name is etymologically related to the Hebrew phrase "I am," which may mean "the Pre-existent One." YHWH is especially God's covenant name for his chosen people Israel. The name appears 6,828 times in the Hebrew Bible.[1]

In Judaism, the name came to be viewed as so holy that it must not be spoken. Instead of reading it aloud, rabbis would replace the word with *hashem*, meaning "the Name," or would say *adonai*, meaning "Lord" or "Master."

1. This number comes from my search of the Hebrew word in *Biblia Hebraica* in Accordance Bible Software.

When vowel marks were introduced into the Hebrew text, the name YHWH was frequently pointed with the vowel marks for *adonai* to remind readers to substitute the word *adonai* in oral reading. Unfortunately, later translators, who were unaware of this substitution, read YHWH with the vowel marks for *adonai* and so mispronounced the divine name as "YaHoWaH" or "Jehovah." The American Standard Version, for example, uses this mispronunciation "Jehovah" as a translation for YHWH throughout.

The translators of the Septuagint (LXX), the Greek translation of the Hebrew Scriptures (see Question 23), followed the Jewish pattern of substituting YHWH with a general word for "Lord," and so translated YHWH with the Greek word *kyrios*, a common word for "Lord." So throughout the LXX, as well as in quotations of the Old Testament in the Greek New Testament, YHWH is translated as *kyrios*.

Most English versions follow this same pattern. Instead of transliterating the divine name as *Yahweh*, they translate it as "LORD." To distinguish it from *kyrios*, they use a capital with small caps "LORD" for Yahweh in the Old Testament and then use a capital with lower case "Lord" for *adonai* in the OT and for *kyrios* in the NT.

There are a few exceptions. For example, the King James Version used "Jehovah" four times, in Exodus 6:3, Psalm 83:18, Isaiah 12:2, and Isaiah 26:4. As noted above, the ASV used "Jehovah" throughout the OT, a total of 6,779 times. The New Jerusalem Bible uses "Yahweh" for YHWH throughout the Old Testament, a total of 6,342 times. The HCSB, by contrast, uses "Yahweh" selectively in the Old Testament, 654 times, or less than 10 percent of the 6,800 appearances of the Hebrew YHWH.[2] The introduction to the HCSB seeks to justify this partial use. It notes that while normally rendering YHWH (Yahweh) as "LORD,"

> the HCSB OT uses Yahweh, the personal name of God in Hebrew, when a biblical text emphasizes Yahweh as a name: "His name is Yahweh" (Ps 68:4). Yahweh is also used in places of His self-identification as in "I am Yahweh" (Is 42:8). Yahweh is used more often in the HCSB than in most Bible translations because the word LORD in English is a title of God and does not accurately convey to modern readers the emphasis on God's personal name in the original Hebrew.

The problem with this, of course, is the subjectivity in deciding which instances merit the use of "Yahweh" and which do not. The Christian Standard

2. The number 654 comes from my search of the 2009 edition of the HCSB in Logos Bible Software. My search of the 2003 edition in Accordance Bible Software resulted in 645 appearances.

Bible, the 2017 revision of the HCSB, returned to the traditional use of "LORD" for the Hebrew YHWH throughout.[3]

Using "Thees" and "Thous" in Prayer Language

In early modern English, second-person pronouns were distinguished according to their function and number. In the singular, "thou" was used for the subject, "thee" for the object, and "thy" (or "thine") for the possessive. So you would say, "*Thou* [subject] shalt protect *thy* [possessive] family." And, "They shall protect *thee* [object]." The plural forms were "ye" (subject), "you" (object), and "your(s)" (possessive). In the sixteenth and seventeenth centuries the English language simplified, and these different forms began to disappear, being replaced by "you" and "your(s)." When the King James Version was being translated (1611), "thee," "thou," "thy," and "ye" were already in decline, but were still common in formal writing, such as Bible translation. In the centuries that followed they disappeared almost completely.

In time the KJV became the standard English translation of the Bible, and its now archaic pronouns and accompanying verbs (like "shalt") came to indicate for many readers holy or sacred language. This sense of piety became so deeply entrenched in the English language that revisions of the KJV, while adopting contemporary pronouns elsewhere in the text, continued to use archaic pronouns and verb forms in contexts addressing God in prayer. For example, the Revised Version (RV) of 1885, the first major revision of the KJV, practiced this policy. Consider Matthew 26:39–41 RV. When Jesus prays to the Father he uses "thou," but when he speaks to Peter he uses "you":

> And going a little farther he fell on his face and prayed, "My Father, if it be possible, let this cup pass from me; nevertheless, not as I will, but as <u>thou wilt</u>."
>
> And he came to the disciples and found them sleeping; and he said to Peter, "So, could <u>you</u> not watch with me one hour? Watch and pray that <u>you</u> may not enter into temptation; the spirit indeed is willing, but the flesh is weak."

The ASV of 1901, the American counterpart to the RV, continued this practice, as did the 1952 RSV and the 1971 NASB. Only in the 1980s did this practice

---

3. Tom Schreiner, general editor of the CSB, gives four reasons for this change: (1) the inconsistency of usage in the HCSB; (2) the fully consistent translation of יהוה as "Yahweh" (more than six thousand times) would overwhelm readers; (3) the unfamiliarity of Yahweh trips up readers; and (4) the pattern of the New Testament, like the LXX, is to use the title *kyrios* ("Lord") rather than a personal name "Yahweh" (Thomas R. Schreiner, "Q&A: Translation Decisions for the Christian Standard Bible," Christian Standard Bible, January 2017, https://csbible.com/wp-content/uploads/2017/01/Translation-Decisions-QA.pdf, p. 2).

begin to disappear. The NKJV (1982) uses "you" and "your(s)" throughout, as does the NRSV (1989) and the ESV (2001). While the 1995 NASB continued to use thees and thous, the 2020 has finally dropped them.

The strongest argument for dropping them in contemporary English versions is that the original languages have no special forms for the second-person pronouns. To introduce this language into translations is to artificially introduce archaisms into the biblical text.

Capitalizing Pronouns for Deity

As in the case of using thees and thous in prayer, capitalizing pronouns for God is commonly viewed as a way to show reverence for the divine. Psalm 95:2 NKJV reads, "Let us come before His presence with thanksgiving; Let us shout joyfully to Him with psalms." Notice that while the pronoun "us" is not capitalized because it refers to human beings, the pronouns "His" and "Him" are capitalized because they refer to God. This practice has become so commonplace in religious writing that I have students express concern when they come across Bible versions that do not use capitals for God or for Jesus Christ.

But, in fact, the practice of capitalizing pronouns for God is a relatively recent phenomenon. The King James Version, for example, did not do so. Psalm 95:2 in the KJV reads, "Let us come before his presence with thanksgiving, and make a joyful noise unto him with psalms." Most modern versions have followed suit. One of the first versions to introduce capitalized pronouns for God was Young's Literal Translation of 1862. Today, only a few major versions continue this tradition. These include the Amplified Bible, NASB, NKJV, and HCSB. The CSB, the 2017 revision of the HCSB, returned all pronouns to lowercase. Among the many contemporary versions that do *not* capitalize pronouns are RSV, NRSV, ESV, CSB, NIV, NET, CEB, NEB, REB, NLT, GNT, NCV, GW, CEV, JB, NJB, NAB, and others. There are a variety of reasons for this:

(1) The early Hebrew and Greek alphabets did not contain capital letters, so the original manuscripts did not capitalize any pronouns. This confirms, at the least, that *not* capitalizing pronouns does not indicate a lack of reverence for God. The original inspired text did not capitalize them.

(2) Most English stylebooks advise against capitalizing pronouns. While the church is certainly not bound by such stylebooks, we generally want our translations to follow good English style with reference to punctuation, grammar, and syntax.

(3) Capitalizing pronouns with reference to Jesus in the New Testament can create confusion and even mistranslation. This is because a capitalized pronoun suggests that the person speaking considers Jesus to be God. But this is not always the case. For example, in John 19:7 NASB, the Jewish leaders of Jerusalem argue with the governor Pontius Pilate about Jesus: "The Jews answered him, 'We have a law, and by that law <u>He</u> ought to die, because <u>He</u> made <u>Himself</u> out to be the Son of God!'" Capitalizing "He" and "Himself" suggests

that these Jewish leaders consider Jesus to be divine. But in fact they are denying this very thing! The capitalization confuses the meaning of the text.

(4) Similar problems arise with Old Testament messianic prophecies. Consider three OT passages that are identified in the NT as fulfilled by Christ:

Psalm 2:7 (Acts 13:33)

NKJV You are My Son, Today I have begotten You.
NASB He said to Me, 'You are My Son, Today I have fathered You.
HCSB He said to Me, "You are My Son; today I have become Your Father.

Psalm 16:10 (Acts 2:27)

NKJV For You will not leave my soul in Sheol
NASB For You will not abandon my soul to Sheol
HCSB For You will not abandon me to Sheol

Psalm 22:1 (Mark 15:34)

NKJV My God, My God, why have You forsaken Me?
NASB My God, my God, why have You forsaken me?
HCSB My God, my God, why have You forsaken me?

Notice the inconsistencies. While all the pronouns related to God the Father are capitalized, some of the ones referring to Jesus are not. In Psalm 2:7, all three versions capitalize "You/Your." But in Psalm 16:10, none of them capitalize "me/my." In Psalm 22:1, the NKJV capitalizes "Me" but the NASB and HCSB do not. The problem here is that while all these passages were "fulfilled" by Christ, some are fulfilled *typologically* rather than uniquely (see Question 20). In the original psalm, the referent might be one of the kings from David's line or an unnamed righteous sufferer. Jesus fulfills the prophecy typologically because he is the last and greatest of the Davidic kings and the ultimate righteous sufferer. The versions are in a quandary because capitalizing the pronoun might incorrectly suggest that the original human referent is divine.

For all these reasons, it seems best to follow the now standard practice of keeping all pronouns in the lowercase.

Red-Letter Editions of the Bible

Another issue related to God language in the Bible concerns so-called red-letter editions, where the words of Jesus are printed in red. As with archaic "thees" and "thous" and capitalized pronouns, this practice is sometimes viewed as sacrosanct, and any attempt to depart from it is viewed by some as sacrilege. Yet, as in the case of these other practices, red-letter editions are a relatively recent phenomenon—first appearing at the turn of the twentieth century—and without ancient precedent.

The idea of printing the words of Jesus in red was first conceived by Louis Klopsch (1852–1910), editor of the *Christian Herald* magazine.[4] Klopsch had a passion for publishing and distributing Bibles, and in 1899 he published a New Testament with the words of Christ in red, entitled *The New Testament . . . With All the Words Recorded Therein, as Having Been Spoken by Our Lord, Printed in Color*. Two years later, in 1901, he published a full Bible, *The Holy Bible: Red Letter Edition*. In this edition he not only printed the words of Christ in the New Testament in red, but also Old Testament prophecies which were spoken by him or which referred to him. Klopsch chose red because his original inspiration came from Luke 22:20, "This cup is the new covenant in my blood, which is poured out for you." As the color of Christ's blood, red served as a symbol of his great sacrifice and our salvation. In the introduction to his Red Letter Edition, Klopsch wrote:

> Modern Christianity is striving zealously to draw nearer to the great Founder of the Faith. Setting aside mere human doctrines and theories regarding Him, it presses close to the Divine Presence, to gather from His own lips the definition of His mission to the world and His own revelation of the Father. . . . The Red Letter Bible has been prepared and issued in the full conviction that it will meet the needs of the student, the worker, and the searchers after truth everywhere.[5]

The success of Klopsch's work inspired others, and many publishers quickly followed suit with their own red-letter editions. While Klopsch's Bible was no doubt inspired by a passion for Jesus and a love for God's Word, nevertheless this practice of singling out Jesus's words has some deficiencies of its own:

(1) A red-letter edition may suggest that the words of Christ have greater authority than the rest of Scripture. Yet, *all Scripture* is God-breathed and has equal authority (2 Tim. 3:16–17). We should beware of creating a canon within the canon, where certain words are viewed as more valuable than others.

---

4. This material was taken from Steve Eng, "The Story Behind: Red Letter Bible Editions," *Bible Collectors' World*, January/March 1986, International Society of Bible Collectors, http://www.biblecollectors.org/articles/red_letter_bible.htm; Charles M. Pepper, *Life-Work of Louis Klopsch* (New York: Christian Herald, 1910); Robert W. Funk, Roy W. Hoover, et al., *The Five Gospels* (New York: Macmillan, 1993), 37; Philip Sellew, "Red Letter Bible," in *The Oxford Companion to the Bible*, eds. Bruce M. Metzger and Michael D. Coogan (New York: Oxford University, 1993), 619.
5. Louis Klopsch, "Explanatory Note," in *The Holy Bible: Red Letter Edition* (New York: Christian Herald, 1901), xvi.

(2) Why are the words of Jesus given special emphasis, but the words of God the Father and the Holy Spirit are not? Shouldn't these be printed in a distinct color (perhaps purple for royalty) since their authority is just as great as that of Jesus?

(3) The words of Jesus in the Gospels are in fact the words of the inspired and authoritative evangelists—Matthew, Mark, Luke, and John. *They* are the inspired authors, who remembered, translated, interpreted, summarized, explained, and arranged Jesus's words into a Spirit-inspired account of his ministry. The actual (Aramaic) words of Jesus are for the most part unknown to us. But we believe that the Spirit guided these four to write the true and authoritative Word of God. This means that the narrative around Jesus's words, as well as the narrative comments and explanations made by the evangelists themselves, have just as much authority as the quoted words of Jesus.

Summary

Translating the divine name YHWH can be a challenge for translators. Since the Jews would not utter the name because of its holiness, the Greek Septuagint translated it as *kyrios*, meaning "Lord." Most modern versions follow this model, translating the name as "LORD," with small caps. A few versions use "Yahweh" (NJB; HCSB [sometimes]) or "Jehovah" (ASV). Some versions use archaic pronouns like "thee" and "thou" followed by archaic verb forms when addressing God or referring to him in prayer. Though meant to indicate piety, there is no precedence for this in the original text of Scripture. The same is true of capitalizing pronouns for God and for printing the words of Jesus in red letters.

REFLECTION QUESTIONS

1. What difficulties arise in translating the divine name YHWH? How do most versions render it?

2. Why do some versions use archaic pronouns and verb forms in prayer language? When did this practice begin?

3. Why do some versions capitalize pronouns for deity? When did this practice begin? What are some arguments for and against this practice?

4. Why do some versions print the words of Jesus in red? When did this practice begin? What are some arguments for and against this practice?

5. What is your own opinion on the various practices discussed in this chapter?

PART 4

The History of (English) Bible Translation

QUESTION 23

What Were the Earliest Translations of the Bible?

Ancient Jewish Versions of Scripture

Although Jesus accused the Pharisees of crossing land and sea to make a single convert (Matt. 23:15), there is little evidence for widespread proselytizing by the Jews of antiquity. Jewish translations of the Hebrew Bible were not generally initiated for evangelistic purposes, but rather to provide the Scriptures for Jews who no longer spoke Hebrew. This was certainly the case for the first two languages into which the Bible was translated, Greek and Aramaic.

The Greek Septuagint

The first and most important translation of the Hebrew Bible is the Greek version known as the Septuagint, probably beginning to be translated in the mid-third century BC. The name "Septuagint" comes from the Latin *septuaginta*, meaning "seventy," a rounded-off reference to the legend that seventy-two scholars translated the work in seventy-two days. The Septuagint is commonly abbreviated as "LXX," the Roman numeral for "seventy."

The account of its origin comes from the *Letter of Aristeas*, an ancient document that purports to be a letter from a man named Aristeas to his "brother" (or friend) Philocrates. It recounts how, during the reign of the Egyptian king Ptolemy II Philadelphus (284–247 BC), Demetrius, the chief librarian of the great library of Alexandria, sent a request to Eleazar, the Jewish high priest in Jerusalem, to produce a Greek translation of the Torah, the great Jewish book of law. Eleazar sent seventy-two scholars, six from each of the twelve tribes, with Hebrew Torah scrolls to Egypt to do the work. According to the letter, the work was completed in seventy-two days and then read to the Jewish community in Alexandria, who rejoiced at its accuracy. In light of the divine providence behind its production, the priests and elders pronounced a curse on anyone who would change the text in any way.

Today most scholars consider the *Letter of Aristeas* to be a pseudonymous document written near the end of the second century BC, a hundred years after the events it describes. Its primary purpose seems to be apologetic, a theological defense of Judaism as a religion and more specifically of the Septuagint as a translation.

While the details of the story are probably legendary,[1] it may contain a kernel of truth. A Greek translation of the Pentateuch was probably produced in Alexandria in the middle of the third century BC, perhaps during the reign of Ptolemy II Philadelphus. Following the conquests of Alexander the Great (fourth century BC), Greek had become the *lingua franca* of much of the Eastern Mediterranean. Most Jews of the Diaspora no longer spoke Hebrew, resulting in the need for a Greek translation of the Hebrew Scriptures. The Torah was likely translated first, and the rest of the Hebrew Bible (the Prophets and the Writings) followed over the next century.

The LXX is a mixed translation, sometimes more literal, sometimes more free.[2] Like the Hebrew Scriptures and the Greek New Testament, it also has its own textual history of transmission and recension. The influence of the Septuagint runs in two directions. On the one hand, it was shaped by the Judaism of its day and so helps us to understand the theological milieu leading up to the time of Christ. On the other hand, the Septuagint itself shaped Judaism and early Christianity. For example, the LXX helped to bridge the gap between Jews and Gentiles by expanding the meaning of Greek words to include Hebrew concepts. For example, in classical Greek, the term *doxa* generally carried the sense of "opinion." By using this word to translate the Hebrew word *kevod*, the LXX emphasized the sense of divine "glory." In this way the LXX helped introduce a Jewish worldview into the Greek world and gave the Christians a ready-made vocabulary for preaching a message whose foundations lay in Judaism and the Hebrew Scriptures.

The LXX provided the early Christians with a Bible that was understandable throughout the Mediterranean world. Christians could use it when preaching to both Jews and Gentiles. It thus became a powerful apologetic tool for the early church. Most Old Testament quotations in the NT are taken from the LXX. An example of this apologetic value may be seen in Isaiah 7:14, where the Hebrew term *'almah* ("young woman") was translated in the LXX as *parthenos*, a Greek term with strong connotations of virginity (cf. Matt. 1:23). Using the LXX, Christians could point to this Old Testament text as evidence for the virgin birth of Christ.

---

1. The account of the story became even more fanciful over time. The first-century Alexandrian Jewish philosopher Philo recounts a version whereby all the scholars working independently produced an identical Greek text—proof positive of the text's divine inspiration! See Karen Jobes and Moisés Silva, *Invitation to the Septuagint* (Grand Rapids: Baker, 2000), 36; Sidney Jellicoe, *The Septuagint and Modern Study* (Oxford: Clarendon, 1968), 38–47.
2. Ernst Würthwein, *The Text of the Old Testament* (Grand Rapids: Eerdmans, 1979), 51–53.

Other Greek Versions

Three Greek versions of note followed the Septuagint, those of Aquila, Symmachus, and Theodotion.[3] Aquila of Sinope was a convert to Christianity, who later converted to Judaism and became a disciple of the famous Rabbi Akiba. Around AD 130 Aquila produced a highly literal Greek version of the Hebrew Scriptures, whose primary purpose may have been to challenge the Septuagint's dominance. No copies of the full version have survived, although many of its readings are known to us from Origen's *Hexapla* (see below).

Sometime in the late second or early third century, Symmachus produced a new Greek version, which Jerome praised as more elegant and clear than the literal version of Aquila. According to Eusebius and Jerome, Symmachus was an Ebionite (a Jewish-Christian sect), although Epiphanius claims he was a Samaritan who had converted to Judaism. Only fragments of this work remain.

Somewhere between the literal work of Aquila and the idiomatic work of Symmachus was the Greek translation of Theodotion, whose second-century translation was evidently a revision of an earlier Greek translation, though whether this was the Septuagint or another version is unclear. Early church tradition claimed Theodotion was a convert to Judaism from Ephesus, although Jerome identifies him as an Ebionite.

These three Greek versions are known to us primarily because of the monumental work of scholarship known as the *Hexapla*, compiled by Origen, the third-century scholar and theologian (c. 186–253).[4] Origen's *Hexapla* (produced c. 230–45) was a six-column edition of the Old Testament, with columns dedicated, respectively, to (1) the Hebrew text; (2) a Greek transliteration of the Hebrew; (3) the translation of Aquila; (4) the translation of Symmachus; (5) Origen's own revision of the Septuagint; and (6) the edition of Theodotion. The whole work was massive, comprising more than 6,500 pages in fifteen volumes.[5] Kept in Caesarea, the manuscripts were probably never copied fully and were likely destroyed in the Arab invasions of the early seventh century. Only parts of the work are preserved, appearing in various authors who utilized Origen's work.

The Aramaic Targums

During and after the Babylonian exile, Aramaic gradually replaced Hebrew as the language of the Jewish people (see Question 1). For this reason, readings from the Hebrew Scriptures in the synagogues were usually followed

3. Würthwein, *Text of the Old Testament*, 53–55.
4. Paul Wegner, *The Journey from Texts to Translations: The Origin and Development of the Bible* (Grand Rapids: Baker, 1999), 198–99; Würthwein, *Text of the Old Testament*, 55–57; D. C. Parker, "Hexapla of Origen, The," *Anchor Yale Bible Dictionary* (New York: Doubleday, 1992), 188–89.
5. Parker, "Hexapla," 188–89.

by a *targum*, an Aramaic translation or paraphrase of the Hebrew text, provided by an interpreter (*meturgeman*). These Aramaic readings, or *targumim*, were written down over time and formalized. While some targums are very literal, others are paraphrastic interpretations, providing insight into how the Hebrew text was applied by the rabbis of that day. For example, the Targum of Jonathan ben Uzziel on the Prophets interprets the fourth Servant Song, Isaiah 52:13–53:12, as referring to the Messiah, but interprets the suffering as applying to the nation Israel.[6] Unfortunately, the traditions found in the targums can be very difficult to date, and so the beliefs expressed in them are difficult to identify with specific Jewish communities.

Early Christian Versions of Scripture

As a missionary religion, Christianity sought to proclaim the gospel to the ends of the earth. This created a need to render God's Word into the diverse languages of the world. With the dawn of Christianity, the age of Bible translation began in earnest.

Old Latin Versions and the Vulgate

The term "Old Latin" refers to a variety of Latin versions that were produced prior to the translation of the Vulgate. These were likely first produced in the late second or early third centuries, perhaps in Carthage, and circulated in North Africa, Italy, Gaul, and Spain. Most were translations from the Greek, often very woodenly, and some may have begun as interlinear readings in Greek manuscripts.[7] Their diversity and low quality caused Augustine to complain that it seemed that anyone who got his hands on a Greek manuscript of the NT would translate it into Latin, no matter how little they knew of either language! Jerome similarly (and hyperbolically) complained that there were almost as many Latin versions as there were manuscript copies.[8] While Tertullian of Carthage (c. 160–220) wrote in Latin, his biblical quotes appear to be translated directly from the Greek. The first evidence of the use of a Latin text comes from Cyprian of Carthage (c. 200–258), and the Bible of St. Augustine of Hippo (354–430) was almost certainly the Old Latin.[9] Old Latin manuscripts are identified with a lowercase "it" and a superscript identifying the manuscript: it^{a}, it^{b}, it^{c}, it^{d}.

The inconsistencies found in the Old Latin called for a revision, and in AD 382 Pope Damasus I commissioned the early church father Jerome (c.

---

6. Wegner, *Journey from Texts to Translations*, 202–3.
7. Bruce M. Metzger and Bart D. Ehrman, *The Text of the New Testament: Its Transmission, Corruption, and Restoration*, 4th ed. (New York: Oxford University Press, 2005), 101.
8. Kurt Aland and Barbara Aland, *The Text of the New Testament*, 2nd ed., trans. Errol F. Rhodes (Grand Rapids: Baker, 1989), 187.
9. Aland and Aland, *Text of the New Testament*, 187; Wegner, *Journey from Texts to Translations*, 251.

345–420), the leading biblical scholar of his day, to produce a new Latin edition. This version, known today as the Vulgate (the "common" version), was destined to become the official Bible of the Roman Catholic Church. Jerome produced a copy of the Gospels within a year and followed this with a translation of the Psalms. Scholars debate whether the rest of the New Testament was also translated at this time and what role Jerome played in its production.[10] Eventually, recognizing the need to translate the Old Testament directly from the Hebrew, Jerome moved to Bethlehem and continued his work there under the tutelage of Jewish rabbis. He completed the Old Testament around AD 405.

Jerome famously spoke of his work as both a labor of love and a perilous and presumptuous endeavor. In a letter to Damasus in the preface to the four Gospels, he writes:

> You urge me to revise the old Latin version, and, as it were, to sit in judgment on the copies of the Scriptures which are now scattered throughout the whole world; and, inasmuch as they differ from one another, you would have me decide which of them agree with the Greek original. The labour is one of love, but at the same time both perilous and presumptuous; for in judging others I must be content to be judged by all; and how can I dare to change the language of the world in its hoary old age, and carry it back to the early days of its infancy? Is there a man, learned or unlearned, who will not, when he takes the volume into his hands, and perceives that what he reads does not suit his settled tastes, break out immediately into violent language, and call me a forger and a profane person for having the audacity to add anything to the ancient books, or to make any changes or corrections therein?[11]

Since the Septuagint was generally considered the "real Bible," Jerome faced severe criticism for using the Hebrew text for his Old Testament. Yet the Vulgate weathered this criticism and by the eighth or ninth centuries had gained ascendancy over the Old Latin. It wasn't until the Council of Trent in 1546, however, that the Vulgate was declared to be the only true and authentic Bible of the Roman Catholic Church.

---

10. Metzger and Ehrman, *Text of the New Testament*, 105.
11. Philip Schaff and Henry Wace, eds., *Jerome: Select Works and Letters*, vol. 6 of A Select Library of the Nicene and Post-Nicene Fathers of the Christian Church, Second Series, Accordance electronic ed. (New York: Christian Literature, 1890), para. 41, 489.

Syriac (Aramaic) Versions, Including the Peshitta

Syriac, also known as Syrian Aramaic, is the name given to a version of Aramaic that emerged in the first century and became the main literary language of Christian communities living in Syria and throughout the Near East. Syriac flourished from the fourth to the eighth centuries as a liturgical language for Christians of the East as far away as India and even China.

In much the same way that the disparate Old Latin versions gave way to the standardized Vulgate, so in the fifth century a standard Syriac version, the Peshitta, was produced. When the Syrian Church split in AD 431, two major recensions emerged, the Eastern (Nestorian) and the Western (Jacobite). Scholars debate whether the OT of the Peshitta was originally produced by Jews or Christians.[12] The former is likely, since the OT seems to have been translated from the Hebrew text and influenced by the Aramaic targums. Yet the text was apparently revised in later centuries using the Septuagint. Another debate swirls around the NT Gospels. Since Jesus spoke Aramaic, some have claimed that the Aramaic recorded here are the original words of Jesus. This, however, is unlikely, since the NT Peshitta is a fifth-century translation from the Greek, with no direct link to the Aramaic spoken by Jesus.[13]

Coptic Versions

Coptic refers to a group of related dialects that descended from the ancient Egyptian language. Although Greek became the common language for trade and diplomacy in Egypt following the conquests of Alexander the Great in the fourth century BC, Coptic remained the language of everyday discourse. As Christianity spread to Egypt, missionary translations of the New Testament were produced in Coptic. Most Coptic manuscripts are in two major dialects, the Sahidic of Upper (southern) Egypt, a version likely translated in the early third century, and the Bohairic of Lower (northern) Egypt, of uncertain date, though perhaps from the fourth century.[14] Both tend to follow the Alexandrian text type.

Although Arabic replaced Coptic as the primary spoken language of Egypt following the Muslim conquests of the seventh century AD, Coptic remains today as the liturgical language of the Coptic Orthodox Church.

Armenian and Georgian Versions

In a number of places, no written version of a language existed, and so Christian missionaries had first to produce alphabets before translating the Scriptures. According to tradition, St. Mesrop (361–439), a soldier turned

---

12. Würthwein, *Text of the Old Testament*, 80–81.
13. F. F. Bruce, *The Books and the Parchments*, 5th ed. (London: Marshall Pickering, 1991), 190; Wegner, *Journey from Texts to Translations*, 244.
14. Metzger and Ehrman, *Text of the New Testament*, 110–12.

missionary, developed a new alphabet for the Armenian language around AD 406 and, with the help of others, translated the Bible into Armenian. The Armenian version is sometimes called the "queen of the versions" because of its beauty and accuracy.[15]

The first versions in Georgian, the unique language of the rugged region north of Armenia in the Caucasus Mountains, were probably produced in the fifth century either from the Armenian or Old Syriac versions. Armenian tradition ascribes both the Georgian alphabet and this first Bible version to the same Mesrop who translated the Armenian version.[16]

Old Slavonic Versions

Perhaps the most famous example of alphabet-creating and language-shaping missionaries are the brothers Cyril and Methodius, the "apostles to the Slavs."[17] Sons of a wealthy official in Salonica (Thessalonica), the brothers learned the Slavonic language from immigrants who had settled there from Eastern Europe. Sent by the eastern emperor Michael III to evangelize the Moravians, the brothers trained clergy and translated the Bible. Their translation work not only became the basis for versions into a variety of Slavonic languages, but Cyril is credited with creating the Glagolitic and Cyrillic alphabets, the latter still used today for Russian and other languages across Eurasia.

Ethiopic Versions

While some church traditions attribute the evangelization of ancient Ethiopia (also called Abyssinia) to the Ethiopian eunuch of Acts 8, others attribute the church there to the work of the apostles Matthew or Bartholomew. In any case, inscriptions of King Ezana confirm the establishment of Christianity there by the mid-fourth century. While our earliest Ethiopic NT manuscripts come from the tenth century, the text was likely translated first in the fifth or six centuries.

Summary

The earliest translations of the Hebrew Scriptures were the Greek Septuagint and the Aramaic targums. Both were produced in contexts where Jews no longer spoke Hebrew and needed the Scriptures in their new languages. Early versions produced by Christians arose in missionary contexts, as the gospel advanced to new cultures and languages. The most important early versions were translations into Latin, Syriac, Coptic, Armenian, Georgian, Slavonic, and Ethiopic.

---

15. Metzger and Ehrman, *Text of the New Testament*, 117.
16. Wegner, *Journey from Texts to Translations*, 48; Aland and Aland, *Text of the New Testament*, 205, 209.
17. Metzger and Ehrman, *Text of the New Testament*, 121–22.

REFLECTION QUESTIONS

1. Why were new translations of the Bible into Greek and Aramaic necessary for the Jews?
2. What was the primary reason the early Christians translated Scripture?
3. What is the Septuagint? When and where was it likely translated?
4. What significance did the Septuagint have for Judaism? For the early church?
5. What is the story behind the translation of the Latin Vulgate?

QUESTION 24

What Were the Earliest English Translations of the Bible?

Although Christianity arrived in Britain during the Roman period, in the early fourth century, we have no records of vernacular Bible translations from that period. The language of the old British church was Latin. The Germanic invasions of the Angles, Saxons, and Jutes in the fifth century mostly wiped out Christianity in Britain. It wasn't until Pope Gregory the Great sent monks to England in AD 597 and the Irish monk Columba evangelized Scotland that Christianity was once again established in the British Isles.

The Bible in Old English (Anglo-Saxon)

The earliest known Christian literature written in Old English are the poems of Caedmon, written around AD 670. These did not contain the biblical text, but stories from the Bible put to verse for recitation and singing. The earliest known Scripture text in Old English was a translation of the Psalms said to have been produced by Aldhelm, bishop of Sherborne in Dorset, sometime around AD 700. The Venerable Bede (673–735), the scholar and Benedictine monk whose *Ecclesiastical History of the English People* earned him the title "the father of English history," is said to have translated several portions of the NT into Old English. Unfortunately, none of these have survived. The English king Alfred the Great (871–901), a scholar in his own right, translated Bede's *Ecclesiastical History* and other great works into Old English. He also produced a law code, which he introduced with English translations of several great legal sections of the Bible, including the Ten Commandments, the Book of the Covenant from Exodus 21–23, the letter from the Jerusalem Council in Acts 15:23–29, and the Golden Rule.[1]

1. F. F. Bruce, *History of the Bible in English: From the Earliest Versions*, 3rd ed. (New York: Oxford University Press, 1978), 6–7.

Other examples of vernacular translations from this time include interlinear glosses in Old English added to Latin manuscripts. Most famous is the Lindisfarne Gospels, an illuminated Latin manuscript of the Gospels written by Bishop Eadfrith of Lindisfarne near the end of the seventh century. A tenth-century monk named Aldred added a literal English rendering between the lines of the Latin. The work is now housed in the British Museum. F. F. Bruce notes other versions from this period. The Wessex Gospels from the mid-tenth century is the oldest surviving independent (non-interlinear) version of the Gospels. Later in the tenth century, the abbot Aelfric of Eynsham in Oxfordshire produced a translation of the first seven books of the OT as well as homilies that incorporate other portions of the OT.[2]

The Norman Conquest of England in 1066 mostly ended this period of translation into English for the next three centuries. Norman French replaced Anglo-Saxon among the upper class and Latin was the language of the Norman-controlled church. Old English gradually disappeared as a literary language.

John Wycliffe (1382/1388)

The first full Bible to be translated into English was produced under the direction of John Wycliffe (c. 1330–1384). Wycliffe, a leading Oxford theologian, is known as "the Morningstar of the Reformation" because of his progressive views on the authority of Scripture and his denial of papal authority. Wycliffe believed the Bible was the sole authority for Christian doctrine, superior to any ecclesiastical office or authority, and that it should be available to all Christians everywhere. These views, a hundred and fifty years before the Protestant Reformation, were radical in the church of his day and made Wycliffe many enemies. In 1382 he was brought before a synod in London, and his essays and sermons were condemned as heretical. Wycliffe's powerful position protected him from personal harm, but not from hatred and slander. Sir Thomas More would later refer to Wycliffe as the "great arch-heretic" who undertook "of a malicious purpose" to translate the Bible into English and "purposely corrupted the holy text."[3] Many of Wycliffe's followers were harassed and imprisoned. Some were burned at the stake. In 1408 a synod of clergy at Oxford ruled that no one could translate or even read a vernacular version of the Bible without church approval. In 1428, forty-three years after Wycliffe's death, Pope Martin V ordered that his remains be dug up and burned.[4]

Two editions of the Bible are associated with Wycliffe's name, though how much of the actual translation work he did is uncertain. The first edition came out prior to his death in 1382. It was a very wooden, literal version,

---

2. Bruce, *History of the Bible in English*, 7–11.
3. Cited by Bruce, *History of the Bible in English*, 22.
4. Bruce M. Metzger, *The Bible in Translation: Ancient and English Versions* (Grand Rapids: Baker, 2001), 57.

translated from the Latin Vulgate rather than the Hebrew or Greek texts. A second, more idiomatic version was published around 1388 by his secretary, John Purvey, after Wycliffe's death. Purvey not only improved the quality of the translation but also consulted a variety of Vulgate manuscripts to improve its textual basis. Since it was produced before the invention of the printing press, the text had to be hand-copied. Nevertheless, it had a significant influence both among Wycliffe's followers and with the general public. About 180 manuscripts of the whole or part of Wycliffe's Bible survive today.[5]

William Tyndale (1526/1534)

William Tyndale (c. 1494–1536) has the distinction of producing the first printed edition of the New Testament into English, as well as the first English version translated directly from the Greek. Two landmark events paved the way for Tyndale's work: the invention of the printing press and movable type by Johannes Gutenberg around 1450; and the first printed edition of the Greek New Testament, produced by the scholar Erasmus in 1516. Tyndale had studied at both Oxford and Cambridge and was proficient in Hebrew and Greek. Like Wycliffe before him, Tyndale was passionate about God's Word and believed it should be available to all people everywhere.

When Tyndale faced opposition to his work in England, he moved to Germany in 1524, where the Protestant Reformers had more freedom to produce vernacular versions. Luther's German NT had been published in 1522 and the complete Bible in German would be finished in 1534. When Tyndale finished his English NT in 1525 or 1526, copies were smuggled into England. The bishop of London is said to have purchased as many copies as he could to burn them. But Tyndale used the royalties to revise the text and publish more copies.

Tyndale continued his work and by 1530 had finished translating the first five books of the Old Testament. He also evidently translated the historical books from Joshua through 2 Chronicles. Though not published during his lifetime, these were incorporated into Matthew's Bible of 1537 (see below). Tyndale produced a second edition of the NT in 1534. It is this one that is considered the standard Tyndale New Testament.

While Tyndale pushed forward, his enemies relentlessly pursued him. In 1535 he was kidnapped from his home in Antwerp, imprisoned in a fortress near Brussels, and tried for heresy. On October 6, 1536, he was executed by strangulation and his body was burned. Tyndale's last words were reputed to be "Lord, open the king of England's eyes."[6]

Tyndale's version was a great improvement in accuracy and English style over that of Wycliffe. Though condemned by Tyndale's opponents, the version

---

5. Bruce, *History of the Bible in English*, 12–23; Metzger, *Bible in Translation*, 56–58.
6. Bruce, *History of the Bible in English*, 24–52 (quote on p. 52; from Foxe's *Book of Martyrs*).

captured the hearts of the people and became the basis for most English versions that followed. Its widespread use also became a key factor in the growing acceptance of vernacular versions by the reading public. J. Isaacs writes:

> Tindale's honesty, sincerity, and scrupulous integrity, his simple directness, his magical simplicity of phrase, his modest music, have given an authority to his wording that has imposed itself on all later versions. With all the tinkering to which the New Testament has been subject, Tindale's version is still the basis in phrasing, rendering, vocabulary, rhythm, and often in music as well. Nine-tenths of the Authorized New Testament is still Tindale, and the best is still his.[7]

The Coverdale Version (1535)

Miles Coverdale (1488–1569) has the distinction of producing the first complete Bible printed in English. Wycliffe's version had been hand-copied, not printed, and Tyndale had not completed a full edition of the Bible by the time of his death. Coverdale, who was educated at Cambridge, developed a passion for biblical studies and, like Tyndale, spent much of his life seeking to make the Bible available in the English language. At one time an Augustinian friar, Coverdale left his order because of his growing Protestant convictions and in 1528 fled to Germany. There he worked for a time as an assistant to Tyndale in Hamburg.

Although Coverdale's Bible was published in 1535, a year before Tyndale's execution, the political winds in England were already changing. This resulted in a very different reception to Coverdale's work. King Henry VIII, in order to validate his divorce from Catherine of Aragon, had broken with the Roman Catholic Church and appointed himself head of the Church of England (the Act of Supremacy of 1534). When Thomas Cranmer, a Protestant, became archbishop of Canterbury in 1533, he petitioned Henry to encourage the translation of the Bible into English. Seeing this opening, Coverdale dedicated his new Bible to Henry with a flattering introduction. When Henry appointed his bishops to report on this new Bible, they returned with a negative report but, when pressed, could point to no actual errors or heresies. Henry reputably responded, "If there be no heresies, then in God's name let it go abroad among our people."[8] With these changes in political and ecclesiastical attitudes, English versions began to multiply.

7. J. Isaacs, "The Sixteenth-Century English Versions," in *The Bible in Its Ancient and English Versions*, ed. H. W. Robinson (Oxford: Clarendon, 1940), 160, cited by Bruce, *History of the Bible in English*, 44.
8. Bruce, *History of the Bible in English*, 56.

Although Coverdale had the same passion as Tyndale for making God's Word available to all people, unlike Tyndale, he was not an expert in Hebrew or Greek (something he humbly acknowledged). He therefore used Tyndale's work for the New Testament, the Pentateuch, and the book of Jonah, but translated the rest of the Bible from Latin and German editions. In the dedication of his version, he speaks of using "five sundry interpreters." According to Bruce, these likely refer to Tyndale, the Vulgate, a new Latin version produced by Sanctes Pagninus in 1528, Luther's German version, and an adaptation of Luther into a Swiss dialect.[9]

Coverdale's version was the first English version to separate out the books of the Apocrypha and place them at the end of the Old Testament. Coverdale's passion for the English Bible continued in the years that followed. He edited the Great Bible of 1539 (see below) and later did work on the Geneva Bible of 1560.

Matthew's Bible (1537)

If Coverdale's Bible was an attempt to finish Tyndale's work using other versions, Matthew's Bible sought to complete that work with Tyndale's own unpublished works. Scholars believe that the name "Thomas Matthew," which appears on the cover page of this version, is a pseudonym for a man named John Rogers, an associate of Tyndale. While Tyndale had apparently finished translating the historical books up to 2 Chronicles, he was not able to publish them before his death. Rogers compiled this material, together with Tyndale's New Testament and Coverdale's version of the rest of the Old Testament and the Apocrypha. He likely published pseudonymously out of concerns that his well-known association with Tyndale would result in the translation's rejection.

Like Coverdale's version, Matthew's Bible received widespread acceptance primarily because of the support of Protestant leaders like Oliver Cromwell. Both versions included flattering dedications to the king and both Matthew's Bible and Coverdale's second edition of 1537 received tacit approval from Henry VIII, bearing on their title pages the words, "Set forth with the kinges most gracyous lycence."[10] Some fifteen years later, however, Rogers would become a victim of the to-and-fro of British politics. When Mary Tudor ascended to the throne in 1553, Rogers was arrested and imprisoned. In February of 1555 he was burned alive at Smithfield, the first Protestant martyr under "Bloody Mary's" attempt to restore Roman Catholicism in the Church of England.

The Great Bible (1539)

While the Bibles of Miles Coverdale and Thomas Matthew (= John Rogers) were well received by most, they were viewed as too Protestant by many clergy. This was especially true of the marginal notes in Matthew's

9. Bruce, *History of the Bible in English*, 59.
10. Bruce, *History of the Bible in English*, 64–65.

Bible. Oliver Cromwell, vicar-general under Henry VIII, therefore advocated for a new, more neutral edition that would be acceptable to all. Cromwell appointed Coverdale to oversee the work. The basis for the text was to be Matthew's Bible, but without the notes. The result was the Great Bible, which became the first officially sanctioned Bible of the Church of England. On the bottom of the first page of the second edition (1540), a note reads, "This is the Byble apoynted to the use of the churches." The designation "Great Bible" refers to its large size, which was designed to sit on church lecterns. Ironically, a Bible based on Tyndale's vilified work had now become the official Bible of the Church of England.

The Geneva Bible (1560)

During the reign of Mary Tudor (1553–58), further translation and publication of the Bible became impossible in England, and a number of English Protestant scholars moved to Geneva, Switzerland, where Protestantism was flourishing among Reformers like Theodore Beza and John Calvin. William Whittingham, formerly of All Souls College in Oxford, was one of the leaders of this group. Whittingham married John Calvin's sister and succeeded John Knox as pastor of the English church in Geneva. He and his colleagues also produced a New Testament in 1557, based primarily on Matthew's edition of Tyndale, with some revision drawn from the Great Bible. They then set out to produce a version of the full Bible, which was published in 1560. The Geneva Bible was based primarily on the Great Bible in the Old Testament and the Tyndale Bible in the New, but with close consultation of the Hebrew and Greek.

The exceptional level of scholarship in and around Geneva made the Geneva Bible superior to any English edition that had yet appeared. It also had copious notes, most of which provided historical or geographical contexts, or which explained difficulties in the text. Other notes, however, were theological and practical. These notes are infamous for irking King James I and in this way providing impetus for the Authorized, or "King James," Version (see next question).

Even after the publication of the King James Version, the Geneva Bible would remain the favorite among many Protestants. It became the official Bible of the Church of Scotland (Presbyterian), and the Pilgrims brought it, instead of the KJV, to New England. It was also Shakespeare's Bible, and its language and cadences appear throughout his plays and sonnets.

The Bishops' Bible (1568)

The superiority of the Geneva Bible to the Great Bible was obvious to most of the Anglican leadership, but it was inconceivable that they would adopt the former considering its Calvinistic and anti-monarchist notes. A revision of the Great Bible was deemed essential. The work was initiated by Matthew Parker, archbishop of Canterbury. The directions given stipulated that the text was to follow the Great Bible, except when that version did not accurately represent the meaning of the Hebrew and Greek. Any notes that were added on controversial passages should present a balanced perspective.

The Bishop's Bible could be deemed a success in that it went through nineteen editions and superseded the Great Bible as the official Bible of the Church of England. But it was not widely used outside the Anglican Communion because of the superior quality of the Geneva Bible.

Summary

Although portions of the Bible were produced in Old English as early as the seventh century, the first full English Bible was inspired by John Wycliffe and appeared in 1382. The first printed New Testament translated directly from the Greek was that of William Tyndale, published in 1526. Tyndale was martyred for his efforts, but his work inspired a flourishing of English Bible translations, including the Coverdale Version (1535), Matthew's Bible (1537), the Great Bible (1539), the Geneva Bible (1560), and the Bishops' Bible (1568). All of these paved the way for the Authorized, or King James, Version of 1611.

REFLECTION QUESTIONS

1. Why did the church oppose Bible translations into vernacular languages (the common languages people speak)?
2. What was unique about John Wycliffe's Bible version?
3. What was unique about William Tyndale's Bible version?
4. What was unique about the Geneva Bible, and why did some Anglicans dislike it?
5. What was the impetus behind the Great Bible? The Bishops' Bible?

QUESTION 25

What Is the King James Version, and How Did It Come to Be?

The most influential English translation of all time is without doubt the King James Version (KJV), also known as the Authorized Version (AV), because it was authorized for use in churches by King James I of England. The KJV arose during tumultuous religious, political, social, and cultural changes in England. Understanding this history will help us understand the KJV's rise to prominence.[1]

The Puritans in Elizabethan England

The long and illustrious reign of Queen Elizabeth I (b. 1522; reigned 1558–1603) was a golden age in sixteenth-century England, as the nation grew to worldwide prominence politically, militarily, and culturally. Great works of English literature emerged during this period, coming from authors like Ben Jonson, Christopher Marlowe, Edmund Spenser, and, of course, William Shakespeare. During this golden age, English became enshrined as the language of national identity for the United Kingdom and its colonies. Militarily, the defeat of the Spanish Armada in 1588 signaled the end of the threat that a Spanish conquest could reinstitute Roman Catholicism in England by force.

Yet while Elizabeth's reign was marked by an enormous rise in the influence of Great Britain, it was also a period of internal religious conflict. This was caused not only by the continuing struggle between Roman Catholics and Protestants, but also by conflicts within Protestantism between traditional Anglicans on the one side and the growing Puritan movement on

1. See especially Alister McGrath, *In the Beginning: The Story of the King James Bible and How It Changed a Nation, a Language, and a Culture* (New York: Anchor Books, 2001); David G. Burke, ed., *Translation That Openeth the Window: Reflections on the History and Legacy of the King James Bible* (Atlanta: American Bible Society, 2009).

the other. Elizabeth, always the diplomat, sought compromise and balance. Under her Settlement of Religion, the Church of England retained an essentially Catholic structure, with clerical robes and bishops, but maintained a basically Protestant set of beliefs.[2]

Drawing their inspiration from the Protestants of Geneva, the Puritans emerged during Elizabeth's reign as a powerful reform movement within the Anglican Church. Elizabeth had kept them on a tight rein, requiring the clergy to wear vestments and to use the Anglican Prayer Book. These and other rules were despised by the Puritans, especially those who had returned from exile in Geneva after the death of Mary Tudor. They considered such traditions to be idolatrous vestiges of England's Catholic past.

When Elizabeth died in 1603, the Puritans saw their opportunity. They were (at first, at least) delighted in the choice of successor, King James VI of Scotland, soon to be James I of England. Since James had successfully reigned over Presbyterian Scotland, the English Puritans were convinced that he would be on their side and would move England away from the Anglican rule by bishops toward a Presbyterian style of governance like those in Geneva and Zurich. What they did not know was that, while James was a wily politician who had maintained positive relations with his Scottish subjects, he disliked Presbyterianism, believing that the Anglican rule of bishops was the only way to maintain the authority of the monarchy. Not only did James despise the Puritans, whom he viewed as radical Protestants, but he especially hated the Geneva Bible, which was their favorite.

Competing Bibles: Geneva versus Bishops'

We have discussed the origin of the Geneva Bible in the previous question. This translation was overseen by William Whittingham and published in Geneva in 1560. Drawing on the wealth of biblical scholarship generated by Calvin and his colleagues in Geneva, the Geneva Bible is widely viewed as the most accurate Bible of its day. The Bible was particularly noteworthy for its extensive system of exegetical and theological notes, which increased its appeal and made it the Bible of choice among many Protestants.

Yet these same notes were loathed by the Anglican leadership, because they challenged certain cherished Anglican traditions. The Bishops' Bible of 1568 remained the officially sanctioned version of the Church of England and the only one permitted to be read in public services. King James, in particular, wished to see the demise of the Geneva Bible. He viewed its notes as anti-monarchist and opposed to the divine right of kings. One example of this is Psalm 105:15, which in the Geneva Bible reads, "Touch not mine anointed, and do my prophets no harm." The "anointed" was commonly interpreted as

2. McGrath, *In the Beginning*, 125.

the king, God's anointed vice-regent. Yet the Geneva Bible had a note identifying the term with God's people in general.

King James I and the Hampton Court Conference of 1604

James's opportunity to replace the Geneva Bible came about through an unusual series of events. When James came to the throne, the Puritans saw their opportunity to gain the religious upper hand. Assuming the Scottish king would have Presbyterian sympathies, they met him as he journeyed south from Edinburgh to London for his coronation. They presented him with a document signed by more than a thousand clergy members, approximately 10 percent of the church's leadership. Though respectful in tone and presenting the Puritans as loyal subjects, the document included a long list of demands for religious reform. Among these were the abolition of certain clerical vestments, the rejection of the apocryphal books, no more use of the sign of the cross, and other practices that the Puritans considered too "Catholic." To deal with these demands, James called a conference to be held in January 1604 at the palace of the Hampton Court.

James himself presided over the Hampton Court Conference. John Reynolds, president of Corpus Christi College in Oxford, led the Puritan delegation. Richard Bancroft, the bishop of London, represented the Anglicans. Bancroft was a staunch and powerful opponent of the Puritans. Although he was at first suspicious of King James, since he, like the Puritans, suspected James would favor Presbyterianism, he also knew that James held firmly to the divine right of kings. Bancroft gained the king's ear and convinced him that the true enemies of the monarchy were the Puritans on the one side and the Catholics on the other. The only way to maintain religious stability in England and ensure the power of the monarchy was to support the Anglican cause and the ecclesiastical rule of bishops. James could not agree more.

Although the Puritans saw the conference as an opportunity to gain their demands, in fact the deck was stacked against them. Only four Puritans were invited to attend, and these were chosen by James and his advisors, not by the Puritans themselves, who would have selected more radical leaders. The rest of the council was made up of the king and his advisors, and nine bishops and deans representing the Anglicans.

James began the conference with a long speech defending his right as king to oversee the affairs of the church. He also affirmed the religious status quo as established by Elizabeth but welcomed proposals for reform. On the second day of the conference, John Reynolds set out four Puritan demands. These were, in his words,

1. That the doctrine of the church might be preserved in purity according to God's word.
2. That good pastors might be planted in all churches, to preach the same.

3. That the church government might be sincerely administered according to God's word [meaning Presbyterian rule].
4. That the Book of Common Prayer might be fitted to more increase of piety [meaning its abolition or at least a major revision].[3]

King James was not inclined to honor any of these demands, and one by one shot them down. The Hampton Conference was headed for disaster, with growing frustration on the side of the Puritans. It seemed destined to create an even greater rift between Anglicans and Puritans and between the Puritans and the Crown. At this point, however, John Reynolds made a surprising proposal, recommending the production of a new Bible translation. The motivation behind this proposal is unclear. Perhaps the Puritans assumed that the Geneva Bible would never be authorized by the Anglican Church and hoped that a new translation could reflect the accuracy of the Geneva Bible without its controversy.

Bishop Bancroft had rejected every Puritan proposal and scoffed at this one as well. He said, "If every man's humour were followed, there would be no end of translating."[4] Yet James saw in this proposal a great opportunity. By agreeing to this one demand, he could, in effect, throw the Puritans a bone. This could save the conference and mollify his critics. Furthermore, a new translation that was "Puritan-approved" would likely result in the demise of the Geneva Bible, which he so despised. It could be a double win for James, who immediately endorsed the proposal, declaring that he had yet to see "a Bible well translated into English," and adding, "of all, that of Geneva is the worst."[5] So it was out of this political and ecclesiastical compromise—an attempt both to satisfy the Puritans and to keep them in check—that the KJV version was born.

The Production of the KJV

Although Bishop Bancroft had at first opposed the project, when the king affirmed it, he quickly had a change of heart, and the king appointed him chairman of the new translation. Forty-seven biblical scholars were chosen to produce the work. Six panels of translators were set up, three for the Old Testament, two for the New Testament, and one for the Apocrypha. Two groups met at Westminster, two at Oxford University, and two at Cambridge. The translators were not paid, since neither the Crown nor the Parliament had sufficient resources. Rather, the churches were encouraged to provide paid positions for the translators as they did their work.

---

3. McGrath, *In the Beginning*, 159–60.
4. McGrath, *In the Beginning*, 161.
5. McGrath, *In the Beginning*, 162.

Bancroft wrote and James approved a list of fifteen translation rules. Here are five of the most significant of these (with comment):[6]

Rule 1: "The ordinary Bible read in the Church, commonly called the *Bishops' Bible*, to be followed, and as little altered as the Truth of the original will permit." The official Bible of the Anglican Church was to be the foundation. The goal here was continuity with the present Church of England and its leadership.

Rule 3: "The Old Ecclesiastical Words to be kept, *vis.* the Word *Church* not to be translated *Congregation* &c." Tyndale had used innovative terms like "congregation," which some thought promoted a less centralized and institutional form of church government and so undermined the authority of the bishops.

Rule 6: "No Marginal Notes at all to be affixed, but only for the explanation of the Hebrew or Greek Words." The notes of the Geneva Bible—and the party politics they were thought to engender—were to be avoided.

Rule 11: "When any Place or special Obscurity is doubted of, Letters to be directed by Authority, to send to any Learned Man in the Land, for his Judgment of such a Place." The best resources were to be consulted and the best counsel of scholars sought.

Rule 14: "These translations to be used when they agree better with the Text in the Bishops' Bible: *Tindoll's*, *Matthew's*, *Coverdale's*, *Whitchurch's*, *Geneva*." The goal was to determine the meaning of the text, and all important predecessors—even the Geneva Bible—should be consulted. This new version was to stand on the shoulders of giants.

The Completion and Reception of the KJV

Work on the translation began in 1604, and the last assignments were due in 1610. Richard Bancroft died on November 2, 1610, and so never saw the fruit of his labor. The editing work was completed by Miles Smith and Thomas Bilson, who included a dedication to James I and a lengthy preface, "Translators to the Reader," which set out the goals and principles of the translators. The task of publication was assigned to Robert Barker, the king's printer, and took place at Barker's printing house in central London. The first printing occurred in 1611.[7]

The reception of the KJV, like its inauguration, was marked by a good measure of political intrigue. The new version was at first received with little interest and a great deal of criticism. The Pilgrims, for example, in 1620 refused to take the new version on the Mayflower, preferring the Geneva Bible. Hugh Broughton, one of the leading biblical scholars of his day, had been passed over in the translation process—probably because of his reputation

6. See McGrath, *In the Beginning*, 173–74, for all fifteen rules.
7. For a detailed description of the technology involved, see McGrath, *In the Beginning*, 200–5.

as a caustic and curmudgeonly old man! When the new version arrived on his desk, he wrote venomously against it, saying that "The late Bible . . . bred in me a sadness that will grieve me while I breathe, it is so ill done. Tell His Majesty that I had rather be rent in pieces with wild horses, than any such translation by my consent should be urged upon poor churches. . . . The new edition crosseth me. I require it to be burnt."[8]

The Eventual Triumph of the KJV

In contrast to the KJV's tepid reception, the Geneva Bible continued to be extremely popular and the favorite of the Puritans, that is, until historical and political events led to its demise. In 1616 James banned the publication of the Geneva Bible in the United Kingdom to promote sales of his new version. Printers, however, were able to circumvent the ban by printing Bibles in Amsterdam and Dort and importing them to England. As the better product, the Geneva Bible continued to outsell the KJV. It had a clearer Roman typeface (the KJV had a dark Gothic type that was difficult to read), was produced on better paper, was available in smaller personal editions, and was significantly cheaper. When Charles I succeeded his father James, he promoted William Laud to archbishop of Canterbury. Laud shared Charles's anti-Puritan views and sought to further suppress the Geneva Bible. He banned its importation, claiming that sales of the Bible were unpatriotic, since they represented unfair competition for British publishers. As the supply was cut off, sales of the KJV naturally rose. The situation changed somewhat when Charles I was imprisoned and executed, and the Puritan commonwealth was established under Oliver Cromwell. Yet by this time the Geneva Bible had lost much of its influence. Indeed, during the time of its ban, editions of the KJV were printed with the Geneva's notes!

The final death knell to the Geneva Bible came with the restoration of the monarchy in 1660. The nation as a whole was sick of the Puritan movement and all that it stood for. The Geneva Bible, viewed now as both a foreign import and a Puritan relic, was out of favor. Alister McGrath puts it this way:

> With the restoration of the monarchy, to popular acclaim, the "Battle of the Bibles" had ended. The King James Bible had finally triumphed over its rival. The grounds of that triumph may partly rest in its eloquence, or in the excellence of its translation. Yet the most significant factor in its final triumph appears to have been the fact that it was associated with the authority of the monarchy at a time when such authority was viewed positively. In marked contrast, the Geneva Bible was

8. Cited by F. F. Bruce, *History of the Bible in English*, 3rd ed. (New York: Oxford University Press, 1978), 107.

> marginalized, not on account of the quality of its translation or English prose, but because it had been the preferred translation of the detested Puritan faction, who had now been comprehensively routed, militarily and politically.[9]

What is curious is that for the first 150 years of its existence, almost nobody commented on the noble prose or exalted style of the KJV, its most respected traits today. Why did it take so long for its literary quality to be appreciated? Perhaps because this exalted style was more a perception than a reality, a result of the gradual assimilation of its rhythm and cadence into the religious subconscious of its readers. McGrath continues:

> When, why, and how did this [adulation] take place? It is impossible to say. Perhaps an increasing distance from the origins of the translation began to allow the work to be endowed with the characteristics of a classic. Perhaps a fading of memories allowed rival versions—such as the Geneva Bible or the Bishops' Bible—or hostile initial reactions to be forgotten. Perhaps familiarity dulled the senses to the weakness of the translation, or allowed well-known words to become embedded in the memory. Whatever the reasons—and these remain less than fully understood—there is no doubt that a decisive and irreversible change came about in the esteem in which the King James Bible was held in England and beyond.[10]

McGrath's intuitions may be correct. Indeed, to my ears, those sections of the KJV that sound the most noble and exalted are the ones that are most familiar, the ones I have heard and memorized since childhood. Contemporary Bible versions still sound wrong because they are not written in Elizabethan English (which everyone knows is the language of God!), and because they do not sound familiar in their rhythm and cadence. Whatever the diverse reasons for its remarkable success, no one can deny the enduring impact of the language of the KJV on both church and society.

Summary

The King James Version arose in the context of political and ecclesiastical conflict between King James I and his Puritan subjects within the Church of England. James saw a proposal for a new translation as an opportunity both to mollify the Puritans (who had proposed the translation) and to replace the Puritan's Geneva Bible, which he despised. The translation process utilized

---

9. McGrath, *In the Beginning*, 289.
10. McGrath, *In the Beginning*, 290.

the best biblical scholars of the time and took seven years to complete. The first edition was published in 1611. While many at first ignored, rejected, or criticized the KJV, it eventually became the Bible of choice among English speakers, a position it would hold for almost four hundred years.

REFLECTION QUESTIONS

1. What key political events led up to the production of the KJV?

2. Why did King James dislike the Geneva Bible?

3. What were some of the most significant rules of translation for the KJV?

4. How was the KJV at first received?

5. What factors does McGrath suggest helped to make the KJV the premier English Bible?

QUESTION 26

Is the King James Version the Most Accurate English Version Today?

The King James Version is universally recognized as the most influential English translation of all time. For four hundred years, the KJV remained nearly unchallenged among English versions. The impact of the KJV on the language, culture, and literature of the English-speaking world is incalculable. It has been called "the noblest monument of English prose."[1] Hundreds of English idioms considered commonplace today were introduced by the King James Version or its immediate predecessors (see Question 12 for some of these). I grew up reading, studying, and memorizing the KJV and—to me at least—many verses simply sound "wrong" when translated in any way other than the KJV.

For some people today, there is no other Bible. The so-called King James Only crowd claims that the KJV is the only divinely authorized English translation. Some would even say the only divinely authorized Bible of any language—period. The extreme side of this movement has produced books with titles like *God Wrote Only One Bible*; *The Paraphrased Perversion of the Bible*; *The Corruption of the Word*; *New Age Bible Versions*; and *The Bible "Babel."*[2]

I don't know how many times I've heard that old joke, "If the KJV was good enough for the apostle Paul, it's good enough for me!" But of course the KJV was not Paul's Bible. He didn't speak Elizabethan English, and he read his Bible (our Old Testament) in Hebrew, Aramaic, and Greek.

1. Preface to the *Revised Standard Version* (New York: Thomas Nelson, 1952), iii.
2. James Jasper Ray, *God Wrote Only One Bible* (Eugene, OR: Eye Opener Publishers, 1983); Gene Nowlin, *The Paraphrased Perversion of the Bible* (Collingswood, NJ: The Bible for Today, 1974); James Kevin, *The Corruption of the Word* (Williamsburg, NM: Micro-Load Press, 1990); Gail Riplinger, *New Age Bible Versions* (Munroe Falls, OH: A.V. Publications, 1993); Gail Riplinger, *Which Bible Is God's Word?* (Oklahoma City: Hearthstone, 1994); Peter Ruckman, *The Bible "Babel"* (Pensacola, FL: Bible Baptist Bookstore, 1964).

Yet while the KJV is the greatest English version of all time, it is not the most reliable or accurate *today*.[3] Here's an analogy I use with my students: "The KJV is the greatest Bible of all time in the same way the Macintosh 512K is the greatest personal computer of all time." The Mac 512K was my first personal computer. It was introduced in 1984, the second-generation MacIntosh. It was incredibly innovative. While Apple did not invent the computer mouse, the "windows" format, or the intuitive user-friendly interface using icons, the company popularized them for a mass audience. For someone like me, who had never used a computer, this was revolutionary—perhaps the greatest advance in writing and research since the invention of the codex![4] Yet by today's standards, the MacIntosh 512K is a dinosaur. It was a beige box-like unit with a small, 9-inch monochrome screen. It had *no* hard drive for data storage, only one internal "floppy" drive. A floppy at that time could hold about a megabyte (1 MB) of data (storage for about one photograph).[5] To get some perspective, my present iPhone has 256 GB of memory, 250,000 times as much!

My point is that while the Macintosh 512K could be called the greatest personal computer of all time, it is hopelessly outdated today. In the same way, although the KJV is the greatest translation of all time, it is outdated in two main areas: its language and its source text. Concerning its language, the English language has changed, so that the KJV is full of archaic language. Much of it is obscure and difficult to understand. Some of it is inaccurate and misleading, because the meaning of words has changed. The second major difficulty is that the New Testament of the KJV was based on a very limited number of late Greek manuscripts. We have much older and more reliable manuscripts available today. We will look at the first difficulty, archaic language, in this question and will examine the textual basis of the KJV New Testament in the next.

Before proceeding, however, I must make a strong qualification. I am *not* saying that you should not read and use the KJV. If this is the Bible you grew up with and you love, by all means, keep reading! The best Bible

---

3. See Mark Ward, *Authorized: the Use and Misuse of the King James Bible* (Lexham Press, 2018); Roy E. Beacham & Kevin T. Bauder, eds., *One Bible Only? Examining Exclusive Claims for the King James Bible* (Grand Rapids: Kregel, 2001); James R. White, *The King James Only Controversy: Can Your Trust the Modern Translations?* (Minneapolis: Bethany House, 1995); D. A. Carson, *The King James Version Debate: a Plea for Realism* (Grand Rapids: Baker, 1979).
4. The codex is the "book" form of manuscripts as opposed to the scroll. While scrolls must be laboriously rolled open to locate a particular passage, the codex had individual pages bound together and written on both sides, so that the reader can immediately turn to any passage.
5. At the computer store where I bought the computer, I asked the clerk whether I should get an external floppy drive to supplement my internal one, so that I could run my MS Word software program on one floppy (1 MB) and store my data on the other (1 MB). His response was (with a straight face), "You'll never need that much memory!"

translation for you is the one you will read. People can certainly profit enormously and hear God speak to them through the KJV. Yet for most contemporary English readers, the KJV is neither the most accurate nor the most readable version.

Archaic Language in the KJV

The simple truth about language is that it changes over time (see Question 10), so translations must be periodically updated to keep up with the English language. To say someone is "gay" means something very different today than it did even fifty years ago. So when the KJV says that you should not show greater honor to someone "that weareth the gay clothing" (James 2:3), the contemporary reader will likely misunderstand this as a reference to same-sex attraction rather than as a warning against preferential treatment for the rich. Consider 2 Corinthians 6:11–13 in the KJV, which is quite incomprehensible for a contemporary reader:

> O ye Corinthians, our mouth is open unto you, our heart is enlarged. Ye are not straitened in us, but ye are straitened in your own bowels. Now for a recompence in the same, (I speak as unto my children,) be ye also enlarged.

Below are some statements in the KJV that are likely to be either unknown or misunderstood by readers because of changes in the English language. We will give two kinds of examples: (1) obscurities and (2) inaccuracies. In each case I will compare the KJV to a modern version that represents the meaning more accurately in contemporary English.

Archaisms Resulting in Obscurity

Leviticus 22:22

KJV	Blind, or broken, or maimed, <u>or having a wen, or scurvy, or scabbed</u>, ye shall not offer these unto the LORD, nor make an offering by fire of them upon the altar unto the LORD.
CSB	You are not to present any animal to the LORD that is blind, injured, maimed, <u>or has a running sore, festering rash, or scabs</u>; you may not put any of them on the altar as a food offering to the LORD.

Deuteronomy 22:19

KJV	And they shall <u>amerce</u> him in an hundred shekels of silver
NIV	They shall <u>fine</u> him a hundred shekels of silver

Joshua 9:4–5

KJV They did work wilily
NLT They resorted to deception

Judges 1:23

KJV And the house of Joseph sent to descry Bethel
NRSV The house of Joseph sent out spies to Bethel

Judges 16:7

KJV And Samson said unto her, If they bind me with seven green withs that were never dried, then shall I be weak, and be as another man.
NKJV And Samson said to her, "If they bind me with seven fresh bowstrings, not yet dried, then I shall become weak, and be like any other man."

1 Samuel 21:13

KJV And he changed his behaviour before them, and feigned himself mad in their hands, and scrabbled on the doors of the gate, and let his spittle fall down upon his beard.
NIV So he pretended to be insane in their presence; and while he was in their hands he acted like a madman, making marks on the doors of the gate and letting saliva run down his beard.

Job 41:18

KJV By his neesings a light doth shine, and his eyes *are* like the eyelids of the morning.
CEV When this monster sneezes, lightning flashes, and its eyes glow like the dawn.

Psalms 5:6

KJV Thou shalt destroy them that speak leasing
NIV You destroy those who tell lies

Isaiah 3:24

KJV Instead of sweet smell there shall be stink; and instead of a girdle a rent
NLT Instead of smelling of sweet perfume, she will stink. She will wear a rope for a sash

Isaiah 11:8

KJV The weaned child shall put his hand on the cockatrice' den.
GW Toddlers will put their hands into vipers' nests.

Isaiah 32:7

KJV The instruments also of the churl *are* evil
NLT The smooth tricks of scoundrels are evil

Haggai 1:4

KJV *Is it* time for you, O ye, to dwell in your cieled houses?
NIV Is it a time for you yourselves to be living in your paneled houses?

Matthew 14:8

KJV Give me here John Baptist's head in a charger.
NIV Give me here on a platter the head of John the Baptist.

Luke 9:29

KJV And as he prayed, the fashion of his countenance was altered
ESV And as he was praying, the appearance of his face was altered

Acts 19:38

KJV Wherefore if Demetrius, and the craftsmen which are with him, have a matter against any man, the law is open, and there are deputies: let them implead one another.

NIV If, then, Demetrius and his fellow craftsmen have a grievance against anybody, the courts are open and there are proconsuls. They can press charges.

Romans 11:2

KJV Wot ye not what the scripture saith of Elias?
CEB Or don't you know what the scripture says in the case of Elijah?

Romans 13:13

KJV Let us walk honestly . . . not in chambering and wantonness
NET Let us live decently . . . not in sexual immorality and sensuality

2 Thessalonians 2:8

KJV And then shall that Wicked be revealed, whom the Lord shall consume with the spirit of his mouth, and shall destroy with the brightness of his coming.
NIV And then the lawless one will be revealed, whom the Lord Jesus will overthrow with the breath of his mouth and destroy by the splendor of his coming.

James 1:21

KJV Wherefore lay apart all filthiness and superfluity of naughtiness.
TEV So get rid of every filthy habit and all wicked conduct.

1 Peter 2:18

KJV Servants, be subject to your masters with all fear; not only to the good and gentle, but also to the froward.
NKJV Servants, *be* submissive to *your* masters with all fear, not only to the good and gentle, but also to the harsh.

Archaisms Resulting in Inaccuracies

While the previous examples are words and phrases that don't make sense to most modern readers, in many other cases, the KJV gives the *wrong* meaning from the perspective of contemporary English usage.

Exodus 23:13

KJV And in all *things* that I have said unto you be circumspect.
ESV Pay attention to all that I have said to you.

Comment: To be "circumspect" today means to be wary and unwilling to take risks. But the Hebrew means to pay heed to what is said.

Exodus 30:35

KJV And thou shalt make it a perfume, a confection after the art of the apothecary.
CEB Like a skilled perfume maker, carefully blend them together and make incense.

Comment: A confection made in an apothecary sounds like the production of marijuana edibles. In fact, this is the preparation of incense for the tabernacle.

1 Kings 11:1

KJV But king Solomon loved many strange women
NKJV But King Solomon loved many foreign women

Comment: "Strange" in contemporary English means odd or unusual. But the problem with Solomon's wives was not that they were quirky, but that they were *foreign* and worshipped other gods.

Nehemiah 13:26

KJV nevertheless even him [Solomon] did outlandish women cause to sin.
NAB yet even he was led into sin by foreign women.

Comment: Similar to the previous example, "outlandish" in English today means looking or sounding bizarre or unfamiliar. But Solomon did not marry bizarre women; he married foreign ones.

2 Kings 3:9

KJV they fetched a compass of seven days' journey
NIV After a roundabout march of seven days

Comment: To "fetch a compass" in contemporary American English would mean to go get a compass (a direction-finding instrument). The Hebrew actually means to take a roundabout path.

Song of Songs 2:12

KJV The flowers appear on the earth . . . and the voice of the turtle is heard in our land
REB the turtle-dove's cooing is heard in our land

Comment: Modern readers of the KJV will wonder what a turtle sounds like.

Isaiah 3:18

KJV In that day the Lord will take away the bravery of *their* tinkling ornaments about their feet, and their cauls, and their round tires like the moon, the chains, and the bracelets, and the mufflers
NLT On that day of judgment the Lord will strip away everything that makes her beautiful: ornaments, headbands, crescent necklaces, earrings, bracelets, and veils

Comment: In the KJV it sounds like God takes away not only the beautiful jewelry, but also the car parts—tires, mufflers, and chains!

1 Corinthians 16:13

KJV Watch ye, stand fast in the faith, quit you like men, be strong.
NIV Be on your guard; stand firm in the faith; be courageous; be strong.

Comment: Paul tells the Corinthians to be like men and quit?!

1 Thessalonians 5:14

KJV comfort the feebleminded, support the weak, be patient toward all *men*
CSB comfort the discouraged, help the weak, be patient with everyone

Comment: The Greek word (*oligopsychos*) does not mean "feebleminded" or unintelligent. It means discouraged or disheartened. It also sounds like it is especially the men who are weak and feebleminded.

2 Timothy 2:15

KJV Study to shew thyself approved unto God
NLT Work hard so you can present yourself to God and receive his approval

Comment: The Greek word translated "study" (*spoudazō*) actually means to "work hard" or "do your best."

Hebrews 4:12

KJV For the word of God *is* quick, and powerful
NKJV For the word of God is living and powerful

Comment: Growing up I wondered how God's Word was "quick," unless this meant you could read it fast. In fact, the Greek word means "living" or "alive."

1 Peter 2:9

KJV But ye *are* a chosen generation, a royal priesthood, an holy nation, a peculiar people
NIV But you are a chosen people, a royal priesthood, a holy nation, God's special possession

Comment: Christians are sometimes odd or peculiar, but that is not what the Greek here means. It means something special that is acquired.

Summary

Although the KJV is certainly the most influential and enduring English Bible translation of all time, it has serious deficiencies today because of its archaic language and its inferior Greek textual basis. We provide evidence for the former here, including two categories of archaic language: (1) translations that are obscure or incomprehensible to most readers today, and (2) translations that are inaccurate or misleading because of changes in the meaning of English words.

REFLECTION QUESTIONS

1. What Bible version(s) (if any) did you use growing up? What, if any, impact did the King James Version have on you?

2. What does the author mean that the KJV is the "greatest English translation of all time"? How can this claim be compatible with the further claim that the KJV is outdated for most readers today?

3. What does the author say are the two most important problems of the KJV for contemporary readers?

4. In approximately what percentage of the KJV examples above did you recognize the meaning without looking at the contemporary translation?

5. Some say we should simply resist the changing state of English by refusing to accept changing definitions of words. How would you respond to this?

QUESTION 27

What's Wrong with the NT Manuscripts Behind the King James Version?

In addition to its archaic language, the other major problem with the King James Version is its use of inferior Greek manuscripts for the New Testament.[1] To understand this phenomenon, we must explore, first, the textual basis for the New Testament of the KJV (known as the "Textus Receptus") and, second, the development of modern textual criticism and the establishment of the Critical Text. This historical survey may be supplemented with the fuller discussion of the method of textual criticism in Question 8.

The Textual Basis for the King James Version New Testament

The New Testament of the King James Version was translated from the Greek New Testament produced by Erasmus in the early sixteenth century. The impetus for Erasmus's text was the invention of the movable type printing press by Johannes Gutenberg around 1440.

As we have seen (Question 8), prior to the invention of the printing press, all books had to be hand-copied, a process that inevitably resulted in errors. Gutenberg's press created a revolution in literature for two main reasons: (1) it allowed near-perfect copies to be made, and (2) it enabled mass production. The first major book to be printed by Gutenberg was the Latin Vulgate.

The first Greek New Testament to be printed was part of a magnificent five-volume polyglot (multi-language) Bible, known as the Complutensian Polyglot. The work was overseen by the cardinal primate of Spain, Francisco Ximenes de Cisneros (1436–1517). The NT, contained in the fifth volume, was printed first, in January 1514. It included the text of the Greek New Testament and the Latin Vulgate side by side. The OT was done in volumes

1. See the references cited in Question 26, n. 3.

1 to 4 and was published in 1517. It included the Hebrew text, the Latin Vulgate, and the Greek Septuagint side by side. The Pentateuch (Genesis–Deuteronomy) included the Aramaic Targum of Onkelos at the foot of the page, with a Latin translation.[2]

Although the Complutensian Polyglot was the first Greek NT to be printed, it was prohibitively expensive and not designed for mass distribution. Seeing an opportunity, a printer named Johann Froben approached the Dutch biblical scholar and humanist Desiderius Erasmus and encouraged him to prepare a Greek edition of the NT suitable for mass production. Spurred on by Froben to beat other competitors, Erasmus produced his text in a remarkably short time. Printing of the work began in October of 1515 and was completed by March 1516. Although a significant accomplishment for its time, Erasmus's Greek text had some major shortcomings:

(1) Erasmus had a very limited number of Greek manuscripts available to him, only about a half dozen. All of these were later manuscripts from the Byzantine family. The oldest was from the eleventh century AD. Today we have Greek manuscripts that are much older, from the second, third, fourth, and fifth centuries.

(2) In various places, Erasmus gave in to pressure to conform to the Latin Vulgate—even when it conflicted with the Greek text. Since the fourth century, the Vulgate had been the official Bible of the church. To go against it seemed like heresy to many. The most famous example of this comes from 1 John 5:7–8, the so-called "three-witnesses" passage. The Vulgate of Erasmus's day included the longer reading on the right:

1 John 5:7–8 (Greek text)	**1 John 5:7–8 (Vulgate reading)**
For there are three that testify: the Spirit, the water and the blood; and the three are in agreement.	For there are three that testify <u>in heaven: the Father, the Word, and the Holy Spirit; and these three are one. And there are three that testify on earth</u>: the Spirit, the water, and the blood; and these three agree as one.

The underlined words were not found in any of Erasmus's Greek manuscripts nor in manuscripts of the Latin Vulgate until about AD 800. They first show up in some Old Latin manuscripts around AD 500. When Erasmus was criticized for leaving these words out of his first and second editions, he responded that if anyone could show him a single Greek manuscript with this passage in it,

2. Bruce M. Metzger and Bart D. Ehrman, *The Text of the New Testament: Its Transmission, Corruption, and Restoration*, 4th ed. (New York: Oxford University Press, 2005), 137–42.

he would include it. One appeared shortly after (almost certainly prepared for Erasmus's benefit!).[3] Today only five late Greek manuscripts have this reading: one from the fourteenth century (629), two from the sixteenth century (61, 918), one from the seventeenth century (2473), and one from the eighteenth century (2318). Four more manuscripts have it added as a variant reading (88, 221, 429, 636). Considering its omission from every Greek manuscript for the first twelve hundred years of the church, it is virtually certain that this passage was not part of the original text of 1 John.

(3) In other places Erasmus introduced words from the Latin Vulgate that are found in only a few late Greek manuscripts. For example, in the episode about the Ethiopian eunuch in Acts 8, we learn that "as they traveled along the road, they came to some water and the eunuch said, 'Look, here is water. What can stand in the way of my being baptized?'" (Acts 8:36 NIV). Evidently a copyist did not like that the man's conversion was not actually described, so he added: "And Philip said, 'If you believe with all thine heart, you may.' And he answered and said, 'I believe that Jesus Christ is the Son of God.'" Only a few late Greek manuscripts have these two sentences.

(4) Erasmus only had one manuscript of the book of Revelation (copied in the twelfth century), but it was missing the last leaf with the last six verses. Erasmus therefore translated from Latin back into Greek. This has resulted in the odd situation that there are several words in Erasmus's Greek text at the end of Revelation that do not appear *in any Greek manuscripts*.[4]

Erasmus's text was revised several times by Erasmus himself and then picked up and used by others in subsequent editions of the Greek NT. It was essentially Erasmus's Greek New Testament that a century later became the basis of the New Testament of the KJV. The name "Textus Receptus" that is given to this Greek text came from an edition produced by the Elzevir brothers in 1633. The preface to this edition said that this Greek text was the "text which is now received by all"—in Latin, *textus receptus*.[5]

The Rise of Modern Textual Criticism

Textual criticism of the New Testament arose as a discipline in the eighteenth and nineteenth centuries through the groundbreaking work of textual scholars like J. Griesbach, K. Lachmann, L. F. C. Tischendorf, and most significantly B. F. Westcott and F. J. A. Hort. Westcott and Hort (WH) are credited with bringing the growing consensus of scholarship together into a coherent system. Their method examined both external and internal textual evidence (see Question 8 for definitions of these). WH identified four manuscripts families, which they called the Syrian, Western, Alexandrian, and Neutral families.

3. Metzger and Ehrman, *Text of the New Testament*, 146–48.
4. Metzger and Ehrman, *Text of the New Testament*, 143, 145.
5. Metzger and Ehrman, *Text of the New Testament*, 152.

By comparing variant readings and following widely accepted rules of internal evidence (see below), they concluded that Syrian readings were generally inferior, resulting from expansion, correction, clarification, and harmonization. They concluded that this family likely arose from the standardization of the text in the fourth century. Using these same rules of textual transmission, WH further claimed that two fourth-century majuscule manuscripts, Codex Sinaiticus (א) and Codex Vaticanus (B), represented the purest form of the text, which they called the "Neutral" text. When these two agreed with each other on a particular reading, WH viewed that reading as practically certain.

Most textual critics today follow a modified version of the WH method, weighing both external and internal evidence and making textual decisions on a case-by-case basis. Westcott and Hort's Syrian text is known today as the Byzantine family. In agreement with WH, most scholars view Byzantine readings as generally later and less reliable than other families. In contrast to WH, however, few speak of a "neutral" text, or give so much weight to the two oldest majuscules, Codex Sinaiticus (א) and Codex Vaticanus (B). Instead, these two are viewed as good examples of the Alexandrian family, which *in general* represents the earliest and most reliable family.

Concerning internal evidence (evaluating the tendencies of copyists and authors), the methods of WH are generally followed today. Below are four of them illustrated.

(1) *Choose the reading that best explains the origin of the others.* This is the most basic rule of internal textual evidence. It is asking: Did reading A likely arise from reading B, or did B arise from A? Consider Mark 1:2–3, where some manuscripts read, "As it is written <u>in Isaiah the prophet</u>," while others read, "As it is written <u>in the prophets</u>." It is easy to see why a copyist would replace "Isaiah the prophet" with "the prophets," since Mark quotes Malachi 3:1 before quoting Isaiah 40:3 (he cites two prophets, not just Isaiah). On the other hand, it is inexplicable why a copyist would make the text *harder* by changing the plural "prophets" into the singular "Isaiah." The first reading is almost certainly original, since it is easy to explain how the second arose from it.

(2) *The harder reading is usually the better reading.* This rule generally holds true because copyists were more likely to smooth out a difficult reading than to make an easy one more difficult. For example, in Galatians 1:18, Byzantine manuscripts read, "I went up to Jerusalem to get acquainted with <u>Peter</u> and stayed with him fifteen days" (cf. Gal. 2:11, 14). Alexandrian manuscripts here read "Cephas" (the Aramaic version of his name) instead of "Peter." Cephas is rare in the NT (9x) while Peter is very common (156x). It is easy to see why a copyist would change Cephas to Peter, but very difficult to explain the inverse.

Or consider Matthew 27:16, where most manuscripts read, "At that time they had a notorious prisoner, called Barabbas." A few manuscripts read, "called Jesus Barabbas." Jesus (or *Yeshuah/Joshua*) was a very common Jewish name in the first century and may well have been Barabbas's first name. It is easy to see why a Christian copyist would drop the name and simply call him "Barabbas," not wanting to identify this criminal with the name Jesus.

Similarly, during Jesus's crucifixion in Mark 15, Byzantine manuscripts introduce an OT quotation: "So the Scripture was fulfilled which says, 'And He was numbered with the transgressors'" (Mark 15:28 NKJV). Alexandrian manuscripts do not have this citation. Again, it is easy to see why a copyist would introduce this fulfillment formula into Mark's gospel, especially considering the parallel in Luke 22:37. But it is almost inconceivable why a copyist would intentionally omit it.

This example brings up an important question about so-called "missing verses" in some Bible versions. As a result of this textual decision, most modern versions move directly from Mark 15:27 to 15:29, skipping 15:28 (see NIV; NLT; ESV; NASB; CSB; etc.). This has caused great concern among some Christians and angry accusations that modern versions are removing verses from the Bible! But this is not correct. We must remember that there were originally no chapter or verse divisions in the Bible (see Question 21). The numbering system of chapters and verses that we have today was introduced *after* the Byzantine text became the dominant family. So numbers were given to many "verses" that were not in fact part of the original text. Translators are not *removing* verses from the Bible. They are *restoring* the text to its original form by removing later scribal additions.

(3) *The non-harmonized reading is usually the better reading.* This is because copyists tended to harmonize parallel accounts, especially in the Synoptic Gospels. In Matthew 9:13 most Alexandrian manuscripts read, "I have not come to call the righteous, but sinners." Byzantine manuscripts add "<u>to repentance</u>," harmonizing the text to the parallel passage in Luke 5:32. It is easy to explain why a copyist would add the phrase because of their familiarity with the Lukan parallel. It is almost impossible to explain why they would remove it if it were already there.

Similarly, in John 6:11, Alexandrian manuscripts read, "Jesus then took the loaves, gave thanks, and distributed to those who were seated as much as they wanted." Byzantine manuscripts add that "Jesus . . . distributed to <u>the disciples, and the disciples to</u> those who were seated." This harmonizes John's account with the Synoptics (Matt. 14:9; Mark 6:41; Luke 9:16). Again, it is easy to explain why copyists would add these words, but almost impossible to explain why they would drop them.

(4) *The shorter reading is usually the better reading.* This rule comes from the fact that copyists tended to expand the text to include variant readings, explain obscurities, and add natural complements. Natural complements are additions that bring the text in line with common expressions used elsewhere, such as when "Jesus" is expanded to "the Lord Jesus" or "Jesus Christ." In these cases, the shorter, unexpanded phrase is almost certainly original,

since a copyist is more likely to add a natural complement than to delete one. Consider these examples:[6]

Reference	Alexandrian Reading	Byzantine Reading
Acts 19:4	Jesus	Christ Jesus
1 Cor. 9:1	Jesus	Jesus Christ
2 Cor. 4:10	Jesus	Lord Jesus
Heb. 3:1	Jesus	Christ Jesus
1 John 1:7	Jesus	Jesus Christ
Rev. 1:9	Jesus	Jesus Christ
Rev. 12:17	Jesus	Jesus Christ
1 Thess. 3:11	Jesus our Lord	our Lord Jesus Christ
2 John 1:3	Jesus Christ	The Lord Jesus Christ
2 Cor. 5:18	Christ	Jesus Christ
Acts 15:11	Lord Jesus	Lord Jesus Christ
Acts 16:31	Lord Jesus	Lord Jesus Christ
1 Cor. 5:4	Lord Jesus	Lord Jesus Christ
2 Cor. 11:31	Lord Jesus	Lord Jesus Christ
2 Thess. 1:8	Lord Jesus	Lord Jesus Christ
2 Thess. 1:12	Lord Jesus	Lord Jesus Christ
Acts 19:10	the Lord	the Lord Jesus
1 Cor. 16:22	the Lord	the Lord Jesus Christ
Acts 6:3	the Spirit	the Holy Spirit
Acts 8:18	the Spirit	the Holy Spirit
1 Cor. 2:13	the Spirit	the Holy Spirit

The fact that Alexandrian readings tend to be supported by both external and internal evidence has convinced most NT scholars of the reliability of this method of textual analysis. Not only are Alexandrian manuscripts our earliest, but their readings tend to be confirmed by recognized patterns of textual transmission. Further confirmation has come from the discovery of biblical papyri over the last two centuries (see Question 8). These papyri

6. See James R. White, *The King James Only Controversy: Can You Trust the Modern Translations?* (Minneapolis: Bethany House, 1995), 45–46.

manuscripts, which represent our earliest NT documents, have tended to follow Alexandrian readings.

The Critical Text and Contemporary Versions

The Greek text that results from using this method of textual criticism is called the Critical Text. It is represented in two main printed editions, the United Bible Societies' (UBS) *Greek New Testament*, now in its fifth edition, and the Nestle-Aland *Novum Testamentum Graece*, currently in its twenty-eighth edition. Both editions include an apparatus listing textual variants and their supporting manuscripts.

Almost all contemporary English versions of the New Testament follow the Critical Text. The only exception is the New King James Version, which follows the Textus Receptus. In its notes, however, the NKJV provides variant readings from both the Critical Text (marked as "NU" = Nestle-Aland/United Bible Societies) and the Byzantine family (marked as "M" = "Majority" text, since Byzantine readings always represent the majority of manuscripts).

Summary

While the KJV is the most influential English translation of all time, it suffers today from two important weaknesses: its archaic language (see previous question) and an inferior Greek text behind its New Testament translation. Today we have access to earlier Greek manuscripts, whose reliability can be confirmed using the tools of textual criticism.

REFLECTION QUESTIONS

1. What is the Textus Receptus, and how did it come to be? What role did Erasmus's Greek NT play in its development?

2. What role did Westcott and Hort play in the establishment of contemporary methods of textual criticism?

3. What is the Byzantine family of manuscripts? What is the Alexandrian family?

4. What are the main rules textual critics use for evaluating textual variants, causing them to arrive at the Critical Text? Why is the "harder" reading usually the better one?

5. Which contemporary English versions follow the Critical Text? Which follow the Textus Receptus?

QUESTION 28

When Was the King James Version Revised and Why?

As we have seen, contrary to those who claim the KJV is the only real Bible, it was in fact part of a long line of English versions and revisions, which included Wycliffe, Tyndale, Coverdale, Matthew's, the Great Bible, the Bishops' Bible, and the Geneva Bible. The KJV translators themselves acknowledged this in the lengthy preface that was originally published with the KJV. They write, "Truly, good Christian Reader, we never thought from the beginning that we should need to make a new translation, nor yet to make of a bad one a good one . . . but to make a good one better."[1] No translation is perfect, they assert, but all versions that are faithful to the text communicate God's Word:

> We affirm and avow, that the very meanest translation of the Bible in English set forth by men of our profession . . . containeth the word of God, nay, is the word of God. . . . No cause therefore why the word translated should be denied to be the word, or forbidden to be current, notwithstanding that some imperfections and blemishes may be noted in the setting forth of it.[2]

Though all translations—including their own—contain "some imperfections and blemishes," these do not detract from their value as the Word of God. Nor should this prevent translators from improving on the translation in subsequent revisions.

1. "The Translators to the Reader," preface to the King James Version, reproduced in Appendix C of Dewey M. Beegle, *God's Word into English* (New York: Harper & Brothers, 1960). For this quote see p. 146.
2. "The Translators to the Reader," 142.

Revising the KJV

That the 1611 edition of the KJV was never a perfect translation is evident from the fact that subsequent editions corrected errors and made minor improvements. Some of these were grammatical or stylistic errors. Others were printing mistakes. Perhaps the most infamous printing error came in an edition of 1631 in which the word "not" was inadvertently omitted from the Seventh Commandment, so that it read, "Thou shalt commit adultery"! The edition became known as the "Wicked Bible," and the king's printer was fined three hundred pounds by Archbishop Laud. Less scandalous but still humorous was an Oxford edition of 1717, which became known as the "Vinegar Bible" because the chapter heading in Luke 20 had "The Parable of the Vinegar" instead of Vineyard. An edition published in Oxford in 1795 was dubbed the "Murderer's Bible" after the printer accidentally replaced "Let the children be filled" with "Let the children be killed" in Mark 7:27. F. F. Bruce points out that all these changes may be summed up by a misprint in Psalm 119:161: "Printers have persecuted me without a cause" (the text should have read "Princes").[3]

Revisions to the 1611 edition were made in new Cambridge editions in 1629 and 1638. More comprehensive corrections were made by Thomas Paris in a 1762 edition from Cambridge and by Benjamin Blayney in 1769 from Oxford.[4] Blayney's edition is viewed by many as the "standard" KJV.

Others sought to improve the text by revising the KJV on the basis of the discovery of earlier Greek manuscripts and the changing views of textual criticism. Between 1718–24, Edward Wells produced a revised edition of the KJV called *The Common Translation Corrected*. In 1729 Daniel Mace published a critical Greek text with the KJV beside it, the latter corrected in line with the Greek text. William Whiston, who succeeded Sir Isaac Newton in the chair of mathematics at Cambridge, published *The Primitive New Testament* in 1745. In it he "corrected" the KJV in line with the Greek text of Codex Bezae (D). Similarly, in 1840 Samuel Sharpe published *The New Testament, Translated from the Greek of J. J. Griesbach*, a revision of the KJV that followed Griesbach's critical Greek text.[5]

Other revisions of the KJV had different kinds of improvements in mind. In 1768 John Wesley produced a revision "for plain, unlettered men who understand only their Mother Tongue." In it he made about twelve thousand changes to the KJV. In 1833 the American lexicographer and philologist Noah Webster produced his own edition of the KJV, replacing many archaic words with modern equivalents and updating the style to reflect contemporary idioms.[6]

---

3. All examples here are from F. F. Bruce, *History of the Bible in English: From the Earliest Versions*, 3rd ed. (New York: Oxford University Press, 1978), 108–9.
4. Bruce M. Metzger, *The Bible in Translation: Ancient and English Versions* (Grand Rapids: Baker, 2001), 78.
5. Bruce, *History of the Bible in English*, 127–34.
6. Metzger, *Bible in Translation*, 90–92.

The Revised Version (RV, 1885)

While there were many private attempts to revise the King James Version through the years, the first to gain official church support began as a proposal by Bishop Wilberforce of Winchester at the Anglican Convocation of Canterbury in 1870. The proposal called for the establishment of a committee "to report upon the desirability of a revision of the Authorized Version of the New Testament . . . in all those passages where plain and clear errors, be found to exist."[7] While the proposal at first mentioned only the New Testament, it was quickly revised to include the Old. The impetus for the new version was in part the changing English language, which increasingly rendered KJV language obsolete. More important, however, was the increasing scholarly consensus that the KJV New Testament was based on inferior Greek manuscripts. The translation was not to be a new translation, but a revision of the KJV. The translators were to "introduce as few alterations as possible into the Text of the Authorized Version consistently with faithfulness" and "to limit, as far as possible, the expression of such alterations to the language of the Authorized and earlier English versions."[8] This was similar to language used by the original KJV translators with reference to its predecessor, the Bishops' Bible. Like the KJV, the Old Testament was to be based on the standard Hebrew text (the Masoretic Text). The New Testament, however, was to be based on the updated Greek text of Wescott and Hort (see Questions 8 and 27), both of whom served on the revision committee.

The New Testament took eleven years to produce and was released in 1881 to significant fanfare. Two million copies were sold in Britain in a few days; 110,000 copies were sold in Philadelphia and two Chicago newspapers published the entire New Testament in their May 22 edition. The full Bible was published in 1885.

The greatest strength of the Revised Version (RV) was its use of the earlier and more reliable Greek manuscripts for the New Testament. The Old Testament also represented a major improvement in accuracy over the KJV, because of significant advances in biblical scholarship since the seventeenth century. Where the RV was doomed to failure, however, was in its English style. The revisers followed a more consistently literalist approach than the KJV translators and paid less attention to readability and stylistic elegance. The great English preacher Charles Haddon Spurgeon is purported to have said that the Revised New Testament was "strong in Greek, weak in English."[9] As a result, the RV never seriously challenged the KJV in terms of popular appeal.

---

7. Bruce, *History of the Bible in English*, 135.
8. Bruce, *History of the Bible in English*, 137.
9. Metzger, *Bible in Translation*, 104.

The American Standard Version (ASV, 1901)

It was originally hoped that a single version of the RV would become standard for both the British and American public, and early in the process an American committee was established. The Americans, however, found it hard to operate under the strict terms established by the revision committee. Furthermore, in the days before air travel, meeting together was impractical. Proposals on sections of text would be sent to America for input and then returned with comment. American proposals had to gain the approval of two-thirds of the British committee to be accepted. For the differences that remained, the American committee would yield its preference. The most significant differences would then be published in an appendix to the Revised Version. By this agreement, no distinct American version could be published until fourteen years after the RV's release.

At the publication of the full Bible of the RV in 1885, the American committee decided to continue its work until a final decision on its publication would be made. In the meantime, unauthorized editions of the RV incorporating the American readings from the appendix were published in New York and Philadelphia. Since these included only some of the American changes, the American committee continued its work, and in 1901 the American Standard Version (ASV) was published. The name "Standard" was added to distinguish its official status from the unauthorized copies.[10]

The ASV introduced about six hundred readings preferred by the Americans. Its strengths and weaknesses are similar to those of the RV. Although utilizing the better Greek NT manuscripts, it suffers from an overly literal approach to translation and is stylistically less readable. The greatest idiosyncrasy was rendering the divine name YHWH in the Old Testament as "Jehovah," instead of as "LORD" (see Question 22). The ASV also retains the Hebrew transliteration "Sheol" where the KJV had translated "the grave," "the pit," or "hell." Other notable changes include the use of "Holy Spirit" instead of the KJV's "Holy Ghost" and "love" instead of "charity" in 1 Corinthians 13.

The Revised Standard Version (RSV, 1952)

The ASV of 1901 was considered by many to be overly literal, and discussions for its revision began in 1928, when its copyright was acquired by the International Council of Religious Education. The Standard Bible Committee was appointed, originally comprised of fifteen scholars, with the charge of making further revision to the text of the ASV. Lack of funding because of the Great Depression in America slowed the pace considerably, until Thomas Nelson and Sons, publishers of the ASV, agreed in 1936 to fund the project with advance royalties. While it was hoped that British scholars could be included, the Second World War made this impossible. Work in America

10. Metzger, *Bible in Translation*, 102–3.

continued through the war years, and the New Testament was published in February 1946. The full Bible followed in September 1952.

The Bible was released with huge fanfare and an unprecedented first printing of nearly a million copies. The Revised Standard Version (RSV) had much going for it. Its translation committee was made up of some of the leading OT and NT scholars in the world, with names such as H. J. Cadbury, F. C. Grant, A. T. Robertson, and the famed archaeologist William F. Albright. The committee also had extensive denominational diversity, including Congregationalists, Methodists, Episcopalians, American Baptists, Southern Baptists, Presbyterians, Disciples of Christ, Quakers, and Lutherans. Its publicity placed it squarely in a position to become heir to the KJV tradition—updated in terms of contemporary English and advances in biblical scholarship.

Yet while some evangelicals celebrated its release and wrote in praise of its accuracy, many others were skeptical or openly critical. The most scathing attacks came from the fundamentalist camp, which subjected the RSV to unrelenting castigation. The passage that raised the most ire was Isaiah 7:14, where the RSV had translated the Hebrew term *ʿalmah* as "young woman" instead of "virgin." From the perspective of the RSV translators, this was a more accurate rendering of the Hebrew word, which most commonly referred to a young woman of marriageable age, not specifically to a virgin. Hebrew had a more specific term for virgin, *betulah*, which was not used in the Hebrew text here. Yet in the wake of the modernist-fundamentalist controversies of the 1920s, where the virgin birth and other "fundamentals" of the faith had been under attack, this seemed to many conservatives to be clear evidence of a liberal conspiracy. One pastor held up a copy of the RSV in front of his congregation with the word "fraud" written on it and then ripped out and burned the page bearing Isaiah 7:14. Another sent Luther Weigle, chairman of the RSV committee, a metal box containing the ashes of a book he claimed was the RSV. Pamphlets appeared with titles like "The New Per-Version of the Bible" and "The Devil's Masterpiece."[11]

Many other passages in the RSV were similarly criticized. The RSV used the term "expiation" instead of the KJV's "propitiation" in Romans 3:25. While "expiation" carries the sense of a sacrifice that covers or atones for sins, "propitiation" includes the idea of the appeasement of God's wrath. Critics claimed that the RSV had gone soft on God's righteous wrath and the critically important doctrine of penal substitution.

Romans 9:5 became another crux verse, since it relates to the deity of Christ. The KJV had punctuated the phrase "God blessed forever" in apposition to "Christ":

11. See Peter Thuesen, *In Disconcordance with the Scriptures: American Protestant Battles over Translating the Bible* (New York: Oxford University Press, 1999), 97–98.

KJV Whose are the fathers, and of whom as concerning the flesh Christ came, who is over all, God blessed for ever. Amen.

The RSV interpreted the phrase "God blessed forever" as a closing doxology related to God the Father, not Christ:

RSV to them belong the patriarchs, and of their race, according to the flesh, is the Christ. God who is over all be blessed for ever. Amen.

To be fair to the RSV, it is *not* true, as some critics claimed, that the RSV intentionally denied the deity of Christ. Passages like Romans 9:5 were translated this way because of grammatical considerations. The RSV included many other strong statements of Jesus's deity in passages like John 1:1, Titus 2:13, and 2 Peter 1:1.

The RSV was also heavily criticized for its textual decisions, since it followed the Critical Text instead of the Textus Receptus. Opponents did not seem to care that the earlier RV and ASV had also utilized contemporary methods of textual criticism. Those weaned on the KJV were aghast that the longer ending of Mark was relegated to a footnote.

There is little doubt that these attacks were for the most part theologically rather than exegetically driven. Fundamentalist opponents considered the National Council of Churches (NCC), the sponsoring body of the RSV, a liberal organization whose goal was the unification of all denominations into one "Superchurch." It was galling to them that the NCC claimed the RSV was the "new authorized" version. Carl McIntire, who published one of the most influential anti-RSV pamphlets, wrote, "We have here an effort on the part of the NCC to elevate itself to a position in the Protestant world where it will be 'the authority.'"[12]

One of the strangest accusations against the RSV was that it was pro-communist. During the heyday of McCarthyism in the 1950s, the politically liberal sentiments of some of the translation committee members became tinder for the fires already raging around the RSV. In 1960 the US Air Force Reserve published a counter-subversive training manual that "warned recruits to avoid, among other things, the communist-tainted RSV Bible."[13] The RSV was not just a red-letter Bible. It was a Red Bible through and through!

In retrospect, it would be difficult to assert that *any* of the RSV readings so vehemently criticized were in fact "wrong"—at least from the perspective of biblical scholarship. They are all possible interpretations of the biblical text. Indeed many were right—that is, almost certainly more accurate than earlier

12. Thuesen, *Disconcordance*, 101.
13. Thuesen, *Disconcordance*, 104.

versions. This is especially the case with reference to its Greek base text. Yet the RSV became the victim of an ideological debate raging in the church, namely, the modernist/fundamentalist controversy. The result was that, although the RSV experienced significant commercial success and critical acclaim, it never became a standard translation for the evangelical world and so never came close to usurping the KJV as "the church's Bible."

We will discuss later revisions to the KJV, including the NASB, NKJV, NRSV, and ESV under part 5: "Contemporary English Versions."

Additional Note: Formal Equivalent Versions Outside the KJV Tradition

The examples given above demonstrate that most formal equivalent versions used today are part of the KJV tradition. Yet there are several notable exceptions to this. One of the most famous was Robert Young's *Literal Translation of the Bible*.[14] Young, an Edinburgh bookseller best known for his *Analytical Concordance to the Bible*, produced an English version that had as its goal one-to-one correspondence with the Hebrew and Greek. By following the word order of the original Hebrew and Greek and seeking strict lexical and syntactic concordance, Young's obscure work may best be viewed as confirming the impossibility of literal translation. It functioned best as a crib for seminary students who forgot to prepare their Hebrew or Greek lessons for class.

Another extremely wooden-literal version close to the time of Young's was that of Julia Evelina Smith, the first woman to translate the entire Bible into English. Julia and her sister Abby were followers of the millenarian theology of William Miller, whose interpretation of the book of Daniel resulted in predictions that Christ would return in 1843. Smith became an avid student of the Bible, learning Latin, Hebrew, and Greek and translating the Bible from the Greek (New Testament and Septuagint), the Latin (Vulgate), and the Hebrew (Masoretic Text). Her translation was eventually published in 1876 as *The Holy Bible: Containing the Old and New Testaments; Translated Literally from the Original Tongues*. Like Young's, it was extremely literal and at times incomprehensible, seeking one-to-one correspondence between English words and Hebrew, Latin, and Greek counterparts.[15]

---

14. Robert Young, *The Holy Bible, Containing the Old and New Covenants Literally and Idiomatically Translated out of the Original Languages* (Edinburgh: A. Fullarton, 1862).
15. Metzger, *Bible in Translation*, 92–98. For more on the fascinating story of the production of this Bible and the Smith family legacy, see Kathleen L. Houseley, *The Letter Kills but the Spirit Gives Life: The Smiths—Abolitionists, Suffragists, Bible Translators* (Glastonbury, CT: Historical Society of Glastonbury, 1993); Susan J. Shaw, *A Religious History of Julia Evelina Smith's 1876 Translation of the Holy Bible: Doing More Than Any Man Has Ever Done* (San Francisco: Mellen Research University Press, 1993).

Summary

Minor revisions to the KJV began shortly after its publication. While most of these were minor corrections and improvements, others tried to improve the text by adapting it to the earlier Greek manuscripts or by clarifying its sometimes-archaic English. The first major revision with broad ecclesiastical support was the Revised Version of 1885 and its American counterpart, the American Standard Version of 1901. While both utilized the better Greek manuscripts, both also followed an even more literalistic approach, reducing their popular appeal. The next major revision came in the Revised Standard Version of 1952. It was produced by world-class biblical scholars and had wide denomination support. Yet its cutting-edged critical scholarship could also be seen as its liability, since innovative translations like "young woman" instead of "virgin" in Isaiah 7:14 and "expiation" instead of "propitiation" with reference to Christ's death (Rom. 3:25; Heb. 2:17; 1 John 2:2; 4:10) were seen as dangerous condescension to a liberal agenda. This resulted in relentless attacks from fundamentalist opponents.

REFLECTION QUESTIONS

1. Why were revisions to the KJV considered necessary by many scholars?
2. What goals were set out for the Revised Version (RV)?
3. How did the ASV differ from the RV?
4. Who was behind the RSV and what advantages did it have as a translation?
5. What kinds of attacks did the RSV endure?

QUESTION 29

What Have Been the Main Roman Catholic Versions of the Bible?

As we have noted previously, the Latin Vulgate, translated by Jerome in the fourth century AD, became the official Bible of the Roman Catholic Church.[1] For much of its history, the church discouraged vernacular translations of the Bible. This was in part due to the fear that independent-minded Bible readers might interpret Scripture differently from the official teachings of the church. This, of course, is what happened during the Protestant Reformation, when Martin Luther challenged the Scriptural basis for Catholic practices like the selling of indulgences and papal infallibility.

This points to a basic difference in how Protestants and Roman Catholics view the authority of Scripture. For Protestants the Bible is the church's highest authority for faith and practice. *Sola Scriptura* ("Scripture alone") was the rallying cry of the Protestant Reformation. Accurate translation and interpretation of the Bible is therefore essential for determining Christian doctrine. Roman Catholics have a more nuanced perspective. The Roman Catholic Church (RCC) also considers the Bible to be infallible and authoritative, but only when it is interpreted in line with authentic apostolic tradition. And this tradition is maintained and protected by the magisterium, or church leadership, as represented by the pope. "Catholics insist that there is a need for a teaching magisterium to rule on just what is and is not authentic apostolic tradition," so that "infallible guidance in

1. We have not included a question on English versions of the Eastern Orthodox Church because the Orthodox churches do not officially endorse any English version. For the Old Testament, Orthodox believers consider the Septuagint to be the inspired text and for the New Testament, the Byzantine Greek text. For this reason, Orthodox Christians have historically tended to favor the King James Version over contemporary English versions because of its use of Byzantine New Testament manuscripts (see Questions 8 and 27). In 2008 Thomas Nelson published *The Orthodox Study Bible,* which utilizes the St. Athanasius Academy Septuagint for its OT text and the New King James Version for the NT text.

interpreting the Bible comes from the church."[2] The Council of Trent of 1546 concluded that no one could interpret "Sacred Scripture . . . contrary to the unanimous consent of the Fathers."[3] This means that in practice, the RCC magisterium establishes doctrine and becomes the final arbiter on disputed issues.

In this context, vernacular translations were not only unnecessary for establishing truth, but could be dangerous by encouraging erroneous doctrines. Yet this also created a tension for the church, since awareness of the story of Scripture and its teaching is important for Christian growth and maturity. The proliferation of Protestant Bible versions in the sixteenth and seventeenth centuries resulted in recognition by many Roman Catholics of the need for devotional Bible study. Since the late sixteenth century, therefore, several Roman Catholic English versions have received sanction from the RCC. Official approval or license for publication by the RCC is known as *imprimatur*. To receive such imprimatur, a Bible must contain the deuterocanonical books (Apocrypha; see Question 7). Here we will briefly survey various Roman Catholic English versions.

The Douay-Rheims Bible (NT, 1582; OT, 1610)

The first complete Roman Catholic Bible in English was the Douay-Rheims Bible. This version has a history (ironically) parallel to the Geneva Bible. While the Geneva Bible was produced by Protestants who had fled England during the reign of the Catholic Queen Mary Tudor, the Douay-Rheims version was produced by Roman Catholics who fled England during the Protestant reign of Elizabeth I. During this time, a Catholic seminary was established at Douay in Flanders for the training of English priests. Recognizing the need for a Catholic version in English to rival the flourishing Protestant versions, a translation project was launched under the leadership of Jesuit scholar Gregory Martin. The seminary moved to Rheims in 1578, and the New Testament was completed in 1582. Financial pressures delayed completion of the whole Bible until 1610.

The Douay-Rheims version was translated from the Latin Vulgate, the official Bible of the RCC. At times its literal style mimics the Latin, making it almost unintelligible. The Lord's Prayer, for example, asks God to give us today "our supersubstantial bread" (Matt. 6:11); in the parable of the good Samaritan, the Samaritan tells the innkeeper that he will repay "whatsoever thou shalt supererogate"; John the Baptist and Jesus call on the people to do "penance," because the kingdom of God is at hand.[4]

---

2. Norman L. Geisler and Ralph E. MacKenzie, *Roman Catholics and Evangelicals: Agreements and Differences* (Grand Rapids: Baker, 1995), 180–81.
3. Geisler and MacKenzie, *Roman Catholics and Evangelicals*, 181–82.
4. F. F. Bruce, *History of the Bible in English: From the Earliest Versions*, 3rd ed. (New York: Oxford University Press, 1978), 118–21.

Like the Geneva Bible, the Douay-Rheims version had a full set of notes defending its theology. This was intended to respond to Protestant teaching and support the Counter-Reformation. At points these notes pulled no punches. In the note on Matthew 6:24, the "two masters" that compete for allegiance are explained as "two religions, God and Baal, Christ and Calvin, Masse and Communion, the Catholike Church and Heretical Coventicales."[5]

The Douay-Rheims-Challoner Revision (NT, 1749; OT, 1750)

The Douay-Rheims version underwent minor revisions through the years, but by the middle of the eighteenth century it was largely unintelligible to many readers. The task of a major revision fell to Bishop Richard Challoner (1691–1781), Vicar Apostolic of the London District. The revised New Testament was published in 1749 and the Old Testament in 1750. Challoner was a converted Protestant and so very familiar with the KJV, and the revision draws heavily from the language and cadence of the KJV. The Douay-Rheims-Challoner Bible was authorized for Roman Catholics in the United States in 1810.

Ronald A. Knox's *The Holy Bible, A Translation from the Latin Vulgate* (NT, 1945; OT, 1949)

Born the son of an Anglican priest, Ronald Knox was a gifted writer and scholar who studied classics at Eton and Oxford. At age twenty-nine he converted to Roman Catholicism and in 1939 began work on a Bible translation. Although a papal decree in 1943 allowed Catholics to translate from the Hebrew and Greek rather than the Latin Vulgate (see discussion below), Knox had already translated much of the New Testament from the Vulgate and so continued on this course. His version was the first officially approved English version for Catholics since Douay-Rheims-Challoner. Knox was a gifted writer, and his translation was meant to be a literary rather than a literal translation. In his book *Trials of a Translator*, Knox claims to be following the translation principle of Hilaire Belloc, asking not, "How shall I make this foreigner talk English?" but rather, "What would an Englishman have said to express the same?"[6] Yet in many places Knox's prose is not as fluid as one might hope. In 1 Corinthians 1:10, Paul calls the church to unity:

---

5. Bruce M. Metzger, *The Bible in Translation: Ancient and English Versions* (Grand Rapids: Baker, 2001), 69.
6. From Ronald A. Knox, *Trials of a Translator* (New York: Sheed & Ward, 1949), 75–76. Cited by Sakae Kubo and Walter F. Specht, *So Many Versions? 20th Century English Versions of the Bible*, rev. ed. (Grand Rapids: Zondervan, 1983), 63.

Knox	Only I entreat you, brethren, as you love the name of our Lord Jesus Christ, use, all of you, the same language.
NIV	I appeal to you, brothers and sisters, in the name of our Lord Jesus Christ, that all of you agree with one another in what you say.

Curiously, while Knox does not reproduce the poetry of the Old Testament in verse structure, he does seek to preserve the structure of Hebrew acrostic psalms. For example, he reproduces Psalm 118 (Vulgate/LXX = Psalm 119 MT), with each line of the first stanza starting with a word that begins with an "A"; the second stanza, a "B," and so on. By skipping certain letters (Q, X, Y, Z), he kills two birds with one stone, reducing the English alphabet to the same number of letters as the Hebrew alphabet (22), and avoiding the nearly impossible task of finding meaningful words that begin with these rare letters.

The Confraternity Version (NT, 1941; OT, 1948–69)

The Douay-Rheims-Challoner version served the Catholic Church well for almost two hundred years. But by the mid-twentieth century there was a need for a significant revision. This task was undertaken by the Episcopal Committee of the Confraternity of Christian Doctrine. In 1941 a major revision of the NT was released with the name *The New Testament of Our Lord and Savior Jesus Christ*. Though the work remained a translation of the Vulgate, the translators had incorporated insights from the Hebrew and Greek into the translation and included notes alerting readers to places where the Greek and Latin texts differed. The Old Testament followed and was released in stages, between 1952 and 1969.

New American Bible (NAB, 1970)

In 1943 an encyclical was issued by Pope Pius XII declaring that the original Hebrew and Greek texts of Scripture had greater authority than ancient or modern versions. The encyclical, known as *Divino afflante spiritu*, read in part:

> We ought to explain the original text which was written by the inspired author himself and has more authority and greater weight than any, even the very best, translation whether ancient or modern. This can be done all the more easily and fruitfully if to the knowledge of languages be joined a real skill in literary criticism of the same text.[7]

7. "Preface to the New American Bible Old Testament," in *The Revised New American Bible* (Washington, DC: Confraternity of Christian Doctrine, 1991).

Prior to this, Roman Catholic versions were translated only from the Latin Vulgate. The New Testament of the Confraternity Version (see above) was translated before this encyclical and so was translated from the Vulgate. The Old Testament, however, had been translated after the encyclical, and so the Hebrew was used. When it came to publishing the whole Bible, the committee decided it was only appropriate to re-translate the New Testament from the original Greek.

The complete Bible was released in 1970 as the New American Bible (NAB). The NAB is more idiomatic than Douay-Rheims-Challoner but more literal than the Jerusalem Bible and the New Jerusalem Bible (see below). The NAB is also more ecumenical than previous Catholic versions. Five of the fifteen members of its committee were Protestants, including Frank M. Cross, J. A. Sanders, David Noel Freedman, W. D. Davies, and John Knox. A revised version of the NAB appeared in 1986, which incorporated, among other changes, the moderate use of gender-inclusive language (see Questions 18–20). The foreword states:

> When the meaning of the Greek is inclusive of both sexes, the translation seeks to reproduce such inclusivity insofar as this is possible in normal English usage, without resort to inelegant circumlocutions or neologisms that would offend against the dignity of the language.[8]

Inclusive language is thus preferred, but only in keeping with faithfulness to the original text and maintaining good English style. A revised edition of the Old Testament was begun in 1994 and a fourth edition of the whole NAB was released in 2011.

Jerusalem Bible (JB, 1966)

The Jerusalem Bible (JB), like the NAB, arose in part in response to the 1943 encyclical mentioned above. As a result of the decree, a group of Dominican scholars at the École Biblique in Jerusalem translated the Bible into French, the *Bible de Jérusalem*, which was published in 1956. This version was widely acclaimed for its accuracy and literary qualities, so an English edition was proposed. While the work was inspired by the French edition, the English translators first worked from the Hebrew and Greek texts, then compared this closely with the *Bible de Jérusalem*. The work was published in 1966. The Jerusalem Bible is more idiomatic than the New American Bible. One unique feature is its rendering of the divine name (the Tetragrammaton: YHWH) as Yahweh, rather than with the traditional LORD. The JB was revised

8. "Preface to Revised Edition" (New Testament) in *The Revised New American Bible* (Washington, DC: Confraternity of Christian Doctrine, 1986).

over the years for various purposes and in various ways. The next three versions, NJB, NCB, RNJB, are all revisions of it.

New Jerusalem Bible (NJB, 1985)

When a new edition of the *Bible de Jérusalem*, the predecessor of the JB, was published in 1973, the decision was made to update the Jerusalem Bible. The chief editor of the new edition was Henry Wansbrough of Ampleforth Abbey, Yorkshire. It was published in 1985 as the New Jerusalem Bible (NJB). The NJB is slightly more literal than its predecessor (JB) but somewhat freer than the NAB. Like the JB, the NJB translates the Tetragrammaton (YHWH) as "Yahweh." For the traditional "Lord of hosts," the NJB has "Yahweh Sabaoth." When the Hebrew idiom "son of man" means "human being," the NJB translates it uniquely as "child of Adam" (Num. 23:19; Ps. 8:4; Heb. 2:6).

The NJB, like the 1986 revision of the New American Bible, adopted the moderate use of gender-inclusive language. The preface states, "Considerable efforts have been made, though not at all costs, to soften or avoid the in-built preference of the English language, a preference now found so offensive by some people, for the masculine; the word of the Lord concerns men and women equally."[9]

New Catholic Bible (NCB, 2007)

In 2007, the Catholic Truth Society published the New Catholic Bible (NCB), a revised version of the original Jerusalem Bible (1966) intended to bring its text in line with the lectionaries used in most English-speaking countries. These changes were in line with directives of the Congregation for Divine Worship and the Discipline of the Sacraments and the Pontifical Biblical Commission. The Tetragrammaton (YHWH), which the Jerusalem Bible had rendered as "Yahweh," was returned to the traditional "Lord" throughout the Old Testament. The Psalms of the JB were completely replaced with the 1963 Grail Psalter, an earlier revision of the JB Psalms. The revision also contained new introductions, text notes, and liturgical notes, many of them integrating material from the NJB.[10]

Revised New Jerusalem Bible (RNJB—NT and Psalms, 2018; Full Bible, 2019)

A new edition of the New Jerusalem Bible, known as the Revised New Jerusalem Bible (RNJB) was released in the New Testament and Psalms in 2018 and as a full Bible in 2019. Henry Wansbrough again served as chief editor. Some of the significant changes in this edition include introducing more

9. Foreword to *The New Jerusalem Bible* (New York: Doubleday, 1985).
10. Henry Wansbrough, foreword to *The New Catholic Bible* (London: Catholic Truth Society, 2007).

gender-inclusive language and returning to the tradition of translating the Tetragrammaton (YHWH) as "Lord" instead of "Yahweh." Ancient measurements are also more commonly translated using modern metric equivalents. The new edition also seeks to reflect shifts in contemporary English, such as the increasing use of "will" over "shall" in emphatic or prophetic futures.

Catholic Editions of "Protestant" Bibles

Since the 1960s, a number of traditionally Protestant versions have produced "Catholic Editions." The main difference between these and their Protestant counterparts is the inclusion of the Apocrypha (see Question 7). The first of these was the Revised Standard Version Catholic Edition (RSVCE), published in 1965–66. Under the editorship of Bernard Orchard OSB and Reginald C. Fuller, the Catholic Biblical Association adapted the RSV text for use by Catholics. The deuterocanonical (Apocryphal) books were placed in the traditional order found in the Vulgate. In their introduction, the editors state their goal of making "the minimum number of alterations, and to change only what seemed absolutely necessary in the light of Catholic tradition."[11] A revised edition appeared in 2006.

The Catholic Living Bible, a Catholic edition of the enormously popular Living Bible, received an imprimatur from the Roman Catholic Church in 1976.[12] It contains the deuterocanonical books and an introduction written by Pope John Paul II entitled "Why Read the Bible?" Other Catholic editions of traditionally Protestant versions include the New Revised Standard Version Catholic Edition (NRSVCE, 1993), the Good News Translation Catholic Edition (GNTCE, previously TEV, 1979/1993), the New Living Translation Catholic Edition (NLTCE, 2001/2015), and the English Standard Version Catholic Edition (ESV-CE; 2018; see Question 31 for more on this).

Summary

The flurry of Bible translations in vernacular languages provoked by the Protestant Reformation became impetus for the RCC to produce its own vernacular versions. While these were at first translated only from the Latin Vulgate, the official Bible of the RCC, a papal decree in 1943 encouraged translations directly from the Hebrew and Greek. In addition to translations produced by RCC scholars, a number of originally Protestant versions have come out in Catholic editions that include the deuterocanonical books.

---

11. From the "Introduction to the 1966 Edition," *Revised Standard Version, Second Catholic Edition*. (San Francisco: Ignatius Press, 2005).
12. *The Catholic Living Bible* (Carol Stream, IL: Tyndale House, 1976). Imprimatur: Leo A. Pursley, Bishop of Fort Wayne-South Bend, January 9, 1976.

REFLECTION QUESTIONS

1. What was the first official Roman Catholic translation of the Bible into English?
2. What was distinctive about Ronald Knox's Roman Catholic version?
3. How would you describe the origin of the New American Bible?
4. How would you describe the origin of the New Jerusalem Bible?
5. What Protestant Bibles have appeared in Roman Catholic editions? What is the difference between these Protestant and Roman Catholic editions?

QUESTION 30

What Were the Earliest Natural-Language English Versions?

Many Bible versions appeared in the early twentieth century that sought to reproduce the Bible in natural, idiomatic English. The rationale for these was that since the Greek of the New Testament was Koine or "common" Greek—the language of everyday discourse—then the Bible should be translated into common or natural English. These translations in many ways paved the way for the many dynamic equivalent and functional equivalent versions that appeared in the latter part of the twentieth century.

The Twentieth Century New Testament (1900/1904)

This remarkable version was unique in that it was not only the first truly modern-English version but also it was produced primarily by laypeople, not by professional scholars. The work was initiated in 1891 by two people, Mary Higgs of Oldham, England, the wife of a congregational minister, and Ernest de Mérindol Malan, a signal and telegraph engineer from Hull, whose grandfather had been a Swiss minister and hymn writer. They had been brought together by W. T. Stead, editor of *The Review of Reviews*, after both had independently written letters encouraging the production of a contemporary version of the Bible that young people could understand. They solicited volunteers for the work, and over time, approximately twenty people were involved in the translation. Some were ministers, but most were educated laypeople. Most of the time they worked independently, communicating by mail. As the work progressed, at times they consulted with scholars, most notably the classicist Richard F. Weymouth, who would shortly produce a modern-English version of his own. The process took more than ten years, and the complete New Testament was published in 1901 as *The Twentieth Century New Testament: A Translation into Modern English Made from the Original*

Greek (Wescott & Hort's Text). A second edition, taking into account suggestions made by readers of the first edition, was published in 1904.

The text is ordered following natural paragraph divisions, with verse numbers noted in the margin. Topical section headings are given every few paragraphs. The books of the New Testament are ordered somewhat differently from their traditional order. The preface clarifies: "The order in which the Books and Letters of the New Testament appear in this translation is due to the desire not to inconvenience a reader, familiar with the old order, more than is necessary, but, at the same time, to make an advance in the direction of such a chronological arrangement, as modern research has rendered possible." Three sections are distinguished by genre: (1) Historical Books: Mark, Matthew, Luke, John, Acts (Mark first since most scholars think it was written first); (2) Letters: James, 1–2 Thessalonians, Galatians, 1–2 Corinthians, Romans, Colossians, Philemon, Ephesians, Philippians, 1–2 Timothy, Titus, Hebrews, 1–2 Peter, Jude, 1–3 John; and (3) Revelation.

This version has been widely praised for its accuracy and readability. It is often noted how remarkable, even miraculous, this is, since it was not produced by biblical scholars. Yet perhaps we should not be so surprised. The meaning of the biblical text is generally quite clear. It is reproducing that meaning into clear and accurate English that can be the greater challenge. Scholars, with their constant eye on the Hebrew and Greek, tend to translate into "Biblish" (or "Greeklish") an awkward hybrid of English and Hebrew/Greek idiom. English speakers, by contrast, speak and write in standard English. This is why, increasingly, Bible translation committees are including English stylists in addition to biblical scholars. Perhaps we should have learned that lesson 120 years ago when this version first appeared!

R. F. Weymouth's *The New Testament in Modern Speech* (1903)

Richard F. Weymouth was a classical scholar who had served as headmaster of Mill Hill School and as a teaching fellow at University College, London. He had also been a consultant for the *Twentieth Century New Testament*. In 1862 he published an edition of the Greek New Testament called *The Resultant Greek Testament*, which was based on the majority consensus of the main Greek editions of the nineteenth century. The Greek text included an apparatus at the bottom of the page indicating where his text differed from the Textus Receptus or other recent Greek editions. Recognizing from his many years of teaching Greek the need for a contemporary-language translation of the Bible, Weymouth set out to produce one, basing its text on his own Greek edition. Weymouth died in 1902, before his work was published, but the work was completed by Ernest Hampden-Cook, a Congressional minister, who had worked on the *Twentieth Century New Testament*. The volume was published in 1903 and entitled *The New Testament in Modern Speech, an*

Idiomatic Translation into Every-day English from the Text of "The Resultant Greek Testament."

Being a fastidious schoolmaster as well as a classical scholar, Weymouth paid special attention to grammatical accuracy and Greek tense function. Weymouth's text was therefore not just simplified English. For example, he was willing to retain archaic language if it was still understandable in his day and if it contributed to "the dignity of style that befits the sacred themes."[1] In this way Weymouth sought to be sensitive to the register, or reading level, at which the original texts were written. Weymouth states in his preface that his goal is not to replace the traditional versions like the AV and RV, but rather to supplement them for better understanding. At the same time, he expresses hope that his work would become the basis for a new version that might one day replace the AV and RV.[2] This suggests that Weymouth really did believe that using contemporary English made the text not only more comprehensible but also *more accurate*.

James Moffatt's *The New Testament: A New Translation* (NT, 1913; OT, 1924; Full Bible, 1928)

James Moffat's translation is perhaps the best known of the single-translator Bibles of the first half of the twentieth century. Moffatt was a Scottish biblical scholar who held teaching positions at Mansfield College in Oxford, United Free Church College in Glasgow, and eventually at Union Theological Seminary in New York. In 1901, Moffatt published *The Historical New Testament*, a new translation of the New Testament documents arranged in what he considered to be their chronological order. He was awarded an honorary doctor of divinity from the University of St. Andrews for this work. In 1913 he published *The New Testament: A New Translation* and followed this in 1924 with *The Old Testament: A New Translation*. The two were combined into *A New Translation of the Bible* in 1928.

Moffatt's translation was well respected for its high level of scholarship and for its fine idiomatic English. Yet it was also controversial because of its idiosyncrasies and liberal bent. First, the New Testament was based on the recently published Greek text of Hermann von Soden, which came to be viewed by scholars as full of defects. Second, and more importantly, Moffatt was willing to adopt a good number of textual emendations—changes not based on manuscript readings, but on scholarly conjecture. For example, in the puzzling passage about preaching to spirits in prison in 1 Peter 3:19, Moffatt translated, "Enoch also went and preached to the imprisoned spirits"—even though no Greek manuscripts have "Enoch" here. The translation also gained a reputation for being liberal because of Moffatt's use of various font styles to distinguish different sources

1. R. F. Weymouth, *The New Testament in Modern Speech* (London: James Clarke, 1908), viii.
2. Weymouth, *New Testament in Modern Speech*, ix.

as delineated in the Documentary Hypothesis, the critical theory related to the sources behind the Pentateuch, the first five books of the Old Testament. Other (more orthodox) idiosyncrasies include the use of "The Eternal" for the divine name Yahweh (YHWH or LORD) and the use of the transliteration "Logos" instead of the translation "the Word" in John 1.

E. J. Goodspeed's *An American Translation* (NT, 1923; OT, 1927; Full Bible, 1931)

The New Testament of *An American Translation* was the work of Edgar J. Goodspeed, who was professor of New Testament at the University of Chicago from 1900 to 1937. After giving a paper in 1920 pointing out problems in various modern-speech versions, Goodspeed was encouraged by representatives of the University of Chicago Press to produce a translation of his own. Goodspeed agreed, with encouragement from his wife, and the New Testament was published in 1923 as *The New Testament: An American Translation.* An Old Testament edition was subsequently requested, and Goodspeed recruited an Old Testament colleague, J. M. Powis Smith, to supervise the work. It was completed in 1927, and the full Bible was published in 1931.

This version may be viewed as an American counterpart to Moffatt's Scottish-English version. Goodspeed himself indicates this in his preface, where he points out that "for American readers, especially, who have had to depend so long upon versions made in Great Britain, there is room for a New Testament free from expressions which, however familiar in England or Scotland, are strange in American ears."[3] Despite this very real need, sometimes good English is simply good English, and Goodspeed's version received high praise on both sides of the Atlantic. Perhaps not surprising, because of the nature of the American market, the version also received some criticism, especially because it was produced by the "liberal" University of Chicago divinity school. Yet in reality it was significantly more conservative than Moffatt's.

Helen Barrett Montgomery's *The Centenary Translation of the New Testament* (1924)

Helen Barrett Montgomery was an American educator, writer, and social reformer. In 1921 she was elected as the first woman president of the Northern Baptist Convention. As an activist she raised money in support of many causes, including colleges for women in China. She also worked for her church with boys who lived on the streets, where she came to recognize the deficiencies of the archaic language of the King James Version. Having studied Greek at Wellesley College, she was inspired by the Weymouth New Testament (1903)

3. E. J. Goodspeed, *The New Testament: An American Translation* (Chicago: University of Chicago Press, 1923), vii.

to produce a new version in natural English. This work was published in 1924 by the American Baptist Publication Society as *The Centenary Translation*, in celebration of the society's one-hundredth anniversary. It was later reprinted as *The New Testament in Modern English*. Montgomery was the first woman to produce a translation published by a professional publishing house.[4]

In addition to a highly accessible text, Montgomery utilized various features to aid in reading, including indented paragraphs with verse numbers in the margins, adding explanatory section headings, and italicizing citations of the Old Testament in the New. Her egalitarian inclinations are evident in that she often adopts interpretations that support a more active role for women: (1) Phoebe is identified as a "minister" (*diakonos*) in Romans 16:1; (2) Junia is taken as a woman's name, and she and Andronicus are referred to as "notable among the apostles" (Rom. 16:7); (3) 1 Corinthians 11:13 is taken as a statement rather than a question, so that Paul concludes, "It is fitting that a woman should pray to God with her head unveiled"; (4) the silence of women enjoined in 1 Corinthians 14:34–35 is treated as a Corinthian slogan, which Paul disagrees with in verse 36; (5) in 1 Timothy 2:15 women will be saved by "the Child-bearing" (i.e., by Christ), not by the maternal role of giving birth to children; and (6) in 1 Timothy 3:11 *gynaikes* ("wives" or "women") is interpreted as "deaconesses".[5] Overall this is an excellent translation, both scholarly and readable. One must wonder whether its general neglect has been, at least in part, because of the gender of its translator.

J. B. Phillips's *The New Testament in Modern English* (PME, 1958)

Like Helen Barrett Montgomery, John Bertram Phillips was motivated to translate the Bible while working with young people who found it difficult to understand the KJV. Phillips was training to be an Anglican minister and working with a youth group in south London when he began translating portions of the New Testament into common English to help his students understand. In 1947 he published Paul's letters as *Letters to Young Churches* and followed this with *The Gospels in Modern English* in 1952, *The Young Church in Action* in 1955, and *The Book of Revelation* in 1957. The whole New Testament was published together in 1958. The appeal of Phillips's translation was not just its simplicity, but also its dynamic style and vivid relevance. It was perhaps the most popular of the modern English versions until the remarkable success of Kenneth Taylor's Living Bible.

---

4. Julia E. Smith (see Question 28) had self-published her translation at her own expense.
5. See Sharyn Dowd, "Helen Barrett Montgomery's 'Centenary Translation of the New Testament', Characteristics and Influences," *Perspectives in Religious Studies* 19, no. 2 (1992): 133–50, available at www.godswordtowomen.org/Dowd.htm.

Kenneth Taylor's The Living Bible (NT, 1967; Full Bible, 1971)

The Living Bible began from the desire by Kenneth Taylor to help his ten children understand the difficult language of the KJV during family devotions. His success at rephrasing biblical passages in simple language gave him the idea that a clear and natural translation might be helpful for others as well. In 1962 Taylor published *Living Letters*, a paraphrase of the New Testament Epistles that he had produced mostly while commuting by train to Chicago. Other volumes followed. The full New Testament was published in 1967 and the whole Bible in 1971 as the Living Bible (LB). The natural English and lively style of Taylor's work made it extremely popular, especially among young people. Another major part of its success was the Bible's conservative credentials. In 1963 *Living Letters* was endorsed by the Billy Graham Evangelistic Association and offered on Graham's television program. Sales skyrocketed. In 1972 the Living Bible was the bestselling book in the United States, with four million dollars in royalties. By 1974 it accounted for 46 percent of Bible sales in the United States.[6] The explosive growth provoked Taylor to form his own publishing house, Tyndale House Publishers, to manage sales.

The term "paraphrase" normally means the restatement of a text in different words, usually for the purpose of clarification. In this sense, the LB is a true "paraphrase," since Taylor's method was to simplify the very literal American Standard Version into everyday language. The primary strength of the LB is its vivid relevance for contemporary readers. Its primary weakness is that as the work of a single translator, who himself was not a biblical scholar, its paraphrases are not always as accurate to the original meaning of the text as they could be. An attempt to remedy this would come with the publication of the New Living Translation, a major revision of the LB meant to retain its readability while improving its accuracy (see Question 32).

Others of Notable Mention

Space does not permit a review of the many other contemporary English versions of the early to mid-twentieth century. A few of notable mention include the following: American Baptist scholar Charles B. Williams, *The New Testament: A Translation in the Language of the People* (1937); Greek scholar and Presbyterian minister Gerit Verkuyl, *The Berkeley Version* (NT, 1945; full Bible, 1959); Methodist missionary and educator Charles Kingsley Williams, *The New Testament in Plain English* (1952); Lutheran Church–Missouri Synod (LCMS) pastor and seminary professor William F. Beck, *The New Testament in the Language of Today: An American Translation* (1963).

---

6. Jack P. Lewis, *The English Bible, from the KJV to the NIV: A History and Evaluation*, 2nd ed. (Grand Rapids: Baker, 1991), 238.

Summary

A number of modern English versions appeared in the early decades of the twentieth century, a preview of the proliferation of functional equivalent versions later in the century. These versions were almost all single-translator projects, rather than committee works. One exception is the *Twentieth Century New Testament*, a committee work. This version is itself unique, however, in that it was translated almost exclusively by laypeople, rather than by biblical scholars.

Of these natural-language versions, the most impactful was Kenneth Taylor's Living Bible, whose skyrocketing sales demonstrated the immense hunger to hear God's Word as a clear, contemporary, and relevant message for today.

REFLECTION QUESTIONS

1. What is the *Twentieth Century New Testament*, and how did it come to be?

2. What are some unique characteristics of James Moffatt's NT translation?

3. What was unique about Helen Barrett Montgomery's *The Centenary Translation of the New Testament*?

4. Who was J. B. Phillips, and what prompted him to produce a New Testament in modern English?

5. What is the Living Bible and how did it come to be?

PART 5

Contemporary English Versions

Since there has been a consistent stream of Bible translations into the English language since the beginning of the twentieth century, it is impossible to draw a strict line (or a specific date) as to what constitutes a "contemporary" English version. The versions we will survey in the next three questions are considered contemporary because they are (1) still read and used widely today, and (2) readily available in print or electronic form; that is, they must be popular and accessible. We will divide them into three questions related to their translation philosophy: (1) formal equivalence, (2) functional equivalence, and (3) mediating. (See Question 3 for the meaning of these terms.)

QUESTION 31

What Are the Most Popular Formal Equivalent Versions Today?

New American Standard Bible (NASB—NT, 1963; Full, 1971)

The New American Standard Bible (NASB) was produced under the auspices of the Lockman Foundation, the same nonprofit that sponsored the Amplified Bible. The NASB was a revision of the American Standard Version (ASV) of 1901, the American counterpart to the Revised Version (RV, 1885). The NASB is thus in the line of the KJV and "based on the time-honored principles of translation of the ASV and KJV."[1] It was produced, in part, as a response to the perceived liberalism of the Revised Standard Version (RSV) of 1952 (see Question 28). The foreword to the 1977 edition begins with this emphasis:

> The New American Standard Bible has been produced with the conviction that the words of Scripture as originally penned in the Hebrew, Aramaic, and Greek were inspired by God. Since they are the eternal Word of God, the Holy Scriptures speak with fresh power to each generation, to give wisdom that leads to salvation, that men may serve Christ to the glory of God.[2]

The NASB was produced by fifty-eight conservative evangelical scholars from various Protestant denominations and traditions, including Baptist, Presbyterian, Methodist, Nazarene, and Congregationalist. These translators

1. Preface to The New American Standard Bible (La Habra, CA: Lockman Foundation, 1977).
2. Foreword to The New American Standard Bible (La Habra, CA: Lockman Foundation, 1977).

were originally kept anonymous, but later were disclosed.[3] The NT appeared in 1963 and the whole Bible in 1971, with significant revisions in 1977, 1995, and 2020.

The NASB is probably the most consistently literal English version widely available today, explicitly claiming to adhere to "the principles of formal equivalence translation."[4] We have noted in previous questions what this entails, especially *lexical concordance* and *grammatical correspondence* (see Question 3). One of the ways the NASB seeks to maintain formal equivalence is by using *italics* to indicate words that are not found in the original Hebrew, Aramaic, or Greek but are implied by it,[5] an issue discussed in Question 15. Another unique feature meant to retain formal equivalence is the noting of Greek historical presents with an asterisk.[6] The Editorial Board claims two main goals: "to adhere as closely as possible to the original languages of the Holy Scriptures, and to make the translation in a fluent and readable style according to current English usage."[7] By most accounts, the NASB has succeeded admirably in the first point, but fallen short in the second.

Some other distinct features of the NASB were meant to reflect reverence for the sacred text, such as capitalizing personal pronouns when referring to deity and retaining archaic personal pronouns ("thou," "thee,") and verbal forms (e.g., "saith") when addressing God in prayer. For example, while Peter and John address the Sanhedrin as "you" in Acts 4:19, in the prayer of the church that follows they address God as "Thou" and "Thy" (4:27). As noted in Question 22, neither capitalized pronouns nor archaic forms have precedent in the Hebrew or Greek texts.

The 1995 edition increased overall readability, updated some archaic language, and, significantly, eliminated the pronouns "thou," "thee" and "thy" in prayer language to God. The preface to the 2020 edition claims to build on the strengths of the 1995 version by improving accuracy, modernizing language, and improving readability. Most remarkably, however, the 2020 edition adopts gender-inclusive language. Under the category "Gender Accuracy," the 2020 preface states:

---

3. "Translators of the New American Standard Bible," WholesomeWords.org, accessed December 8, 2021, https://www.wholesomewords.org/nasbtran.html.
4. "Version Information: New American Standard Bible," BibleGateway.com, https://www.biblegateway.com/versions/New-American-Standard-Bible-NASB/#vinfo.
5. Foreword to the NASB (1977).
6. For the nature of the historical present tense, see Daniel B. Wallace, *Greek Grammar Beyond the Basics: An Exegetical Syntax of the New Testament* (Grand Rapids: Zondervan, 1996), 526–32. The NASB is not altogether consistent here, and a number of historical presents are not marked.
7. Foreword to the NASB (1977).

> In past editions it was common practice to translate the Greek word *anthrōpoi* as "men" and the Hebrew *adam* when used in the plural as "men," as well as all the pluralistic uses of *ish* and similar words. The same was true for singulars, as masculine. This was never intended to be gender-exclusive when the context indicated that women were included; it was assumed at that time that readers inferred the inclusion of women. Gender accuracy is important, however, so in this edition Greek and Hebrew words that are not actually exclusive in gender as they are used in a given context are rendered by inclusive terms, such as "people." Just as important, when the words in the original languages are in fact referring only to males or females, the distinction is maintained in English.

The next paragraph notes that previous editions of the NASB translated the Greek *adelphoi* as "brethren" because this term was still used to address members of a profession, society, or church, regardless of gender. English has changed, however, and "brethren" is now archaic. While the natural replacement would be "brothers," this term is perceived by most readers as exclusive of men and so is inaccurate in these contexts. So when the author or speaker is clearly referring to women, the NASB 2020 now translates "brothers *and sisters*," with the latter in italics to indicate it is not in the Greek.

While it is refreshing to see the NASB move toward greater gender accuracy, the solution of introducing italics is still linguistically flawed (see Question 15). Neither "brothers" nor "sisters" is in the Greek (so both should be in italics!). The Greek word is *adelphoi*, which in this context means "siblings" (i.e., "brothers and sisters") not "brothers." To refer to "brothers" as the "literal meaning" is a lexical fallacy (see Question 10).

Linguistics aside, not everyone is happy with innovation, especially with reference to gender accuracy, and a group of scholars from John MacArthur's Master's Seminary were clearly unhappy with the NASB 2020 edition. They received approval to produce a version of the NASB that would not introduce these gender changes. This version has been renamed the *Legacy Standard Bible* (LSB) and represents a minor revision of the 1995 NASB.[8] According to the translators, the LSB "seeks to be an improvement upon the NASB '95, while simultaneously preserving its faithful legacy."[9] For these scholars, the NASB 2020 was evidently a (gender-inclusive) bridge too far.

---

8. See the Legacy Standard Bible homepage: https://lsbible.org.
9. Legacy Standard Bible (LSB), Lockman Foundation, accessed January 31, 2023, https://www.lockman.org/legacy-standard-bible-lsb.

New King James Version (NKJV—NT, 1979; Full, 1982)

A good number of English translations have been revisions of the King James Version or revisions of revisions. Only a few, however, have taken its name, including the *King James II Version* (KJVII, 1971) and the New King James Version. These two have in common an attempt to retain the majestic style and cadence of the KJV, while updating its archaic words. Both also sought to return to the Greek text used by the 1611 translators, the Textus Receptus (see Question 27). The former was produced by Jay Green and published in 1971. Today it is a relic of history. The NKJV, by contrast, has been well marketed and remains one of the most popular English versions. For years, it moved back and forth with the NLT for the third spot in English Bible sales, consistently behind only the NIV and the KJV.

The NKJV was conceived by Arthur Farstad of Dallas Theological Seminary and Samuel Moore, president of Thomas Nelson Publishers of Nashville, Tennessee. More than 130 evangelical scholars did the translation work over a seven-year period. The New Testament appeared in 1979, and the whole Bible followed in 1982. The NKJV seeks to update the KJV in word order, grammar, spelling, and vocabulary.[10] The archaic pronouns "thou," thee," "thy," and "thine" were replaced with "you," "your," and "yours," even in prayer language.

As just mentioned, the most notable difference between the NKJV and other KJV revisions is its New Testament textual basis, which reverts to the Textus Receptus (TR), the family of Greek editions of the New Testament behind the King James Version (see Question 27). Virtually all other modern versions use the Critical Text, derived from what are considered older and more reliable Greek manuscripts. Notably, however, footnotes in the NKJV point out manuscript differences between the TR and the Critical Text.[11]

The NKJV is one of the most literal, or formal equivalent, of the modern versions, competing with the NASB for this distinction. We have noted previously that the KJV is not as literal as some suppose, and at times the translators intentionally chose variety over consistency to achieve better English style. The NKJV revision, by contrast, tends toward more formal consistency and so sometimes fall short of the style and literary achievement of its predecessor.

New Revised Standard Version (NRSV, 1990/2022)

After the RSV was published in 1952, its translation committee continued to meet every few years to make minor corrections to the text and consider new directions. Significant advances in biblical scholarship were taking place

10. For a good discussion of these changes, see Sakae Kubo and Walter F. Specht, *So Many Versions? 20th Century English Versions of the Bible*, rev. ed. (Grand Rapids: Zondervan, 1983), 275–91.
11. These also note variants in the Majority (= Byzantine) Text; see Questions 8 and 27.

during this period, particularly in the comparative studies of Semitic languages. The Dead Sea Scrolls also continued to provide new insights into the culture and background of the biblical text. Considering these and other developments, in 1974 the National Council of Churches, which held the copyright to the RSV, authorized its Division of Christian Education to produce a new edition, to be called the New Revised Standard Version. Bruce Metzger of Princeton Theological Seminary chaired the translation committee. The complete Bible was published in 1990.

The NRSV was the first English version to consistently and comprehensively introduce gender-inclusive language for masculine generic terms in Hebrew and Greek (see Question 18). The mandate for the committee was that "masculine-oriented language should be eliminated as far as this can be done without altering passages that reflect the historical situation of ancient patriarchal culture."[12]

Like its predecessors (KJV; RV; ASV; RSV), the NRSV is a formal equivalent version. But it is somewhat more idiomatic than these and more sensitive to Greek and Hebrew idioms. In this sense it is closer to the "mediating" spectrum of translation than these others. The NRSV is especially respected and widely used in academic circles—the translation of choice for many scholars. It is also one of the most ecumenical versions, widely used in mainline denominations. It is offered in three formats: a Protestant format without the Apocrypha, a Roman Catholic edition with the Apocrypha, and a Common Edition with all the books of the Protestant, Catholic, and Eastern Orthodox canons.

A new edition was released in 2022. In addition to improving clarity and taking account of advances in biblical scholarship, this revision seeks greater sensitivity toward people by avoiding demeaning terms and not identifying them by their disabilities. Mark 14:69 now speaks of a "female servant" instead of a "servant-girl." Matthew 4:24, which previously referred to "demoniacs, epileptics and paralytics," now refers to "people possessed by demons or having epilepsy or afflicted with paralysis."

English Standard Version (ESV, 2001)

In 1997 Lane Dennis, president of Crossway publishers, negotiated with the National Council of Churches to obtain the rights to revise the 1971 edition of the Revised Standard Version (RSV). The rights were granted in 1998, and the new edition was published in 2001 as the English Standard Version (ESV). The ESV translation committee consisted of fourteen members from various evangelical denominations and was chaired by Lane Dennis.

The ESV is a revision of the RSV, changing the text somewhere between 5 and 8 percent. The ESV removes the RSV's archaic "thees" and "thous" in

12. Preface to The New Revised Standard Version (New York: Division of Christian Education of the National Council of Churches of Christ, 1989).

prayer language and generally moves the text in a more consistently literal direction. The goal of the translators was to produce an "essentially literal" version and to remove the perceived liberal bias of the RSV. Notable changes in this regard included changing the RSV's "expiation" to "propitiation" (Rom. 3:25; Heb. 2:17; 1 John 2:2; 4:10) and changing "young woman" to "virgin" in Isaiah 7:14. The ESV also moves the RSV in a more gender-inclusive direction, for example, removing the words "man" and "men" almost seven hundred times from the RSV. While consistently retaining the translation "brothers" for *adelphoi*, a footnote at the word's first occurrence in each NT book acknowledges that in these contexts the word means "brothers and sisters."

The ESV went through minor revisions in 2007 and in 2011. In 2016 a third revision was released in which fifty-two words were changed in twenty-nine verses. This version was announced as the "ESV Permanent Text Edition" in which "the text of the ESV Bible will remain unchanged in all future editions printed and published by Crossway." This announcement was met with derision by many biblical scholars and was reversed a month later in order "to allow for ongoing periodic updating of the text to reflect the realities of biblical scholarship such as textual discoveries or changes in English over time."[13]

The ESV Study Bible, an exceptionally well-developed product, was released in 2008 and became a huge seller. This, together with the ESV's endorsement by well-known evangelical statesmen like John Piper and J. I. Packer, has made the ESV a particularly popular product, especially with those inclined toward Reformed theology and a complementarian view of gender relations.

The ESV has also broadened its base into new territory. In 2009 Oxford University Press published the English Standard Version Bible with Apocrypha. In this version the Apocrypha was placed after the Old Testament and was intended to be used for liturgical readings and for historical purposes. In 2018, the Conference of Catholic Bishops in India published the English Standard Version Catholic Edition (ESV-CE), in which the text was modified by a team of Catholic scholars to adhere to Catholic teaching. The Catholic edition was published in North America by the Augustine Institute, a private Catholic graduate school, as *The Augustine Bible*.[14]

In 2013 the Gideons International transitioned from the NKJV to the ESV for their distribution of free Bibles. Yet it was stipulated that they could

---

13. Jeremy Weber, "Crossway Reverses Decision to Make ESV Bible Text Permanent," *Christianity Today*, September 28, 2016, https://www.christianitytoday.com/news/2016/september/crossway-reverses-decision-esv-bible-text-permanent-mistake.html. See also Joe Carter, "Nine Things You Should Know about the ESV Bible," *The Gospel Coalition*, May 31, 2020, https://www.thegospelcoalition.org/article/9-things-you-should-know-about-the-esv-bible.
14. Peter Jesserer Smith, "Augustine Institute Publishes Major New Catholic Bible," *National Catholic Register*, May 13, 2020, https://www.ncregister.com/interview/augustine-institute-publishes-major-new-catholic-bible.

modify the text to agree with the Textus Receptus over the Critical Text. The Gideons' ESV text is thus altered in approximately fifty places to agree with the KJV and the Textus Receptus.

Summary

The four most widely used formal equivalent English versions today are the NASB, NKJV, NRSV, and the ESV. All four are revisions in the line of the KJV, with the NASB revising the ASV, and the NRSV and ESV revising the RSV. Of these four, only the NKJV follows the Textus Receptus—the family of Greek editions behind the KJV NT. Of the four, the NASB is probably the most literal, the NRSV the most respected among biblical scholars, the NKJV the most traditional, and the ESV the leading seller.

REFLECTION QUESTIONS

1. What did you find most interesting or surprising about each of the four versions surveyed here?

2. Have you used any of the four Bible versions discussed in this question? What was your impression?

3. What distinguishes the NKJV from the others?

4. The NRSV is the most ecumenical of the four. How is this demonstrated?

5. What factors have contributed to the popularity of the ESV?

QUESTION 32

What Are the Most Popular Functional Equivalent Versions Today?

As we have seen, many versions appeared in the early twentieth century that placed a high priority on natural, contemporary English (see Question 30). Edgar J. Goodspeed described his goal in producing one of these: "I wanted my translation to make on the reader something of the impression the New Testament must have made on its earliest readers."[1] This kind of vivid relevance was also the concern of J. B. Phillips in his *New Testament in Modern English* (1958) and Kenneth Taylor in his enormously popular *Living Bible, Paraphrased* (1967, 1971). For many readers, Taylor's dynamic and idiomatic renderings brought to life what had previously been a closed and incomprehensible book. Additional impetus for natural-language translations came from the world of international Bible translation and the linguistic theories associated especially with Eugene Nida, the United Bible Societies, and Wycliffe Bible Translators (SIL). As we have seen (Question 3), Nida originally referred to his method as "dynamic equivalence," later adopting the more appropriate designation "functional equivalence."[2] The second half of the twentieth century may rightly be called the heyday of functional equivalence in English Bible translation. Below we will survey five of the most important of these versions.

Today's English Version/Good News Translation (TEV/GNT—NT, 1966; Full Bible, 1976)

The first English version to consciously adopt the method of dynamic equivalence was a New Testament published by the American Bible Society in 1966, entitled *Good News for Modern Man: The New Testament in Today's English*

1. Edgar J. Goodspeed, *New Chapters in New Testament Study* (New York: Macmillan, 1937), 113.
2. See Jan de Waard and Eugene A. Nida, *From One Language to Another: Functional Equivalence in Bible Translating* (Nashville: Nelson, 1986), 7–8.

Version (TEV). The New Testament was translated by Robert Bratcher, Research Associate of the Translations Department of the American Bible Society. New editions followed in 1967 and 1971. In 1976 the fourth edition was published together with an Old Testament under the title *Good News Bible*. While the New Testament was produced almost completely by Bratcher, the Old Testament was produced by a seven-member panel of biblical scholars chaired by Bratcher. In 2001 the translation was renamed the Good News Translation (GNT). The reason for this change was to emphasize that the TEV was a true *translation*, not simply a paraphrase.

The original impetus for the TEV/GNT came from requests from Africa and Asia for an English translation suitable for those speaking English as a second language. Its clarity and natural English, however, widened its appeal to a much broader audience. The foreword to the translation states, "The Good News Bible in Today's English Version is a new translation which seeks to state clearly and accurately the meaning of the original texts in words and forms that are widely accepted by people who use English as a means of communication." It seeks "to set forth the biblical content and message in the standard, everyday, natural form of English."[3] Bratcher emphasizes the need to translate Hebrew and Greek words according to their meaning in context, rather than with a single English word. Clarity and simplicity are key. "Caesar" becomes "Emperor" or "Roman Emperor." "Centurion" is rendered in various ways depending on the context: "army officer, "captain in the Roman army," "commander," and so on. "The Sanhedrin" is "the Council." Technical theological terms are avoided. The traditional "justify" is usually rendered "put right with God" (Rom. 2:13; 3:20, 24, 26; 5:1, 9, etc.) The technical term "propitiation" becomes in 1 John 2:2 "the means by which our sins are forgiven." The popularity of the version is reflected in its exceptional sales. In its first six years, thirty-five million copies were sold.[4]

While praised for its clarity, the TEV/GNT has sometimes been criticized for oversimplifying the text and for imposing a uniform pedestrian style on the different authors and genres of Scripture. A revised edition was introduced in 1992 that updated the translation generally and incorporated a moderate use of gender-inclusive language (see Question 18).

New Century Version (NCV, 1987) and the International Children's Bible (ICB, 1987)

This version is one of the most basic and easy-to-read English Bibles—but with a complicated history of titles and publishers. It was originally produced as a version for deaf people by the World Translation Center in Fort Worth, Texas, a subsidiary of Bible League International (associated with the

3. "About the Good News Translation," GNT, accessed January 31, 2023, https://gnt.bible/about.
4. Sakae Kubo and Walter F. Specht, *So Many Versions? Twentieth Century English Versions of the Bible*, rev. ed. (Grand Rapids: Zondervan, 1983), 171.

Churches of Christ). The New Testament was published in 1978 by Baker Book House with the title *English Version for the Deaf* (EVD). Vocabulary selection was based upon *The Living Word Vocabulary* by Edgar Dale and Joseph O'Rourke, the standard used by the editors of *The World Book Encyclopedia.*

Realizing its potential for broader appeal, Baker then published an edition for a more general audience, entitled the Easy-to-Read Version (1980). It was geared toward a third-grade reading level. Recognizing its value for younger readers, this version was revised and published by Sweet Publishing (Ft. Worth, TX) in two separate editions, the International Children's Bible (ICB—NT, 1983; full Bible, 1987) and the New Century Version (NCV—NT, 1984; full Bible, 1987). Sweet Publishing subsequently merged with Worthy Publishing and in 1988 produced a special edition, known as *The Everyday Bible*, a version endorsed by Billy Graham.

When Sweet/Worthy was acquired by Word Publishing in 1991, the NCV was revised to a slightly higher reading level, with longer sentences and a more fluid style. In 1992 Word Publishing was acquired by Thomas Nelson, which continues to publish both the NCV and the ICB. In the 2000s, the NCV achieved a measure of marketing success through the publication of Thomas Nelson's Biblezines, with names like *Revolve* (2003), *Becoming* (2004), *Refuel* (2005), and *Explore* (2006). These are glossy magazines with the complete New Testament text of the NCV surrounded by pictures and articles, geared for teens and young adults. A new edition of the NCV was produced in 2005, with Tremper Longman III (Old Testament), Daniel Taylor (English stylist), and me (New Testament) serving as editors. The three of us later came together to produce the Expanded Bible (2011), a version that used the NCV as its base text with various in-text amplifications, expansions, alternate interpretations, more formal renderings, traditional translations, commentary, cross references, and textual variants (see Question 35).[5]

The NCV and ICB are simple-language functional equivalent versions. The NCV preface says the version is guided by two basic premises: faithfulness to the original text of Scripture, and clarity so that anyone can read and understand the Bible.[6] Difficult words are replaced with more easily understood terms: "justify" becomes "make right"; "genealogy" becomes "family history" (Matt. 1:1). Geographical names are clarified. "Lake Galilee" is consistently used instead of variants like the "Sea of Kinnereth," "Lake Gennesaret," and "Sea of Tiberias." Many rhetorical questions, which are potentially confusing for children, are reworded as statements (see Question 14). For example, "To whom will you liken me that we may be compared?" (Isa. 46:5 NIV) becomes in the NCV/ICB, "No one is equal to me or like me." Figures of speech are simplified, and idiomatic expressions are clarified. "Truly, truly, I say to you" (John 10:7 NASB) becomes in the NCV/ICB simply, "I tell you the truth." The difficult

5. *The Expanded Bible* (Nashville: Thomas Nelson, 2011).
6. Preface of The Holy Bible: New Century Version (Nashville: Thomas Nelson, 2005).

idiom "Then David slept with his fathers" (NASB) is translated simply as "Then David died" (1 Kings 2:10 NCV/ICB). The description of Canaan as "a land flowing with milk and honey" (Exod. 3:8 NIV) becomes in the ICB, "This is a land where much food grows" and in the NCV, "This is a fertile land." This last example illustrates the small differences between the NCV and the ICB.

Contemporary English Version (CEV—NT, 1991; Full, 1995)

Like the TEV/GNT, the Contemporary English Version (CEV) is a functional equivalent version produced by the American Bible Society. It was a committee work, overseen by international Bible translator and linguist Barclay Newman. The NT appeared in 1991 and the full Bible in 1995. A revision was released in 2005. As a successor to the TEV/GNT, the CEV applies even more consistently the principles for international Bible translation developed by Eugene Nida and his associates (see Question 3). The CEV utilizes short sentences and a simplified vocabulary. Sentences are reordered for clearer logic, making it particularly useful for children and remedial readers. Traditional Bible language is replaced to an even greater extent than in the TEV/GNT. God's "grace" is usually translated as God's "kindness"; "parable" becomes "story"; "Hosanna" is translated as "Hooray!" (Matt. 21:9).

The CEV's strength is simplicity, clarity, and readability. The introduction identifies the version as a companion rather than a replacement for traditional versions—a missionary version that seeks to cross cultural boundaries that other versions do not. The introduction also stresses that since more believers around the world *hear* the Bible rather than reading it for themselves, the CEV is designed especially for oral presentation and public reading:

> The *Contemporary English Version* has been described as a "user-friendly" and a "mission-driven" translation that can be *read aloud* without stumbling, *heard* without misunderstanding, and *listened to* with enjoyment and appreciation, because the language is contemporary and the style is lucid and lyrical.[7]

One common criticism of the CEV is that it sometimes oversimplifies the text, missing important nuances of meaning. Compare 2 Corinthians 5:17 in the CEV and the NIV:

CEV	Anyone who belongs to Christ is a new person. The past is forgotten, and everything is new.
NIV	Therefore, if anyone is in Christ, the new creation has come: The old has gone, the new is here!

7. "Welcome to the Contemporary English Version," in The Holy Bible: The Contemporary English Version (Nashville: Thomas Nelson, 1995).

The CEV is clear and straightforward, but misses important components of meaning: (1) the consequential "therefore," linking Paul's statement to his previous discussion; (2) the "new creation" language, so important for Paul's eschatology framework; and (3) the incorporation "in Christ" language that is central to Paul's soteriology.

God's Word (GW, 1995)

God's Word translation was produced by God's Word to the Nations Bible Society, which is (unofficially) affiliated with the Lutheran Church–Missouri Synod (LCMS). The work began as a revision of William F. Beck's *New Testament in the Language of Today* (see Question 30), with the intention of completing the full Bible, but eventually it became a complete retranslation of both the OT and the NT. Five scholars, seventeen technical reviewers, and four English reviewers did the work.[8] The first edition was published by World Publishers of Iowa Falls, Iowa, in 1995. In 2008 Baker Publishing Group acquired rights to the translation.

In its preface the version claims to be using neither formal equivalence nor functional equivalence, but rather "closest natural equivalence"—a translation policy that avoids the awkwardness of literal versions and the loss of meaning of idiomatic ones. Despite this attempt to distinguish itself as unique, God's Word clearly fits into the genre of functional equivalent versions like the TEV, NCV, CEV, and NLT. It is generally accurate and readable, comparable to these others in style and quality.

New Living Translation (NLT, 1996/2004)

The New Living Translation is today the most popular of the functional equivalent versions and consistently ranks in the top four or five in sales among English Bible versions. The NLT (1996) was a major revision of the enormously popular Living Bible. While the LB was the work of a single translator, Kenneth Taylor, the NLT is a committee work involving some ninety evangelical scholars from various denominations. While the Living Bible identified itself as a paraphrase, meaning a simplification and clarification of another English version (in this case the American Standard Version), the NLT is promoted as a true translation, which follows the translation philosophy of dynamic, or functional, equivalence. "The goal of this translation theory is to produce in English the closest natural equivalent of the message expressed by the original-language text, both in meaning and in style."[9] The transition from paraphrase to functional equivalence can

8. "God's Word Translation," accessed September 5, 2022, https://en.wikipedia.org/wiki/God%27s_Word_Translation.
9. Introduction to The Holy Bible: New Living Translation (Carol Stream, IL: Tyndale House, 2015).

be seen in John 1:1. The LB originally read, "Before anything else existed, there was Christ." The NLT has "In the beginning, the Word already existed," retaining both the allusion to Genesis 1:1 and the christological title "the Word."

A major revision of the NLT was subsequently released in 2004. A "Note to Readers" explains how this new edition came about:

> While the NLT's [1996] influence was rapidly growing, the Bible Translation Committee determined that an additional investment in scholarly review and text refinement could make it even better. So shortly after its initial publication, the committee began an eight-year process with the purpose of increasing the level of the NLT's precision without sacrificing its easy-to-understand quality. This second-generation text was completed in 2004, with minor changes subsequently introduced in 2007, 2013, and 2015.[10]

The significant scope of these changes may be seen by a close examination of the LB (1971), the original NLT (1996), and the NLT revision (2004). Compare the three editions on Romans 3:23–25:

Living Bible	NLT 1st ed.	NLT 2nd ed.
23 Yes, all have sinned; all fall short of God's glorious ideal; 24 yet now God declares us "not guilty" of offending him if we trust in Jesus Christ, who in his kindness freely takes away our sins. 25 For God sent Christ Jesus to take the punishment for our sins and to end all God's anger against us. He used Christ's blood and our faith as the means of saving us from his wrath. In this way he was being entirely fair, even though he did not punish those who sinned in former times. For he was looking forward to the time when Christ would come and take away those sins.	23 For all have sinned; all fall short of God's glorious standard. 24 Yet now God in his gracious kindness declares us not guilty. He has done this through Christ Jesus, who has freed us by taking away our sins. 25 For God sent Jesus to take the punishment for our sins and to satisfy God's anger against us. We are made right with God when we believe that Jesus shed his blood, sacrificing his life for us. God was being entirely fair and just when he did not punish those who sinned in former times.	23 For everyone has sinned; we all fall short of God's glorious standard. 24 Yet God, in his grace, freely makes us right in his sight. He did this through Christ Jesus when he freed us from the penalty for our sins. 25 For God presented Jesus as the sacrifice for sin. People are made right with God when they believe that Jesus sacrificed his life, shedding his blood. This sacrifice shows that God was being fair when he held back and did not punish those who sinned in times past,

10. "A Note to Readers," in *New Living Translation* (2015).

To determine which edition of the NLT you are using, look at the date on the copyright page. Also, the logo for the 1996 edition is set in a square box; the 2004 edition is a diamond shape on top of the square.

Summary

Five of the most popular functional equivalent versions were surveyed here. The TEV/GNT was the first English Bible to consistently follow the translation principles of dynamic/functional equivalence developed by Eugene Nida and his colleagues involved in international Bible translation. The NCV was originally developed as a translation for the deaf and subsequently revised into a general-purpose idiomatic translation (NCV) and a children's Bible (ICB). God's Word (GW) translation is a high-quality functional equivalent version produced in Lutheran circles. The CEV is a major revision of the TEV, seeking even greater clarity and fluidity when read aloud. The NLT is the best selling of functional equivalent versions. It is a major revision of Kenneth Taylor's Living Bible, this time overseen by a committee of biblical scholars. The 1996 NLT itself went through a major revision in 2004.

REFLECTION QUESTIONS

1. What are the goals of functional equivalent versions?
2. What was distinctive about the TEV? What is the significance of its translation approach?
3. How did the NCV get its start? Why is this significant with reference to its translation goals?
4. What is distinctive about the CEV? What is its goal with reference to public reading?
5. What is the origin of the NLT? How is it different from the LB? What does the text say about the 2004 revision of the NLT?

QUESTION 33

What Are the Most Important Mediating Versions Today (apart from the NIV)?

The best-selling mediating version in the English language is the New International Version (NIV). The NIV is also the best-selling Bible in the world and the only version to have surpassed the King James Version in year-to-year Bible sales. For this reason, we have devoted a question to its history, nature, and revisions (see Question 34). The following versions are NIV-like in that they steer a clear middle course between formal and functional equivalence. In addition, all have in common that they are new translations (not revisions of the KJV) and committee translations (rather than the work of a single translator).

New English Bible (NEB—NT, 1961; Full, 1970) and Revised English Bible (REB, 1989)

The New English Bible was initiated in 1946 with an overture from the Presbytery of Stirling and Dunblane to the General Assembly of the Church of Scotland recommending the translation of the Bible be made in present-day language. After negotiations with several Protestant denominations of Great Britain and the University Presses of Oxford and Cambridge, a committee was formed and commissioned with the work. Four panels of scholars did the translation. The convener of the Old Testament panel was G. R. Driver of Oxford University. The Apocrypha panel was led by G. D. Kilpatrick, also of Oxford. C. H. Dodd, professor emeritus at Cambridge, oversaw the New Testament panel and served as general director of the entire project.[1]

The translation was intentionally not bound to the language of the Authorized Version. The introduction states that their goal was to "render

1. Bruce M. Metzger, *The Bible in Translation: Ancient and English Versions* (Grand Rapids: Baker, 2001), 132–33.

the Greek, as we understood it, into the English of the present day, that is, into the natural vocabulary, constructions, and rhythms of contemporary speech. We have sought to avoid archaism, jargon, and all that is either stilted or slipshod."[2] The New Testament was published in 1961 and the full Bible a decade later in 1970, together with a revision of the New Testament.[3]

Some literalists criticized the NEB for adding words not found in the original text. Metzger provides a list of some of these (italicized here, not in the NEB): "Those who sleep *in death*" (1 Thess. 4:13); "in *the province of* Asia" (Rev. 1:4); "*human* body" (Rom. 12:4); and "tongues *of ecstasy*" (1 Cor. 13:8). In most of these, the words in italics represent implicit meaning, which we have elsewhere noted is appropriate if contemporary readers might miss that meaning (see Question 15). The NEB also renders some traditional language in innovative ways. "Scribes" becomes "doctors of the law" (Mark 15:31, etc.); the parable of the "talents" is the parable of the "bags of gold" (Matt. 25:14–30); "saints" becomes "God's people" (Col. 1:2, etc.); "beloved" as an address becomes "dear friends" (1 John 4:7, etc.).[4] These kinds of translations have become commonplace in other recent mediating versions, like the NIV, CSB, and NET, since they capture the original meaning more clearly. For example, the "scribes" of Judaisms were not copyists, as the name suggests, but teachers or experts in the Mosaic law (cf. NIV; NET). "Talents" were not abilities, as most readers will assume, but rather a huge measure of gold worth millions of dollars. "Dear friends" (cf. NIV; CBT; NET) is a close English approximation to what the Greek word *agapētoi* communicated. Few people today would address their friends as "Beloved."

The NEB was also criticized for its British colloquialisms. In Joshua 15:18, Caleb's daughter Achsah arrives to see her father riding on a donkey. The KJV's translation, "and she lighted off *her* ass," has provoked giggles through the centuries. But the NEB only made it worse by rendering the phrase, "she broke wind." Other NEB translations are similarly odd or perplexing. Proverbs 1:16 says that sinners "hasten hot-foot into crime." Jesus's teaching in his hometown synagogue raises the ire of his hearers, who "fell foul of him" (Mark 6:3), and Stephen's critical speech in Acts 7 "touched them on the raw" (Acts 7:54). Paul warns the Corinthians to "have nothing to do with loose livers" (1 Cor. 5:9), and in Revelation, the great and wicked city of Babylon is "bedizened" with gold and silver and pearls (Rev. 18:16).[5]

Shortly after the publication of the NEB in 1970, a committee was formed to assess criticism of the text. What was intended to be a minor

---

2. Cited by Metzger, *Bible in Translation*, 133.
3. The New English Bible (Oxford: Oxford University Press, 1970).
4. Metzger, *Bible in Translation*, 133–34.
5. Metzger, *Bible in Translation*, 136.

revision turned into a major one under a new name, the Revised English Bible (REB), published in 1989. The "thees" and "thous" used for prayer in the NEB are removed, the highbrow style is muted, and certain idiosyncratic readings changed. Greater consistency is achieved. For example, the Greek *ekklēsia* had been rendered a variety of ways in the NEB: church, congregation, meeting, community. The REB more consistently uses "church." The REB also introduced a moderate use of gender-inclusive language (see Questions 18–20).

New English Translation (NET, 2006/2017)

The NET Bible is another new version (not a revision), produced by twenty-five biblical scholars. It is available free online at Bible.org and other sites. The NET has two distinctive features. The first is its inclusion of more than sixty thousand footnotes that provide commentary on the biblical text. The preface to the first edition reads:

> This level of documentation is a first for a Bible translation, making transparent the textual basis and the rationale for key renderings (including major interpretive options and alternative translations). This unparalleled level of detail helps connect people to the Bible in the original languages in a way never before possible without years of study of Hebrew, Aramaic, and Greek. It unlocks the riches of the Bible's truth from entirely new perspectives.

The second distinctive feature of this version is an Internet format that allows the text to be constantly updated. The acronym "NET" is a play on words, referring both to the version's name, New English Translation, and to this Internet (online) format. The goal was to produce printed versions every decade or so with accumulated changes. After releasing "Beta" editions of the New Testament in 1998 and the whole Bible in 2001 and 2003, the official first edition was published in 2006 and a second edition in 2017.

The NET is a mediating version that steers a middle course between formal and functional equivalence. Its notes are particularly helpful for those interested in Bible translation, since they allow readers to "look over the shoulder" of translators to see why decisions were made. Although produced by conservative evangelical scholars, the NET translators were not afraid to follow contemporary scholarship into controversial areas. For example, Isaiah 7:14 in the NET renders the Hebrew *'almah* as "young woman" rather than as "virgin." An extensive note provides the justification for this translation. The NET Bible is also one of the very few translations to follow much contemporary scholarship in rendering the Pauline phrase *pistis christou* as a subjective genitive, the "faithfulness of Christ" rather than traditionally as an objective genitive, "faith in Christ" (see Rom. 3:22, 26; Gal. 2:16, 20; 3:22; Eph. 3:12; Phil. 3:9).[6]

(Holman) Christian Standard Bible (HCSB—NT, 1999; Full, 2004; CSB, 2017)

The HCSB originally arose from a project initiated by Arthur Farstad, who had served as the general editor for the New King James Version. Farstad favored the Greek Majority Text (see Questions 8 and 27) and had published a Greek edition of it with coeditor Zane Hodges in 1982. His goal was to produce a modern English version based on the Greek Majority Text. Together with Edwin Blum, a faculty member at Dallas Theological Seminary, Farstad produced some portions of a translation of the New Testament.

In 1998, Farstad and Blum were approached by representatives of Holman Bible Publishers and LifeWay Christian Resources, the publishing arm of the Southern Baptist Convention (SBC). The SBC was seeking an alternative to the NIV for their curriculum because of the high cost of NIV royalties and the NIV's move toward gender-inclusive language. Farstad and Blum agreed to produce the version. Tragically, Farstad died just a few months into the project. Without his influence, the shift was made away from the Majority Text back to the Critical Text—bringing it in line with all other modern versions except the New King James Version. Some of Farstad's influence remained, however, in that the HCSB provides in its footnotes many alternative readings from the Textus Receptus and the Majority Text.

The HCSB was produced by an interdenominational team of one hundred scholars and proofreaders. The New Testament was published in 1999 and the full Bible in 2004. A second edition appeared in 2009. The HCSB is generally more literal than the NIV but less so than formal equivalent versions. According to its introduction, the HCSB strives for neither formal nor functional equivalence, but "optimal equivalence," which (not surprisingly) means the perfect balance between form and function.

Though well publicized and well received in many circles, the HCSB never achieved a significant market share of Bible sales. In June 2016 Broadman and Holman announced a revision of the translation, dropping the name "Holman" and renaming it the Christian Standard Bible (CSB). The Translation Oversight Committee was co-chaired by Tom Schreiner (Southern Baptist Theological Seminary) and David Allen (Southwestern Baptist Theological Seminary). Its translation philosophy was the same as

6. For the subjective genitive, see Richard B. Hays, *The Faith of Jesus Christ: The Narrative Substructure of Galatians 3:1–4:11*, 2nd ed. (Grand Rapids: Eerdmans, 2002). For support for the objective genitive, see A. Hultgren, "The *Pistis Christou* Formulations in Paul," *Novum Testamentum* 22 (1980): 248–63; J. D. G. Dunn, "Once More, ΠΙΣΤΙΣ ΧΡΙΣΤΟΥ," *SBL Seminar Papers* (Atlanta: Scholars Press, 1991), 730–44.

the HCSB, optimal equivalence, which "places equal value on fidelity to the original and readability for a modern audience, resulting in a translation that achieves both goals." [7]

The CSB rolled back some of the unique features of the HCSB:

1. The HCSB had translated the divine name YHWH as "Yahweh" in many contexts. Yet this was inconsistently done. The CSB returned to the traditional translation as "Lord" (small caps), a policy followed by almost all English versions (see Question 22).
2. The HCSB had capitalized pronouns for God (see Question 22). The CSB follows standard English grammar in returning these to lowercase.
3. The HCSB had touted its use of "Messiah" over "Christ," when the term *christos* is used as a title. The CSB continues this policy but significantly reduces the number of times the term is translated "Messiah" from 112 times to 55.
4. The HCSB had also touted its use of "slave" over "servant," since the Hebrew (*ʿebed*) and Greek (*doulos*) commonly indicate ownership. The CSB editors, however, recognizing how jarring "slave" sounded in many of these contexts, returned many of them to "servant." The word "slave(s)" occurred 316 times in the HCSB but only 188 times in the CSB. The use of "servant" increased from 771 (HCSB) to 921 (CSB).
5. The HCSB was intentionally conservative in its use of gender-inclusive language. The CSB significantly increased the use of inclusive terms (see Question 18).
6. The HCSB tended to use the term "languages" instead of "tongues" because the latter was considered archaic. Some critics viewed this as indicating an anti-charismatic agenda, and so the CSB committee returned to the traditional "tongues."

In summary, the CSB rolled back some of the idiosyncrasies of the HCSB while significantly improving its use of gender-inclusive language. Together these changes may make the version more appealing for a broader audience.

Common English Bible (CEB, 2011)

The Common English Bible, like the NEB, NIV, NET, and HCSB, is a new translation, not a revision of an existing version. Like these others, it takes an intentionally middle ground between formal and functional equivalence and claims its primary goals as accuracy and clarity. The preface states: "The CEB translators balanced rigorous accuracy in the rendition of ancient texts with an equally passionate commitment to clarity of expression in the

7. Introduction to Christian Standard Bible (Nashville: Holman Bible Publishers, 2017).

target language."[8] The version was sponsored by the Christian Resources Development Corporation, a consortium of Christian publishers that included Chalice Press (Disciples of Christ), Westminster John Knox Press (Presbyterian Church, USA), Church Publishing, Inc. (Episcopal Church), Pilgrim Press (United Church of Christ), and Abingdon Press (United Methodist Church).

The project was launched in 2008 and completed in 2011, the work of 120 biblical scholars from twenty-two faith traditions. The best way to describe the CEB might be as an NIV-style translation with a more ecumenical target audience. Most editions of the CEB include fourteen deuterocanonical (Apocryphal) books, including those found in both the Roman Catholic and Eastern Orthodox canons.

The textual basis for the New Testament was the twenty-seventh edition of the Nestle-Aland *Greek New Testament*. The Old Testament translators used as their base the Masoretic text as represented in the *Biblia Hebraica Stuttgartensia* and the *Biblia Hebraica Quinta*, while consulting biblical texts found in the Dead Sea Scrolls and Greek readings from the Septuagint.

The CEB often translates the Hebrew idiom *ben 'adam* (traditionally, "son of man") as "human being" in the Old Testament. Daniel 7:13 reads, "I suddenly saw one like a human being coming with the heavenly clouds." Similarly, in the book of Ezekiel, when the prophet is addressed by God as *ben 'adam* (93x), the CEB translates this as "human one." Uniquely, however, the CEB also renders the Greek equivalent (*ho huios tou anthrōpou*) as "the Human One" when Jesus refers to himself with this title in the Gospels. While readers may find this departure from the traditional "Son of Man" jarring, it is in fact a fair representation of the meaning of the phrase.

Summary

"Mediating" versions steer a middle ground between formal and functional equivalence. All the mediating versions surveyed here are new versions (NEB; NET; HCSB; CEB) or revisions of new versions (REB; CSB). None are in the direct line of the KJV. The NEB and REB are distinctly British versions. The NET Bible has the distinction of a massive number of footnotes dealing with textual and interpretational issues. The (H)CSB is a Southern Baptist version with a presumed goal of challenging the preeminence of the NIV. The CEB is a more ecumenical version with similar aspirations.

8. "Preface to the Common English Bible," Common English Bible (Nashville: Common English Bible, 2011).

REFLECTION QUESTIONS

1. What is meant by a "mediating" version?
2. In what ways did the NEB/REB depart from the KJV tradition?
3. What is most distinctive about the NET Bible?
4. In what ways did the CSB revise the HCSB?
5. What is distinctive about the CEB?

QUESTION 34

What Is the Most Popular English-Language Bible Today?

The New International Version (NIV) is the best-selling English-language Bible today, both in the United States and worldwide. The NIV was the result of a trans-denominational effort by more than one hundred scholars, sponsored by the nonprofit New York Bible Society (NYBS). Following the success of the NIV, in 1988 the NYBS was renamed the International Bible Society (IBS) to more accurately reflect its mission as an international Bible translation and distribution ministry. In 2009 it was again renamed Biblica. While Biblica holds the copyright to the NIV and publishes editions for ministry purposes, Zondervan Publishers has the primary rights to commercial publication in the United States and Hodder and Stoughton has the same rights in the United Kingdom. There is an Anglicized edition of the NIV published in the United Kingdom.

A Brief History of the NIV

The vision for the NIV began in the 1950s with a Christian businessman named Howard Long.[1] An avid evangelist, Long found the King James Version increasingly inadequate for sharing his faith. Though he personally loved the KJV's style and noble prose, he was often met with incomprehension and derision when quoting verses from it to others. A member of the Christian Reformed Church (CRC), Long approached his pastor, Peter De Jong, who showed great interest and began to advocate within the denomination for a new translation. After a series of delays and setbacks, a proposal for a new translation was eventually approved at the 1958 annual Synod of the CRC.

1. Much of the following material comes from John H. Stek, "The New International Version: How It Came to Be," in *The Challenge of Bible Translation: Communicating God's Word to the World*, Festschrift Ronald F. Youngblood, eds. Glen G. Scorgie, Mark L. Strauss, Steven M. Voth (Grand Rapids: Zondervan, 2003), 235–63.

Meanwhile, similar proposals for a new Bible translation were making their way through committees of the National Association of Evangelicals (NAE). Made up of thirty denominations and hundreds of individual churches, the NAE had been formed in 1942 in response to the liberalizing tendencies of the National Council of Churches.

To make a long story short, the NAE and the CRC eventually came together and formed a joint committee, which in 1965 called a conference on Bible translation at Trinity Christian College in Palos Heights, IL. Present at this conference were members of twenty-eight evangelical theological institutions and a wide variety of denominations (Assemblies of God, Baptist, Presbyterian, Lutheran, Methodist, Nazarene, Mennonite, and Christian Reformed). Though diverse, these groups were all "evangelical" in the sense of Christians who held a high view of Scripture as the inspired and authoritative Word of God. A number of papers on the contemporary state of translation were presented. The conference participants concluded that the Revised Standard Version, though a significant improvement over the KJV in many respects, was too linked to higher criticism of the Bible and liberal theology. The recently published New American Standard Version, though reflecting a high view of Scripture, was deemed to be plagued by faulty linguistic assumptions and an overly wooden translation policy.

The conclusion the conference reached was that a new version was needed. On August 27, 1965, the proposal was made that "the preparation of a contemporary English translation of the Bible should be undertaken as a collegiate endeavor of evangelical scholars."[2] A committee of fifteen members—called the Committee on Bible Translation (CBT)—oversaw the project. The translation process itself involved more than a hundred evangelical scholars. Funding came from the New York Bible Society, which almost went bankrupt in the process. Board members of the NYBS mortgaged their homes to keep the society alive and the translation moving forward. Zondervan Publishers eventually stepped in and provided advanced royalties to see the project through to completion.

Production of the NIV

The NIV is a committee translation as opposed to the work of a single translator. And it is a new version translated directly from the Hebrew and Greek, rather than a revision of a previous English version (see Question 9 for these distinctions). Like most modern versions, the basic text used for the Old Testament was Kittel's *Biblica Hebraica* (and later, *Biblia Hebraica Stuttgartensia*) and for the New Testament, the latest critical edition published by the United Bible Societies, together with the latest edition of Eberhard Nestle's *Novum Testamentum Graece*. These texts were assigned, book by book, to translation teams made up of two translators, two translation consultants (biblical scholars), and a stylist consultant (when available).

---

2. Stek, "The New International Version," 244.

These teams produced an initial translation following a translation manual produced by the CBT. The translation was then submitted to three successive editorial committees, which included examinations not only by biblical scholars but also by theologians and English stylists. The theologians were to represent the concerns of various confessional traditions; the stylists were to make sure the text represented good English and read well orally. Final decisions were made by the fifteen-member CBT.

The New Testament of the NIV was released in 1973 and the whole Bible in 1978. The CBT continued to meet annually to examine, discuss, and vote on proposals for revision. A supermajority vote of 70 percent of the CBT is required to make changes to the text. In 1984, a new edition was released incorporating decisions made by the CBT since 1978. This 1984 edition was the standard edition of the NIV until the latest revision in 2011.

The NIV's Success

The NIV's popularity soared in the years following its publication, and by the mid-1980s it was annually outselling the KJV. At one point it achieved close to 40 percent of the English Bible translation market. The publication of the popular NIV Study Bible (NIVSB) in 1985 helped to propel this success forward. The NIVSB was one of the first study Bibles with notes that were primarily exegetical (helping to explain the meaning of the text), rather than theological (defending theological propositions from the text), which made it particularly helpful for Bible study.

Today, more than 500 million copies of the NIV have been sold worldwide, and millions more distributed freely by Biblica. Two decisive factors working in tandem appear to have contributed to the NIV's remarkable success: first, its readability by virtue of its mediating translation philosophy, and second, its evangelical credentials.

By adopting a modified dynamic/functional equivalent translation philosophy, the NIV was far more readable than its more literal predecessors like the RSV and NASB. Of course other versions available around the same time, like the Living Bible and Today's English Version, were written in even more natural English. Yet for people who grew up in the church, these were mere "paraphrases." Neither sounded like the "real Bible," that is, the King James Version. Stuffy biblical scholars would scoff that these versions were fine for devotional reading and remedial readers, but they were inadequate for serious study. This was the beauty of the NIV. Though it was clear and understandable, it still *sounded* like the real Bible. The translators consciously sought to keep the cadence and rhythm of the KJV, particularly in well-known passages. One of my favorite examples is Psalm 23, which the NIV rendered, "The LORD is my shepherd, I shall not be in want." As noted ealier (p. 25), the phrase "be in want" is hardly natural English. But this is perhaps the most beloved and well-known psalm in the Psalter, and the KJV reads, "I shall not want." The NIV still reverberated with the sound and rhythm of the KJV, but in more contemporary—if here somewhat awkward—English. This balanced approach—idiomatic yet traditional—helps to explain why the NIV surpassed its evangelical competitors.

The second factor that contributed greatly to the NIV's success was its evangelical credentials. The version was developed by a broad and influential coalition of evangelical scholars who first produced and then promoted the translation. The one hundred–plus translators came from a wide range of evangelical theological institutions. The fifteen original CBT members included scholars from Southwestern Baptist Theological Seminary, Westminster Theological Seminary, Nazarene Theological Seminary, Gordon Divinity School, Covenant Theological Seminary, Conservative Baptist Theological Seminary, Trinity Evangelical Divinity School, Bethel College, Houghton College, Dallas Theological Seminary, Calvin Theological Seminary, and Goshen Biblical Seminary. Replacements after death or retirement included scholars from Regent College, Westmont College, Tyndale Theological Seminary, Wheaton College, and others.[3] While it is true that the RSV had a strong coalition of *mainline* denominational support, the NIV's *evangelical* credentials brought much greater acceptance in the conservative Christian world. (And it is evangelicals who buy the most Bibles!)

The preface to the NIV makes this theological perspective clear, noting that "the translators were united in their commitment to the authority and infallibility of the Bible as God's Word in written form."[4] All NIV translators were required either to sign the Evangelical Theological Society statement of faith (which reads, "The Bible alone, and the Bible in its entirety, is the Word of God written, and is therefore inerrant in the autographs") or a similar evangelical confession.[5]

New International Reader's Version (NIrV—NT, 1994; Full, 1996)

The New International Reader's Version (NIrV) is an English version based on the translation philosophy of the NIV but written in a simpler style of English, with a smaller vocabulary and simplified grammar. It is designed especially for children, adults with lower reading skills, and those for whom English is a second language. It has been identified as geared for a third-grade reading audience. The translation was commissioned in 1992 by Biblica and

---

3. For lists of names, see Stek, "New International Version," 245; and Michael Marlowe, "The NIV Committee on Bible Translation," accessed January 31, 2023, www.bible-researcher.com/niv-translators.html.
4. Preface to the *The Holy Bible: New International Version* (Grand Rapids: Zondervan, 1984).
5. These include, "The Westminster Confession, the Belgic Confession, the New Hampshire Confession, or the creedal basis of the National Association of Evangelicals; or some other comparable statement" (Stek, "New International Version," 246).

the work accomplished by forty translators from fourteen denominations. The NIrV NT was published in 1994 and the full Bible in 1996, with revisions in 1998 and 2014.

Compare the NIV with the NIrV on a complex theological passage like Romans 3:22–26:

NIV	NIrV
[22] This righteousness is given through faith in Jesus Christ to all who believe. There is no difference between Jew and Gentile, [23] for all have sinned and fall short of the glory of God, [24] and all are justified freely by his grace through the redemption that came by Christ Jesus. [25] God presented Christ as a sacrifice of atonement, through the shedding of his blood—to be received by faith. He did this to demonstrate his righteousness, because in his forbearance he had left the sins committed beforehand unpunished—[26] he did it to demonstrate his righteousness at the present time, so as to be just and the one who justifies those who have faith in Jesus.	[22] We are made right with God by putting our faith in Jesus Christ. This happens to all who believe. It is no different for the Jews than for the Gentiles. [23] Everyone has sinned. No one measures up to God's glory. [24] The free gift of God's grace makes us right with him. Christ Jesus paid the price to set us free. [25] God gave Christ as a sacrifice to pay for sins through the spilling of his blood. So God forgives the sins of those who have faith. God did all this to prove that he does what is right. He is a God of mercy. So he did not punish for their sins the people who lived before Jesus lived. [26] God did all this to prove in our own time that he does what is right. He also makes right with himself those who believe in Jesus.

The Changing Landscape

The NIV is the only English version since the KJV to come close to becoming the "standard" English version. While it is still the most popular English version, the landscape of Bible translation has changed in recent years and the NIV's position of dominance has waned. A number of factors may have contributed to these changes.

(1) As described in Question 18, a major controversy over gender-inclusive language rocked the evangelical world beginning in 1997. The negative publicity against the NIV generated by this controversy shook some people's confidence in the NIV brand. Ironically, today the changes introduced into the NIV have become quite commonplace in Bible versions, even among the most conservative ones (see Question 18). Yet it is hard to restore full confidence once it has been lost or questioned.

(2) When it was first translated, the NIV was almost alone in occupying a mediating place between formal and functional equivalent versions (see discussion above, and Question 3). This middle ground is now a crowded place, with versions like the (H)CSB, the CEB, and the NET Bible vying for place. These versions also chip away customers from various constituents. The (H)CSB was produced in Southern Baptist Convention (SBC) circles, the largest Protestant denomination in the country and historically a major customer of the NIV. The

CEB is directed toward more mainline denominations, where the NIV has also been historically popular.

(3) Just as new mediating versions have challenged the center of the translation spectrum, so the increased sophistication of functional equivalent versions like the NLT 2014 edition have eroded NIV support from the right side of the translation spectrum. While natural-language versions like the NLT were once dismissed as "mere paraphrases"—inspiring for devotional use but inadequate for serious study—they are now recognized as works of scholarship, the product of highly competent biblical scholars.

(4) On the more formal (left) side of the translation spectrum, improvements in readability in the NASB and, especially, the rising popularity of the ESV, have further chipped away at the NIV's preeminence. Many evangelicals appreciated the scholarship and window on the Hebrew and Greek provided by the RSV but did not like its reputation as a "liberal" version. The ESV, which may be seen as an "evangelicalized" RSV, changed these offensive passages, making it the translation of choice among some who prefer a more formalist approach.

Summary

The NIV is the most popular English-language version in the world. It was produced by a broad coalition of evangelical scholars and denominations and followed a mediating translation philosophy. This approach, together with the NIV's evangelical credentials, have contributed greatly to its success. Today, however, the world of English Bible translation is more crowded, more diverse, and more competitive. It seems unlikely that any single translation will achieve the kind of preeminence that characterized the KJV for centuries and the NIV in recent years.

REFLECTION QUESTIONS

1. What Bible versions have you used in the past? What has been your experience of the NIV?
2. How would you summarize the key events that led to the production of the NIV?
3. What does the author suggest were the keys to the NIV's success?
4. What is the NIrV and how is it related to the NIV?
5. According to the author, how has the world of English Bible translation been changing in recent years?

QUESTION 35

Which Versions Blur the Line Between Translation and Commentary?

How Much Interpretation?

We have seen throughout this book that all translation involves interpretation. This is because there is no one-to-one correspondence between languages. The meaning of each word, phrase, or clause must first be interpreted and understood in the source language before an equivalent word, phrase, or clause can be chosen in the receptor language to replace it. Even the most strict word-for-word version makes an interpretive decision with every word translated.

While every translation is an interpretation, functional equivalent versions certainly interpret more than formal equivalent ones, since their goal is reproducing *meaning* over form. We have seen examples of this throughout this book. Functional equivalent forms: (1) *explain unknown cultural terms* (e.g., translating "phylacteries" as "prayer boxes with Scripture verses inside"; Matt. 23:5 NLT); (2) *make implicit meaning explicit* (e.g., translating "Asia" as "the province of Asia"; Acts 16:6 NIV); (3) *convert weights and measurements to English equivalents* (e.g., translating "a denarius" as "a day's wages," Matt. 20:2 GW; or "sixty stadia" as "seven miles," Luke 24:13 ESV); and (4) *replace Hebrew or Greek euphemisms with English ones* (e.g., translating "Adam <u>knew</u> Eve" as "Adam <u>was intimate with</u> Eve," Gen. 4:1 CSB).

Providing additional interpretation is also helpful when a word or phrase can mean different things and scholars are divided. We have seen examples of this. Does the word *skeuos* ("vessel") in 1 Thessalonians 4:3–4 refer to a man's "body" or his "wife." Is the "the Revelation of Jesus Christ" (Rev. 1:1) a revelation "about" or "from" Jesus Christ? (Both examples are from Question 4.) In cases like these, footnotes are generally needed to alert readers to important alternate interpretations.

Many Bible study tools provide interpretational help. The most important of these are Bible commentaries, but also helpful are study Bibles, background studies, and reference books like Bible handbooks, dictionaries, and encyclopedias. Study Bibles provide notes at the bottom of the page. The NET Bible provides extensive textual and exegetical material in footnotes. Below we will note three Bible versions that provide additional interpretation *within the text*.

Kenneth S. Wuest's *The New Testament: An Expanded Translation* (1961)

In his preface, Wuest describes his New Testament as an "expanded translation," which means he uses "as many English words as are necessary to bring out the richness, force, and clarity of the Greek text."[1] While a noble goal, Wuest's work suffers in two main areas. The first is its awkward English style, a result of seeking to replicate formal features of Greek grammar. For example, Wuest tries to retain the Greek historical present tense by using English present tenses, resulting in an odd mix of tenses.[2] For instance, he translates Mark 3:13, "And He goes up into the mountain and calls for himself and to himself those whom He himself was desiring, and they went off to Him."[3]

Wuest also tries to retain Greek word order whenever possible, because this "places emphasis where the inspired writer put it, and brings out the style of the original."[4] Greek word order, however, is highly flexible because of its developed case system, something not true of English. Wuest's translation of 1 John 1:8 makes Paul sound like Yoda from *Star Wars*: "If we say that we do not have a sinful nature, ourselves we are deceiving." This awkward English sounds very different from how Paul's idiomatic Koine Greek would have sounded to his readers.

Another problem with Wuest's work is that while he claims to be bringing out the "full meaning of each Greek word,"[5] these expansions are often lexical fallacies. For example, in the famous post-resurrection dialogue in John 21 between Jesus and Peter, Wuest assumes a strict distinction between the meaning of *agapaō* and *phileō*.[6] For Jesus's first two questions to Peter, instead of "do you love [*agapaō*] me more than these?" (21:15, 16), Wuest translates *agapaō* as, "Do you have a devotional love for me called out of your heart by my preciousness to you, a love which impels you to sacrifice yourself for me?"

---

1. Kenneth S. Wuest, *The New Testament: An Expanded Translation* (Grand Rapids: Eerdmans, 1961), vii.
2. The NASB indicates Greek historical present tenses with an asterisk (*) but translates them in the past tense. See Question 31.
3. The unusual "He himself" may be Wuest's attempt to place emphasis on the redundant use of the Greek subject pronoun *autos*. But this redundancy may simply be a result of Mark's Semitic style rather than for emphasis. Again, Wuest seems to be overtranslating the Greek.
4. Wuest, *Expanded Translation*, vii.
5. Wuest, *Expanded Translation*, viii–iv.
6. Wuest, *Expanded Translation*, iv–v.

Similarly, in Peter's three replies, instead of "You know that I love [*phileō*] you," Wuest translates *phileō* as, "You know I have a friendly feeling and affection for you." This interpretation assumes that there is a clear distinction of meaning between *agapaō* (God-like love) and *phileō* (human affection). Yet the great majority of Johannine scholars affirm that here, as elsewhere in the gospel, John uses *agapaō* and *phileō* synonymously.[7] The purpose of the dialogue is not to show that Jesus reluctantly concedes to the only lower-grade love that Peter can muster. It is to restore Peter *three times*, since he denied him three times.

Wuest claims to be carrying over the true action of Greek tenses into English, but he does not take into account the diversity of functions within each tense. For example, he assumes that the perfect tense must indicate action completed in the past with present results. So, instead of translating Matthew 4:4 as "It is written . . ." (KJV, etc.), he brings out the full meaning: "It has been written and is at present on record." This, however, does not take into account that the perfect tense can place the emphasis on the present state (an intensive or resultative perfect) or on the completed nature (an extensive or consummative perfect).

Similarly, it was once commonly believed that the aorist tense in Greek prohibitions meant *do not start* something, while the present tense meant to *stop* doing it. So Wuest translates Matthew 5:17 (aorist tense) "Do not begin to suppose that I came to destroy the law or the prophets," and Matthew 6:19 (present tense) as "Stop accumulating treasures upon the earth for yourselves." This use of tense functions in prohibitions has been shown to be an overgeneralization.[8]

Amplified Bible (AMP, 1965/1987/2015)

The Amplified Bible includes "amplifications" that provide explanations, clarifications, expansions, alternate interpretations, and textual variants for the words and phrases in the biblical text. This unique translation was primarily the work of Mrs. Frances Siewert and was published in stages between 1954 and 1965. It was sponsored jointly by the Lockman Foundation and Zondervan Publishers. The Lockman Foundation is a nonprofit founded in

---

7. The Father loves the Son: John 3:35; 16:27; 17:24 (*agapaō*); 5:20 (*phileō*); Jesus loves Lazarus and his sisters: 11:5 (*agapaō*); 11:3 (*phileō*); the disciple whom Jesus loved: 13:23; 19:26 (*agapaō*); 20:2 (*phileō*); believers are loved by the Father and the Son: 14:21, 23 (*agapaō*); 16:27 (*phileō*).
8. See Daniel B. Wallace, *Greek Grammar Beyond the Basics: An Exegetical Syntax of the New Testament* (Grand Rapids: Zondervan, 1996), 485, 713–17. Wallace concludes that the basic force of the aorist in commands or prohibitions is that it views the action as a whole, while the basic force of the present is that it views the action as an ongoing process. In specific contexts, of course, the present could mean "Stop. . ." and the aorist, "Don't start. . . ," but it is the context that determines this.

1942 in La Habra, California, to promote Bible translation, evangelism, education, and benevolence. The same foundation produced the New American Standard Bible (Question 31). The AMP was based on the American Standard Version (ASV) of 1901, the American counterpart to the English Revised Version (RV) and so may be viewed as a formal equivalent version in the KJV line of revision.[9]

In the introduction, the various sigla used in the AMP are explained:

- Parentheses ( ) signify additional phases of meaning included in the original word, phrase, or clause of the original language.
- Brackets [ ] clarify words or comments not actually expressed in the immediate original text, as well as definitions of Greek names.
- Italics indicate various things: (1) textual variants; (2) words which are not found in the original Greek but implied by it; (3) conjunctions "and" and "or" in italics introduce an amplified word or phrase.[10]

To see these in practice, consider Genesis 2:9 AMP:

> And out of the ground the Lord God made to grow every tree that is pleasant to the sight *or* to be desired—good (suitable, pleasant) for food; the tree of life also in the center of the garden, and the tree of the knowledge of [the difference between] good and evil *and* blessing and calamity. [Rev. 2:7; 22:14, 19]

The "or" in italics indicates that "to be desired" is an alternative translation for "pleasant to the sight." Parentheses around "suitable" and "pleasant" suggest that the word translated "good" has more meaning than the English "good" expresses. Adding "the difference between" in brackets clarifies what "knowledge" of good and evil means. The "and" in italics indicates that the experiential knowledge of good and evil is the difference between "blessing" (in Eden) and "calamity" (resulting in expulsion). The final brackets point to cross references to the "tree of life" in the book of Revelation. These amplifications, when reliable, can provide helpful clarification for the text.

An updated edition of the Amplified Bible was released in 1987 and then a major revision in 2015. This latest, a significant improvement in accuracy, became the standard edition (AMP) and the 1987 version was renamed The Amplified Bible, Classic Edition (AMPC).[11]

---

9. "Version Information," Amplified Bible (AMP), Biblegateway.com, accessed December 7, 2021, https://www.biblegateway.com/versions/Amplified-Bible-AMP/.
10. Introduction to The Amplified Bible (La Habra, CA: Lockman Foundation, 1987).
11. "Version Information," Amplified Bible (AMP), Biblegateway.com.

The Amplified Bible can be a helpful tool, since it is certainly true that no single English translation can capture precisely all the meaning of the Hebrew or Greek. At some places, however, the amplifications seem to be guided more by tradition than by scholarship. Its greatest weakness, however, is linguistic, in that the amplifications can give readers the false impression that Hebrew and Greek words are like suitcases packed with theological content to be excavated, and that multiple senses a word can have are all present in each occurrence. This is sometimes called an "all-inclusive meaning fallacy," or more technically, "illegitimate totality transfer."[12] In fact, Hebrew and Greek words, just like English ones, have a range of potential senses, and it is the *context* that gives the word its fuller meaning. The original preface to the Amplified Bible demonstrates this linguistically naivete:

> No matter how perfectly done the work of the translators may be, the difficulties involved in expressing the ideas bound up in one Greek word or phrase in an equivalent English word or phrase are often insurmountable. . . .
>
> To illustrate, let us take the sentence, "Believe on the Lord Jesus Christ and thou shalt be saved" (Acts 16:31). What does the word "believe" mean? It is extremely important, for multitudes are pinning their hope of heaven upon it. Yet that word long since ceased to convey, if it ever did, the sense of the original.
>
> Webster's long definition of "believe" includes such synonymnous expressions as, "to place credence . . . apart from personal knowledge, to expect or hope . . . to be more or less firmly persuaded of the truth of anything, to think or suppose." In this sense, most people believe in Christ—that He lived; that He was a perfect man Who sincerely believed Himself to be the Son of God, and that He died on the cross hoping to save sinners. But this is by no means the meaning of the Greek word which twenty-two New Testament versions out of twenty-four consulted render "believe." Yet they do so because there is no single better word in the English.
>
> The Greek word is "*pisteuo*," and means, "To adhere to, cleave to; to trust, to have faith in; to rely on"—which summed up in, "Believe on the Lord Jesus Christ and thou shalt be saved," means an absolute personal reliance upon the Lord Jesus Christ as Saviour.[13]

12. See James Barr, *The Semantics of Biblical Language* (Oxford: Oxford University Press, 1961), 218.
13. Introduction to The Amplified Bible (La Habra, CA: Lockman Foundation, 1958).

These paragraphs include several linguistic problems. In reality, the Greek word *pisteuō* has approximately the same semantic range as the English word "believe." It can mean authentic trust or mere assent, depending on the context. James 2:19 uses the same verb to say that "Even the demons believe [*pisteuō*]—and they shudder" (CSB). This is certainly not "absolute personal reliance upon the Lord Jesus Christ," as the preface claims. It is the *context*, not the verb alone, that carries this sense of full trust and reliance.

Later editions of the Amplified Bible tended to improve upon these linguistic deficiencies. The preface was modified to say that "the reader gains understanding through the use of amplification," rather than that the amplification gives us the true fuller meaning of the word. Yet the error persists that the translation "believe" is inadequate because it "hardly does justice to the many meanings contained in the Greek *pisteuō*." It is not that many meanings are "contained" in each use of *pisteuō*, but rather that *pisteuō*, like "believe," can have different meanings depending on the context.

Despite these shortcomings, the Amplified Bible remains a helpful tool when used with caution and checked against other reliable study tools.

Expanded Bible (EB, 2011)

The Expanded Bible, published by Thomas Nelson, is similar to the Amplified Bible in that it uses in-text notes to provide additional information to a basic translation.[14] This version uses a modified version of the New Century Version (NCV), a functional equivalent version, as its base text. This base text is printed in bold, with additional information in brackets []. Bracketed material includes:

1. *expansions* [], providing alternate ways of translating, including synonyms, words with slightly different nuances, or more sophisticated diction
2. *alternate interpretations* [*or*], different interpretations of the text (not just an alternate way to say the same thing)
3. *literal or formal equivalent renderings* [ᴸ]
4. *traditional renderings* [ᵀ], providing well-known renderings from past translations, especially the KJV tradition
5. *commentary* [ᶜ], providing historical, cultural, theological, or other explanatory information to help readers better understand a verse or passage
6. *cross-references* [ᴿ] to other biblical passages
7. *textual variants*, footnotes providing significant textual variants

14. I was one of the three primary contributing scholars for the Expanded Bible, together with Tremper Longman III and Daniel Taylor.

A centered dot (·) indicates where the expansion begins. Here is a sample from Romans 3:23–25a EB:

> 23 [LFor; Because] **Everyone has sinned and •fallen short** [*or* is not worthy] **of God's •glorious standard** [*or* glorious presence; Lglory], 24 **and all need to be •made right with God** [justified; declared righteous] **as a free gift by his grace, •by being set free from sin** [Lthrough the redemption that is] **•through** [*or* in] **Jesus Christ.** 25 **God •sent** [*or* appointed; *or* presented] **him •to die in our place to take away our sins** [as a sacrifice of atonement; *or* as the mercy seat; Tas a propitiation; Cthe Greek term could mean the place where sacrificial blood was dripped (the mercy seat) or the sacrifice itself].

The Expanded Bible, like the Amplified Bible, was intended to provide interpretational options and exegetical insights into the meaning of the text in an in-line format. Yet while avoiding some of the linguistic errors of the Amplified Bible, the Expanded Bible has not experienced anything close to its commercial success.

Summary

There is a fine line between translation and commentary, since the goal of both is to guide readers toward the meaning of the text. While supplemental study material (study Bibles, commentaries, etc.) can provide interpretational help, versions like Wuest's *Expanded Translation*, the Amplified Bible, and the Expanded Bible seek to provide additional commentary within the text itself.

REFLECTION QUESTIONS

1. Why does the author say that all translation involves commentary?
2. What do you think constitutes too much commentary in a translation?
3. What were the goals of Wuest's *Expanded Translation*?
4. What are the goals of the Amplified Bible? The Expanded Bible?
5. What are the strengths and weaknesses of these kinds of expanded versions?

QUESTION 36

Which Versions Most Radically Recontextualize the Bible?

Every few years it seems a new translation emerges that captures the imagination of some segment of the Christian public. While diverse in their approach and perspective, these new translations share in common an attempt to recontextualize the text to make it relevant to a contemporary audience. I have elsewhere referred to these as "transculturations," where contemporary relevance or recontextualizing the message takes a higher priority than historical and cultural accuracy.[1] Almost all of these are single-author translations. By far the most popular and influential is *The Message* by Eugene Peterson, though a culturally important predecessor was Clarence Jordan's *Cotton Patch Version*.

Clarence Jordan's *Cotton Patch Version* (1968–1970)

This remarkable recontextualization of the New Testament was produced by pastor and civil rights activist Clarence Jordan. Jordan was the founder of Koinonia Farm in Americus, Georgia, a pioneering interracial farming community in the Deep South. In 1968 he published *The Cotton Patch Version of Paul's Epistles: A Colloquial Modern Translation with a Southern Accent Vigorous and Fervent for the Gospel, Unsparing in Earthiness, Rich in Humor.*[2] Jordan's second volume was published in 1969 as *The Cotton Patch Version of Luke and Acts: Jesus' Doings and the Happenings.*[3] A third volume, *The Cotton Patch Version of Matthew*

1. Gordon D. Fee and Mark L. Strauss, *How to Choose a Translation for All Its Worth* (Grand Rapids: Zondervan, 2007), 32–34.
2. Clarence Jordan, *The Cotton Patch Version of Paul's Epistles* (Clinton, NJ: Association Press, 1968).
3. Clarence Jordan, *The Cotton Patch Version of Luke and Acts* (Piscataway, NJ: Association Press, 1969).

and John,[4] was incomplete at the time of Jordan's death in 1969 and was published posthumously with the whole of Matthew and first eight chapters of John.

The *Cotton Patch Version* sets the story of Jesus in the American South during the Civil Rights Movement of the 1950s and '60s. Jesus is born in Gainesville, Georgia, and his parents escape to Mexico when "Governor Herod" tries to kill him. Jesus is ultimately lynched in Atlanta by the state governor, Pontius Pilate, and his religious cronies, Annas and Caiaphas, co-presidents of the Southern Baptist Convention. In Acts the resurrected Jesus commissions his disciples to be his "agents in Atlanta and throughout Georgia, in the ghetto and across the land."

This radical recontextualization of the New Testament is obviously intended to draw an analogy between the evil world systems that opposed and executed the Son of God and similar power structures of today that promote racism and oppression. Its strength is its ability to jar people into seeing parallels and connections they might otherwise miss. It is not meant to be a translation of the text *per se* (Jordan called it a "version," not a historical translation), but a recontextualization of the *message* to point people to spiritual, social, political, and cultural realities.

P. K. McCary's *Black Bible Chronicles* (1993)

This work, produced by P. K. McCary, has been identified as an "adaptive retelling" of the biblical story.[5] It seeks to translate Scripture into the vocabulary and style of African American Vernacular English (AAVE, or Ebonics). In the foreword Andrew Young, former mayor of Atlanta and UN Ambassador, writes, "The *Black Bible Chronicles* is an attempt to put the most important message of life into the language of the streets."

A first volume, *Black Bible Chronicles: From Genesis to the Promised Land* appeared in 1993.[6] A version of the Gospels, *Rappin' with Jesus: The Good News according to the Four Brothers*, followed the next year.[7] The creation account in Genesis begins under the heading "World Up!":

> Now when the Almighty was first down with his program, He made the heavens and the earth. The earth was a

---

4. Clarence Jordan, *The Cotton Patch Version of Matthew and John* (New York: Association Press, 1970).
5. Freddy Boswell, "Classifying 'Cotton Patch Version' and Similar Renderings as Adaptive Retelling Rather Than Translation (La clasificación de la 'cotton patch version' y de otros tipos de versiones más como reescrituras adaptadoras que como traducciones)," *Hermēneus* 8 (2006): 45–66.
6. P. K. McCary, *Black Bible Chronicle: From Genesis to the Promised Land* (New York: African American Family Press, 1993).
7. P. K. McCary, *Rappin' with Jesus: The Good News according to the Four Brothers* (New York: African American Family Press, 1994).

> fashion misfit, being so uncool and dark, but the Spirit of the Almighty came down real tough, so that He simply said, "Lighten up!"

The fall of humanity (Genesis 3) begins with a description of the serpent:

> Now the serpent was one bad dude, one of the baddest of all the animals the Almighty had made. And the serpent spoke to the sister and asked, "You mean the Almighty told you not to eat of all the trees in the garden?"
>
> And the sister told him, "Yeah, snake, I can eat of these trees, just not the tree of the knowledge or the Almighty said I'd be knocked off."
>
> And that bad ol' serpent told the sister, "Nah, sister, he's feeding you a line of bull. You won't die. The Almighty just knows that if you eat from the tree, you'll be hipped to what's going down."

These volumes have the positive goal of making the Bible's message relevant for a particular audience. Like the *Cotton Patch Version*, they are striving not for historical accuracy but contemporary relevance. More problematic in this case is the challenge of staying current with street language, which is constantly changing. Instead of sounding relevant, the translation sometimes sounds silly, a caricature of the culture it is seeking to connect with.

Eugene Peterson's *The Message* (NT, 1993; Full Bible, 2002)

The Message is the masterpiece of pastor, teacher, and scholar Eugene Peterson, though the publisher states that Peterson's work was "thoroughly reviewed by a team of recognized Old and New Testament scholars to ensure that it is accurate and faithful to the original languages."[8] Peterson's work arose directly from his pastoral ministry. In the preface he states:

> If there is anything distinctive about *The Message*, perhaps it is because the text is shaped by the hand of a working pastor. For most of my adult life I have been given a primary responsibility for getting the message of the Bible into the lives of the men and women with whom I worked. . . . *The Message* grew from the soil of forty years of pastoral work.[9]

---

8. See the list on *The Message* website: https://messagebible.com/about/.
9. Eugene Peterson, preface to *The Message: The Bible in Contemporary Language* (Colorado Springs: NavPress, 2005).

The NT was released in 1993 and the full Bible in 2002. It was a huge success. Peterson was a master of the English language, and his style is often evocative and earthy. One reviewer notes that he "writes with passion and power, almost turning prose into poetry."[10] Peterson repeatedly made it clear that his goal was contemporary relevance more than historical precision. He strove to convert the tone, rhythm, and ideas of the Bible into the way people think and speak today. In this way he viewed his work as a supplement, rather than a replacement, to traditional versions.

> *The Message* is a reading Bible. It is not intended to replace the excellent study Bibles that are available. My intent here (as it was earlier in my congregation and community) is simply to get people reading it who don't know that the Bible is read-able at all, at least by them, and to get people who long ago lost interest in the Bible to read it again.[11]

While *The Message* is certainly thought-for-thought rather than word-for-word, it goes well beyond functional equivalence. Rather than carrying the reader *back* to the world of the text, Peterson's primary goal was to bring its *message* into the world of today. Peterson's unconventional and evocative style is evident from page one. Compare Genesis 1:1–3 in the NIV and *The Message*:

NIV	MSG
In the beginning God created the heavens and the earth. The earth was formless and void, and darkness was over the surface of the deep, and the Spirit of God was moving over the surface of the waters. Then God said, "Let there be light"; and there was light.	First this: God created the Heavens and Earth—all you see, all you don't see. Earth was a soup of nothingness, a bottomless emptiness, an inky blackness. God's Spirit brooded like a bird above the watery abyss. God spoke: "Light!" And light appeared.

John 1:14, which speaks of the Word moving "into the neighborhood," has often been noted as especially memorable in *The Message*:

10. David Dewey, *A User's Guide to Bible Translations: Making the Most of Different Versions* (Downers Grove, IL: Intervarsity, 2004), 182–83.
11. Peterson, preface to *The Message*.

NIV	MSG
The Word became flesh and made his dwelling among us. We have seen his glory, the glory of the one and only Son, who came from the Father, full of grace and truth.	The Word became flesh and blood, And moved into the neighborhood. We saw the glory with our own eyes, The one-of-a-kind glory, like Father, like Son Generous inside and out, True from start to finish.

The Voice **(NT, 2008; Full Bible, 2012)**

This innovative version is a collaboration of Thomas Nelson Publishers and Ecclesia Bible Society, whose president, Chris Seay, is the driving force behind the translation. Seay's stated goal was to produce a new wholistic approach to Scripture that would address the needs of the church in a rapidly changing world. Perhaps the most unique aspect of *The Voice* is that it was produced by a collaborative effort of approximately 120 scholars, pastors, writers, musicians, poets, and artists. According to the preface, four key words summarize the vision of the project: (1) holistic: considers heart, soul, and mind; (2) beautiful: achieves literary and artistic excellence; (3) sensitive: respects cultural shifts and the need for accuracy; (4) balanced: includes theologically diverse writers and scholars. The New Testament was published in 2008 and the full Bible in 2012.

In terms of format, *The Voice* includes several unique features:

(1) *Italic type*. Italics indicate words that "bring out the nuance of the original, assist in completing ideas, and often provide readers with information that would have been obvious to the original audience."[12] Consider Matthew 5:31: "And here is something else: *you have read in Deuteronomy that* anyone who divorces his wife *must do so fairly*—he must give her the requisite certificate of divorce *and send her on her way, free and unfettered*."

The words in italics provide helpful background, noting that Jesus is alluding to Deuteronomy (24:1) and that the original purpose was not to sanction divorce—as the religious leaders were using it—but to protect a woman from exploitation.[13] One problem with adding this information, however, is that it can distract from Jesus's point, which was *not* to indicate the good purpose of the law in Deuteronomy, but to challenge the religious leaders'

12. Preface to *The Voice* (Nashville: Thomas Nelson, 2012).
13. Deuteronomy 24:1–4 says that in the event of the woman's second marriage and another divorce, the first husband was not allowed to remarry her. This prevented the first husband from exploiting her by marrying her to get the dowry she had received at her second marriage.

distortion of that law to gain an easy divorce. The words in italics sometimes seem redundant or distracting.

(2) *Delineated material.* A second feature in *The Voice* is additional cultural, historical, theological, or devotional content set apart in text boxes. For example, after King Herod tells the magi to find the baby Jesus so he can worship him, a text box reads: "Herod, of course, didn't really want to worship the baby Jesus. He wanted to kill Him. He was being crafty, trying to trick the magi into betraying the one they sought. But it didn't work." While this material may be helpful for background or application, its position in the same column as the biblical text could confuse readers about whether it is text or commentary. This potential was especially apparent in the 2008 edition, which oddly used first-person statements in some text boxes. For Matthew's genealogy (1:1–17) the text box began, "I've told you this long genealogy for a good reason"—as though Matthew was speaking here! The 2012 full Bible wisely modified this to "This long genealogy is given for a good reason."

(3) *Screenplay dialogue.* A third feature of *The Voice* is a "screenplay" format used to identify dialogue. Consider Matthew 4:3–7:

The Devil: If you are the Son of God . . .

Jesus: It is written, "Man shall not live by bread alone . . . "

The Devil: If you are the Son of God . . .

Jesus: That is not the only thing Scripture says . . .

While some readers may find the screenplay format helpful, others will find it distracting. It seems odd to me that a translation that intentionally seeks to present Scripture as *story* would introduce a format that reads more like a script than a narrative.

Some words are translated in *The Voice* in unusual ways: "apostle" is "emissary"; "Christ/Messiah" is often "God's Anointed, *the Liberating King*"; in the Old Testament, the Hebrew *Yahweh* (YHWH), traditionally rendered LORD (see Question 22), is translated as the "Eternal (One)." Though these renderings are unconventional, they are intentionally so and for the most part represent legitimate translations. Many scholars, for example, believe the divine name YHWH is etymologically related to God's self-designation as "I AM" = the Self-Existent One (see Deut. 3:14).

John 1:1 translates the Greek *logos* as the "Voice" instead of the traditional "Word." Compare John 1:1–5 in the NIV and *The Voice*:

NIV	*The Voice* (2012)
In the beginning was the Word, and the Word was with God, and the Word was God. 2 He was with God in the beginning. 3 Through him all things were made; without him nothing was made that has been made. 4 In him was life, and that life was the light of all mankind. 5 The light shines in the darkness, and the darkness has not overcome it.	Before time itself was measured, the Voice was speaking. The Voice was and is God. 2 This *celestial* Word remained ever present with the Creator; 3 His speech shaped the entire cosmos. *Immersed in the practice of creating,* all things that exist were birthed in Him. 4 His breath filled all things with a living, breathing light— 5 A light that thrives in the depths of darkness, *blazes through murky bottoms.* It cannot and will not be quenched.

This passage provides a taste of the creative artistry and translational liberties taken by the version. This approach clearly goes beyond functional equivalence to a creative rewriting of the text. We could spend an entire chapter debating each phrase's adequacy or inadequacy as a representation of John's meaning.

Online reviews of *The Voice* are mixed, though it receives scathing reviews from some conservatives, based often on claims of its "new age" theology and presumed links to the emergent church movement.[14] Brian McClaren, at one time the most influential voice of emergent/postmodern Christianity, was one of the contributing writers. But claims of new age theology would appear to be unfounded.

Some Other Examples

There are other recontextualizations of the Bible, which space limitations do not allow us to review. Elsewhere we mentioned Rob Lacey's *The Word on the Street*, also known as *The Street Bible*[15] (see Question 2), which in tone is somewhere between Peterson's *Message* and McCary's *Black Bible Chronicles*.

One of the latest additions to this genre is *The Passion Translation*, which has achieved great popularity in some charismatic circles. This version is

14. One online reviewer went so far as to say, "Unfortunately, not since the release of the Jehovah's Witnesses' New World Translation of the Greek Scriptures in 1950 has there been a Bible published that so blatantly mangles and distorts God's Word in order to support a peculiar and aberrant theological agenda." Chris Rosebrough, "Review of The Voice New Testament: Part 1," Extreme Theology, November 19, 2008, www.extremetheology.com/2008/11/review-of-the-voice-new-testament---part-one.html.
15. Rob Lacey, *The Street Bible* (Grand Rapids: Zondervan, 2003).

primarily the work of Brian Simmons, formerly a translator with New Tribes Mission, who views this translation as a divine calling on his life. While less radical in its recontextualizations than some others, *The Passion* is deeply marred by idiosyncratic interpretations, many of which the translator claims (without merit) are based on Aramaic originals. In February 2022, *The Passion Translation* was removed from the Bible version site BibleGateway.com, presumably because of its unorthodox translations.[16]

Summary

Some Bible translation may be said to "recontextualize" the Bible, focusing primarily on contemporary relevance rather than historical and cultural accuracy. The primary goal of versions like the *Cotton Patch Version*, *Black Bible Chronicles*, *The Voice*, *The Street Bible*, and (to a lesser extent) *The Message* is to bring the message of the text into today's culture, rather than to transport the reader into the world of the text.

REFLECTION QUESTIONS

1. Have you used any of the versions discussed in this question? What was your impression?
2. Who produced the *Cotton Patch Version*? How does it recontextualize the New Testament?
3. What was the purpose and goal of the *Black Bible Chronicles*?
4. What is *The Voice*, and what are some of its unique characteristics?
5. Who produced *The Message*? What did he view as its goals and limitations?

---

16. Kate Shellnut, "Bible Gateway Removes The Passion Translation," *Christianity Today*, February 9, 2022. https://www.christianitytoday.com/news/2022/february/passion-translation-tpt-bible-gateway-remove-charismatic-pa.html.

PART 6

International Bible Translation

While this book has been concerned primarily with Bible translations into English, these last few questions focus on translating the Bible around the world. With reference to international translation efforts, two distinct goals should be kept in mind. The first is translating the Bible into the most spoken languages of the world to reach as many people as possible with the gospel. Question 37 discusses Bible versions in the most widely spoken languages of the world. A second goal, however, and one more commonly associated with Bible translation agencies, is to produce a Bible in all the seven thousand–plus languages of the world, so that every person can read or hear the message in their mother tongue or "heart language." Question 38 discusses statistics related to this goal and the major ministries involved in it. Question 39 then discusses some of the unique challenges international translators face. Finally, Question 40 deals with perhaps the most controversial issue in recent decades for international translators: the debate over Muslim-sensitive Bible versions.

QUESTION 37

What Are the Main Bible Versions in the World's Major Languages?

The chart below shows the ten most widely spoken languages in the world. The list on the left is ranked by total speakers; the right, by native speakers. Total speakers include those for whom that language may be their second (or more) language. When considering both native and non-native speakers, English is the most widely spoken language in the world, with more than a billion users. English drops to third when first-language speakers alone are counted.

Top Ten Languages Spoken Around the World[1]			
Total Speakers	**(in millions)**	**Native Speakers**	**(in millions)**
1. English	1,452	1. Mandarin Chinese	929
2. Mandarin Chinese	1,118	2. Spanish	475
3. Hindi	602	3. English	373
4. Spanish	548	4. Hindi	344
5. French	274	5. Bengali	234
6. Standard Arabic	274	6. Portuguese	232
7. Bengali	273	7. Russian	154
8. Russian	258	8. Japanese	125
9. Portuguese	258	9. Western Punjabi	93
10. Urdu	231	10. Yue Chinese	85

1. The data for these charts is adapted from *Ethnologue* 2022 (25th ed.), an annual publication of SIL International. Easiest access to this data is via Wikipedia pages reporting *Ethnologue* data, accessed September 13, 2022: https://en.wikipedia.org/wiki/List_of_languages_by_number_of_native_speakers and https://en.wikipedia.org/wiki/List_of_languages_by_total_number_of_speakers.

Bible translation has a long history in some languages and a relatively short one in others. Some languages have many Bible versions (244 English ones by one count!),[2] while others have few, if any (see Question 38). Here we will survey some of the important Bible versions in six of the seven most widely spoken languages of the world by total speakers. We are not including English, since its many versions are discussed throughout this book. The six include Mandarin Chinese, Hindi, Spanish, French, and Arabic. We have included a seventh, German (twelfth most widely spoken with 76 million native speakers and 135 million total), because the Luther Bible in German had such an important role historically in the Protestant Reformation. For each of these languages, we seek to identify the earliest translation(s), the traditional "standard" (KJV-like) Bible, and a few contemporary-language versions.

(Mandarin) Chinese Versions (1.118 Billion Speakers)[3]

Translations of portions of the Bible into Chinese likely began in the seventh century, when Nestorian missionaries introduced Christianity to China. No examples of these versions have been preserved, however, and Bible translation did not begin in earnest until the Protestant missionary movement of the nineteenth century. The first complete translation of the Bible was produced under the editorship of Joshua Marshman and published by the British and Foreign Bible Society (NT, 1813; OT, 1822). A variety of versions followed over the next century.

The closest thing to a "Chinese KJV" is the Chinese Union Version (CUV) of 1919. The project was launched in 1890 with the goal of producing a translation that was both accurate and readable and that could serve as the standard for Chinese Protestants. The translation, which took almost thirty years to produce, was overseen by a panel of translators from a variety of denominations. The translators used the English Revised Version (1885) as their model and checked its readings against the Hebrew and Greek texts. While three versions were originally planned, two classical Chinese versions and a vernacular Mandarin Chinese version, it was ultimately published with one consolidated classical Chinese translation and one vernacular Mandarin version.[4] The CUV is still the Bible of choice among most Chinese Protestants. In the 1980s, a project was launched to update its language while retaining

2. As listed on the Find a Bible website: https://find.bible/languages.
3. Daniel Kam-to Choi, "A History of the Chinese Bible," in *The Oxford Handbook of the Bible in China*, ed. K. K. Yeo (New York: Oxford University Press, 2021), 20–46; Alexander Wylie, "The Bible in China: A Record of Various Translations of the Holy Scriptures," in *Christian Progress in China: Gleanings from the Writings and Speeches of Many Workers*, ed. Arnold Foster (London: Religious Tract Society, 1889), 29–46.
4. Jost Zetzsche, "The Work of Lifetimes: Why the Union Version Took Nearly Three Decades to Complete," in *The Bible in Modern China: The Literary and Intellectual Impact* (Nettetal, Germany: Steyler Verlag, 1999).

as much of the original form as possible. The result was the Revised Chinese Union Version (RCUV). The New Testament was completed in 2006 and the whole Bible in 2010.

A number of contemporary Chinese versions have been produced over the years. Today's Chinese Version (TCV—NT, 1975; full Bible, 1979) was produced by the United Bible Societies and modeled after the English TEV (GNT). The Chinese Living Bible (CLB, 1974) was produced by Living Bibles International and modeled after the Living Bible (LB). It was eventually republished by the International Bible Society (now Biblica) in 1998 as the Chinese Contemporary Bible (CCB). The Chinese New Version (CNV)[5] was completed in 1992 by the Worldwide Bible Society together with the Lockman Foundation (publishers of the NASB and the Amplified Bible). Of these versions, only the TCV, the CUV, and its revision the RCUV, are approved for use in China by the Three-Self Patriotic Movement (or Three-Self Church), the state-sanctioned Protestant church of China. The only Catholic Bible authorized in China is the Studium Biblicum. Although begun by a Franciscan friar, Gabriele Allegra, in 1935, it was not published as a full Bible until 1968.

Hindi (and Urdu) Versions (602 Million Speakers)

We include Urdu together with Hindi here since they are so similar in terms of phonology and grammar that they appear to be the same language. They are different in that Hindi is derived from Sanskrit and written in the Devanagari script, while Urdu draws loanwords from Arabic and Persian and is written in the Perso-Arabic script known as Nastaliq. Urdu is the official language of Pakistan and is also widely spoken in India and elsewhere. Hindi is spoken throughout northern and central India.[6] When categorized together, the two languages are often called Hindustani.

Early Bible translations into Hindi and Urdu were often closely connected, and sometimes the same version would simply be written with different scripts. William Carey (1761–1834), often called "the father of modern missions," was the primary instigator of translations into various languages of India.[7] He was the lead translator for Bengali (see below) and supported the work of translation into Hindi, Oriya, Sanskrit, Marathi, and Assamese. Carey was also a great promoter of education, translating Hindu classics into English. In 1794 he opened a public school system that eventually included girls, something almost unthinkable at that time in India.

5. Originally called the New Chinese Version (NCV) but changed to CNV to avoid confusion with the New Century Version.
6. "Urdu language," *Encyclopaedia Britannica*, accessed January 31, 2023, brittanica.com.
7. Justo L. Gonzalez, *The Story of Christianity*, vol. 2, *The Reformation to the Present Day* (Grand Rapids: Zondervan, 2010), 419.

There are a variety of Hindi and Urdu Bibles available today, including the Hindi Old Version, the Hindi Revised Old Version, the Hindi Common Language Bible, the New Urdu Bible Version, and the Revised Urdu Holy Bible. Most of these are published by the Bible Society of India. The Hindi Easy-to-Read Version (1995) and Urdu Easy-to-Read Version (2003) are published by the Bible Translation Center.[8]

Spanish Versions (548 Million Speakers)[9]

The first complete Bible to be printed in Spanish was edited by Casiodoro de Reina and published in Basel in 1569. It is commonly known as the "Biblia del Oso" ("Bible of the Bear"), because of the printer's image of a bear eating honey on its title page. The 1596 revision of the text was edited by Cipriano de Valera and printed in London. From these two editors, the text came to be known as the Reina-Valera (RV) version, the standard KJV-like Bible of Spanish-speaking Protestants. It has been revised many times. The most popular version today is the 1960 revised edition (RVR).

For traditional Roman Catholics, the most widely accepted traditional version is the *Biblia Torres Amat*, published in 1825. It was translated from the Latin Vulgate by Spanish Bishop Félix Torres Amat (1772–1849) and holds a place in the Spanish-speaking world like the Douay-Rheims version in English (see Question 29). Another highly respected Catholic version today is *La Biblia de Jerusalém*, first published in 1967 and revised in 1973. It is a Spanish edition of the highly acclaimed French *La Bible de Jérusalem* (1956), which appeared in English as the Jerusalem Bible (1966; see Question 29). Other versions respected by Catholics include the *Biblia Latinoamericana* (1979) and *Dios Habla Hoy* (God speaks today) of 1979.

There are many contemporary-language Spanish versions used by Protestants. Notable are the NIV-inspired *Nueva Versión Internacional* (NVI, 1999), published by Biblica; the NLT-inspired *Nueva Traducción Viviente* (NTV, 2010), published by Tyndale Español; the NASB-inspired *La Biblia de las Américas* (LBLA), published by the Lockman Foundation (1986, 1995, 1997), and the *Reina Valera Contemporánea* (RVC, 2011), published by Sociedades Biblicas Unidas (United Bible Societies).

---

8. These and other versions can be found at https://find.bible/languages/hin/ and https://find.bible/languages/urd.
9. J. Atkins, *La Biblia en español: Cómo nos llegó* (Minneapolis: Augsburg Fortress, 2008); José Sánchez, "Historia de la Biblia en España," in M. Pérez and J. Trebollé, *Historia de la Biblia* (Madrid: Editorial Trota, 2006), 311–37; Rafael A. Serrano, *The History of the Spanish Bible: An Introduction* (self-published, 2017).

French Versions (274 Million Speakers)[10]

Portions of the Bible were translated into French as early as the twelfth century by Peter Waldo and his followers, and in the mid-thirteenth century at the University of Paris.[11] The first complete Bible to be published in French was translated by the theologian, humanist, and prolific translator Jacques Lefèvre d'Étaples and published in 1530 in Antwerp. Pierre Robert Olivétan, the cousin of John Calvin, made significant use of Lefévre's work in publishing a full French Bible in Switzerland in 1535. He substantially improved upon Lefévre's work with greater attention to the Hebrew and Greek and better French style. The 1588 edition of Olivétan's version became known as the "Geneva Bible" (not to be confused with the English Geneva Bible) and remained the favorite of French Protestants for the next two centuries.

Lefévre's work was also taken up by Nicholas de Leuze and François de Larben, who produced the *Bible de Louvain* in 1550, which became the basis for most French Roman Catholic Bibles.[12] For Roman Catholics, the most important contemporary French translation is *La Bible de Jérusalem*, published in 1954 and revised in 1973. This French classic was the inspiration for the English Jerusalem Bible (JB) and its revision, the New Jerusalem Bible (NJB).

The closest thing to a KJV-like version for French-speaking Protestants is the Louis Segond Version (LSG). It was translated from Hebrew and Greek texts by Swiss theologian and Old Testament scholar Louis Segond. The OT was published in 1871 in two volumes and the full Bible in 1880. The 1910 version, commissioned and published by the British and Foreign Bible Society, remains the standard edition for most French Protestants. In 2007 the Geneva Bible Society published an updated edition called Segond 21.

Other notable contemporary French versions include *La Bible du Semeur* (BDS; Bible of the sower), a functional equivalent version published by Biblica (1999), and the *Bible en français courant* (BFC; Bible in contemporary French) published in 1987 by the Alliance Biblique Universelle.

Arabic Versions (274 Million Speakers)[13]

The Bible was probably first translated into Arabic in the eighth century AD.[14] Our oldest extant Arabic Bible manuscript is Mt. Sinai Arabic Codex

---

10. See Frédéric Delforge, *La Bible en France et dans la Francophonie: histoire, traduction, diffusion* (Villiers-le-Bel, France: Société biblique française, 1991).
11. J. H. Skilton, "Versions of the Bible, Medieval and Modern," in *Zondervan Encyclopedia of the Bible*, 2nd ed., eds. Merrill C. Tenney and Moisés Silva (Grand Rapids: Zondervan, 2009), 5:1012–13.
12. Skilton, "Versions of the Bible," 1015.
13. Sidney H. Griffith, *The Bible in Arabic: The Scriptures of the "People of the Book" in the Language of Islam* (Princeton, NJ: Princeton University Press, 2013).
14. Bruce M. Metzger and Bart D. Ehrman, *The Text of the New Testament: Its Transmission, Corruption, and Restoration*, 4th ed. (New York: Oxford University Press, 2005), 122–23.

151, which was discovered at St. Catherine's Monastery on Mount Sinai, the same monastery where the famous Codex Sinaiticus was found. The manuscript is dated to AD 867 and includes the name of the translator, Bishr Ibn Al Sirri, a Nestorian Christian from Damascus. It contains the book of Acts, the Pauline Epistles, and the General Epistles.[15]

The mostly widely used Arabic version today is the Van Dyke Version (sometimes spelled Van Dyck[16]), which was sponsored in the 1800s by the Syrian Mission and the American Bible Society.[17] The project was launched in Beirut by Eli Smith and was completed after his death under the oversight of Cornelius Van Alen Van Dyck. The NT was published in 1860 and the OT in 1865. The Van Dyke Version is the closest thing to a KJV of the Arabic-speaking world. It is the standard Arabic Bible of the Coptic Church, the Syrian Orthodox Church, and many Protestant churches. Like the KJV, it is based on the Textus Receptus (see Question 27). Much of its Arabic is today considered archaic and obsolete, and it uses older ecclesial terms difficult for contemporary Arabic speakers to understand. The Bible Society publishes it with a glossary of three thousand words that are unknown or misunderstood.

The primary competitors of the Van Dyke Version are several contemporary Arabic versions that appeared in the latter part of the twentieth century. In 1973 Living Bibles International launched a new version under the guidance of Georges Houssney, a Lebanese Christian based in Beirut. Houssney modeled it after the NIV. The NT was completed in 1988 and named *Kitab al-Hayat ("The Book of Life")*. In 1992, when Living Bibles International merged with the International Bible Society (now Biblica), the version was renamed the New Arabic Version (NAV). The NAV is much clearer and more contemporary than Van Dyke and is widely accepted in the Arabic world. It still uses the old ecclesial terms, which won it friends among traditionalists but has resulted in criticism from progressives.

There have been other contemporary versions. Today's Arabic Version (TAV), also called Good News Arabic (GNA) or the Ecumenical Version, was produced by the Bible Society as a functional equivalent version modeled after the Good News Translation (see Question 32). It was released in 1992. The Easy-to-Read Arabic Version, produced by the World Bible Translation Center, is written in simplified Arabic but still uses traditional ecclesial terms. The Sharif Bible was produced by an Egyptian Christian to help his Muslim friends understand the Bible. It uses contemporary Arabic and avoids foreign

---

15. Harvey Staal, Mt. Sinai Arabic Codex 151, I. *Pauline Epistles*, Corpus Scriptorum Christianorum Orientalium 452 (Leuven: Peeters, 1983).
16. The difference in spelling is due to different Anglicizations of the Dutch "Van Dijk."
17. For details on the Van Dyke Version, see Ghassan Khalaf, *Shedding Light on Boustani-Van Dyck Bible Translation* (Beirut: Bible Society, 2009); and "The Arabic Bible," Arabic Bible Outreach Ministry, www.arabicbible.com/for-christians/the-bible.html.

names and ecclesiastical terms found in more traditional versions.[18] The NT was published in 1990 with the title The Noble Gospel; the full Bible was published in 2000 as The Noble Book. The Arabic word *sharif* means "noble."

German Versions (135 Million Speakers)[19]

German, like English, has a rich history of Bible translation. The earliest known Bible in a Germanic language is the fourth-century Gothic translation of Wulfila (c. 311–380). While there were many German versions produced during the Middle Ages, Bible translation truly flourished with the invention of the printing press. The first printed German version was the Mentel Bible, a high German edition published by Johannes Mentelin in 1466. The Mentel Bible was the first of eighteen printed versions of the Bible in German that preceded the landmark work of Martin Luther, the German monk who sparked the Protestant Reformation.[20]

The Luther Bible is by far the most important translation of the Bible into German. Its prestige and influence in the German-speaking world has been much like that of the KJV in the English-speaking world. Furthermore, like William Tyndale's English version, Luther's was the first German version that made significant use of the Hebrew and Greek texts, rather than relying on the Latin Vulgate. For the NT, Luther used the second edition of Erasmus's Greek New Testament, essentially the same Greek text used for the KJV—what is today called the "Textus Receptus" (see Question 27). Luther completed his NT in 1522 and the whole Bible in 1534. The full Bible was a collaborative effort of Luther and others. He continued to revise his text until his death in 1546.

One of the reasons for the success of the Luther Bible was its idiomatic nature. Luther was remarkably progressive in his view of translation, anticipating functional equivalent translation philosophy centuries before its academic development (see Questions 3 and 5). Luther's Bible, in turn, had a profound impact both on the German language and the German people. On the one hand, its accessibility encouraged Germans to read their Bibles for themselves, and so to think critically about the implications of their faith, rather than relying solely on ecclesiastical authorities. By standardizing the many German dialects into one High German language, the Luther Bible also helped to forge a German national identity.

While Luther's Bible was clear and idiomatic in its day, like all languages German changed over time, so that the Luther Bible (like the KJV) became difficult for contemporary readers to understand. While it is still a German

18. "The Sharif Bible," accessed March 3, 2023, https://sharifbible.cc/the-sharif-bible.
19. H. Volz, "German," in *The Cambridge History of the Bible*, ed. S. L. Greenslade (Cambridge: Cambridge University Press, 1963), 94–110.
20. Skilton, "Versions of the Bible," 1012.

standard (used primarily in its 1984 edition), there are a variety of contemporary German versions, including *Hoffnung für Alle* (Hope for all), *Die Gute Nachricht Bibel* (good news Bible), and the Catholic *Einheitsübersetzung* (unified translation, or unity translation). A popular New Testament called *Das Buch*, originally modeled after Eugene Peterson's *The Message*, was produced in 2009 by German theologian Roland Werner. A third edition (which includes Psalms and Proverbs) was released in 2022.

Summary

Under this question we have surveyed Bible translations in some of the most widely spoken languages of the world, including Chinese, Hindi, Spanish, French, Arabic, and German. For each we have noted the earliest versions, the "KJV-like" version in that language, and some contemporary versions.

REFLECTION QUESTIONS

1. Why is it especially important to produce good Bible versions in the most widely spoken languages of the world?
2. What is the KJV-like version of the Chinese-speaking world? When was it produced?
3. What is the KJV-like version of the Spanish-speaking world? When was it produced and by whom?
4. What is the KJV-like version of the Arabic-speaking world? When was it produced and by whom?
5. What is the most famous German Bible version of all time? When was it produced and by whom?

QUESTION 38

How Many Languages Still Need a Bible, and Who Is Doing This Work?

The Statistics

As of the year 2022, there were approximately 8 billion people in the world and somewhere between six to eight thousand languages. This number is necessarily inexact, because languages are constantly changing and because it is difficult to precisely distinguish languages from dialects. One estimate comes from Wycliffe Bible Translators, who claim that there are 7,378 languages in the world. Of these, about 10 percent (717) have the whole Bible in their language; another 1,582 languages have a complete New Testament; and 1196 have some portion of the Bible (457 million). That makes 3,495 languages with some Scripture, but 3,883 with no Scripture.[1]

The good news is that for almost 90 percent of the people in the world (7.04 billion out of 7.9 billion), some Scripture in their language exists. The bad news is that there are still 860 million people and several thousand languages that still need God's Word.

There are hundreds of organizations involved in Bible translation. Many of them are part of the Forum of Bible Agencies International, an alliance of international Bible agencies and other missions organizations founded in 1990. Its goal is to encourage collaboration and cooperation in the task of promoting Bible translation and Bible knowledge worldwide. In 2006, the Forum launched the website Find a Bible (https://find.bible), a directory providing listings and links to Bibles in the many languages of the world. The website provides comprehensive tables related to international Bible translation, including listings of the following:

1. "2022 Global Scripture Access," Wycliffe Global Alliance, accessed January 31, 2023, www.wycliffe.net/resources/statistics.

1. *Bibles*: 4,979 Bibles in the many languages of world (as well 3,132 Bible films and another 20,777 Bible resources)
2. *languages:* 7,894 languages, including the number of native speakers and Bibles available in each language
3. *countries:* 227 countries in the world, including their population, languages, refugees, degrees of literacy, and level of persecution
4. *agencies:* 1,022 agencies involved in Bible translation and related activities

Some Organizations Doing Bible Translation

The 1,022 agencies noted above shows the vast scope of ministries engaged in Bible translation. The Forum's approximately forty member agencies are divided into full (voting) members, associate members (nonvoting), and one collaborating agency. A list of these appears below, representing some of the most important Bible translation agencies worldwide.

Full Members of the Forum	
American Bible Society	Lifewords
Bible League Canada	Lutheran Bible Translators
Bible League International	OneHope
Biblica	Open Doors
Davar Partners International	Pioneer Bible Translators
Deaf Bible Society	Scripture Union
Deaf Missions	Seed Company
DOOR International	SIL International
Faith Comes by Hearing	Word for the World Bible Translators
Institute for Bible Translation	Wycliffe Bible Translators USA
Jesus Film Project	Wycliffe Global Alliance

Associate Members of the Forum[2]	
4.2.20 Foundation	SIM International
Bibles for China	Spoken Worldwide
Bible Translation Fellowship	Story Runners (A Cru Ministry)
Crossway	Talking Bibles International

2. Former members include Ethnos360 (formerly New Tribes), Global Recordings Network, and Mars Hill Productions.

Associate Members of the Forum[2]	
Digital Bible Society	Taylor U. Center for Scripture Engagement
Global Partners	Virtual Storehouse
Jerusalem Center for Bible Translators	Wycliffe Bible Translators (UK & Ireland)
MegaVoice	YouVersion
Mundo Cristão	

Collaborating Agency
United Bible Societies

Details about these organizations can be found at their respective websites. Here we will briefly discuss the history and mission of two of the most influential, Wycliffe Bible Translators and the United Bible Societies.

Wycliffe Bible Translators and Its Affiliates

Wycliffe Bible Translators was founded in 1942 by William Cameron Townsend (1896–1982) and is named after John Wycliffe, who translated the first complete Bible into English (see Question 24). Townsend was a missionary and linguist whose early missionary work was with the Central American Mission (CAM) among the Kaqchikel Maya people of Guatemala.[3] Through his work with a minority indigenous population, Townsend came to see the plight of these native peoples as both spiritual and social. Their poverty and oppression were due not only to their spiritual darkness but also to illiteracy, lack of education, and monolingual isolation. Their only access to the larger society was through mixed-race bilingual middlemen (speaking both Spanish and the native language), who benefited personally from the status quo and so had no impetus to improve the economic and social position of the native peoples.

Townsend also firmly believed that the Bible provided the ultimate answer to humanity's problems—spiritual, social, and economical—and no people group could thrive without direct access to Scripture in their heart language. Townsend therefore developed a philosophy of mission that encouraged the propagation of economically strong, self-sufficient, and biblically literate communities of faith.

3. For a fuller history of Townsend and his work, see Hugh Steven, *Wycliffe in the Making: The Memoirs of W. Cameron Townsend, 1920–1933* (Wheaton, IL: Harold Shaw, 1995).

In 1933, Townsend left Guatemala and went to Mexico to continue his work of translating into indigenous languages. With support from key Mexican government officials, he founded the Summer Institute of Linguistics (SIL) to train linguist-missionaries for Bible translation. Since the government of Mexico could not directly fund missionary work through its educational system, in 1942 Townsend founded Wycliffe Bible Translators (WBT) as an independent nonprofit. While WBT would focus on missionary activity, SIL would do the technical linguistic research.

The work of Wycliffe and its many affiliate organizations has had a tremendous impact on international translation efforts in general and the proliferation of Bible translations in particular. Early on, Townsend came to recognize that to produce the best translations required advanced knowledge not only of biblical studies but also linguistics. SIL trained and equipped some of the best linguists in the world. Two of its most notable pioneers were groundbreaking linguists and Bible translators Kenneth Pike and Eugene Nida (for the latter, see Question 3 and 6). The following are some Wycliffe affiliates.

Wycliffe Regionals and *Wycliffe Global Alliance* came out of the expansion of Wycliffe Bible Translators globally and the founding of many Wycliffe organizations around the world. These were originally operated as Wycliffe divisions within each country, and in 1980, Wycliffe Bible Translators International was launched to provide organization to these divisions. In 1991 Wycliffe International was restructured into an association of stand-alone organizations, with each country's organization becoming fully independent. In 2011, the new "doing business as" name Wycliffe Global Alliance (WGA) replaced Wycliffe International. Today, WGA is a community and network of one hundred–plus member organizations operating in more than sixty countries. These organizations work together in Bible translation projects around the world. Many are also members of the Forum of Bible Agencies International.

SIL International, formerly Summer Institute of Linguistics, is "a global, faith-based nonprofit that works with local communities around the world to develop language solutions that expand possibilities for a better life."[4] It is the technical linguistic side of Wycliffe, with its main focus on the study, analysis, and documentation of languages, especially lesser-known ones, in order to widen linguistic knowledge, promote literacy, and translate the Bible into the diverse languages of the world. SIL publishes *Ethnologue*, a database of knowledge from its multi-faceted linguistic, anthropological, and sociological research (see Question 37). SIL also produces publications and software that promote language research and learning.

The Seed Company is a subsidiary of Wycliffe USA and part of the Wycliffe Global Alliance. Its primary focus is development and fundraising, linking donors to Bible translation projects where local people are producing

4. See the SIL website at www.sil.org.

a translation in their own language. The organization was launched in 1993 by Bernie May, a former president of Wycliffe USA.

JAARS, which originally stood for Jungle Aviation and Radio Service, is a nonprofit subsidiary of SIL International, founded by William Cameron in Peru in 1948. Its purpose was to provide missionaries and Bible translators safe access to remote language groups. Today, JAARS provides wide-ranging technical support, including transportation by air, land, and sea, information technology, and media support. In 1986, the organization dropped its full name and became simply JAARS, Inc.

Wycliffe Associates (WA) was founded in 1967 in association with Wycliffe Bible Translators, but became fully independent and gained separate tax-exempt status in 1995. Their motto is "Accelerating Bible Translation," and their mission is to "empower and equip national Bible translators—native speakers—to translate Scripture into their heart language using resources and tools provided through Bible translation workshops under the guidance and authority of the local church."[5] The organization made headlines over the last decade on two controversial issues.

First, in 2016 WA pulled its membership from the Wycliffe Global Alliance over the debate related to the translation of "Son of God" in Muslim-idiom translations (see Question 40 for more on this issue).

Second, Wycliffe Associates' translation program MAST, which stands for Mobilized Assistance Supporting Translation, has come under scrutiny and criticism. Advocates of the program claim that it is a highly effective method that produces Bible translations far faster (weeks to months instead of years) and cheaper than ever before. It achieves this by skipping much of the technical work of traditional translation procedures, instead utilizing local church leaders and native language speakers to a much greater degree. Wycliffe Associates has raised millions of dollars in donations based on these claims. Some critics, however, assert that these claims of success have been exaggerated and that Bible translations produced using MAST are of inferior quality. Representatives of WA dispute these claims and continue to assert the extraordinary success of the program. The Evangelical Council for Financial Accountability (ECFA) became skeptical of WA's claims about MAST and launched a review. In response, Wycliffe Associates resigned from the ECFA in February 2020.[6] It would seem the jury is still out on the success and impact of the program.

---

5. See the WA website at https://wycliffeassociates.org.
6. For articles critical of Wycliffe Associates, the MAST method, and their fundraising, see Warren Cole Smith, "When Is a Bible Translation Not a Bible Translation?," *Ministry Watch*, May 14, 2020, https://ministrywatch.com/when-is-a-bible-translation-not-a-bible-translation; Warren Cole Smith, "Claims by Wycliffe Associates in Fundraising Initiatives Raise Questions," *Roys Report*, April 15, 2020, https://julieroys.com/claims-by-wycliffe-associates-in-fundraising-initiatives-raise-questions.

National Bible Societies and the United Bible Societies

Rivaling the impact and influence of Wycliffe and its many affiliates are the many loosely affiliated "Bible Societies" around the world. This movement began with the establishment of the British and Foreign Bible Society, founded in 1804 by a group of Christians associated with the Religious Tract Society. They were inspired by the story of a Welsh girl named Mary Jones, who had saved for six years and then trekked twenty-six miles to purchase a Bible in Welsh. Initially formed to provide affordable Bibles to Welsh-speaking Christians, the vision quickly spread: "If for Wales, why not for the kingdom? And if for the kingdom, why not for the world?"[7] Among the founders were William Wilberforce, the famous abolitionist, and other members of his Clapham Sect. The Clapham Sect was a group of social reformers in the late eighteenth and early nineteenth centuries associated with Clapham, a district in southwest London.

Other Bible societies soon followed, including the National Bible Society of Ireland (1806), the Bible Society of Northern Ireland (1807), the Scottish Bible Society (1809), the Bible Society of India (1811), the Finnish Bible Society (1812), the Russian Bible Society (1813), the Netherlands Bible Society (1814), and others.[8] The American Bible Society (ABS) was formed in 1816.[9] Its first president, Elias Boudinot, served as president of the Continental Congress from 1782 to 1783, near the end of the American Revolutionary War. Other prominent individuals also held this position, including John Jay, the first Chief Justice of the United States Supreme Court. The ABS provided the first Bibles in hotels and distributed pocket Bibles to soldiers in the American Civil War. In the 1830s, the ABS became embroiled in controversy when it unfortunately refused a donation from the American Anti-Slavery Society intended to distribute Bibles to American slaves. The donation instead went to the American Missionary Society.[10] The ABS today publishes and distributes interconfessional translations of the Bible and provides study aids and other tools to help people engage with it. Today's English Version (TEV), also known as the Good News Translation (GNT), and the Contemporary English Version (CEV) were produced by the ABS (see Question 32).

The United Bible Societies (UBS) was established in 1946 by representatives from various of these national societies. It is a global fellowship made up today of approximately 150 Bible Societies operating in more than 240 countries and territories. Its headquarters is in Swindon, England. The UBS identifies itself as interconfessional, interdependent, and integrated. "Interconfessional" means serving and working "with all churches

7. See the "Our History" page on the Bible Society website at www.biblesociety.org.uk/about-us/our-history.
8. See the Wikipedia page "Bible society" for a fuller list and links.
9. See John Fea, *The Bible Cause: A History of the American Bible Society* (New York: Oxford University Press, 2016).
10. Fea, *Bible Cause*, 72–83.

of all traditions and denominations—Catholic, Orthodox, Protestant and Emerging." "Interdependent" means "made up of independent national Bible Societies—choosing to join together as members in an interdependent global organization." "Integrated" means "unique in operating across the full Bible Lifecycle, so that, with God's help, we can meet people and cultures at their point of need."[11] On its website, the UBS affirms that it has translated the entire Bible into the languages of more than half the world's population, which is about seventy percent of Bible translations that exist today. Their goal "over the next 20 years is, by God's provision, to complete 1200 translation projects, which will provide around 600 million people with access to Scripture."[12]

Summary

Today hundreds of organizations around the world are involved in Bible translation, seeking to translate God's Word into all the approximately seven thousand languages of the world. The goal is that all of earth's nearly eight billion people will be able to read or hear God's Word in their own mother tongue—their heart language. While only about 10 percent of the languages in the world have a full Bible, almost 50 percent have some Scriptures. Since there are Bibles or parts thereof in virtually all of the world's largest language groups, approximately 90 percent of the world's population have some parts of Scripture available to them. The challenge remains to make God's Word fully available to all people everywhere.

REFLECTION QUESTIONS

1. How many languages are there in the world? How many have some or all of Scripture translated into them?

2. What percentage of the world's population does not yet have any part of the Bible available to them?

3. What is the ultimate goal for all Bible translation organizations?

4. What is the history behind Wycliffe Bible Translators?

5. What is the history behind the United Bible Societies?

---

11. "Who We Are," United Bible Societies, accessed January 31, 2023, https://unitedbiblesocieties.org/who.
12. "How We're Making a Difference," United Bible Societies, accessed January 31, 2023, https://unitedbiblesocieties.org/how/.

QUESTION 39

What Are Some of the Challenges Faced by International Bible Translators?

Throughout this book we have discussed many of the challenges related to Bible translation, focusing especially on English translation. All of these apply to international translators working with remote groups and tribal languages, including the difficulties in translating words, collocations, idioms, euphemisms, weights and measures, and so on. Here we look at other challenges related especially to international translators.

Logistic Challenges

We can start with logistic challenges, that is, those challenges related to simply doing the work. There are *financial* challenges for international translation. A translation team must be organized, trained, and provided with resources. In addition to costs for administration, there are costs related to moving, housing, and living expenses. In the destination country, native-language consultants must be recruited, trained, and supported in their work.

There are *geographical and environmental* challenges. Remote tribal groups in places like Irian Jaya, Papua New Guinea, or the Amazon rainforest can be difficult to reach and dangerous to approach. Perhaps the most famous account of Christian martyrdom in modern times is the harrowing story of five missionaries, Jim Elliot, Pete Fleming, Ed McCully, Nate Saint, and Roger Youderian, who were speared to death by members of the Huaorani (or Waorani) tribe in Ecuador in 1956 while trying to make contact with this remote people group.[1]

1. See Ruth A. Tucker, *From Jerusalem to Irian Jaya: A Biographical History of Christian Missions*, 2nd ed. (Grand Rapids; Zondervan, 2004), 352–59; Elisabeth Elliot, *Through Gates of Splendor* (New York: Harper, 1957).

Logistic challenges can also include *political* obstacles. Visas can be difficult to obtain in some countries. Translators may face governmental or local opposition in places where there is a majority population of another religion, such as Hindu or Muslim. Authoritarian governments may oppose Christian missionaries they see as threats to their authority. Opposition can also come from those opposed to Christian proselytizing. There are lively debates among anthropologists, linguists, and missiologists as to whether Christian evangelization and Bible translation enriches or adversely affects native cultures.[2]

Challenges of Non-written Languages and Illiterate Populations

In many cases throughout history, the languages in which the Bible was translated already had a rich literary history. For example, when the Hebrew Bible was translated into Greek in the third century BC (the Septuagint [LXX]; see Question 23), Greek had existed as a language in written form for centuries, and there were many Greek religious and philosophical works. This provided the translators with a ready-made vocabulary that could be utilized and adapted to express the religious concepts found in the Hebrew Bible.

By contrast, international translators working in remote tribal regions often encounter languages that have no written form, let alone a history of literary works. In these contexts, the community's history and traditions may have been passed down orally from generation to generation by tribal elders or by a class of tradition-guardians. In situations where no written language exists, Bible translators must first learn the spoken language. This includes learning not only word meanings, grammar, and syntax but also idioms, collocations, cultural connotations, and a host of other societal assumptions that are unique to that language group. Translators must then develop or modify an existing alphabet to record the language. This may include introducing new letters or symbols to indicate sounds that are not part of Western language groups.[3] Then the native language speakers must be taught how to read the language that up to that point had been only spoken.

Of course, even in contexts where a spoken language has a written form, large segments of the population may be unable to read or write. The task of translators in these contexts is not only to produce a written version of the Scriptures in the local language, but also to establish schools and other resources for developing literacy. It may also entail producing audio versions of the Bible translation, which do not require reading skills. It is significant in this regard that throughout church history most Christians have learned the

2. For opposition from an anthropologist, see David Stoll, *Fishers of Men or Founders of Empire? The Wycliffe Bible Translators in Latin America* (London: Zed Books, 1983). For opposition from a linguist, see Lawrence Venuti, *The Translator's Invisibility: A History of Translation*, 2nd ed. (New York: Routledge, 2008), reprinted with a new introduction in 2018. See Question 6.
3. The International Phonetic Alphabet, developed by the International Phonetic Associations, seeks to provide a letter for every sound utilized in languages around the world.

Scriptures through their attendance at church services and catechism, where the Scriptures were orally read or recited rather than privately read.

It is not surprising, considering these linguistic and pedagogical challenges, that international Bible translation organizations like Wycliffe and the United Bible Societies have been on the cutting edge of the development of research methods and resources related to linguistic analysis, language acquisition, literacy training, and even anthropological research. We have previously mentioned *Ethnologue* (Question 38), a database and reference volume published annually by SIL International, a Wycliffe affiliate. First published in 1951, *Ethnologue* provides statistical research widely utilized by both religious and secular organizations.

Challenges Related to Skills and Expertise

We have repeatedly noted that the two most fundamental goals of Bible translation are *accuracy* and *readability* (see Question 2), and this applies to international translation as well. Three areas of expertise are essential to achieve these goals: biblical scholarship, linguistic expertise, and mastery of the receptor language.

(1) *Biblical scholarship*. Ideally, all Bible translators should be biblical scholars, with a thorough knowledge of Hebrew and Greek, training in exegetical methodology, and a mastery of the historical and cultural background to the biblical world. In reality, the level of training for missionaries varies from place to place and from situation to situation. Fortunately, there is a wealth of biblical study material that translators can draw upon, including other Bible translations, commentaries, biblical reference works, Bible software, and Hebrew and Greek study tools.

Some Bible commentary series, such as the SIL Exegetical Summary Series[4] and the United Bible Societies' Handbook Series,[5] are especially geared for international translators. The former summarizes scholarly interpretations of biblical texts, noting perspectives found in various commentaries. The latter is a more traditional commentary, but includes comments geared especially for the challenges faced by international translators. For example, in *A Handbook on the Letter of James*, the authors comment on the phrase "Count it all joy" (RSV) in James 1:2, noting some of the potential challenges translators might face in certain languages:

> A literal translation of the clause *Count it all joy* presents difficulties for translators in many languages. In such languages a more natural translation will be "You should rejoice greatly when . . . ," or more idiomatically "Your hearts [or, stomachs] should feel very warm when . . . ," "Your hearts should dance

4. See the SIL Exegetical Summary Series titles at https://www.sil.org/resources/publications/ess.
5. See the UBS Handbook Series titles at https://thebibletranslator.org.

> when . . . ," or "Your innermost being should ring when . . . " In languages where it will be unnatural to talk about being "joyful" when encountering trials, it will be helpful to translate in a similar way to TEV, "consider yourselves fortunate," and say "You must understand that it is beneficial for you when . . . ," ". . . it is a great advantage for you when . . . ," or even "You must feel great satisfaction when . . . "[6]

In terms of Bible software, Paratext was developed jointly by SIL International and the UBS. It is described as "the world's leading software application for creating and checking new Bible translations, writing study Bibles, and revising existing translations."[7] A more recent fully online tool produced by the UBS is TIPs, which stands for Translation Insights and Perspectives.[8] Of course traditional Bible software programs, like Logos Bible Software (logos.com) and Accordance Bible Software (accordancebible.com), are also valuable tools for all Bible students including translators. Websites like BibleGateway.com provide access to hundreds of Bible translations in a variety languages.

Another way translators seek to maintain biblical accuracy is by using biblical scholars as consultants for their translation projects. A preliminary translation into the receptor language can be tested by producing a "back-translation" and sending it to biblical scholars. A back-translation is a relatively formal translation of the initial receptor-text translation back into English (or whatever is the primary language of the scholar-consultant). This allows the scholar to see approximations of the words and idioms used in the target language. The scholar can then raise questions and dialogue with the translators about whether the draft accurately represents the meaning of the Hebrew or Greek source text.

(2) *Linguistic expertise*. In addition to biblical scholarship, accurate translation requires expertise in linguistics, understanding how languages work. As with biblical scholarship, a PhD in linguistics would be ideal for all translators. But this level of training is not always possible. Organizations like SIL International were established to provide linguistic training for those preparing to do international translation work. There are also a wealth of resources published by Wycliffe, the UBS, and other organizations for linguistic training in preparation for Bible translation.[9]

---

6. I.-J. Loh, and H. Hatton, *A Handbook on the Letter from James* (New York: United Bible Societies, 1997), 11–12.
7. "Reference Tools and Resources: Paratext," United Bible Societies, accessed January 31, 2023, https://translation.bible/tools-resources/paratext.
8. "Translation Insights and Perspectives," TIPS, accessed 3/3/2023, https://tips.translation.bible. For a video introduction to TIPs, see https://tips.translation.bible/wp-content/uploads/2022/02/TIPsAnim.mp4
9. See, for example, Katherine Barnwell, *Bible Translation: An Introductory Course in Translation Principles*, 4th ed. (Dallas: SIL International, 2020); Harriet Hill,

(3) *Fluency in the target/receptor language.* If accuracy in translation requires biblical and linguistic expertise, readability requires first-language translators and consultants who have fluency in the receptor language. We have all had the experience of hearing someone speak in a language that was not their mother tongue. Their words may be understandable, but they often speak in awkward or "broken" language, without the naturalness and fluidity of a first-language speaker (see Question 2). Translations that have not been checked and double-checked by first-language consultants may be rejected or underutilized by members of the receptor culture because they sound foreign and awkward to native speakers.

The Challenge of Linguistic Differences

A fourth major challenge international Bible translators face is navigating the diversity of language systems around the world. As we have noted frequently throughout this book, different languages use not only different words but different grammatical constructions to express the same meaning. Consider, for example, the part of speech known as the article. In English we have a *definite* article ("the") and an *indefinite* article ("a, an"). The former indicates when something specific is in mind ("the book"), while the latter indicates something general or nonspecific ("a book"). Greek, by contrast, has only one article (*ho, hē, to*), whose primary function is *not* to indicate definiteness or indefiniteness.[10] There is no one-to-one correspondence between Greek and English in the use of the article, so in each case the English translator must decide whether to use a definite article, an indefinite article, or no article at all. There are other differences as well. The Greek article is declined (changes form) in line with the gender, case, and number of the noun it modifies. By contrast, English articles do not change form with reference to gender, case, or number. When we move to other languages around the world, things get far more complicated. For example, Mandarin Chinese, unlike Greek and English, has no article at all. The same is true of Japanese, Korean, and Russian. A Chinese noun standing alone can mean "a" or "the." Chinese has other ways to express an idea like the indefinite article, such as using the word *yī* ("one"), followed by the appropriate classifier. Whereas in English and Greek, the article is a separate word, in some languages (like Hebrew), it is a prefix, attached to the front of a word; in others (like Aramaic), it is suffix, attached to the end. While some languages commonly use articles with proper names (Greek: *ho Iēsous*), others, like English, do not. I would not say "the Jesus."

Ernst-August Gutt, Christoph Unger, Rick Floyd, and Margaret Hill, *Bible Translation Basics: Communicating Scripture in a Relevant Way* (Dallas: SIL International, 2011).

10. See Daniel B. Wallace, *Greek Grammar Beyond the Basics: An Exegetical Syntax of the New Testament* (Grand Rapids: Zondervan, 1996), 206–90.

This is just a tiny tip of the linguistic iceberg, since these kinds of differences appear in virtually every part of speech and vary greatly among the seven thousand–plus languages of the world! Consider, for example, first-person plural pronouns (we/us/ours). Some languages have both an "inclusive" *we* and an "exclusive" *we*. The inclusive *we* includes both the speaker and the addressee(s), me, those with me, *and you*; the exclusive includes only me and those with me. Since Hebrew and Greek make no such distinction in the form of the word, translators into languages that do must decide *in each case* purely from the context. Sometimes the decision is easy. When the disciples ask Jesus concerning their attempt to exorcise a demon, "Why couldn't *we* drive it out?" (Matt. 17:19), it is clearly exclusive. And when Jesus says, "*We* are going up to Jerusalem" (Mark 10:33), it is clearly inclusive. Yet other passages are debatable. When the author of 1 John writes, "We write this to make *our* joy complete" (1 John 1:4), is he also referring to the readers' joy? And when the author of the gospel of John writes, "This is the disciple who testifies to these things and who wrote them down. *We* know that his testimony is true" (John 21:24), is he affirming that the readers also know this to be true?[11]

The challenge for translators is discerning the unique linguistic features of both source and receptor languages, and finding ways to communicate the message of the source text clearly and accurately. This involves biblical and linguistic expertise, as well as an enormous amount of time, energy, and patience.

Cultural Challenges

A fifth major challenge international translators face relates to cultural differences (see Questions 15–17). People groups differ not only in the languages they speak, but also in their worldviews, religious convictions, belief systems, cultural customs, and ethical values. These features can radically affect the way one understands the Bible. A well-known example of misunderstanding based on cultural assumptions is found in Don Richardson's autobiographical missionary account known as *Peace Child*.[12] In the book Richardson describes how he and his wife were working to evangelize the Sawi people of Netherlands New Guinea. In their tribal lore, the Sawi celebrated a legendary hero who had exacted revenge on an enemy by first pretending to be his friend and then betraying him. While teaching the story of Jesus to the tribespeople, Richardson was dismayed to learn that they viewed Judas as the hero of the story! Here we see a difference in cultural values that dramatically changes the meaning of the story. Eventually, Richardson overcame this dilemma by connecting the gospel message to another tradition of the tribe known as a "peace child." This was a ritual where the newborn son of a tribal chief would be given over to a warring tribe's chief to raise. As long

---

11. For these and other examples, see Wallace, *Grammar*, 397–99.
12. Don Richardson, *Peace Child*, 4th ed. (Ventura, CA: Regal, 2005).

as the child lived, there would be peace between the two tribes. Richardson taught the tribe about God's gift of his Son Jesus as the "peace child" who brings peace between God and people.

Sometimes the cultural problem is not misunderstanding, but ignorance. The historical and cultural contexts of the ancient Near East and the Greco-Roman world are very different from other contexts around the world. Places and things found in the Bible may be unknown to native populations. How do you translate the words "camel" or "sheep" in a context where these animals are unknown? A classic illustration of this is whether to replace the word "sheep" with "pig" in language groups where sheep are unknown and pigs are used as sacrificial animals.

While there is no single or simple answer here, the best solution is usually to choose a translation that gains more than it loses. To replace "sheep" with "pig" is highly problematic, since sheep and shepherds play such a prominent role in Scripture. The Lord is my shepherd (Ps. 23:1). Jesus is the good shepherd (John 10). Sheep were sacrificed at the Jewish Passover, a festival that is identified in the NT as fulfilled in Christ's death on the cross (1 Cor. 5:7). Furthermore, pigs in Scripture are unclean animals that cannot be eaten or used as sacrifices! In this case, it would seem far better to educate people on the nature of sheep than to replace sheep with such a problematic term.

Summary

In this question we have examined some of the unique challenges faced by international translators, including those related to logistics, geography, literacy, biblical and linguistic expertise, and the sometimes major linguistic and cultural differences between people groups.

REFLECTION QUESTIONS

1. What are some of the physical obstacles that international Bible translators face?
2. What steps must Bible translators take if there is no written version of a tribal language?
3. Identify some unique resources developed for international Bible translators.
4. Why is it important to have fluent native speakers on any translation team?
5. Can you give an example of a translation problem that might arise from the differences between the source language and receptor language cultures?

QUESTION 40

What Is the Controversy in Translating "Son of God" in Muslim Contexts?

One of the most controversial recent topics in the world of international Bible translation concerns translating biblical statements about Jesus as the Son of God and God as Father in the context of outreach to Muslims. This issue, in turn, is part of a larger debate related to what are called "insider movements" within Islam.

Insider Movements in Islam

Insider movements seek to open the door to evangelism among Muslims by providing more indigenous and less Westernized expressions of Christianity. In insider movements, "individuals remain culturally Muslim while affirming belief in 'Isa, the Qur'anic rendering of the name Jesus."[1] Translations that are indigenized for Muslim contexts are sometimes called "Muslim-idiom translations" (MITs).

In addition to the Son of God question, other controversial issues related to insider movements include: (1) how to discuss the doctrine of the Trinity, and (2) whether to use "Allah," the Muslim name for God, in Bible translations. Neither of these issues, however, is as controversial as the Son of God debate. To be sure, the doctrine of the Trinity is apparently rejected in the Qur'an. Surah 5:73 reads, "They do blaspheme who say: God is one of three in trinity: for there is no god except one God" (cf. 4:171).[2] It is debated whether statements like these represent a rejection of the biblical doctrine

1. Cynthia L. Miller-Naudé and Jacobus A. Naudé, "Ideology and Translation Strategy in Muslim-Sensitive Bible Translations," *Neotestamentica* 47, no. 1 (2013): 173.
2. All quotations are taken from *The Qur'an, A Translation*, trans. Abdullah Yusuf Ali, 23rd US ed. (Elmhurst, NY: Tahrike Tarsile Qur'an, 2008).

of the Trinity or a distorted and heretical (Arian) view of the Trinity.[3] But in either case, this is not an issue of translation *per se*, since the word "Trinity" does not appear in the Bible. And it is the word rather than the concept that is the primary negative trigger for Muslims.

Similarly, translating God as "Allah" is much less controversial than identifying Jesus as the Son of God.[4] Almost all Bible translators agree that *allah* was the generic word for God or a god in Arabic even before Islam. And, as Kenneth Thomas notes, "Jews, Christians, and Muslims have used Allah in their citations and translations of the Bible since the first centuries of Islam."[5] Using Allah for God in Arabic translations of the Bible should therefore be no more controversial than the use of *elohim* for God in the Hebrew Old Testament or *theos* for God in the Greek New Testament. These were generic words for God with prior histories, and yet the biblical authors were willing to use them. The English word "god" itself has pagan Germanic roots that predate Christianity. Furthermore, most Arabic scholars believe that *allah* and *elohim* ultimately come from the same root, again suggesting that Allah is acceptable for translating general words for God.

While "Allah" is therefore an acceptable translation for *elohim* (OT) and *theos* (NT) in Arabic versions of the Bible, it should probably not be used when the Hebrew text has *Yahweh* (YHWH), the personal name for God. In this case Arabic translations have generally either transliterated the word as *Yahwah* or have translated it as *rabb* ("lord").[6] This latter, again, follows the precedent of (1) the Hebrew Scriptures, where *Yahweh* is pronounced as *adonai*, "lord," when read aloud; (2) the Greek Bible, where YHWH is translated as *kyrios*, "lord"; and (3) most English versions, where YHWH is rendered as "LORD" in small caps (see Question 22). "Allah" should also be avoided in Bible translations for languages where "Allah" has come to function as a proper name rather than a generic term for God (such as Persian, Amharic, French, and English).[7]

---

3. Some advocates for MITs argue that the Qur'an is not here attacking the biblical doctrine of the Trinity, but rather a distortion of it, the Arabian folk belief that there is a trio of gods consisting of Allah, his wife Mary, and their son Jesus (Rick Brown, in personal correspondence and a draft article of "The Arian Background of the Quran, with Implications for Engagement").
4. See Kenneth J. Thomas, "Allah in Translations of the Bible," *International Journal of Frontier Missions* 23, no. 4 (Winter 2006): 171–74; Mike Tisdell, "Is Allah the God of the Bible?," *Journal of Biblical Missiology*, September 30, 2020, https://biblicalmissiology.org/2020/09/30/is-allah-the-god-of-the-bible.
5. Thomas, "Allah in Translations of the Bible," 171.
6. Thomas, "Allah in Translations of the Bible," 171–72.
7. Tisdell, "Is Allah the God of the Bible?"

The Son of God Debate

The most controversial issue in the context of Muslim insider movements remains how to translate terms related to Jesus's divine Sonship. The difficulty arises because the Qur'an, the Muslim holy book, explicitly denies that Jesus is the Son of God:

> To [Allah] is due the primal origin of the heavens and the earth: how can He have a son when He has no consort? (6:101)[8]
>
> O People of the Book! Commit no excesses in your religion: Nor say of God aught but the truth . . . for God is one God: Glory be to Him: far exalted is He above having a son. (4:171; cf. 5:18; 112:3)

Muslims consider the idea that God had a son to be blasphemous because they misunderstand Jesus's divine Sonship to indicate a biological relationship with God. Rick Brown, perhaps the most articulate defender of MITs, claims that using such language effectively negates evangelism before it can start:

> Not surprisingly [considering these Quranic passages], seekers and believers from Muslim backgrounds regularly single out the term "Son of God" as the biggest obstacle to reading the Gospel. Some will not even touch a Bible because they fear this blasphemous term is in it. . . . The biological meaning of this phrase and its blasphemous connotations are so deeply entrenched in the minds of most Muslims that it is impossible simply to erase it from their minds and hearts.[9]

Some missionaries and translators have therefore tried to resolve this problem by replacing "Son of God" with nonfamilial terms that they claim communicate accurately the meaning of Jesus's status as the Son of God without provoking offense.

While this issue has been a challenge for missionaries since evangelism among Muslims began, it came to the attention of the larger Christian public in recent years, especially following an article by Collin Hansen in *Christianity Today*, published February 4, 2011.[10] In a generally balanced manner, Hansen introduced the key players and the main arguments. A strong negative

8. Cf. Q5:19, 75; 6:101; 9:30–31; 19:35; 72:3; 112:3.
9. Rick Brown, "Delicate Issues in Mission, Part 1: Explaining the Biblical Term 'Son(s) of God' in Muslim Contexts," *International Journal of Frontier Missions* 22 (Fall 2005): 92.
10. Collin Hansen, "The Son and the Crescent," *Christianity Today*, February 4, 2011, 19–23. http://www.christianitytoday.com/ct/2011/february/soncrescent.html.

response followed, including a petition against MITs that garnered 13,000 signatures. The Presbyterian Church of America (PCA) produced a highly critical white paper on the topic, recommending that funds be withdrawn from all translations that avoided familial terms.[11] In August 2011, representatives of Wycliffe Global Alliance and SIL International (see Question 38) met in Istanbul and produced a statement called "SIL International Statement of Best Practices for Bible Translation of Divine Familial Terms."[12] In it they took a generally mediating position, encouraging the retention of familial terms in Bible translation but clarifying their meaning for Muslim readers. Under continuing pressure, in March 2012 Wycliffe and SIL approached the World Evangelical Alliance (WEA) to independently review their principles and practice for translating divine familial language.[13] The WEA formed an independent panel and oversight committee, issuing a report in 2013. At the request of Wycliffe and WEA, the oversight committee continued to meet to review compliance. Their third report came out in February 2017.[14]

Key Issues in the Debate

(1) Advocates of MITs assert that the problem is primarily *linguistic* rather than theological and that "Son of God" does not mean the same thing in Islam as it does in the Bible. Brown points out that for most Muslims, the term "Son of God" has one meaning only, and that is "God's offspring by a sexual union."[15] By contrast, the Bible uses the title "Son of God" in much broader ways. While it often refers to Jesus (Matt. 3:17; 14:33; Mark 3:11; Luke 1:32; John 1:49; etc.), it can also refer to Adam as God's creation (Luke 3:38), angels and heavenly beings (Job 1:6; Ps. 29:1), Israel as God's covenant people (Exod. 4:22; Deut. 32:18), Israel's king as God's vice-regent (Ps. 2:7; 2 Sam. 7:14), Israel's leaders (Ps. 82:6; Ezek. 21:10), and believers in general (Luke 6:35; John 1:12).

---

11. David B. Garner, Robert Berman, Nabeel T. Jabbour, Jonathan Mitchell, Bill Nikides, and Tom Seelinger, *A Call to Faithful Witness (Part One)—Like Father, Like Son: Divine Familial Language in Bible Translation; A Partial Report (Part One of Two Parts) of the Ad Interim Committee on Insider Movements to the Fortieth General Assembly of the Presbyterian Church in America*, May 14, 2012, https://www.pcahistory.org/pca/digest/studies/scim01_2012.pdf.
12. This statement subsequently went through a series of revisions. The April 30, 2012 version with commentary can be found at https://www.sil.org/sites/default/files/files/divine_familial_terms_commentary_full.pdf.
13. A four-point summary of "SIL Standards for Translation of Divine Familial Terms" (September 2015) can be found at www.sil.org/translation/sil-standards-translation-divine-familial-terms.
14. For reports and documentation, including an eighty-eight-page translation procedure document, see "Bible Translation Review," WEA, accessed January 31, 2023, https://worldea.org/bible-translation-review.
15. Brown, "Delicate Issues in Mission," 95.

The references to Jesus as the Son of God in the NT also carry different nuances, some pointing primarily to his role as messianic king (Matt. 16:16; 26:63; Mark 8:29; 14:61; Luke 1:32–33; 4:41; John 1:49) and others to his divine status as the eternal Son (Matt. 11:27; John 1:14, 18; 3:16; Rom. 8:3; Gal. 4:4; Col. 1:15). When the high priest asks Jesus at his trial whether he is "the Messiah, the Son of God" (Matt. 26:63; Mark 14:61), he is not asking whether Jesus is the messianic king and the eternal Son of God (= the Second Person of the Trinity), but rather, whether he is claiming to be the messianic king, who will serve as God's vice-regent and adopted "son" (2 Sam. 7:14; Ps. 2:7). Since "Son of God" in some contexts is a messianic title, some advocates of MITs suggest that it could be replaced by titles like Messiah or Christ.

In response, while it is true that "Son of God" does not always point to Jesus's essential deity, it is *not* true that it is merely synonymous with titles like Christ/Messiah.[16] The familial aspects of the title are important, even in the messianic sense of the phrase. And in many contexts, the term *does* point to Jesus's essential deity. For this reason, the SIL Standards, while recognizing the significant potential for misunderstanding of familial terms applied to God, nevertheless reject their elimination:

> When the words for "father" and "son" refer to God the Father and to the Son of God, these words will always be translated with the most directly equivalent familial words within the given linguistic and cultural context of the recipients.

Yet it is also important to avoid offense and misunderstanding when possible:

> Therefore, in case of difficulties, it is recommended that translators consider the addition of qualifying words and/or phrases . . . in order to avoid misunderstanding. For example, as the biblical context allows, the word for "father" might be rendered with the equivalent of "heavenly Father" when referring to God, and the word for "son" might be rendered with the equivalent of "divine Son," "eternal Son," or "heavenly Son" when referring to Jesus.[17]

16. While in his earlier work Rick Brown asserted that "Son of God" could be synonymous with "Christ" (Brown, "Delicate Issues in Mission," 94), more recently he acknowledges that "terms like 'Christ/Messiah' should be used only to translate *Christos/Meshiach* and should not be used to translate *huios/ben* [i.e., 'son']" (Rick Brown, Leith Gray, and Andrea Gray, "The Terms of Translation: A New Look at Translating Familial Biblical Terms," *IJFM* 28, no. 3 (April–June 2011): 116.
17. "SIL Standards for Translation."

Another argument made by advocates of MITs is that the identification of God as Father and Jesus as Son is metaphorical rather than literal language. These metaphors could be replaced by terms that communicate the analogous intention of the metaphor but don't produce the same misunderstanding. For example, "Son" might be translated as something like "Eternally Beloved One."

Some opponents counter that the Father/Son language of Scripture is not, in fact, metaphorical, but is a metaphysical reality.[18] Some go so far as to claim that the human biological relationship takes its meaning from the reality of divine sonship, rather than vice versa.[19]

While it is certainly true that God reveals the epitome of what a father should be and that we come to know the meaning of true fatherhood by looking to God, this does not mean that God's fatherhood is not metaphorical. For all of us, our initial apprehension of a father is not God, but our human fathers. The term "father" immediately and necessarily draws a metaphorical analogy between God and *the fatherhood we all know* (or idealize)—that of our own experiences as children and/or fathers. God is not a human father, but we understand a little of his divine nature by envisioning the attributes of an ideal human father.

Even if we conclude that the Father/Son language for God is at least partly metaphorical, however, this does not mean we can simply eliminate it without distorting the message of the text. This is because Father/Son language with reference to God is by no means peripheral to the New Testament. It is deep, wide, and pervasive, going to the very heart of the Bible's message. The NT designates God as "Father" 254 times. The ascription of "Son" appears forty times in John's gospel alone.[20] If this metaphor has such prominence in God's self-revelation, the losses made in removing it would seem to outweigh any benefit gained in avoiding offence.

It seems the best solution is to retain divine Sonship language, while seeking to avoid offense by clarifying the meaning for Muslims and others who might misunderstand. This could be done with clarifying words in the text, or with footnotes, glossaries, or other study aids. What must never be done is to distort the meaning of the text to make it more palatable. There are

---

18. David Abernathy, "Jesus the Eternal Son of God," *St. Francis Magazine* 6, no. 2 (2010): 327–94; David Abernathy, "Reflections on the Trinity in Light of 1 John 4:8," *St. Francis Magazine* 6, no. 3 (2010): 471–81; Matthew Carlton, "Jesus, the Son of God: Biblical Meanings, Muslim Understanding, and Implications for Translation and Bible Literacy," *St. Francis Magazine* 7, no. 3 (2011): 1–30; J. Scott Horrell, "Cautions Regarding 'Son of God,' in Muslim-Idiom Translation of the Bible: Seeking Sensible Balance," *St. Francis Magazine* 6, no. 4 (2010): 638–66.
19. Garner, et al., *Call to Faithful Witness*, 56: "The human concept of begotten-ness derives *mutatis mutandis* from the divine relationship of Father and Son. Human begotten-ness is simply one more way in which humans finitely reflect their Creator/Father."
20. Horrell, "Cautions," 649.

fundamental theological differences between Christianity and Islam in terms of the nature of God, the identity of Jesus, the authority of Scripture, and the means of salvation. Muting or clouding these differences will ultimately prove counterproductive.

Summary

The most significant controversy in the context of international Bible translation in recent years has been the translation of divine Sonship language in the context of translations geared toward Muslim evangelism. Advocates of Muslim idiom translations argue that the Qur'an does not necessarily reject a biblical view of the Trinity or Jesus's divine Sonship, but rather a distorted and heretical view that sees Jesus as the physical offspring of a sexual union between God and Mary. Opponents counter that any softening of divine Sonship language distorts God's Word. The best solution, as so often in translation, is to seek a balance that both accurately represents the meaning of the text, while finding ways to communicate this meaning in such a way that clarifies rather than confuses the receptor audience.

REFLECTION QUESTIONS

1. What are "insider movements" in Islam?

2. Why is divine sonship language so controversial when translating the Bible for Muslim audiences?

3. While the doctrine of the Trinity is a critically important issue for evangelism among Muslims, it is not as difficult an issue for Bible translation. Why not?

4. According to the discussion above, when is it acceptable to use "Allah" as a translation for "God" in Arabic translations of the Bible? When should it be avoided?

5. What, in your opinion, is the best way to handle God as Father and Jesus as Son language in Bible translations used in dialogue with Muslims?

Select Resources for Further Study

Barnwell, Katherine. *Bible Translation: An Introductory Course in Translation Principles*. 4th ed. Dallas: SIL International, 2020.

Beekman, John and John Callow. *Translating the Word of God*. Grand Rapids: Zondervan, 1974.

Bruce, F. F. *History of the Bible in English*. New York: Oxford University Press, 1978.

Brunn, Dave. *One Bible, Many Versions: Are All Translation Created Equal?* Downers Grove, IL: IVP Academic, 2013.

Carson, D. A. *The Inclusive Language Debate: A Plea for Realism*. Grand Rapids: Baker, 1998.

de Waard, Jan and Eugene A. Nida. *From One Language to Another: Functional Equivalence in Bible Translating*. Nashville: Nelson, 1986.

Dewey, David. *A User's Guide to Bible Translations: Making the Most of Different Versions*. Downers Grove, IL: Intervarsity, 2004.

Fee, Gordon D. and Mark L. Strauss. *How to Choose a Translation for All Its Worth*. Grand Rapids: Zondervan, 2007.

Greenslade, S. L., ed. *The Cambridge History of the Bible*. Cambridge: Cambridge University Press, 1963.

Kubo, Sakae and Walter F. Specht. *So Many Versions? Twentieth-Century English Versions of the Bible*. Rev. ed. Grand Rapids: Zondervan, 1983.

Metzger, Bruce M. *The Bible in Translation: Ancient and English Versions*. Grand Rapids: Baker, 2001.

Munday, Jeremy. *Introducing Translation Studies: Theories and Applications*. 4th ed. New York: Routledge, 2016.

Nida, Eugene A. and Charles R. Taber. *The Theory and Practice of Translation*. Leiden: E. J. Brill, 1974.

Pym, Anthony. *Exploring Translation Theories*. 2nd ed. London: Routledge, 2014.

Scorgie, Glen G., Mark L. Strauss, and Steven M. Voth, eds. *The Challenge of Bible Translation: Communicating God's Word to the World*. Festschrift Ronald F. Youngblood. Grand Rapids: Zondervan, 2003.

Strauss, Mark L. *Distorting Scripture? The Challenge of Bible Translation and Gender Accuracy*. Downers Grove, IL: InterVarsity, 1998.

Wegner, Paul D. *The Journey from Texts to Translations: The Origin and Development of the Bible*. Grand Rapids: Baker, 1999.

A wealth of information on Bible versions around the world can be found at the SIL International database available at https://find.bible. For Bibles in many world languages, see WorldBibles.org and Biblegateway.com.

Scripture Index

John

Acts

Romans